W9-CFD-632

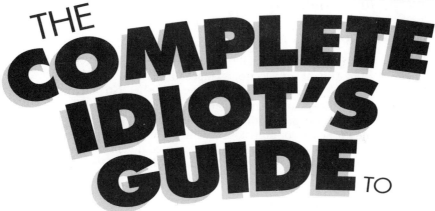

THE COMPLETE IDIOT'S GUIDE TO

the Internet
Third Edition

by Peter Kent

A Division of Macmillan Computer Publishing
201 W. 103rd St., Indianapolis, IN 46290 USA

Another one for the missus.

©1996 Que® Corporation

International Standard Book Number: 0-7897-0862-0
Library of Congress Catalog Card Number: 96-69596

98 97   8 7 6 5 4 3 2

Interpretation of the printing code: the rightmost double-digit number is the year of the book's first printing; the rightmost single-digit number is the number of the book's printing. For example, a printing code of 96-1 shows that this copy of the book was printed during the first printing of the book in 1996.

Screen reproductions in this book were created by means of the program Collage Complete from Inner Media, Inc, Hollis, NH.

Printed in the United States of America

Publisher
Roland Elgey

Publishing Manager
Lynn E. Zingraf

Editorial Services Director
Elizabeth Keaffaber

Managing Editor
Michael Cunningham

Acquisitions Editor
Martha O'Sullivan

Director of Marketing
Lynn E. Zingraf

Product Development Specialists
Faithe Wempen, John Gosney

Technical Editor
Sandy Hagman

Production Editor
Audra Gable

Copy Editors
San Dee Phillips, Tom Lamoureux

Technical Specialist
Nadeem Muhammed

Book Designer
Kim Scott

Cover Designers
Dan Armstrong, Barbara Kordesh

Production Team
*Heather Butler, Angela Calvert, Tricia Flodder, Aleata Howard,
Bob LaRoche, Diana Moore, Sossity Smith, Scott Tullis, Megan Wade, Paul Wilson*

Indexer
Bront Davis

*Special thanks to C. Herbert Feltner for ensuring
the technical accuracy of this book.*

Contents at a Glance

Contents

12 The Giant Software Store: FTP — 143

13 Archie, the Friendly File Librarian — 157

14 Digging Through the Internet with Gopher — 169

18 Telnet: Inviting Yourself onto Other Systems   219

Part 3: Getting Things Done   229

19 Finding Stuff   231

20 Staying Safe on the Internet   241

23 The Future of the Internet   279

Introduction

Welcome to *The Complete Idiot's Guide to the Internet, Third Edition.* Although this is the third edition of this book, it is almost a completely new book. So much has changed since the book was first written late in 1993, that the Internet described in the first edition bears as little relation to today's Internet as the Pony Express does to the modern U.S. Postal Service.

Back in 1993, the Internet boom hadn't begun. Sure, the Internet had been around for more than a couple of decades, but it was a secret kept from most of the world. In 1993, the average American thought the Internet was some kind of international crime conspiracy growing out of the breakup of the Soviet Union. A few months later, though, the media started screaming about this wonderful new tool—about how the Internet would change the world.

Nowadays, if you have a high-tech product to sell, you have to add the word "Internet" to it somehow. If you're selling a program that speeds up printing, you say that it's great for printing information from the Internet. If you're promoting a video card, you say it makes Web pages look great. If you're selling a smart washing machine, you say it cleans off the dust from the information superhighway.

The Internet's Easier Now...

More importantly, though, the Internet actually works very differently from the way it did a few years ago. Or, at least, the manner in which people use the Internet is very different now. Back in 1993, most Internet users were computer geeks. And that was okay because you needed a high degree of geekhood to get anything done on the Internet. For the average business or home computer user, getting an Internet account was like stepping into a time warp. One moment you were in your whiz-bang multimedia mouse-clicking graphical user interface—Windows, OS/2, or the Mac—and the next minute, you were back in the 1970s, working on a dumb UNIX terminal (dumb being the operative word), typing in obscure and arcane, not to mention funky and strange, UNIX commands. You probably found yourself wondering, "What's this **ftp ftp.microsoft.com** thing I have to type?" or "What's **grep** all about and why do I care?" or "Why can't UNIX programmers actually *name* their programs instead of giving them two-letter acronyms?"

Most Internet users these days don't need to know the answers to these ancient questions. These days, the majority of new users are back in the 1990s, working in the graphical user interfaces they love (or love to hate, but that's another issue). Since 1993, thousands of fancy new Internet access programs have been written. Today, it's easier to get on the Internet, and it's easier to get around once you are there.

So Why Do You Need This Book?

Even if you've never stumbled along the information superhighway (or "infotainment superhighway," as satirist Al Franken calls it), you've almost certainly heard of it. A recent survey found that while only 2.3 percent of American high school students could tell you the name of the President of the U.S.A., 93.7 percent knew how to get to the Penthouse Online Web site—and a whopping 112 percent knew how to download bootleg copies of Hootie and the Blowfish songs.

Chances are, though, that if you've picked up this book, you are not an experienced international traveler along the highways and byways of this amazing system called the Internet. You probably need a little help. Well, you've come to the right place.

Yes, the Internet is far easier to get around now than it was in 1993. But there's still a lot to learn. The journey will be more comfortable than it was back in 1993, and you can travel much farther.

Now, I know you're not an idiot. What you do, you do well. But right now, you don't do the Internet, and you need a quick way to get up and running. You want to know what the fuss is about, or maybe you already know what the fuss is about and you want to find out how to get in on it. Well, I'm not going to teach you how to become an Internet guru, but I will tell you the things you really *need* to know, such as:

> ➤ How to get up and running on the Internet

> ➤ How to send and receive e-mail messages

> ➤ How to move around on the World Wide Web (and what is the Web, anyway?)

➤ How to find what you are looking for on the Internet

➤ Protecting life and limb on the information superhighway fast lane

➤ How to participate in Internet discussion groups (that could take over your life and threaten your relationships if you're not careful)

➤ How to talk to Aunt Edna in Walla Walla for $1 an hour—and bankrupt your local long-distance company

I am, however, making a few assumptions. I'm assuming that you know how to use your computer, so don't expect me to give basic lessons on using your mouse, switching between windows, working with directories and files, and all that stuff. There's enough to cover in this book without all that. If you want really basic beginner's information, check out *The Complete Idiot's Guide to PCs* (also from Que), a great book by Joe Kraynak.

How Do You Use This Book?

I've used a few conventions in this book to make it easier for you to follow. For example, when you need to type something, it will appear in bold like this:

type **this**

If I don't know exactly what you'll have to type (because you have to supply some of the information), I'll put the unknown information in italics. For example, you might see the following instructions. In this case, I don't know the file name, so I made it italic to indicate that you have to supply it.

type **this** *file name*

Also, I've used the term "Enter" throughout the book, even though your keyboard may have a "Return" key instead.

In case you want a greater understanding of the subject you are learning, you'll find some background information in boxes. You can quickly skip over this information if you want to avoid all the gory details. On the other hand, you may find something that will help you out of trouble. Here are the special icons and boxes used in this book.

By the Way...

These boxes contain notes, tips, warnings, and asides that provide you with interesting and useful (at least theoretically) tidbits of Internet information.

Technical Babble

The "Techno Talk" icon calls your attention to technical information you might spout off to impress your friends, but that you'll likely never need to know to save your life.

Acknowledgments

Thanks to everyone at Que who helped me put this together, in particular Faithe Wempen and San Dee Phillips, who both know how difficult I can be.

We'd Like to Hear from You!

As part of our continuing effort to produce books of the highest possible quality, Que would like to hear your comments. To stay competitive, we *really* want you, as a computer book reader and user, to let us know what you like or dislike most about this book or other Que products.

You can mail comments, ideas, or suggestions for improving future editions to the address below, or send us a fax at (317) 581-4663. For the online inclined, Macmillan Computer Publishing has a forum on CompuServe (type **GO QUEBOOKS** at any prompt) through which our staff and authors are available for questions and comments. The address of our Internet site is **http://www.mcp.com** (World Wide Web).

In addition to exploring our forum, please feel free to contact me personally to discuss your opinions of this book: I'm on CompuServe, and I'm **lgentry@que.mcp.com** on the Internet.

Thanks in advance—your comments will help us to continue publishing the best books available on computer topics in today's market.

Lorna Gentry
Product Development Specialist
Que Corporation
201 W. 103rd Street
Indianapolis, Indiana 46290
USA

Part 1
The Least You Need to Know

You want to start, and you want to start quickly. No problem. In Part 1, you're going to do just that. First, I'll give you a quick overview of the Internet, and then I'll have you jump right in and use the two most important Internet services: e-mail and the World Wide Web. (The Web is so important these days that many people think the Internet is the Web. I'll explain the difference in Chapter 2.)

By the time you finish this part of the book, you'll be surfing around the Web like a true cybergeek—and you'll be ready to move on and learn the other Internet services.

Chapter 1

The Least You Need to Know

I have some good news for you. The Internet is much easier to use today than it was two and a half or three years ago when the Internet "boom" began. The software has changed dramatically, and procedures that were a real chore a couple of years ago are now quite simple. Still, there's a lot to learn, so we'll begin with a quick overview of these important points. You'll learn more about each of them later.

1. The Internet is a huge computer network—the world's largest—and it's open to the public. Anyone willing to spend the few dollars a month that it costs to buy access to the Internet is allowed on. What started as a tool of the U.S. military-industrial complex is now a tool for everyone from anarchists, to school kids, to corporate America. You'll find a quick Internet history and summary in Chapter 2.

2. E-mail may not be glamorous, but it's the most important tool on the Internet. Millions of people zap e-mail messages across the world each day, from school kids contacting pen pals to business people communicating with colleagues and clients. Most e-mail messages are simple text, but if you know how to use the system, you can also send computer files—pictures, spreadsheets, text, desktop publishing files, and even sounds. Read about e-mail in detail in Chapter 3.

3. The World Wide Web is *not* the Internet; it's just one system running on the Internet. Basically, the Internet is the hardware, and the Web is the software. Still, the Web is one of the most important systems, and certainly the most popular (well, after e-mail).

The Web is a giant hypertext system, a series of millions of documents linked to each other. You view a document in a Web *browser*. You can click one linked word or picture, and another document appears; then click another *link*, and another document pops up. (You can go on like this indefinitely.) There's a lot to learn about the Web, so we'll cover it in Chapters 4–8.

4. There are tens of thousands of discussion groups on the Internet. You'll learn about two main systems for using them: newsgroups and mailing lists. The former requires a special program, a *newsreader*, to display the messages. The latter uses the e-mail system to distribute the group's messages. You'll find groups about the important issues (such as events in Bosnia), the true-but-unreported (alien visitors), the interesting (Greek archaeology), and the trivial (*Melrose Place*). Pick any subject, and somewhere you'll find a related discussion group.

5. Three services—Gopher, FTP, and Telnet—have become submerged in all the fuss about the World Wide Web. Gopher is a menu system that's similar in some ways to the Web. You select a menu option to see another menu or document somewhere else on the Internet—or maybe even somewhere on the other side of the world. Gopher's still alive, but it's not as popular as it used to be (because everyone has rushed to the Web). FTP (File Transfer Protocol) is a file-library system that contains literally millions of computer files in the form of programs, documents, sounds, clip art, and so on. And finally, Telnet is a system by which you can log on to computers all over the Internet so that you can use databases, play games, find information about jobs, and more.

6. The Internet is a communications system; after all, how could it exist without a way to talk to people? Although there are chat systems in cyberspace, the best ones are on the Internet in the online services. On the Internet proper, IRC (Internet Relay Chat) is a system that you either love or hate (thousands seem to love it).

   You don't actually chat—not with your voice anyway. Instead, you type messages that are seen immediately by other participants, and you see their responses right away. You'll learn about these systems in Chapter 15. Then, in Chapter 16, you'll hear about the new voice-on-the-net products (programs that allow you to literally talk to other people) via the Internet's "phone" system. Why pay 50 cents or $1 per minute to phone relatives overseas when you might be able to do so for a $1 or less per *hour*?

7. The Internet is constantly changing. Internet sites come and go, their "addresses" change, and their contents change. Therefore, some of the addresses provided in this book—the Web URLs, Gopher server addresses, and so on—might be wrong by the time you read the book. Hey, don't blame me! That's just the nature of the Internet. Things that you discover on your own or that you read about in other

publications might disappear, too. But this doesn't have to be a problem. If you understand how to search for things on the Internet (see Chapter 19), you can still find what you need.

8. Okay, so you've heard about the dangers of the Internet. You've seen the articles about pornography on the Internet, you've heard Congress debate the subject, and you've been told that shopping on the Internet is dangerous. True? Well, there's no smoke without fire, but you might be surprised at just how safe the Internet really is. (After all, you can always pull the plug!) Credit card companies say that it's actually safer to use your credit card on the Internet than in the "real world." And although there is pornography on the Internet, there's not as much as some critics have claimed (*TIME* even printed a retraction after its "porn on the Internet" article), and you won't just stumble over it. Still, you might want to read Chapter 20 just to make sure you know what it takes to stay safe.

9. The Internet is a hardware system: computers and cables. But it's the software that really makes it run. So you'll need software, you'll need lots of it, and you'll want the latest releases. Luckily there's a lot of cheap—and even free—software ready for the taking at a variety of software archives on the Internet. Systems like TUCOWS (The Ultimate Collection of Winsock Software), the University of Texas Macintosh Archive, and shareware.com (which has software for Windows, Macintosh, and UNIX) make it quick and easy to download new programs and have them running in minutes. In Appendix A, I'll tell you where to find all kinds of software.

10. It's easy for Internet writers to focus on *how* to use the Internet. All too often, we forget a crucial question: *why*? There are thousands of reasons to use the Internet, and I've described just a few of them in Chapter 21. It's a great way for the housebound to keep in touch with the rest of the world (a paradox, perhaps, cyberspace being used as a link to the *real* world). Businesses use it as an essential business tool. Families use it to keep in touch. And people use it to contact others with similar interests. The Internet is such a diverse place that no matter what you plan to use it for now, you may eventually find that it's more important to you in a completely different way. You're on a journey of discovery… Good luck!

Chapter 2

The Internet: What It's All About

In This Chapter

➤ The obligatory "What is the Internet?" question answered

➤ A quick history of the Internet

➤ What sort of information flies across the Internet

➤ Internet services, from Archie to the World Wide Web

➤ Getting a connection to the Internet

➤ Four types of Internet connections

➤ The difference between the Internet and the online services

Yes, this is the obligatory "What is the Internet?" chapter. But before you skip ahead, let me tell you that we'll be covering some other subjects, too, and that I promise not to go into too much detail about Internet history. Quite frankly, most people are tired of hearing about the history of the Internet; they just want to get on the Net and get something done. However, for those of you who may have been holed up in an FBI or ATF siege for the last few years, here's the short history of the Internet.

1. The Internet was created by the U.S. military-industrial complex in the late '60s as a way of enabling government researchers who were working on military projects to share computer files.

2. It *wasn't* set up to figure out how computer networks could be made to survive nuclear war. Yes, yes, I said that in an earlier book, as have a gazillion other Internet authors, but then I read an article by one of the founders and saw the light. This wasn't the initial purpose of the Internet; it was, however, a consideration a few years into its life.

3. Everyone and his dog in academia jumped on the bandwagon. The Internet became a sort of secret academic communication link, connecting hundreds of academic institutions, while America went on watching *Starsky and Hutch*, not realizing what was going on.

4. Eventually, the press figured out what was happening. Granted, it took them almost a quarter of a century, but during that time they were busy being spoon-fed by our political institutions, and the Internet didn't have a public relations company.

5. In 1993, the press started talking about the Internet. In 1994 and 1995, it was about all they could talk about.

6. Ordinary Americans—and then ordinary Brits, Aussies, Frenchies, and others all around the world—began to wake up and realize that the Internet might be worth looking into. And look into it they did—by the millions.

7. The Internet today has become a haven for all sorts of ordinary people, businesses, schools, churches, and the like, as well as some "not-so-ordinary" people.

Okay, that's it. That's my quick history of the Internet. If you want more, you'll have to look elsewhere. I want to move on to what today's Internet really is.

Okay, Then, What Is the Internet?

Let's start with the basics. What's a computer network? It's a system in which computers are connected so they can share "information." (I'll explain what I mean by that word in a moment.) There's nothing particularly unusual about this in today's world. There are millions of networks around the world. True, they are mostly in the industrialized world, but there isn't a nation in the world that doesn't have at least a few. (Okay, I don't know that for sure, but I can't think of one.)

The Internet is something special, though, for two reasons. First, it's the world's largest computer network. Second, and what makes it *really* special is that it's pretty much open to anyone with the entrance fee, and the entrance fee is constantly dropping. Many users have free accounts, and many more are paying as little as $10 to $20 a month sometimes for "unlimited" usage. ("Unlimited" if you can actually connect to the service and stay connected, which is sometimes a problem with very busy services.)

Just how big is the Internet? Well, you should first understand that many of the numbers we've heard in the last few years are complete nonsense. In 1993, people were saying 25 million. Considering that the majority of Internet users at the time were in the U.S., and that 25 million is 10 percent of the U.S. population, and that most people in this great nation thought that computer networks were something used to enslave them in the workplace, it's highly unlikely that anywhere near 25 million people were on the Internet. In fact, they weren't.

These days, estimates vary all over the place, ranging from 8 or 10 million to 30 million or so. Remember, however, that many users are only infrequent visitors to cyberspace. Still, one way or another, there are a whole lot of people out there—and they're all connected to the Internet and capable of sharing information.

What Exactly Is "Information?"

What, then, do I mean by "information?" I mean anything you can send over lines of electronic communication, and that includes quite a lot these days (and seems to include more every day). I mean letters, which are called *e-mail* on the Internet. I mean reports, magazine articles, and books, which are called *word processing files* on the Internet. I mean music, which is called *music* on the Internet.

You can even send your voice across the Internet; you'll learn how to do that in Chapter 16. And let me just say that you'll find it much cheaper than talking long-distance on the phone—as long as you can find someone to talk to at the other end. You can grab computer files of many kinds (programs, documents, clip art, sounds, and anything else that can be electronically encoded) from huge libraries that collectively contain literally millions of files.

A Word About Numbers

When I first started writing about the Internet, I used to try to be specific; I might have said "2.5 million files." However, I've given up that practice for two reasons. First, many of the numbers were made up; no, not by me, but by Internet gurus who were trying to be specific and made "educated" guesses. Second, even if the numbers were correct when I wrote them, they were too low by the time the book got to the editor, *much* too low by the time the book got to the printer, and *ridiculously* low by the time the book got to the readers. But you can be pretty sure that there are at least a few million files available for you to copy.

But "information" could also be a type of conversation. You want to talk about the Unabomber? There's a discussion group waiting for you. Do you want to meet like-minded souls with a passion for day-time soap operas? They're talking right now.

Anything that can be sent electronically is carried on the Internet, and much that can't be sent now probably will be sent in a few months.

The Internet Services

To be specific, take a quick look at the Internet services available to you.

➤ **E-mail.** This is the most used system. Tens of millions of messages wing their way around the world each day, between families, friends, and businesses. The electronic world's postal system, this is very much like the real world's postal system, except that you can't send fruit, bombs, or this month's selection from the Cheese of the Month club. (You *can*, however, send letters, spreadsheets, pictures, sounds, programs, and more. See Chapter 3 for more info.)

➤ **Chat.** Chat's a bit of a misnomer. There's not much chatting going on here, but there is an awful lot of typing. You type a message, and it's instantly transmitted to another person or to many other people, who can type their responses right away. You'll learn more about this in Chapter 15.

➤ **Internet "Phones."** Install a sound card and microphone, get the Internet phone software, and then talk to people across the Internet. This is not very popular today, but just wait a few months. Just think: you can make international phone calls for $1 an hour.... We'll come back to this in Chapter 16.

➤ **FTP.** FTP is the grand old man of the Internet. The whole purpose of the Internet was to transfer files from one place to another, and for years, FTP was how it was done. FTP provides a giant electronic "library" of computer files; you'll learn how to use it in Chapter 12.

➤ **Archie.** FTP's okay, *if* you know where you are going. Archie is like the library's card catalog, telling you which file is kept where. See Chapter 13.

➤ **Gopher.** Gopher, oh, poor old gopher. If not comatose, he's at least been hobbled. Just a couple of years ago, this system (which you'll learn about in Chapter 14) was supposed to revolutionize the Internet by converting a command-line computer system to a menu system. You wouldn't have to remember and use arcane commands anymore; you could just use the arrow keys or type a number corresponding to a menu option. Then along came the World Wide Web....

➤ **World Wide Web.** It's the Web that's really driving the growth of the Internet, 'cause it's *cool*! (Are you sick of that word yet?) Containing pictures, sounds, and animation, the Web is a giant "hypertext" system in which documents around the world are linked to one another. Click on a word in a document in, say, Sydney, Australia, and another document (which could even be from Salzburg, Austria) appears. You'll learn about this amazing system in Chapters 4–8.

➤ **Telnet.** Telnet? Oh, well, may as well talk about it. Very few people use it, but it can be handy. Telnet provides a way for you to log onto a computer that's somewhere out there on the Internet. Once logged on, you'll probably be using arcane commands or a text-based menu system. You may be playing one of the many role-playing *MUD* games (that stands for Multiple User Dungeons or Multiple User Dimensions). Most people are too busy using the Web, but you can read about Telnet in Chapter 18.

➤ **Newsgroups.** Newsgroups are discussion groups. Want to learn all about what's going on in Bosnia? (Or, at least, what the members of the discussion group say is going on?) Want to learn an unusual kite-flying technique? Want to learn about … well, anything really. There are approximately 15,000 internationally distributed newsgroups, and you'll find out how to work with them in Chapters 9 and 10.

➤ **Mailing lists.** If fifteen thousand discussion groups are not enough for you, here are thousands more. As you'll learn in Chapter 11, the mailing lists are another form of discussion group that work in a slightly different manner.

This is not an exhaustive list. Other systems are available; these are simply the most important ones.

But these are all tools, not reasons to be on the Internet. As you read the book, you'll get ideas for how you can actually use the Internet tools for profit and pleasure. And take a look at Chapter 22, "Ideas," which gives loads of examples of how real people use the Internet.

Getting On the Net

So you think the Net sounds great. How do you get to it, though? You might get Internet access in a number of ways:

➤ Your college provides you with an Internet account.

➤ Your company has an Internet connection from its internal network.

➤ You've signed up with an online service such as America Online (AOL), CompuServe, The Microsoft Network (MSN), or Prodigy.

➤ You've signed up with an Internet service provider.

➤ You've signed up with a Free-Net or other form of free community computer network.

The Internet is not owned by any one company. It's more like the world's telephone system: each portion is owned by someone, and the overall system hangs together because of a variety of agreements between those organizations. So there is no *Internet, Inc.* where you can go to get access to the Internet. No, you have to go to one of the tens of thousands of organizations that already have access to the Internet, and get a connection through them.

You'll learn more about finding a connection (and about those Free-Nets) in Appendix B.

The Difference Between the Internet and Online Services

I often hear the questions "What's the difference between the Internet and AOL, or CompuServe, or whatever?" and "If I have an AOL account, do I have an Internet account?"

Right off the bat, let me say that services such as AOL (America Online), CompuServe, Prodigy, GEnie, MSN (The Microsoft Network) and so on, are not the same as the Internet. They are known as *online services*. Although they are similar in some ways (yes, they are large computer networks), they are different in the sense that they are private "clubs."

For instance, what happens when you dial into, say, CompuServe? Your computer connects across the phone lines with CompuServe's computers, which are all sitting in a big room somewhere. All those computers belong to CompuServe (which you can buy, if you want; the parent company H & R Block—yes, the tax people—want to sell).

Now, contrast this with the Internet. When you connect to the Internet, you connect to a communications system that's linked to millions of computers, which are owned by tens of thousands of companies, schools, government departments, and individuals. If the Internet is like a giant public highway system, the online services are like small private railroads.

However, at the risk of stretching an analogy too far (I'm already mixing metaphors, so why not), I should mention that these private railroads let you get off the tracks and onto the public highway. In other words, although AOL, CompuServe, and the others are private clubs, they do provide a way for you to connect to the Internet. So, while the barbarians on the Internet are held at the gates to the private club, the private club members can get onto the Internet.

The online services view themselves as both private clubs and gateways to the Internet. As Russ Siegelman of The Microsoft Network stated, Microsoft wants MSN to be "the biggest and best content club and community on the Internet." So it's intended to be part of the

Internet—but a private part. In fact, although I (and many others) call these services "online services," Microsoft now refers to MSN as an "Internet Online Service."

To summarize:

➤ The Internet is a public highway system overrun with barbarians.

➤ Online services are private railroads or exlusive clubs—or something like that.

➤ Even if you use the Internet, you can't get into the online services unless you're a member.

➤ If you are a member of the online services, you *can* get onto the Internet.

The answer to the second question, then, is "yes." If you have an online-service account (at least with the services mentioned here), you also have an Internet account. Interestingly, these services are now being merged into the Internet. In particular, MSN is making great efforts to appear as an integral part of the Internet. Parts of MSN are already open to the public. And people on the Internet can now access the private areas in MSN if they sign up for the service. They don't have to dial into a phone number provided by Microsoft; they can get onto the Internet any way they like and then use their World Wide Web browser to get into MSN.

What Do You Need?

What does it take to get onto the infotainment superhypeway? Many of you already have Internet accounts; our high-priced research shows that most readers buy this book *after* they have access to the Internet (presumably because they got access and then got lost). However, I want to talk about the types of accounts (or connections) that are available because they all work in slightly different ways. This will help ensure that we are all on the same wavelength *before* we get going.

There are basically four types of Internet connections:

➤ Permanent connections

➤ Dial-in direct connections (SLIP, CSLIP, and PPP)

➤ Dial-in terminal connections (shell accounts)

➤ Mail connections

Generally, if you ask an online service or service provider for an account these days, you'll be given the second type, a dial-in direct connection, even though you won't hear it called that. In fact, different service providers use slightly different terms, and the terminology can become blurred. The following sections define each one, which should clarify things a little.

Service Provider

A company that sells access to the Internet. You dial into its computer, which connects you to the Internet. The online-service providers are an anomaly. Strictly speaking, they are Internet service providers because they provide Internet access. However, they aren't called "service providers"; instead, they are called "online-service providers." The companies called service providers generally provide access to the Internet and little, if anything, more. The online services, on the other hand, have all sorts of file libraries, chat services, news services, and so on, within the services themselves.

Permanent Connections

If you have a permanent connection, your computer connects directly to a TCP/IP (Transmission Control Protocol/Internet Protocol) network that is part of the Internet. Actually, what is more likely is that your organization has a large computer connected to the network, and you have a terminal or computer connected to that computer. This sort of connection is often known as a *dedicated connection*, or sometimes as a *permanent direct connection*.

What's a Protocol?

A protocol defines how computers should talk to each other. It's like a language: if a group of people agrees to speak French (or English or Spanish), they can all understand each other. Communication protocols provide a similar set of rules that define how modems, computers, and programs can communicate.

Permanent connections are often used by large organizations, such as universities, groups of schools, and corporations. The organization has to set up special equipment to connect its network to the Internet, and it has to lease a special telephone line that can transfer data very quickly. Because that organization has a leased line, it is always connected to the Internet, which means there's no need to make a telephone call and use a modem to reach the service provider's computer. Instead, the user simply logs on to the Internet from his terminal.

Dial-In Direct Connections

Dial-in direct connections are often referred to as SLIP (Serial Line Internet Protocol), CSLIP (Compressed SLIP), or PPP (Point-to-Point Protocol) connections. Like the permanent connection, this is also a TCP/IP connection, but it's designed for use over telephone lines instead of a dedicated network. This type of service is the next best thing to the permanent connection. While a permanent connection is out of the price range of most individuals and small companies, a dial-in direct connection is quite cheap (sometimes a dollar or two an hour, but often less).

This is a *dial-in* service. That is, you must have a modem, and you have to dial a telephone number given to you by the service provider or online service. The following figure shows an example of one type of software you can run while working with a dial-in direct or permanent connection. The figure shows Microsoft's FTP site, a large file library that's open to the public. The main reason I'm showing you this right now is so that you can compare it to the horrible-looking dial-in terminal connection we'll talk about next.

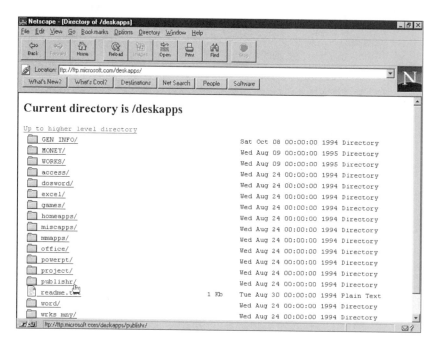

Microsoft's FTP site as viewed from a program running in a dial-in direct connection (SLIP, CSLIP, or PPP).

Dial-In Terminal Connections

With this type of connection, you also have to dial into the service provider's computer. When the connection is made, your computer simply becomes a terminal of the service provider's computer. All the programs you use are running on the service provider's computer. That means that you can transfer files across the Internet to and from your service provider's computer, but not to and from yours. You have to use a separate procedure to move files between your computer and the service provider's.

If you want to see just how ugly this sort of connection really is, take a look at the next figure. This shows Microsoft's FTP site, the exact same service you saw in the first figure. However, if you're working in this, you have to remember all the commands you might want to type or you are lost.

Clearing Up the Confusion

This connection is often called a *dial-up connection*. But that can be confusing because you have to dial a call before connecting to a SLIP account as well. To differentiate between the two, some service providers call this an *Interactive* service—which seems only slightly less ambiguous—or a *shell* account. Throughout this book, I call it a "dial-in terminal connection" because you dial the call to your service provider, and once it's connected, your computer acts as a terminal of the other computer.

Back at Microsoft's FTP site, this time with a dial-in terminal account.

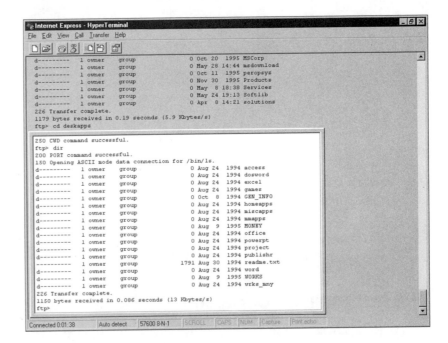

Mail Connections

A mail connection enables you to send and receive Internet e-mail and, perhaps, to read the Internet newsgroups. But you can do nothing more. This is hardly a real Internet account, so I've ignored it in this book. I'll assume you have one of the first three types of accounts.

What Do You Have?

So, where does that leave us, what do you have, and why do you care? Well, we're interested in the permanent, dial-in direct, and dial-in terminal connections. The first two are the most important because...

➤ they are easier to use.

➤ you actually use both in pretty much the same way.

➤ you probably have one of these connections.

If you have an Internet account provided by your employer at work and you access it across your network connection, you have a permanent connection. How do you connect? Ask your system administrator. You might have to log on in some way, or you may find that you are permanently logged on. If your company has set up the network so that you can connect using your graphical user interface—Windows, the Mac, a UNIX graphical user interface, or OS/2—you can use all the fancy Internet software that's available for your particular operating system.

If you have an account through one of the major online service providers, you have a dial-in direct account: PPP, SLIP, or CSLIP. You must use the software the online service provider gives you to dial in and connect, but once you're connected properly, you can use whatever Internet software you want. (You'll learn about various programs as you go through the book.) With any of these accounts, you'll be using "graphical user interface" software with windows, dialog boxes, and so on. In fact, you can use the same sort of software as the permanent connection users.

The dial-in terminal connection is the nasty "I'll use it if I absolutely have to" connection. If you are completely broke and have to use the very cheapest service you can find (perhaps a free service, one of the Free-Nets talked about in Appendix B) or if, perhaps, you are at a college that hasn't yet upgraded its Internet access, you might have to work with a dial-in terminal (shell) account. If so, you'll find yourself working at the command line, where you have to know a bunch of geeky little UNIX commands to get around.

When I first wrote this book in 1993, the book was based on this sort of account because it was pretty much the only type of account available. These days, most users are working with a graphical interface instead of the command line. So this book is based on the newest software. However, if you are still working with a command-line account (if you have a dial-in terminal account, or if your company or college has given you a dumb terminal connected to a UNIX computer connected to the Internet), you can still get help.

The entire first edition of *The Complete Idiot's Guide to the Internet* is on the CD at the back of this book. It's in HTML format (that's the Web-page format) so you can read the book in your Web browser, which you'll learn more about in Chapters 4–8. If you don't have a CD-ROM drive, that CD won't do you much good. If that's the case, use the mail responder. When you get to a subject in which you need more information about the UNIX command line, I'll tell you where to send an e-mail message and what to put in the body of that message. You'll automatically receive a response that includes the relevant chapter from the book.

I Have AOL (CompuServe, MSN, or Such), But Where's the Internet?

I've told you that the online services provide access to the Internet. But when you first install their software and connect to the service, the Internet connection might not be *enabled*. You might see a message telling you that if you want to connect to the Internet you'll have to download some more software. Follow the instructions to do so. Just in case, though, here's how to find out more about setting up an Internet connection on the three most popular online services:

➤ **America Online:** Log on, and then click the **Internet Connection** bar in the main menu or use the keyword **INTERNET**.

➤ **CompuServe:** Log on, and then click the **Internet** button in the main menu or use the GO word **INTERNET**.

➤ **The Microsoft Network:** Choose **Edit, Go to, Other Service**, and then type **INTERNET**.

You Want Help Setting Up?

Unfortunately, I can't help you with the initial set up of your software. There are too many different systems to cover. So here's my (very general) advice: if your service provider or online service can't help you set up, *find another one!*

Don't let me frighten you. In many cases, the initial setup is actually quite easy. You simply run some kind of setup program and follow any instructions, and in a few minutes, you'll be up and running.

Some providers—in particular many of the small service providers—are not terribly helpful. However, things are certainly better than they were two or three years ago, when many service providers had the attitude "we give you the account to connect to, it's up to you to figure out how to do it!" These days, most are making more of an effort. But if you run into a service provider that isn't willing to explain, absolutely clearly, what you need to do to connect, you should move on. This is a very competitive business, and there are many good companies that are willing to help you.

That's All, Folks!

We don't need to talk any more about getting an Internet account. Most of you already have an account, so it's time to move on and get down to the meat of the subject: how to work with the account you have. If, on the other hand, you *don't* have an account yet, flip to Appendix B, in which I explain how to find one and tell you what computer equipment you need. Then turn to Appendix C, in which I tell you all about the software on the CD at the back of this book. In fact, even if you *do* have an account, you should look in these appendices because you might eventually want to swap to a cheaper or more reliable service.

Moving along, we'll assume that you have an Internet account you are completely happy with, and that you know how to log on to that account. (Check with your system administrator or look in your service documentation if you need information about logging on to the Internet.)

The Least You Need to Know

- ➤ The Internet is the world's largest computer network, a huge public information highway.

- ➤ You can do many things on the Internet: send e-mail, join discussion groups, grab files from electronic libraries, cruise the World Wide Web, and much more.

- ➤ There are four types of Internet connections: mail connections, which aren't much good; dial-in terminal connections, which are better, but you're working with the command line or text menus; and permanent connections and dial-in direct (SLIP and PPP) connections, both of which are much better.

- ➤ The Internet is a public system. The online services—America Online, CompuServe, The Microsoft Network, et al—are private services, with "gateways" to the Internet.

- ➤ A member of an online service can use the Internet, but an Internet user cannot use an online service unless he joins.

- ➤ You can get Internet access through your company or school, a small local Internet service provider, a giant Internet service provider (such as AT&T), or an online service.

Chapter 3

The Premier Internet Tool: E-Mail

In This Chapter

➤ Which e-mail program are you using?

➤ All about e-mail addresses

➤ Setting up your e-mail program

➤ Sending a message

➤ Retrieving your messages—then what?

➤ Sending files across the Internet

➤ Avoiding fights!

Ah, some of you think the title of this chapter is a joke. It's not. Although e-mail may not be exciting, "cool," or "compelling," it is the most popular and, in many ways, the most useful Internet service. More people use e-mail on any given day than use any other Internet service. Tens of millions of messages fly across the wires each day—five million from America Online alone.

Despite all the glitz of the Web (you'll learn about that glitz in Chapters 4–8), the potential of Internet Phone systems (Chapter 16), and the excitement—for some—of the many chat systems (Chapter 15), e-mail is probably the most productive tool there is. It's a sort of Internet workhorse, getting the work done without any great fanfare.

After spending huge sums of money polling Internet users, we've come to the conclusion that the very first thing Internet users want to do is send e-mail messages. It's not too threatening, and it's an understandable concept: you're sending a letter. The only differences are that you don't take it to the post office and that it's much faster. So that's what I'm going to start with: how to send an e-mail message.

Dial-In Terminal (Shell) Accounts

If you are working with a dial-in terminal account (also known as a shell account), this information on e-mail won't help you. To learn more about working with e-mail with your type of account, check out the first edition of *The Complete Idiot's Guide to the Internet*, which is on the CD in the back of this book. If that doesn't help (if your system is not set up in such a way that it's obvious how to send a simple message), ask your service provider how to send the first message.

What E-Mail System?

Which e-mail system do you use? Well, if you are a member of an online service, you have a built-in mail system. But, if you are not a member of one of the major online services …who the heck knows what you are using for e-mail! I don't. For that matter, even with an online service, there are different options; CompuServe, for instance, offers a number of different programs you can use.

Basically, it all depends what your service provider set you up with. You might be using Netscape, a World Wide Web browser (discussed in Chapter 4) that has a built-in e-mail program. Likewise, you might be using Microsoft Exchange, which comes with Windows 95. You could be using Eudora, which is probably the most popular e-mail program on the Internet. Or you might be using something else entirely.

Luckily, the e-mail concepts are all the same, regardless of the type of program you are using—even if the actual buttons you click are different.

You Have a New Address!

I recently discovered how you can tell an absolute beginner on the Internet; he often talks about his e-mail "number," equating e-mail with telephones. Well, they are both electronic, after all. However, you actually have an e-mail *address*. That address has three parts:

➤ Your account name

➤ The "at" sign (@)

➤ Your domain name

What's your account name? It's almost always the name you use to log on to your Internet account. For instance, when I log on to my CompuServe account, I have to type 71601,1266. That's my account name. When I log on to MSN I use PeterKent, and on AOL, I use PeKent.

After your account name, you use the @ sign. Why? Well, how would you know where the account name ends and domain name starts, eh?

Finally, you use the domain name, which is the address of your company, your service provider, or your online service. Think of it as the street address. After all, a person can address a real letter to any other person using *your* street address. It's the same with the Internet: one street address (the domain name) can be used for thousands of account names.

Techno Talk
Account Names: They're All the Same

Actually, CompuServe calls the account name a *User ID*, MSN calls it a *Member Name*, and AOL calls it a *Screen Name*. In addition, you might hear the account name called a *user name* or *logon ID*. All of these names mean the same thing: the name by which you are identified when you log on to your account. However, I discovered that WorldNet, AT&T's Internet service, does something odd. You get some strange number as the account name, and you get *another* name to use when using your e-mail. Someone at AT&T gave me a flip answer as to *why* they do this, using a sort of "well of course we *have* to do this, but you probably wouldn't understand" tone of voice; I wasn't convinced.

Where do you get the domain name? If you haven't been told already, ask the system administrator or tech support. (Later in this chapter, you'll learn the domain names of the larger online services.)

Pronouncing Your E-Mail Address Here's the "correct" way to say an e-mail address out loud. You say "dot" for the periods and "at" for the @ sign. Thus, pkent@usa.net is "p kent at u s a dot net."

A Word About Setup

You *might* need to set up your e-mail system before it will work. In many cases, this setup will already be done for you. If you are with one of the online services, you don't need to worry—it's done for you. Some of the Internet service providers also do all this configuring stuff for you. Others, however, expect you to get into your program and enter some information. It doesn't have to be difficult. The following figure shows some of the options you can configure in Eudora.

Eudora Light's Options dialog box, in which you can configure the program before you use it.

Whatever program you have, you might have to enter the following information:

POP (Post Office Protocol) Account This is the "post office" account. When you connect to your service provider, your e-mail program needs to check with the post office (a program running on your service provider's system) to see if any mail has arrived. This post office actually holds the messages that arrive for you until your mail program asks for them. Your account name is usually the same as the account name that you use to log on to your service. You might need to enter the full account name and the POP host name (for instance, in Eudora Light, I enter pkent@mail.usa.net). Or you might have to enter the account name (pkent) in one box and the POP host name (mail.usa.net) in another.

Password You'll need to enter your password so the e-mail program can check the POP for mail. This is generally the same password you use to log onto the system.

Real Name This is, yes, your actual name. Most mail programs will send your name along with the e-mail address when you send e-mail.

SMTP (Simple Mail Transfer Protocol) Host This is another mail program. This one's used to send mail. While the POP holds your incoming mail, the SMTP is used to transmit your messages out onto the Internet. This time, you'll enter a hostname (mail.usa.net) or maybe a number (192.156.196.1) that you've been given by your service provider.

Return or Reply To Address If you want, you can make the e-mail program place a different Reply To: address on your messages. For instance, if you send mail from work but want to receive responses to those messages at home, you'd use a different Reply To address. If you do this, make sure you enter the full address (such as pkent@lab-press.com).

All Sorts of Other Stuff There are all sorts of things you can get a good mail program to do. You can tell it how often to check the POP to see if new mail has arrived, choose the font you want the message displayed in, and/or get the program to automatically include the original message when you reply to a message. You can even tell it to leave messages at the POP after you retrieve them. This might be handy if you like to check your mail from work; if you configure the program to leave the messages at the POP, you can retrieve them again when you get home, using the program on your home machine. You can also define how the program will handle "attachments," but that is a complicated subject that I'll get to later in this chapter.

What Can I Do with My Mail Program? You might be able to do lots of things. Check your documentation or Help files, or simply browse through the configuration dialog boxes to see what you can do. Note, however, that the online services' e-mail programs generally have a limited number of choices. E-mail programs such as Eudora have more choices.

There are so many e-mail programs around, I can't help you configure them all. If you have trouble configuring your program, check the documentation or call the service's technical support. And as I've said before, if they don't want to help, find another service!

Sending a Message

Now that you understand addresses and have configured the mail program, you can actually send a message. So, who can you mail a message to? Well, you may already have friends and colleagues who you can bother with your flippant "hey, I've finally made it onto the Internet" message. On the other hand, why not send yourself a message and kill two birds with one stone: you'll learn how to send one, and then you can see what to do when you receive a message!

So start your e-mail program, and then open the window in which you are going to write the message. You may have to double-click an icon (such as Eudora, for instance) or choose a menu option that opens the mail's Compose window. In Eudora, once the program is open, you click the **New Message** icon or choose **Message, New Message**.

Online Services

If you are working in one of the CompuServe CIM programs, choose **Mail, Create/Send Mail**. In AOL, you choose **Mail, Compose Mail**. And in MSN, you click the big E-mail bar in MSN Central. If you are using Netscape's e-mail program, click the little envelope icon in the lower-right corner or choose **Window, Netscape Mail**. Then you might need to use another command to open the Compose window. In MSN, for instance, choose **Compose, New Message**.

In all of the e-mail programs, the Compose window has certain common elements. In addition, some have a few extras. Here's what you might find:

To: This is the address of the person you are mailing to. If you are using an online service and you are sending a message to another member of that service, all you need to use is the person's account name. For instance, if you are an AOL member and you're mailing to another AOL member with the screen name of PeKent, that's all you need to enter. To mail to that member from a service *other than* AOL, however, you enter the full address: pekent@aol.com. (I explain more about mailing to online services in the section "We Are All One—Sending E-Mail to Online Services," later in this chapter.)

From: Not all mail programs show this, but it gives your e-mail address, which is included in the message "header" (the clutter at the top of an Internet message). It lets the recipient know who to reply to.

Subject: This is a sort of message title—a few words summarizing the contents. The recipient can scan through a list of subjects to see what each message is about. (Some mail programs won't let you send a message unless you fill in the subject line; others don't mind if you leave it blank.)

Cc: You can enter an address here to send a copy to someone other than the person whose address you placed in the To: line.

Bc: This means "blind copy." As with the Cc: line, a copy of the message will be sent to the address (or addresses) you place in the Bc: (or Bcc:) line; however, the recipient of the original message won't be able to tell that the Bcc: address received a copy. (If you use Cc:, the recipient of the original message sees a Cc: line in the header.)

Attachments: This is for sending computer files along with the message. (Again, I'll get to that later in this chapter, in the section "Sending Files—It *Should* Be Easy.")

A big blank area: This is where you type your message.

E-mail programs vary greatly, and not all programs have all of these features. Again, the online service mail programs tend to be a bit limited. The following figures show the Compose window in two very different mail programs.

This is Eudora, a popular mail program.

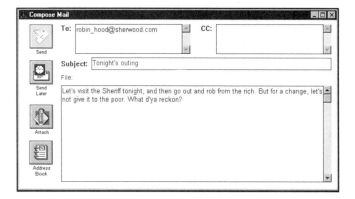

This is America Online's mail composition window.

Go ahead and type a To: address. Why not use your own address? If you are in an online service, you might as well use the entire Internet address. The message will probably go out onto the Internet and then turn around and come back to you. I'll explain those online service addresses in the next section.

We Are All One—Sending E-Mail to Online Services

One of the especially nice things about the Internet, from an e-mail point of view, is that because all the online services are now connected to the Internet, you can send e-mail between e-mail services. Perhaps you have an America Online account because ...well, because they sent you a disk in the mail. And perhaps your brother has a CompuServe account because ...well, because he's a geek, and that's where the geeks have been hanging out for years. (Before you e-mail me to complain, I've had a CompuServe account for more than a decade.) You can send e-mail to each other, using the Internet as a sort of bridge. How? Well, you just have to know the other person's account name on that service and that service's domain name.

For instance, CompuServe has this Internet domain name: compuserve.com. Say you want to send an e-mail message to someone at CompuServe who has the account name (well, User ID they call it on CompuServe) of 71601,1266. You add the two together with the @ in the middle. Then you have 71601,1266@compuserve.com. However, you can't have a comma in an Internet address. So you replace it with a period, and you end up with 71601.1266@compuserve.com.

The following table lists a few other services and tells you how to send e-mail to them.

Sending E-Mail to Other Services

Service	Method of Addressing
Prodigy	Add @prodigy.com to the end of the user's Prodigy address.
America Online	Add @aol.com to the end of an America Online address.
GEnie	Add @genie.geis.com to the end of a GEnie address.
MCImail	Add @mcimail.com to the end of an MCImail address.
MSN	Add @msn.com to the end of the MSN Member name.

These are quite easy. Of course, there are more complicated Internet addresses, but you'll rarely run into them. If you have trouble e-mailing someone, though, call and ask *exactly* what you must type as his or her e-mail address.

Write the Message

Now that you have the address on-screen, write your message—whatever you want to say. Then send the message. How's that done? There's usually a big Send button, or maybe a menu option that says Send or Mail. What happens when you click the button? That depends on the program and whether or not you are logged on at the moment. Generally, if you are logged on, the mail is sent immediately. Not always, though. Some programs will put the message in a "queue," and won't send the message until told to do so. Others will send immediately, and if you are not logged on, they will try to log on first. Watch closely, and you'll usually see what's happening. A message will let you know if the message is being sent. If it hasn't been sent, look for some kind of Send Immediately menu option, or perhaps Send Queued Messages. Whether the message should be sent immediately or put in a queue is often one of the configuration options available to you.

Where'd It Go? Incoming E-Mail

You've sent yourself an e-mail message, but where did it go? It went out into the electronic wilderness to wander around for a few seconds, or maybe a few minutes. Sometimes a few hours. Very occasionally, it even takes a few days. (Generally, the message comes back in a few minutes, unless you mistyped the address, in which case you'll get a special message telling you that it's a bad address.)

Now it's time to check for incoming e-mail. If you are using an online service, as soon as you log on, you'll see a message saying that e-mail has arrived. If you are *already* online, you may see a message telling you that mail has arrived, or you may need to check; you may find a Get New Mail menu option. If you are working with an Internet service provider, you generally won't be informed of incoming mail; rather, your e-mail program has to go and check. Either you can do that manually (for instance, in Eudora, there's a File, check Mail command), or you can configure the program to check automatically every so often.

Fancy Fonts Some of the online services allow you to use fancy text formatting features. For example, MSN, lets you use colors, indents, different fonts, bold and italic, and so on. If you buy a special add-on program for CompuServe, you can do the same sort of thing. But these only work in messages sent *within* the online services. Internet e-mail is plain text—nothing fancy. As a matter of fact, you might as well not bother getting fancy in your Internet e-mail because all that attractive stuff will be stripped out when the message is sent out onto the Internet.

What Now?

What can you do with your incoming e-mail? All sorts of things. I think I'm pretty safe in saying that *every* e-mail program allows you to read incoming messages. Most programs also let you print and save messages (if your program doesn't, you need another). You can also delete them, forward them to someone else, and reply directly to the sender.

These commands should be easy to find. Generally, you'll have toolbar buttons for the most important commands, and more options available if you dig around a little in the menus, too.

A Word About Quoting

It's a good idea to "quote" when you respond to a message. This means that you include part or all of the original message. Some programs automatically quote the original message. And different programs mark quoted messages in different ways; usually, you'll see a "greater than" symbol (>) at the beginning of each line. The following figure shows a reply message that contains a quote from the original message.

You should quote the original message when responding, to remind the sender what he said.

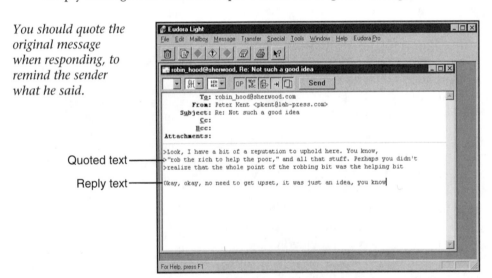

You aren't required to quote. But if you don't, the recipient might not know what you are talking about. I receive dozens of messages a day, and I know people who get literally hundreds. (Of course, the radiation emitted from their computer screens is probably frying their brains.) If you respond to a message without reminding the recipient exactly which of the 200 messages he sent out last week (or which of the five he sent to you) you are responding to, he might be slightly confused.

Quoting is especially important when sending messages to mailing lists and newsgroups (discussed in Chapters 9 and 11), where your message might be read by people who didn't read the message to which you are responding.

Sending Files—It *Should* Be Easy

Oh, I hate this bit. Not because it's so difficult to send files across the Internet (though it is), but because it's, well, sort of embarrassing to admit how difficult it is. Now before you misunderstand, let me say that I *do* know how to send files across the Internet. However, very few people do. And unless both parties involved (the sender and the recipient) understand the process, things won't work. Here's a quick explanation of the problem (and solutions).

Files are commonly sent across cyberspace in one of four ways:

UUENCODE   This is a system in which a computer file is converted to plain ASCII text. It may start out as a sound file or a word processing file, but once it's converted, it looks like gibberish text. This is called *uuencoding*. An encoded file can be placed into an e-mail message and sent. The person at the other end must then save the message as a text file and *uudecode* it—convert it back to its original format.

MIME   Multimedia Internet Mail Extensions is a system designed to make sending files across the Internet easier. It converts the file to text, sends it with the message, and converts it back at the other end. (You can only send text files in the Internet's e-mail system, hence the need to convert files to text.) What's the difference between UUENCODE and MIME? UUENCODE is a sort of quick fix. MIME was intended to be a nicely integrated system that works transparently so that all you have to do is select the file you want to send, and MIME does the rest. Also, it has a method for identifying the type of file that is being transferred. MIME is now used on the World Wide Web to identify multimedia files linked to Web pages.

BinHex   This is a system used on the Macintosh, and it's very similar to UUENCODE. Files are converted into text and then converted back at the other end.

Online Service Systems   Each of the online services has a file-transfer system. In AOL, you can attach a file to a message and then send it to another AOL member. In CompuServe, you can send a file as a message (you cannot attach it to a message, as you can't type anything into the message) and send it to another CompuServe member. In MSN, you can insert all sorts of things, such as pictures, formatted text, or computer files, directly into messages and then send them to other MSN members.

Now, here's the problem. If you want to send a message to another person on the Internet, you have to know which system to use. The following guidelines can help you make a good decision:

1. Check to see if the other person has an account on the same online service you do. Even if you've been given an Internet e-mail address that is obviously not an online service, ask just in case. It's far more reliable to send a file between CompuServe accounts, between AOL accounts, or between MSN accounts, for instance, than to use MIME, BinHex, or UUENCODE. (You'll find that many people—especially geeks—have accounts on two or more services.)

2. If you have to use the Internet e-mail system, check to see which system the recipient can work with (MIME, UUENCODE, or BinHex). *Don't* simply pick one and send the file because if the recipient doesn't have the right software, he won't be able to use the file.

3. Consider which system you have built into your e-mail program. If you are lucky, the system that's built into your e-mail program is the same system the recipient uses. For example, because Eudora Light has both MIME and BinHex, you can send files to anyone using MIME or BinHex—but you cannot send to someone using UUENCODE. (At least, Eudora can't help directly. However, you'll see in a moment how to send uuencoded messages even if it's not built into your e-mail program.)

What if you don't have a match? Or what if you have one of the online services? CompuServe and AOL currently don't work with either MIME or UUENCODE, for instance. There are things you can do, but they may be a hassle. Say you want to send someone a file using UUENCODE because that's the only thing he can work with. But you have a CompuServe account, which means your e-mail program won't automatically uudecode files. You can go to one of the software archives mentioned in Appendix A and download a UUENCODE program. (For instance, if you use Windows, you can use a program called Wincode.) Then you use that program to convert the file to a text file, you copy the text from the file and paste it into the message, and you send the message. (Oh, and then you cross your fingers.)

How about MIME? Say someone just sent you a MIME encoded file; what can you do? Go to the software libraries and search for MIME. For instance, there are little DOS programs I use called Mpack and Munpack. You can save the message as a text file (virtually all e-mail programs let you do this, generally with the File, Save As command), and then use Munpack to convert that text file to the original file format. (Mpack and Munpack are also available for the Macintosh and for UNIX systems.)

If you are lucky, though, your e-mail program has MIME and UUENCODE built in, as well as some kind of command that lets you insert or attach a file. For instance, in Eudora

Light, choose **Message**, **Attach File** and use the small drop-down list at the top of the Compose window to choose between **BinHex** and **MIME**. If you are using an online service, it's easy to send a file to another person within that service. In AOL, for example, click the **Attach** button; in CompuServe, use the **Mail**, **Send File** command.

Cool Things You Can Do with E-Mail

Once you understand your e-mail system and realize that it won't bite, you might actually begin to enjoy using it. The following list contains suggestions of some things you might want to do with your e-mail program.

➤ *Create a mailing list.* You can create a special mailing list that contains the e-mail addresses of many people. For instance, if you want to send a message to everyone in your department (or family, or club) at the same time, you can create a mailing list. Put all the addresses in the list, and then send the message to the list. Everyone on the list receives the message, and you save time and hassle. Some programs will have a mailing list dialog box of some sort; others let you create a "nickname" or "alias" for the mailing list and then associate the addresses with it.

➤ *Create an address book.* Virtually all e-mail systems have address books, and they're usually quite easy to use. You can store a person's complicated e-mail addresses and then retrieve it quickly using the person's real name.

➤ *Work with mail while you're offline.* Most programs these days let you read and write e-mail offline. This is of particular importance with the online services, which are often expensive. Figure out how to use these systems—it's worth the effort.

➤ *Forward your mail.* After being on the Internet for a while, there's a risk of attaining real geekhood—and getting multiple Internet accounts, such as one with your favorite online service, one at work, one with a cheap service provider, and so on. (Right now, I have about eight, I think.) That's a lot of trouble logging on to check for e-mail. However, some services let you forward your e-mail to another account so that if a message arrives at, say, the account you use at home, you can have it automatically sent on to you at work. Very handy. Ask your service provider how to do this; you may need to log on to your *shell* account to set this up (discussed in Chapter 21). While most Internet service providers let you do this, the online services generally *don't*.

➤ *Create a "vacation" message.* When you go on vacation, your e-mail doesn't stop. In fact, that's why so many cybergeeks never go on vacation or take a laptop if they do: they can't bear the thought of missing all those messages. Still, if you manage to break away, you may be able to set a special "vacation" message, an automatic response to any incoming mail, that says basically, "I'm away, be back soon."

(You get to write the response message.) Again, ask your service provider. And again, the online services generally *don't* have this service.

➤ *Filter your files.* Sophisticated e-mail programs have file-filtering capabilities. You can tell the program to look at incoming mail and carry out certain actions according to what it finds. You can place e-mail from your newsgroups into special inboxes, grab only the message subject if the message is very long, and so on.

Caution: E-Mail Can Be Dangerous!

The more I use e-mail, the more I believe that it can be a dangerous tool. There are three main problems: 1) people often don't realize the implications of what they are saying, 2) people often misinterpret what others are saying, and 3) people are comfortable typing things into a computer that they would never say to a person face to face. Consequently, online fights are common both in private (between e-mail correspondents) and in public (in the newsgroups and mailing lists).

The real problem is that when you send an e-mail message, the recipient can't see your face or hear your tone of voice. Of course, when you write a letter, you have the same problem. But e-mail is actually replacing conversations as well as letters. The U.S. Post Office is as busy as ever, so I figure e-mail is *mainly* replacing conversations. That contributes to the problem because people are writing messages in a chatty conversational style, forgetting that e-mail lacks all the visual and auditory "cues" that go along with a conversation.

In the interests of world peace, I give you these e-mail guidelines to follow:

➤ *Don't write something you will regret later.* Lawsuits have been based on the contents of electronic messages, so consider what you are writing and whether you would want it to be read by someone other than the recipient. A message can always be forwarded, read over the recipient's shoulder, printed out and passed around, backed up onto the company's archives, and so on. You don't *have* to use e-mail—there's always the telephone. (Oliver North has already learned *his* lesson!)

➤ *Consider the tone of your message.* It's easy to try to be flippant and come out as arrogant, or to try to be funny and come out as sarcastic. When you write, think about how your words will appear to the recipient.

➤ *Give the sender the benefit of the doubt.* If a person's message sounds arrogant or sarcastic, consider that he or she might be trying to be flippant or funny! If you are not sure what the person is saying, ask him or her to explain.

➤ *Read before you send.* It will give you a chance to fix embarrassing spelling and grammatical errors—and to reconsider what you've just said.

➤ *Wait a day—or three.* If you typed something in anger, wait a few days and read the message again. Give yourself a chance to reconsider.

➤ *Be nice.* Hey, there's no need for vulgarity or rudeness (except in certain newsgroups, where it seems to be a requirement for entrance).

➤ *Attack the argument, not the person.* I've seen fights start when someone disagrees with another person's views and sends a message making a personal attack upon that person. (This point is more related to mailing lists and newsgroups than e-mail proper, but we are on the subject of avoiding fights....) Instead of saying, "anyone who thinks *Days of Our Lives* is not worth the electrons it's transmitted on must be a half-witted moron with all the common sense of the average pineapple," consider saying "you may think it's not very good, but clearly many other people find great enjoyment in this show."

> *Check This Out...*
>
> **You're Being Baited** Some people send rude or vicious messages because they actually *enjoy* getting into a fight like this—where they can fight from the safety of their computer terminals.

➤ *Use smileys.* One way to add some of those missing cues is to add smileys—keep reading.

Smile and Be Understood!

Over the last few years, e-mail users have developed a number of ways to clarify the meaning of messages. You might see **<g>** at the end of the line, for example. This means "grin" and is shorthand for saying, "you know, of course, that what I just said was a joke, right?" You may also see **:-)** in the message. Turn this book sideways, so that the left column of this page is up and the right column is down, and you'll see that this is a small smiley face. It means the same as **<g>**, "of course, that *was* a joke, okay?"

Emoticons Galore

Little pictures are commonly known as "smileys." But the smiley face, though by far the most common, is just one of many available symbols. You *might* see some of the emoticons in the following table, and you may want to use them. Perhaps, you can create a few of your own.

Techno Talk

Share the Smiles

Many people simply call these character faces "smiley faces." But if you'd like to impress your friends with a bit of technobabble, you can call them *emoticons*. And if you really want to impress your colleagues, get hold of *The Smiley Dictionary* by Seth Godin. It contains hundreds of these things.

Commonly Used Emoticons

Emoticon	Meaning
:-(	Sadness, disappointment
8-)	Kinda goofy-looking smile, or wearing glasses
:->	A smile
;-)	A wink
*<|:-)	Santa Claus
:-&	Tongue-tied
:-o	A look of shock
:-p	Tongue stuck out
,:-) or 7:^]	Ronald Reagan

Personally, I don't like smileys much. They strike me as being just a *tiiiny* bit too cutesy. However, I do use them now and again to make *absolutely* sure that I'm not misunderstood!

Message Shorthand

There are a couple of other ways people try to liven up their messages. One is to use obscure acronyms like the ones in this table.

Online Shorthand

Acronym	Meaning
BTW	By the way
FWIW	For what it's worth
FYI	For your information
IMHO	In my humble opinion
IMO	In my opinion
LOL	Laughing out loud (used as an aside to show your disbelief)
OTF	On the floor, laughing (used as an aside)
PMFBI	Pardon me for butting in
PMFJI	Pardon me for jumping in
RTFM	Read the &*^%# manual

Acronym	Meaning
ROTFL or ROFL	Rolling on the floor laughing (used as an aside)
ROTFLMAO	Same as above, except with "laughing my a** off" added on the end. (You didn't expect me to say it, did you? This is a family book, and anyway, the editors won't let me.)
TIA	Thanks in advance
YMMV	Your mileage may vary

The real benefit of using these is that they confuse the average neophyte. I suggest that you learn them quickly, so you can pass for a long-term cybergeek.

You'll also see different ways of stressing particular words. (You can't use bold and italic in Internet e-mail, remember?) You might see words marked with an underscore on either side (_now!_) or, perhaps less frequently, with an asterisk (*now!*).

The Least You Need to Know

➤ There are many different e-mail systems, but the basic procedures all work similarly.

➤ Even if your online service lets you use fancy text (colors, different fonts, different styles) within the service, that text won't work in Internet messages.

➤ Sending files across the Internet is often tricky, but it's easy to do so *within* the online services.

➤ On the Internet, the most common file-transfer methods used are MIME and UUENCODE. These are often built into mail programs, or you can use external utilities to convert the files.

➤ Don't send a file until you know which system the recipient is using.

➤ Get to know all the neat little things your e-mail program can do for you, such as create mailing lists and carry out file-filtering.

➤ Be careful with e-mail; misunderstandings (and fights) are common.

Chapter 4

The World of the World Wide Web

In This Chapter

> ➤ What is the Web?

> ➤ Which browser should you use?

> ➤ The home page

> ➤ Moving around the Web

> ➤ The history list and bookmarks

> ➤ Using the URLs

The World Wide Web is also known as *The Web*, *WWW*, and sometimes (among really geeky company) *W3*. And, in really confused company, it's called *the Internet*. I'd better clear up that little confusion about the Web and the Internet right away.

The World Wide Web is *not* the Internet. It's simply one software system running on the Internet. Still, it's one of the most interesting and exciting systems, so it has received a lot of press, to the extent that many people believe that the terms Web and Internet are synonymous. However, the Web seems to be taking over roles previously carried out by other Internet services, and at the same time, Web programs—*browsers*—are including utilities to help people work with non-Web services. For instance, you can send and receive e-mail with some Web browsers, and you can read Internet newsgroups with some.

What's the Web?

Imagine that you are reading this page in electronic form, on your computer screen. Then imagine that some of the words are underlined and colored. Use your mouse to point at one of these underlined words on your screen and press the mouse button. What happens? Another document opens, a document that's related in some way to the word you clicked.

That's a simple explanation of *hypertext*. If you've ever used Apple's Hypercard or a Windows Help file, you've used hypertext. Documents are linked to each other in some way, generally by clickable words and pictures. Hypertext has been around for years, but until recently most hypertext systems were limited in both size and geographic space. Click a link, and you might see another document held by the same electronic file. Or maybe you'll see a document in another file, but that's on the same computer's hard disk, probably the same directory.

The World Wide Web is like a hypertext system without boundaries. Click a link, and you might be shown a document in the next city, on the other side of the country, or even on another continent. Links from one document to another can be created without the permission of the owner of that second document. And nobody has complete control over those links. When you put a link in your document that connects to someone else's, you are sending your readers on a journey that you really can't predict. They will land at that other document, from which they can take another link somewhere else—another country, another subject, or another culture—from which they can follow yet another link...and on and on.

The Web has no capacity limit, either. Web pages are being added every minute of the day, all over the world. In fact, the Web is really pushing the growth of the Internet. It's so easy to create and post a Web page that thousands of people are doing it, and more are joining them each day.

If you haven't seen the Web, this may all sound a little mundane. Okay, so one document leads to another that leads to another...I try to avoid the Internet hype we've been inundated with over the last couple of years, but the Web really is a publishing revolution. It has made publishing to an international audience quick and simple. I don't mean to imply (as some Internet proponents seem to), that every Web page is a jewel that is widely read and appreciated (much of it is closer to a sow's ear than to silk). But it's a medium with which people can make their words available so that they *can* be widely read if they have some value.

Let's Start

If you want to listen to a CD, you need a CD player. If you want to watch a video, you need a video player. And if you want to view a Web page, you need a Web player: a *Web browser*.

There are actually two parts to the Web equation. First, there's a *Web server*, a special program running on a host computer (that is, a computer connected directly to the Internet). This server administers a Web site, which is a collection of World Wide Web documents. The second part is the *browser*, a program on your PC that asks the server for the documents and then displays the documents so that you can read them.

There are really two big contenders in the Web browser war (yes, there's a war going on). One is Netscape Navigator. Right now, somewhere around 80% of all Web users are working with Netscape. Netscape is available in versions for Windows 3.1, Windows 95 and NT, the Macintosh, and various flavors of UNIX. The following figure shows the Netscape Navigator Web browser.

Servers and Clients If you hang around on the Internet long enough, you'll hear the terms "server" and "client" used over and over. A *server* is a program that provides information that a *client* program can use in some way.

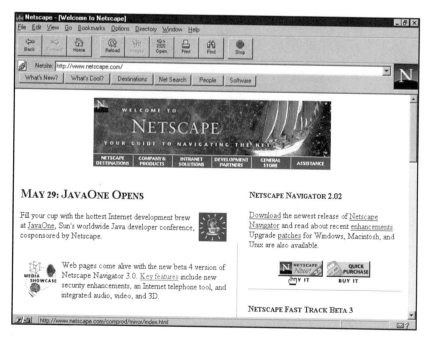

Netscape Navigator is currently the most popular browser on the Web.

Netscape Navigator

This browser is manufactured by Netscape Communications. You might think that it would be known as Navigator for short, but it's not. It's known as Netscape mainly for "historical" reasons. The Netscape programmers came from the NCSA (National Center for Supercomputing Applications). They originally created the first graphical Web browser, called *Mosaic*. Netscape was originally known as *Netscape Mosaic*, and the company was Mosaic Communications. Thus, the browser was known as Netscape to differentiate it from Mosaic.

The second most popular browser is Internet Explorer from Microsoft (shown in the following figure). Originally, this ran only on Windows 95 and Windows NT, but now it's available for the Mac and Windows 3.1.

MS Internet Explorer, Microsoft's latest weapon in the Web war with Netscape.

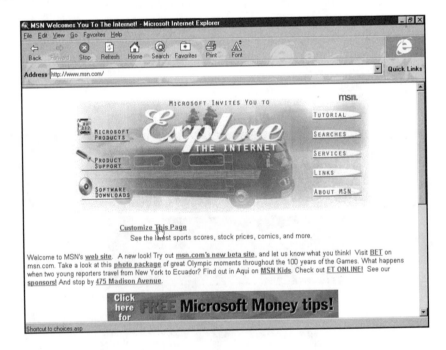

Now, I'm going to keep my head down because what I'm about to say may incite an assault by Web purists. Netscape is not the "be all and end all" of Web browsers. It is undoubtedly a good browser, but you shouldn't feel that if you don't have Netscape you're missing out on something. There are dozens of other browsers available, ranging from pretty awful to very good. Probably the best two are Netscape and Internet Explorer. Personally, I think Explorer is better than Netscape—at least the Windows 95 version is. But I'll concede that they may be neck and neck.

Getting a Browser

Which browser should you use? If your service provider has given you one, I suggest you start with that. You'll probably be given either Netscape or Explorer. Up to now, most service providers have given Netscape, but it looks like that's changing. For example, America Online will (by the time this book is published) be distributing Explorer.

If you have to pick a browser, I suggest that you try Explorer first (if you are using Windows NT or Windows 95); then try Netscape later and see if you like it. If you are using a Mac or Windows 3.1, do it the other way around: start with Netscape (even though the new Explorer for the Mac is getting good reviews). If you are using UNIX, you'll have to go with Netscape; Explorer doesn't currently have a UNIX version. If you want to find Netscape or Explorer, or if you want to see what other browsers are available, see Appendix A.

For now, I'm going to assume that you have a Web browser installed, and that you have opened it and are ready to start. One nice thing about Web browsers is that they all work similarly—and they look very similar, too. So whatever browser you use, you should be able to follow along with this chapter.

Browsing Begins at Home

At the *home page*, that is. When you open your browser, you see your home page. That, by definition, is the first page you see. (I like that kind of definition; it's easy to understand.) For instance, in the earlier figures, you see the default home pages for the Netscape and Explorer browsers (yours will look a little different because this page changes frequently).

Ideally, the home page is a page that has lots of useful links, which take you to places on the Web that you will want to go to frequently. You can create your own home page by using something called HTML, the Web document language (see Chapter 8), or even using one of the fancy new customizing systems you'll find on the Web. (Both Netscape and Microsoft have systems that automatically create customized pages for you, if you have their browsers. Go to **http://www.netscape.com/custom/index.html** for the Netscape system or **http://www.msn.com/** for the Microsoft system. I'll explain how to use these "addresses" later in this chapter, in the section "A Direct Link—Using the URLs.")

Techno Talk

Home Page, Start Page

Internet Explorer actually calls the home page the *start page*, for good reason. The term home page originally meant the page that appeared when you opened your browser or when you used the Home button. Then all of a sudden, everybody was using the term to mean a person or company's main Web page (the page you see when you go to that Web site) such as NEC's home page, Netscape's home page, and so on. So Microsoft's programmers evidently thought it made more sense to rename the home page to "start page." Unfortunately, they're using *both* terms, so Internet Explorer 3.0 has a Home button on the Toolbar (although 2.0 has a Start Page button) and a Go Start Page menu option.

Moving Around on the Web

Let's move around a little. Whatever browser you are using, you'll almost certainly find links on the home page. These are the colored and underlined words. You may also find pictures that contain links, perhaps several different links on a picture (a different link on each part of the picture). Point at a piece of text or a picture; if the mouse pointer changes shape—probably into a pointing hand—you are pointing at a link. (Just to confuse the issue, some pictures contain links, even though the pointer doesn't change shape.)

Click one of the links—whatever looks interesting. If you are online (I'm assuming you are!), your browser sends a message to a Web server somewhere, asking for a page. If the Web server is running (it may not be) and if it's not too busy (it may be), it transmits the document back to your browser, and your browser displays it on your screen.

You've just learned the primary form of Web "navigation." When you see a link you want to follow, you click it. Simple, eh? But what about going somewhere actually useful, somewhere interesting? Most browsers these days either have toolbar buttons that take you to a useful Web page, or come with a default home page with useful links. For example, in Netscape, you can click one of these Directory-bar buttons:

What's New? A selection of new and interesting Web sites from the people at Netscape.

What's Cool? Web sites chosen for their usefulness or CQ—coolness quotient. (Personally, I'm getting tired of the word *cool*. But hey, that's my job: Internet Curmudgeon.)

Destinations More interesting sites, this time broken down by subject—Sports, Travel, Technology, Finance, and so on.

Net Search Web sites that help you search for a subject you are interested in. You'll be looking at these in Chapter 19.

People Links to sites that can help you track down other Internet users.

> **Where Are the Buttons?** You can turn the Directory bar on and off using the **Options, Show Directory Buttons** menu command. These commands are also available from the Directory menu. (I'm assuming that you are using Netscape 3; earlier versions have different buttons.)

How Does It Know Which Server?

How does your browser know which server to request the document from? What you see on your computer screen is not quite the same document that your browser sees. Open the source document—which you probably do using the **View**, **Source** menu option—and you'll see what the Web document *really* looks like. It's just basic ASCII text that contains all sorts of instructions. One of the instructions says, in effect, "if this guy clicks on this link, here's which document I want you to get." You don't normally see all these funky commands because the browser *renders* the page, removing the instructions and displaying only the relevant text.

Internet Explorer 3.0 has a special QuickLinks toolbar (click **QuickLinks** in the Address toolbar to open the QuickLinks toolbar). On that bar, you'll find the Services and Today's Links buttons that take you to useful starting points. The QuickLinks toolbar also has many useful links from the home page and a Search button in the main toolbar that takes you to a page from which you can search the Web (see Chapter 19).

Whatever browser you are using, take a little time to go on a journey of exploration. Go ahead...go as far as you want...get lost. Then come back here, and I'll explain how to find your way back to where you came from.

Link Colors

Some links change color after you click them. You might not know it right away, but if you return to the same page later, you'll find that the link is a different color. The color change indicates that the particular link points to a document that you've already seen. The "used-link" color does expire after a while, and the link changes back to its original color. How long it takes for this to happen is something that you can generally control with an option in the program's Preferences or Options.

The Hansel and Gretel Dilemma: Where Are You?

Hypertext is a fantastic tool, but it has one huge drawback: it's easy to get lost. If you are reading a book and you flip forward a few pages, you know how to get back. You flip back, right? But with hypertext, after a few moves through the electronic library, you can become horribly lost. How, exactly, do you get back to where you came from? And *where* did you come from anyway?

Over the years, a number of systems have been developed to help a person find his or her way around this rather strange freeform medium. This table explains some tools you can use in most Web browsers to move through the pages and sites you've seen.

Web Page Navigation Tools

Button	Description
Back	Click the **Back** button or choose **Back** from a menu (probably the **Go** menu) to return to the previous Web page.
Forward	Click the **Forward** button or choose the **Forward** menu option to return to a page you've just come back from.
Home	Click the **Home** (or **Start**) button to go all the way back to your home page or start page.
Bookmarks	You can set bookmarks on pages you think you'll want to come back to; these can be very helpful because you don't have to struggle to find your way back the next time.
History	This is a list of pages you've seen previously. The **Back** and **Forward** commands take you back and forward through this list. But you can also go directly to a page in the history list by selecting it from the **Go** menu. (In Explorer 2.0, you select from the **File** menu.)

Bookmarks and History

The bookmark system (known as Favorites in Internet Explorer) and the history list are essential tools for finding your way around. Get to know them soon. In most browsers, you can just click a button or select a menu option to place a bookmark. Each system works a little differently, of course. In Netscape, choose **Bookmarks**, **Add Bookmark**, and the bookmark is added to the bottom of the Bookmark menu (you can move it to a folder or submenu later). In Internet Explorer, choose **Favorites**, **Add to Favorites**. In Explorer, you can decide where to put the bookmark when you set it. Both systems have both Bookmarks windows and an associated Bookmarks menu. (Well, okay, in Explorer they're called the Favorites window and menu.) Creating a folder in the window automatically creates a submenu in the menu.

To open Netscape's Bookmarks window choose **Bookmarks**, **Go to Bookmarks** or choose **Window**, **Bookmarks** (depending on which version you have). In Explorer, click the **Open Favorites** button or choose **Favorites**, **Open Favorites Folder**.

A Little History

The history list varies tremendously. Netscape's history list is not very helpful. It lists some, but not all, of the pages you've visited in the current session. Other browsers show much more, often listing pages from previous sessions. Explorer, for instance, keeps a record of up to 3,000 pages (including all the pages from the current session and earlier sessions). You can view the list in a window (see the following figure) sorted by date or by name. You can even search the list by using the Windows 95 **Find** tool on the **Start** menu, for example. Double-click an entry to open that Web page.

In or Out? In Internet Explorer 2.0, the window is separate from the browser window; in version 3.0, the history list is shown within the browser window.

Whatever system you have, though, using the history list is simple. Select the entry from the **Go** menu if you're using Netscape or Internet Explorer 3.0; in Internet Explorer 2.0, you'll find the entries on the File menu. You can also open the history window. In Explorer, choose **Go**, **Open History Folder** in version 3.0, or choose **File**, **More History** in version 2.0. In Netscape, choose **Window**, **History**.

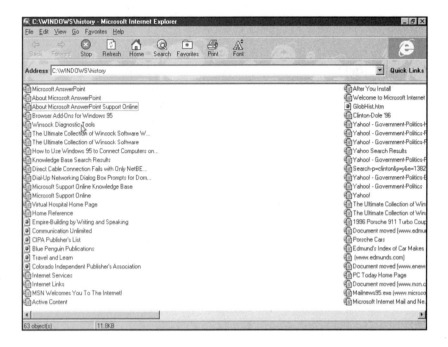

Internet Explorer's history list lets you go back days or even weeks in your Web travels. Each icon represents a Web page you've seen before.

A Direct Link, Using the URLs

Earlier in this chapter, I mentioned a couple of *URLs*. URLs are Web addresses, such as **http://www.msn.com/** or **http://www.netscape.com/**. These provide a direct link to a particular Web page. Therefore, instead of clicking links to try to find your way to a page, you can tell your browser the URL and say "go get this page."

URL This stands for Uniform Resource Locator, which is a fancy name for "Web address."

Most browsers have a bar near the top in which you can type the URL of the page you want to go to. In Netscape make sure that the **Options**, **Show Location** menu command is chosen to display this bar; in Internet Explorer, choose **View**, **Toolbar**. Then click in the box, type the address, and press **Enter**.

If you don't want the bar there all the time (after all, it takes up room that is sometimes better given to the Web pages themselves), you can leave it turned off. If you keep it turned off, you can generally use a shortcut key to display a dialog box in which you can type a URL. In Netscape, press **Ctrl+L** to open the box; in Internet Explorer, choose **File**, **Open** or press **Ctrl+O**. In either case, you type the URL in the box that appears, just as you would in the text box on the toolbar.

The URL Explained

Let's take a look at a URL and see how it works. Here's a longer one:

> http://www.microsoft.com/isapi/msdownload/new2.idc

A URL can be broken down into certain distinct parts. Using the URL above as an example, here's what each part means:

http://	This tells the browser that the address is for a Web page. In addition to http://, you might see similar prefixes for an FTP site or a Gopher menu (we'll look at those in a moment). Http:// stands for *HyperText Transfer Protocol*, the system used on the Internet to transfer Web pages.
www.microsoft.com/	This is the host name, the name of the computer holding the Web server that is administering the Web site you want to "visit."
isapi/msdownload/	This is the directory in which the Web server has to look to find the file you want. In many cases, multiple directories will be listed, so the Web server looks down the "directory tree" in subdirectories. In this example, in fact, it has to look in msdownload, which is a subdirectory of the isapi directory.
New2.html	This is the name of the file you want, the Web page. These are generally .HTM or .HTML files (that means HyperText Markup Language, the "coding" used to create Web pages).

The URL is really nothing complicated, just an address so your browser knows where to look for a file. However, there are different types of URLs, each of which is identified by a different *protocol* portion of the address. The Web page URLs all begin with http://. This table lists some other protocols you'll see on the Internet.

Other Internet Protocols

Protocol Prefix	Description
gopher://	The address of a Gopher site (see Chapter 14).
ftp://	The address of an FTP file library; you'll learn more in Chapter 12.
news:	The address of a newsgroup, discussed in Chapter 9. Note that this doesn't have the // after the name; neither does mailto: (below). However, Netscape has recently been modified to accept news://, too.
mailto:	When you use this URL, the browser's e-mail program opens so you can send mail. Web authors often create links using the mailto: URL so that when someone clicks the link he or she can quickly send a message to the author.
telnet://	The address of a Telnet site (see Chapter 18).
tn3270://	The address of a tn3270 site. This is very similar to Telnet and is also covered in Chapter 18.
wais://	The address of a WAIS site; WAIS is a little used database-search tool, and you probably won't run into many WAIS links.

Forget http://

In most browsers these days (including Netscape and Internet Explorer), you don't need to type the full URL. You can omit the http:// piece, and the browser will assume that the http:// piece should be added. And if you type something beginning with gopher (as in gopher.usa.net, for instance) or ftp (as in ftp.microsoft.com), you can omit the gopher:// or ftp:// part, too.

What Will You Find on Your Web Journey?

When you journey around the Web, you'll find a lot of text documents of course. However, there is much, much more than that. As a system administrator at a Free-Net once said to me, "The Web is for people who can't read!" It was a slight exaggeration, perhaps, but his point was that on the Web, the nontext stuff is often more important than the actual words.

While traveling around the Web, you'll find these sorts of things:

➤ **Pictures:** You'll find these both inside the text documents and on their own. Sometimes, when you click a link (at a museum site, for example), a picture—not a document—is transferred to your browser.

➤ **Forms:** These days, most browsers are forms compatible. In other words, you can use forms to interact with the Web site to send information about yourself (to subscribe to a service, for instance), to search for information, or to play a game, for example.

➤ **Sounds:** Most browsers can play sounds such as voices and music. Many Web sites contain sounds. For instance, IUMA (the Internet Underground Music Archive) has song clips from many new bands.

➤ **Files:** You'll find many Web sites that have files you can download, such as shareware, demos of new programs, and documents of many kinds. When you click a link, your browser begins the file transfer.

➤ **Multimedia of other kinds:** There are all sorts of strange things on the Web: 3D images, animations, Adobe Acrobat .PDF hypertext files, videos, slide shows, 2D and 3D chemical images, and plenty more. Click a link, and the file starts transferring. If you have the right software installed, it automatically displays or plays the file. For instance, in the following figure, you can see a WebShow slide show. (See Chapters 6 and 7 to learn more about multimedia.)

Check This Out...

Where Do I Find What I Want on the Web?

You can follow any interesting links you find, as discussed earlier in this chapter. You can also search for particular subjects and Web pages by using a Web search site, as discussed in Chapter 19.

An ASAP WebShow slideshow presentation in Netscape.

Speeding Up Your Journey by Limiting Graphics

The Web used to be a very fast place to move around. The first Web browsers could display nothing but text, and text transfers across the Internet very quickly. These days, though, things move more slowly. The things I just mentioned—pictures, video, sounds, and so on— really slow down the process. While video is the slowest thing on the Web (moving at an almost glacial pace in most cases), it's actually the pictures that are more of a nuisance; very few sites use video, but *most* use static pictures.

Most browsers provide a way for you to turn off the display of pictures. In Netscape, for instance, choose **Options**, **Auto Load Images**, and remove the check mark from the menu option to turn off images. Because the images are no longer transmitted to your browser, you see the pages much more quickly.

Of course, you often need or want to see those images. Many images have links built into them, and while some Web pages have both graphic links and corresponding text links (for people using a browser that can't or doesn't display pictures), other Web pages are totally unusable unless you can see the pictures. However, you can usually grab the picture you need quickly. Where there *should* be a picture, you'll see a little icon that functions as a sort of placeholder.

In Netscape, you can right-click the placeholder and choose **Load Image** from the shortcut menu that appears. Or you can click the **Images** button in the toolbar to see all of them. In Internet Explorer, you can turn off images in the Options dialog box, *and* you can turn off sounds and video, too. Choose **View**, **Options** and click the **General** tab to see the options that are available. To view an image when you have images turned off, right-click the placeholder and choose **Show Picture** from the shortcut menu.

There's Plenty More!

There's a lot more to say about the Web than I've said in this chapter. In fact, one could write a book about it (actually, I already have: *Using Netscape 3.0* and *Using Internet Explorer*). In the next couple of chapters, you'll learn a few advanced Web-travel tips and a little bit about creating your own Web pages.

The Least You Need to Know

➤ The World Wide Web is a giant hypertext system running on the Internet.

➤ The two best browsers available are probably Netscape and MS Internet Explorer.

➤ The home page (or Start page, in Internet Explorer) is the page that appears when you open your browser.

➤ Click a link in a document to see another document. To find your way back, use the **Back** or **Home** button.

➤ The history list shows where you've been. In Netscape, it includes just some of the pages you've seen in the current session; in some other browsers, it includes all of the pages from the current and some pages from previous sessions.

➤ A URL is a Web "address." You can use the URL to go directly to a particular Web page.

More About
the Web

You've seen the basic moves, now you are ready to learn more techniques to help you find your way around the Web. In the last chapter, you learned how to move around on the Web using a Web browser such as Netscape or Internet Explorer. In this chapter, you'll find out how to run multiple Web sessions at the same time, how to deal with the cache, how to save what you find, and so on. You need to know these advanced moves to work efficiently on the Web.

Multiple Windows—Ambidextrous Browsing

These days, most browsers allow you to run more than one Web session at the same time. Why would you want to do that? Well, there could be many reasons. Everyone's in such a hurry these days.... While you wait for an image to load in one window, you can read something in another window. Or maybe you need to find information at another Web site but don't want to "lose your place" at the current one. (Yes, you have bookmarks and the history list, but sometimes it's just easier to open another window.) You can open one or more new browser windows, as shown in the following figure, so that you can run multiple Web sessions.

Opening multiple windows is a good way to keep from getting lost, or to do more than one thing at a time.

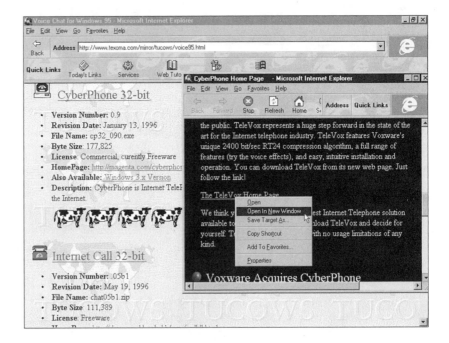

Exactly how you open a new window varies between browsers; however, you'll probably find that most are similar. Here's how the two most popular browsers, Netscape and Internet Explorer, let you open windows.

Netscape gives you two ways to do this:

➤ Right-click the link that you want to "follow" in a new window, and then choose **Open in New Window**. A new Netscape window opens, and the referenced document opens in that window.

➤ Choose **File**, **New Web Browser** or press **Ctrl+N** to open a new window displaying the home page.

Internet Explorer gives you four options:

➤ Right-click the link you want to follow, and then choose **Open in New Window**. A new window opens, displaying the referenced document.

➤ Press **Tab** until the link becomes highlighted, and then press **Shift+Enter**.

➤ Choose **File**, **New Window** or press **Ctrl+N** to open a new window that displays the same document as the one you've just viewed.

➤ Type a URL into the Address text box, and then press **Shift+Enter** to display that document in a new window.

As you might guess, you could encounter some problems when running multiple sessions. First, there's the memory problem. Web browsers are turning into real memory hogs, so you may find that you simply don't have enough memory to run multiple sessions or to run more than one additional session. And remember that there's only so much work your modem can do. If you have several Web windows open and each is transferring things at the same time, every transfer will be slower than if it were the only thing the modem had to do.

Automatic Multiple Sessions

Now and then, you'll find windows opening automatically. In fact, if you are working in Netscape and suddenly notice that the history list has disappeared, it may be that when you clicked a link, a secondary window opened and you didn't notice. (Netscape doesn't transfer history lists to new windows. Internet Explorer does, but even though it clears the entries from the Go menu, you can still view them by opening the history folder.) Web authors can create codes in their Web pages that force browsers to open "secondary" or "targeted" windows.

Your Hard Disk as Web Server?

If you enjoy working on the Web and spend most of your waking hours there, eventually, you'll end up with .HTM or .HTML files on your hard disk. You'll have them in your cache (discussed next), you may save documents using the **File**, **Save As** command, and perhaps you'll even create your own Web pages (see Chapter 8). Your browser provides a way to open these HTML files.

In Internet Explorer choose **File, Open**. Then, in the dialog box that appears, click the **Browse** button. You'll see a typical Open box from which you can select the file you want to open.

HTM or HTML?
Depending to some degree on the operating system you use, the file extension of the HTML Web files might be .HTM or .HTML. Originally, the Web was developed using UNIX computers, and Web files had the extension .HTML. Later, when Windows 3.1 machines started appearing on the Web, the .HTM extension came into use because Windows 3.1 could work only with three-character file extensions. Today, you commonly see both extensions; even though Windows 95 can accept three-letter extensions, not all Windows HTML-editing programs can. And many Windows 3.1 machines are still being used to create Web pages.

Here's a geek trick for you. If you know the exact path to the file you want to open, and if you can type quickly, click in the **Address** or **Location** text box. Then type the entire path and file name, such as **C:/Program Files/ Netscape/Navigator/ownweb.htm**. This should work in both Netscape and Internet Explorer. In some browsers, however, you may need to use the more formal (and older) method by entering the file path in this format: **file:///C|/ Program Files/Netscape/Navigator/ownweb.htm**. Notice that in the second format, you precede the path with **file:///** and replace the colon after C with a pipe symbol (|).

Turbo Charging with the Cache

You need to know about a critical feature of a Web browser—one that seems to make it work really fast. Have you noticed that when you return to a Web document that you've previously viewed, it appears much more quickly? That's because your browser isn't taking it from the Internet; instead, it's getting it from the *cache*, an area on your hard disk or in your computer's RAM (memory) in which it saves pages. This capability is really handy because it greatly speeds up the process of working on the Web. After all, why bother to reload a file from the Internet when it's already sitting on your hard drive? (Okay, you may think of some reasons to do so, but we'll come back to those when we talk about the Reload command.)

Forward Slash or Backslash

UNIX computers use a forward slash (/) between directory names. DOS computers use a backslash(\). As the Web was developed on UNIX computers, URLs use forward slashes. Thus C:/Program Files/Netscape/ Navigator/ownweb.htm is correct, even though in normal DOS notation this would appear as C:\Program Files\Netscape\Navigator\ownweb.htm. However, you can type it whichever way you please when you're opening a file on your hard disk or a page on the Web; both Internet Explorer and Netscape will figure it out.

Here's how this all works. When the browser loads a Web page, it places it in the cache. You can generally control the size of the cache. Not all browsers let you do so, but Netscape, Internet Explorer, and many others do. When the cache fills up, the oldest files are removed to make room for newer ones.

Each time the browser tries to load a page, it *might* look in the cache first to see if it has the page stored. (Whether or not it does depends on how you set up the cache.) If it finds that the page is available, it can retrieve the page from the cache...very quickly.

Putting the Cache to Work

You'll probably want to take advantage of the cache's benefits. To configure the cache in Netscape, choose **Options**, **Network Preferences**, and then click the **Cache** tab. The following figure shows Netscape's cache information.

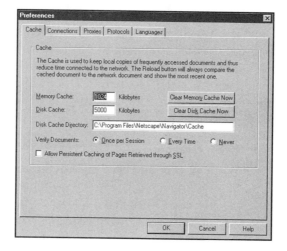

Here's where you set up Netscape's cache.

Configure any of the available settings to meet your needs:

Memory Cache   You can tell Netscape how much of your computer's memory you want to assign to the cache. Netscape stores a few documents in the memory so that it can retrieve them extremely quickly. The button to the right of this option enables you to remove all the pages from the memory cache.

Disk Cache   You can also tell Netscape how large the disk cache should be—that is, how much of your disk space you want to give to Netscape. How much should you give? That all depends on how much disk space you have free. (I always say that you can never have too much hard-disk space, money, or beer; I've been proven wrong once or twice, though.) The button to the right of this option enables you to clear out the disk cache, which is handy when you finally run out of disk space.

Disk Cache Directory   You can tell Netscape *where* to place the disk cache. If you have several hard disks, put it on the fastest disk or the one with most room.

Verify Documents   Now for the complicated one. This tells Netscape when to verify documents. When you request a document (by clicking a link or entering a URL), Netscape can send a message to the Web server saying (basically) "has this document changed since the last time I grabbed it?" If it has changed, Netscape downloads a new copy. If it hasn't changed, Netscape grabs the page from the cache. You can configure Netscape to ask the Web server to verify documents **Once per Session** (in which case, it checks the first time you try to retrieve a document, but it doesn't bother after that); **Every Time** (so that it checks every time you try to get a document, regardless of how many times you view that document in a session); or **Never** (in which case, Netscape doesn't even bother to check to see if it's been updated, unless you use the Reload command).

Allow Persistent Caching of Pages Retrieved Through SSL   This is a new feature related to Internet security. SSL stands for "secure sockets level" (which probably means no more to you than SSL, so I'm not really sure why I told you that). An SSL Web browser can use secure transmission of information; the information is encrypted before being transmitted. (See Chapter 21 for a discussion of encryption.) This feature simply tells the browser not to cache pages that were sent in a secure manner.

Check This Out...

The Hard Disk Cache   Note that you are not reserving an area of your hard disk for the cache. For instance, if you have a 30,000K (almost 30M) disk cache, your browser doesn't create a 30,000K file that prevents other programs from using that disk space. You're just telling the browser that it can use up to that much disk space for the cache *if it's available*—if other programs don't use up the space first.

Internet Explorer uses a very similar system. Choose **View**, **Options**, and click the **Advanced** tab to see the cache information. The following figure shows Explorer 3.0's settings. Although Explorer's programmers—ever the innovators—have taken to referring to the cache as Temporary Internet Files, they are the same thing.

Near the top of the box, you can tell the browser when to check to see if there's a newer version of the file. You can tell it to check **Once per Session**, or you can turn it off altogether (select **Never**).

Notice also that you can modify the size of the cache, this time by dragging a slider to set the percentage of the drive you want to use (instead of by entering an actual MB value). You can clear the cache using the **Empty Folder** button and select the cache directory using the **Move Folder** button. But, notice that Explorer offers something extra: a View Files button. Click the **View Files** button to display a list of the files stored in the cache; then you can double-click a file to open it in the browser.

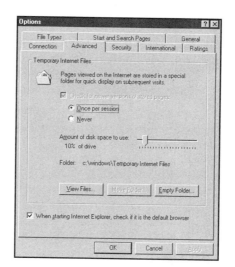

Internet Explorer allows you to modify the cache and view its contents directly.

Decisions, Decisions

Which of the cache options should you use? I prefer Never because it makes my Web sessions *much* quicker. Whenever I tell a browser to go to a Web page that's already in the cache, it loads the page from the hard disk right away, without sending a verification message to the server first. Even if the browser doesn't have to retrieve the page again—because the page hasn't changed—simply checking with the Web server can slow you down noticeably.

On the other hand, I have to remember to keep using the Reload command to make sure I'm viewing the latest version of the Web pages. Some people may prefer to use the Once Per Session option to ensure that they're always looking at the latest page.

What Is Reload?

Sometimes you *do* want to get a file from the Web again. Reload is a "cure" for the cache. If you get a page from the cache, you are not getting the latest document. Sometimes getting the most recent document doesn't matter, but in a few cases, it *does*.

For instance, say you want to return to a site you visited several weeks ago. If you have a very large cache, that document may still be available. If you have the Never option button selected in the Preferences dialog box, your browser displays the *old* document, without checking to see if the corresponding document stored on the Web has changed. Or perhaps, you are viewing a Web document that changes rapidly, such as a stock-quote page. Even if you viewed the page only a few minutes ago, it could already be out of date.

The cure for replacing those old, stale Web pages is to reload them. Click the **Reload** button or choose **View**, **Reload**. Internet Explorer's programmers, in their attempt to rename everything they can, use the term Refresh instead of Reload. (The fact that Reload is a term the Web's been using for several years and that Refresh has a different meaning—Netscape has a Refresh command that simply "repaints" the display using the contents of the memory cache—doesn't seem to matter.) The Reload command (Refresh in Explorer) tells the browser "throw away the copy held in the cache and go get the latest version."

More specific Reload commands are appearing. Netscape has a Reload Cell command that will reload the contents of a single cell in a table. And it also has a Reload Frame command, which reloads just one frame in a framed document. We'll look at frames later in Chapter 6.

Long Documents—Finding What You Need

Some Web pages are large. In fact, some are very large—dozens of pages long—with links at the top of the document that take the user to "sections" lower on the same page. Many Web authors prefer to create one large page than to create lots of small linked ones, the advantage being that once the page has been transferred to your browser, you can use links to move to different parts of the page very quickly.

Virtually all browsers have some kind of Find command—generally Edit, Find or a Find button on the toolbar. Internet Explorer's programmers (as you might guess), have a command called Edit, "Find (on this page)," which I must admit is a very good idea. This command tells the browser to search the current page instead of the Web itself; I'm sure some new users get confused about that issue. (On the other hand, Explorer's Search toolbar button is *not* the same as the Find command; it's for searching the Web.) You'll learn how to search the Web in Chapter 19.

Check This Out...

Don't Forget Find Don't forget the Find command. It can come in very handy for searching long Gopher menus (see Chapter 14) and FTP file listings (Chapter 12), as well as large Web documents.

The Find command works in a way that's very similar to what you've probably used in other programs (in particular, in word processors). Click the **Find** button, or choose **Edit, Find**, and the Find dialog box opens. Type the word or words you are looking for, choose **Match Case** (if necessary), and then click **Find Next**. The browser moves the document so that the first line containing the word or words you are searching for is at the top of the window.

Remember to Right-Click

Remember to use the shortcut menus that appear when you right-click on items. Both Netscape and Internet Explorer use them, as do some other browsers. The shortcut menu is a new toy in the programmer's toy box—and a very nice one at that. Experiment by right-clicking links, pictures, and the background, and you'll find all sorts of useful commands, such as those listed here:

> **Copy Shortcut** or **Copy Link Location**: Copies the URL from the link to the Clipboard.

> **Open**: Opens the related document, just as if you clicked the link.

> **Open in New Window**: Opens a new window and loads the document referenced by the link you clicked.

> **Save Target As** or **Save Link As**: Transfers the referenced document and saves it on your hard disk without bothering to display it in the browser first.

> **Add Bookmark** or **Add to Favorites**: Places an entry for the document referenced by the link in the bookmark or Favorites system.

That's not all, of course. Look to see what else is available. You'll find commands for moving back through framed documents, saving image files, saving backgrounds, and so on. Oh, which reminds me: maybe you should learn how to save such things from the Web, eh?

Is It Worth Saving?

A lot of it really is. Yes, I know that multimedia consultant and author William Horton has called the Web a "GITSO" system. You've heard of GIGO, haven't you? Garbage In, Garbage Out. Well, the Web is a Garbage In, Toxic Sludge Out system.

There really is a lot of sludge out there. But obviously, it's not all sludge. Much of it really is worth saving. And now and then, that's just what you'll want to do: save some of it to your hard disk. Let's look at two aspects in particular: how to save and what you can save.

You can save many, many things from the Web. Most browsers work in much the same ways, though one or two have a few nice little extra "save" features. Here's what you can save:

➤ **Save the document text.** You can copy text from a browser to the Clipboard and then paste the text into another application. Or, you can use the **File**, **Save As** command, which enables you to choose to save the document as plain text (that is, without all the little codes used to create a Web document; you'll look at those in Chapter 8).

Check This Out...

It's Not Yours
Remember that much of what you come across on the Web is copyrighted material. Unless you are sure that what you are viewing is not copyrighted, you should assume that it *is*.

➤ **Save the HTML *source* document.** The source document is the HTML (HyperText Markup Language) document used to create the document that you actually see in your browser. The source document has lots of funky little codes, which you'll understand completely after you read Chapter 8. Once you begin creating your own Web pages (you were planning to do that, weren't you?; everyone else and his dog is), you may want to save source documents so you can "borrow" bits of them. Use **File**, **Save As** and choose to save as HTML.

➤ **Save the text or HTML source for documents you haven't even viewed.** You don't have to view a page before you save it (though to be honest, I haven't yet figured out why you would want to save it if you haven't seen it). Simply right-click the link and choose **Save Target As** or **Save Link As** from the shortcut menu.

➤ **Save inline images in graphics files.** You can copy images you see in Web pages directly to your hard drive. Right-click an image and choose **Save Image As** or **Save Picture As**.

➤ **Save the document background.** Internet Explorer even lets you save the small image that is used to put the background color or pattern in many documents. Right-click the background and choose **Save Background As**.

➤ **Create Windows wallpaper.** Internet Explorer also lets you quickly take an image or background from a document and use it as your Windows wallpaper image. Right-click the picture or the background and choose **Set as Wallpaper**.

➤ **Copy images to the Clipboard.** With this neat Explorer feature, you can copy images directly to the Clipboard. Right-click, and then choose **Copy** or **Copy Background** from the shortcut menu.

➤ **Print the document.** Most browsers have a File, Print command and maybe even a Print button. Likewise, you'll often find a Page Setup command that lets you set margins and create headers and footers.

➤ **Save URLs to the Clipboard.** You can save URLs to the Clipboard, so you can copy them into another program. Copy the URL directly from the Address or Location text box, or right-click a link and choose **Copy Shortcut** or **Copy Link Location**. Some versions of Netscape also allow you to drag a link onto a document in another program; the link's URL will appear in the document.

➤ **Grab files directly from the cache.** Remember that the cache is dynamic; the browser is constantly adding files to and removing files from it. If you have something you want to save, you can copy it directly from the cache. Internet Explorer makes this easy; you simply click the **View Files** button in the Options dialog box. With Netscape, you can view the directory holding the files. However, Netscape renames files, making them hard to identify. Explorer names each file with its URL.

➤ **Save computer files referenced by links.** Many links do not point to other Web documents; they point to files of other formats—which opens a whole can of worms that we'll explore right now.

Grabbing Files from the Web

I like to group these nondocument files into the two following types:

➤ **Files that you want to transfer to your hard disk.** A link might point to an .EXE or .ZIP file (a program file or a .ZIP archive file) that contains a program you want to install on your computer. (See Appendix A for a list of sources of shareware programs, which would fall into this category.)

➤ **Files that you want to play or view.** Other files are not things you want to keep; instead, they are files containing items such as sound files (music and speech), video, graphics of many kinds, word processing documents, and so on, that are part of the Web site you are viewing.

These types of files are the same in one way: whatever you want to do with them— whether you want to save them or simply play them—you *must* transfer them to your computer. However, the purpose of the transfer is different, and the way it's carried out is different.

In the second case (when you want to play or display a file), you might have to configure a special viewer, helper application, or plug-in so that when the browser transfers the file, it knows how to play or display it. We'll look at such things in detail in Chapter 7. For now, we're only interested in the first type of file—a file that you want to transfer and save on your hard disk.

Web authors can distribute computer files directly from their Web documents. A couple of years ago, pretty much the only file libraries were FTP sites (covered in Chapter 12). Now, though, many Web sites have links to files. Companies that want to distribute their programs (shareware, freeware, or demo programs) and authors who want to distribute non-Web documents (PostScript, Word for Windows, Adobe Acrobat, and Windows Help documents, for example) can use Web sites to provide a convenient way to transfer files.

Those Darned Acrobat Files Again

Adobe Acrobat files are special hypertext document files that can be displayed in a free viewer (which you can get at one of the software sites in Chapter 14). I just told you that Acrobat files and others are in the second category. And so they are—but they're in the first, too. It all depends on what you want to do. If you simply want to view the file right now, it would fall into the second category: viewers. If you want to save the file on your hard disk, perhaps for later use, it would fall into the first category: save.

Which category a file fits also depends on the manner in which the file has been saved. In its normal format (the Adobe .PDF format), it could fall into either category. In some compressed formats, it would fall into the first category only because you'd have to save it to your hard disk and decompress it before you could view it. (Compressed formats are explained in Chapter 15.)

Save It

To see how you can save a file, go to TUCOWS (The Ultimate Collection of Winsock Software at **http://www.tucows.com/**). (Its logo is, as you may have guessed by now, two cows.) This site contains a fantastic library of Internet software for Windows computers.

Winsock? What's this Winsock thing? Winsock is a contraction of Windows Sockets, the name of the TCP/IP "driver" used to connect Windows programs to the Internet's TCP/IP system. Just as you need a print driver to connect a Windows program to a printer, you also need a special driver to connect a program to the Internet. The term Winsock refers to programs that can connect to a TCP/IP network.

Suppose you find a link to a program that you want to transfer. You click it as usual, and what happens? Well, if you're using Netscape, and if the file is an .exe or .com file, you'll probably see a File Save box. If so, choose the directory into which you want to save the file (by the way, we'll discuss download directories in Chapter 15). However, you might see the Unknown File Type dialog box (shown in the next figure). This box appears whenever Netscape tries to transfer a file that it doesn't recognize; Netscape wants you to tell it what to do. You can click the **Save As** button to get to the Save As dialog box, and then you can proceed to tell it where you want to save the file.

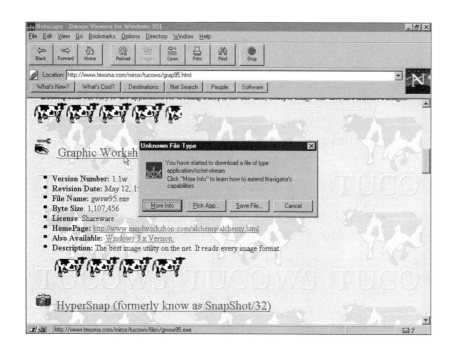

Netscape doesn't know what to do with this file type, so you have to tell it.

Explorer uses a slightly different method. First it displays a dialog box showing that a file is being transferred. After a moment or two, you'll see another dialog box (you can see both in the following figure).

Configuring Always Save

In Chapter 7, you'll learn how to configure a viewer. You should configure the application/octet stream format as an Always Save format. Then Netscape won't bother to display the Unknown File Type box; instead, it will go directly to the Save As box.

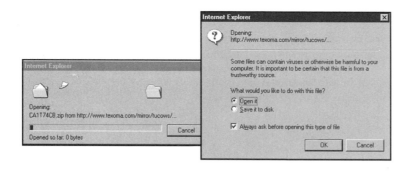

Internet Explorer uses a slightly different method for managing file transfers.

You now have two choices:

➤ You can tell Explorer to **Open it**, in which case Netscape transfers the file to your desktop and runs the file. This is actually a pretty lousy idea, for a couple of reasons. First, if it's a compressed archive file, you'll be expanding all files held by the archive onto the desktop, making a huge mess and mixing them in with all the other files already there. Second, the file may be a program file that will run automatically. If, by chance it contains a virus, you could be in trouble. You should check program files with virus-check software before running them. (You'll learn more about that subject in Chapter 15.)

➤ You can **Save it to disk**. This is the preferable option. Choose this and click **OK**, and the transfer will continue. Once the file has been transferred to your hard disk, you'll see a Save As dialog box in which you can choose where to place the file.

Notice the check box entitled "Always ask before opening this type of file." If you clear the check box, the next time you download a file, Explorer will automatically transfer it and open it, even if you chose the Save it to disk option button the first time. (To recheck this check box, choose **View**, **Options** and click the **File Types** tab. Then click **Application** in the list box, click **Edit**, click **Confirm Open After Download**, and click **OK**.)

The Least You Need to Know

➤ If your computer has enough memory, you can open a second Web document in a new window and keep the current window open.

➤ You'll probably end up saving Web documents on your hard disk; you can reopen them using the **File**, **Open** command.

➤ The cache stores documents you've seen on your hard disk. The browser can get those documents from the cache the next time you want to see them, which speeds up work tremendously.

➤ Reload throws away the version of the page held in the cache and grabs a new one from the Web site. You can configure the cache to do this automatically once every session.

➤ You can copy, print, and save all sorts of things: document text, the document source file, images, background images, and more.

➤ If you click a link to a nondocument file, your browser may ask you what to do with it. You can save it to your hard drive if you want.

Chapter 6

Forms, Applets, and Other Web Weirdness

In This Chapter

➤ Unexpected things you'll run into on the Web

➤ Using tables and forms

➤ Getting into password-protected sites

➤ Using frames and secondary windows

➤ Web programming: Java, JavaScript, and ActiveX

➤ Pushing, pulling, and multimedia

A couple of years ago, you wouldn't have needed this chapter. You would have understood the Web by now. That's because a couple of years ago, the Web was filled with static documents that contained pictures and text. But the Web has changed and is still changing; it's starting to come alive. You'll find all sorts of things that make the Web active. No longer is it just a static medium that you view.

In this chapter, you're going to take a quick look at some weird and wonderful things you might find on the Web, such as tables, forms, password-protected sites, "secondary" or "targeted" windows, and frames. You'll also learn about Java, JavaScript, and ActiveX applets, as well as push and pull commands and multimedia.

Working with Tables

A *table* is...well, you know, a table. It's a set of columns and rows in which you organize text and (sometimes) pictures. Most browsers these days can display tables. So if you are using a recent one (such as Netscape or Internet Explorer), you'll have no problems. Tables are often used to display, well, tabular data. But they can also be used as a simple page layout tool, to get pictures and text to sit in the correct places. (The following figure shows a table being used in this way.) And, recent improvements to the way that HTML handles tables allow authors to use different background colors in each cell.

The Discovery Channel (http:// www.discovery.com/) page formatted using the table feature.

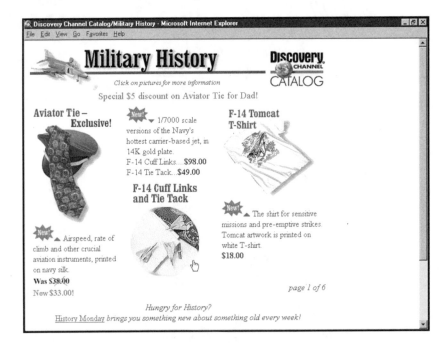

Interactive Web Pages—Using Forms

A *form* is a special *interactive* Web document. It contains the sorts of components that you've become familiar with while working in today's graphical user interfaces: text boxes, option buttons, command buttons, check boxes, list boxes, drop-down list boxes, and so on. You'll find forms at the search sites (see Chapter 19). You use them just like you would a dialog box: you type a search word into a text box, select any necessary options by clicking option buttons, and then click a command button.

Forms are also used to collect information (you might have to enter your name and address when downloading demo software) and make sales. You can choose the products you want to buy and enter your credit-card information into a form. The next figure shows an example form that helps you search for information at the Travelocity Web site (**http://ps.worldview.travelocity.com/PS/generated/browse/destination/6/**).

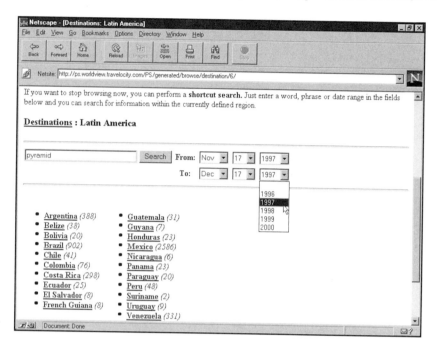

Enter a search word, select dates from the drop-down list boxes, and then click the Search button.

Playing It Safe—Secure Sites

When you enter information into a form and send that information back to the Web server, there is a slight chance that it could be intercepted by someone and read. (It's not very *likely* that your information will be intercepted, but that's another story—which I'll get to in Chapter 20). Netscape, Internet Explorer, and some other browsers, provide a way to send information *securely*. If the form you are viewing comes from a special https:// server (a secure server), the information is *encrypted* before it's sent back from the form to the server. When the server receives the information, it decrypts the information. While the encrypted data is between your computer and the server, the information is useless; anyone who intercepted the information would end up with a load of garbled rubbish.

In most browsers, you know when you are at a secure site. In Internet Explorer, the little lock icon in the lower-right corner is locked. In Netscape, the key in the lower-left corner is whole (it's broken on non-secure sites), and a blue bar appears just below the toolbars when the site is secure. Other browsers use similar but slightly different methods to indicate that you are at a secure page.

One indicator of a secure site is visible in any Web browser. As you can see in the following figure, the URL of a secure Web page begins with **https://** instead of **http://**. If you send information to this site or receive information from it, you can be sure that the information will be transmitted in a secure, encrypted manner.

Netscape uses a number of indicators to show that a site is secure.

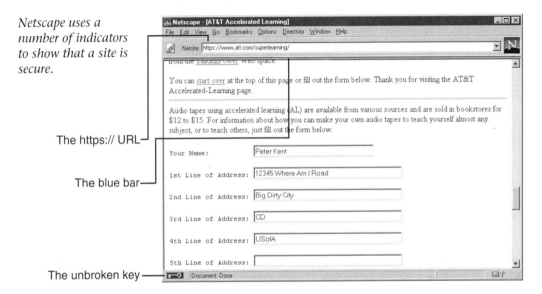

The https:// URL

The blue bar

The unbroken key

For Your Eyes Only: Password-Protected Sites

One day people will actually start spending money online. Right now, however, people seem to want everything to be free. If you've paid your service provider, you don't want to pay *again* when you get where you are going, right?

Because of this, you may not find a huge number of password-protected sites right now. These are Web sites that you can't view unless you enter a password, which is given to you when you go through a registration process (which probably includes some form of wallet surgery).

How Adult Sites Benefit from the CDA I find it amusing that the Communications Decency Act has actually led to higher profits for the owners of porn sites. Because all but the softest of softcore has now been moved into password-protected sites, anyone looking for these materials must pay. Just a few months ago, these sites had to provide "teasers" to get people in. Now they just say, "Sorry, you'll have to join if you want to view."

You *will* find password-protected sites, however, if you enjoy Web sites with, um, lewd and lascivious content. Many adult-oriented sites use password protection as a way to keep out underage users and to force people to pay for what they want to view.

These aren't the only password-protected sites, of course. The following figure shows the Netscape Development Partners site, which is only accessible to people who have coughed up some huge sum for the privilege. In this case, you have to enter your User ID and password into a form; in other cases, the browser opens a dialog box into which you type the information.

The Netscape Development Partners site; you'd better have a password if you want to get in.

Dealing with Secondary Windows

I should know better, but once or twice I've been confused when I've suddenly discovered that Netscape's history list has disappeared. What happened? I clicked a link and then looked away for a moment. While my eyes were averted, another browser window opened automatically. I continued, unaware of what had happened.

If they want to, Web authors can set up a link so that when you click it a new window opens, and the referenced document appears in that window. It's a very handy feature when used properly. These windows are called *targeted* windows. (I prefer to use an older hypertext term: *secondary* windows.)

Public Letter to Web Authors Dear Web authors: it's bad interface design to open a secondary window full-screen. Please open your windows slightly less than full screen, so it's obvious to your users what's going on! Signed, Confused in Denver.

Check This Out...

73

When a targeted window opens in Netscape, the history list disappears from the previous window because Netscape's history list is linked to a particular window. Internet Explorer doesn't have quite the same problem because its history list is managed in a very different way. While the Back and Forward commands stop working in Internet Explorer, you can still access the full history list and get back to a previous page from where you are.

Panes or Frames

Another new feature you may find while browsing on the Web is *frames*. (In other earlier hypertext systems, these were sometimes known as *panes*). The following figure shows an example of frames. When you open a framed document, you find that it displays two or more documents, each within its own pane. The frames around each document may be moveable (if the author set them up that way), and you may have scroll bars in each pane.

The How We See demo shows a good use of framed documents. Click parts of the eye in the left frame to see information in the right frame.

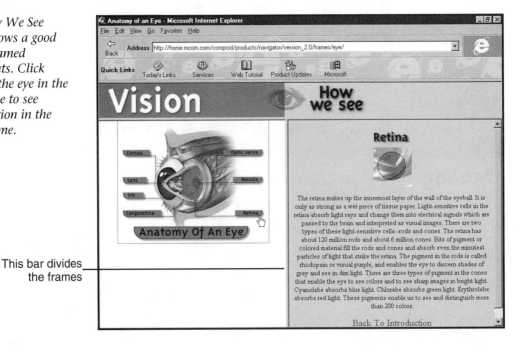

This bar divides the frames

Netscape has special commands to manage the history list and reloads in frames; other browsers will probably follow suit soon. Click inside a frame and then choose **View, Reload Frame** to reload the contents of that one frame. The other frames remain as they are. In addition, some versions of the Netscape browser have a **Back in Frame** command with which you can move back to the previously viewed document within the frame (instead of having to go all the way back to the previous nonframed document).

Animated Icons

Animated icons are becoming popular these days. These are little pictures embedded into Web documents that appear to be in motion. They are relatively easy for Web authors to create, so you can expect to see many more of them appearing on the Web. They add a little motion to a page (this is known in Web jargon as "making a page more compelling"), without causing a lot of extra stuff to be transmitted to your computer.

If you find large and complicated things in motion, you've stumbled across some kind of video or animation file format (see Chapter 7) or perhaps an actual Web program created in Java or ActiveX.

Web Programs: Java, JavaScript, and ActiveX

You may have heard of Java by now. I'm not talking about a chain of coffee bars; I'm talking about a new programming language that will (if you believe the hype) make the Web more exciting, make every appliance from toasters to dishwashers talk to you in Swahili, bring about world peace, and lead to a complete and total eradication of body odor.

That may be true, but for the moment Java is pretty much a programmer's toy. It may take over the world one day, but right now you'll find that Java applications (sorry, "Java applets") are mostly fairly small programs that do nothing more extravagant than add some life to an otherwise-dull Web page. Still, you may be surprised when you arrive at a Web site and see a moving text banner or bouncing heads. That's probably Java at work.

In order for these programs to work, you must be using a Java-compatible Web browser—and even then they may not work (which tends to reduce the believability of their total Web infiltration somewhat!). Netscape 2.0 or later and Internet Explorer 3.0 are Java-compatible. When you reach a Web page that has an embedded Java applet, the Java program is transmitted to your computer, and the browser then runs the program. The program may be a game of some sort (like the one in this figure), a multimedia display, a financial calculator of some kind, or just about anything else. You can find links to Java apps at Gamelan (**http://www.gamelan.com/**).

Check This Out...

Java Interpreters
Java-compatible browsers are Java "interpreters." In effect, an interpreter is a program that can run another program, coordinating between the computer's operating system and the program. So a Java applet can run on any operating system (Windows 3.1, Windows 95, Macintosh System 7, and UNIX of various flavors) as long as it has an interpreter created for that operating system.

This Alien Invasion game is a Java applet.

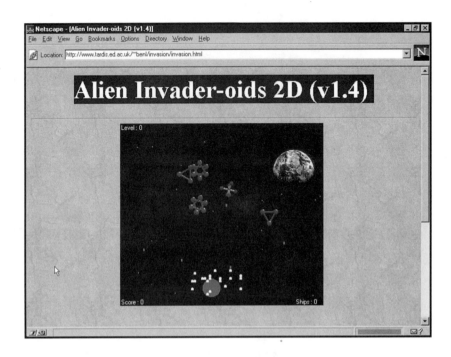

I think Java has been greatly over-hyped (could you tell?). For all the overblown projections, Java applets remain rarely used, unreliable, and slow. (And, in many cases, pointless.) Quite frankly, I don't really see the point of using Java to turn your Web browser into a command-line interface, as one Java applet I saw does. (You have Telnet for that; see Chapter 18.) Searching for interesting or useful Java applets is an experience in frustration and disappointment, with only an occasional surprise. Maybe someday Java will fulfill its promise. But it won't be soon, so don't hold your breath.

Check This Out...

Applications Across the Net

You may have heard the theory that pretty soon, instead of buying software and installing it on your hard drive, you'll "rent" programs across the Internet, paying for the time you use. If this *ever* happens (and there are good reasons to suspect it won't), it will be a very long time from now. Internet connections are currently about as reliable and efficient as a drunk at a beer tasting, and until they are as reliable as the electricity supply, this system simply won't work. I've added this projection to my "yeah, right, don't hold your breath" list.

What About JavaScript and ActiveX?

JavaScript is Java's baby brother. It's a scripting language in which programs are written within the Web page. In other words, a JavaScript-compatible browser reads the Web page, extracts the JavaScript commands, and runs them. JavaScript is not as powerful a programming language as Java, but it's a bit easier to use. You can find loads of JavaScript programs at Gamelan (**http://www.gamelan.com/noframe/Gamelan.javascript.html**) and The JavaScript Index (**http://www.c2.org/~andreww/javascript/**). The following figure shows an example of a JavaScript application, taken from a book I wrote on the subject.

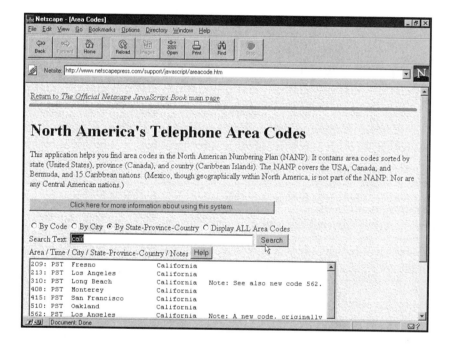

My Area Code program, written in JavaScript.

Finally, there's ActiveX. Right now ActiveX is an almost unknown quantity. A competitor to Java, it's a new system from Microsoft, designed to allow Web authors to easily incorporate multimedia and programs into their Web pages. Currently the only ActiveX browser is Internet Explorer, and you can probably expect it to stay that way for a while. With Netscape as the most popular browser, there's not much incentive for Netscape Communications to add ActiveX to Netscape and help their major competitor! (On the other hand, if Internet Explorer begins to gain Web share—which it seems to be doing—that situation may change.)

Just a Little Shove—Pushing and Pulling

Web authors can set up their Web pages to do things by themselves. Currently, information arrives at your screen because you've directly requested it—by clicking a link or entering a URL. However, Web pages will soon be using *server push* and *client pull*.

The first of these, *server push*, occurs when the Web server continues sending information even though you haven't requested it. For instance, suppose you click a link to display a Web page, and just a few minutes later, the Web page changes. Even if you don't request more information, the server sends updated information and continues to send periodic updates until you close the page.

Client pull is similar, except that the request for updates comes from Netscape. For instance, suppose that you open a page. At the same time the server sends the page, it sends a special program (you don't see this; it all happens in the "background"). This program tells Netscape when to request updates. After the defined interval, Netscape sends a request to the server asking for the information. Again, this will continue until you leave the page.

These systems work so similarly that you usually won't know which method is being used. They are very useful when you're viewing information that changes rapidly, such as stock quotes, weather reports, news headlines, or auctions. At this time, they're not in wide use, but they may become more popular in time.

Check This Out...

The Web Gets More Complicated

As you'll see in Chapter 8, creating a Web page is really quite easy. And even many of the more advanced Web-authoring techniques are not particularly complicated. Sure, there are special codes to learn, but it's all reasonably straightforward.

But now we're seeing the introduction of things that the average Web author will find much more complicated to use. Technologies such as Java, JavaScript, ActiveX, and push and pull require some programming skills. As a result, it's becoming harder for Web authors to keep up with the Joneses (technologically speaking), which may be a good thing. Now they can concentrate on function instead of form, forget about the glitz, and compete by making their Web sites interesting and content-rich instead of just trying to be "cool."

The Multimedia Experience

You'll find all sorts of file formats on the World Wide Web. You'll find a variety of still pictures, video and animations, sounds, electronic documents, 3-D images, and so on. Any file format that you can play or display on your computer can be linked to a Web page.

When you click a link that takes you to one of these file formats, Netscape handles the file itself, if it can. It displays the document or picture in the window in the normal way. But if the file is a format that Netscape can't handle, it has two options. It may send the file directly to a program that *can* handle it (known as a *plug-in, viewer,* or *helper*), or it may ask you what to do. We'll take a look at this subject in Chapter 7.

The Least You Need to Know

➤ The Web is far more diverse than it was a year or two ago; it's much more than just text with pictures.

➤ You'll find lots of tables and forms.

➤ Framed documents allow an author to split a document into multiple pieces, each of which is displayed in its own frame.

➤ Java, JavaScript, and ActiveX are Web programming languages that let authors bring their pages to life. They're currently not much used, though, despite all the hype.

➤ Client pull is a system by which a browser automatically requests updates to a page. Server push is a system by which a server automatically sends updates.

➤ A wide range of multimedia formats must be displayed in viewers or plug-ins; you'll learn about those in Chapter 7.

Web Multimedia

In This Chapter

➤ How does a browser handle different file formats?

➤ Finding plug-ins and viewers

➤ Types of plug-ins and viewers you may want

➤ Installing plug-ins

➤ Installing viewers in Netscape

➤ Installing viewers in Internet Explorer

It's only logical that as the Web gets older, and as people start using it more, it's going to store more types of computer files. You'll find animations, videos, pictures of various formats, sounds that play once they've transferred to your computer, sounds that play *as* they transfer to your computer, "slide" presentations, and all sorts of other weird and wonderful things. Think of this as the *multimedia* content of the Web—literally "multiple media."

Today's Web browsers are designed to handle *any* computer-file format. So when you click a link to a file, that file is transferred to your computer. Your browser can then use it in one of three ways:

➤ **On its own**   The file format may be one that the browser can handle directly. Many Web browsers can play or display Web pages (.HTM or .HTML), text documents (.TXT), some graphics formats (.GIF, .XBM, .JPG, and .JPEG), and some sound formats.

➤ **With a plug-in**   The browser may open a *plug-in*, a special add-on program that plays or displays the file within the browser window.

➤ **With a viewer (or helper)**   The browser may send the file to a *viewer* or *helper*—another program that recognizes the file format—and open a window in which that program can play or display the file.

When you first get your browser, it probably *won't* recognize all of the file formats you'll encounter. When the browser comes across a file format that it doesn't recognize, it will ask you what to do; you can then install a new plug-in or viewer to handle that file type.

Two Types of Multimedia Inclusions

There are basically two ways to include a multimedia file in a Web page. The author may include the file as a *live object* (a file that is automatically transferred to your computer along with the Web page). For instance, a live object may play a background sound or display a picture in a special high-resolution format. The file is, in effect, embedded within the Web page. On the other hand, the author can include the file as an *external* file; you click a link and that file (without a Web page) is transferred to your computer.

What's Available?

Which Plug-Ins Are Installed?   You can quickly find out which plug-ins are installed in Netscape by choosing **Help, About Plug-ins**. You'll see a page showing you each plug-in and its file name. You'll also find a link to the Inline Plug-Ins page.

Scores of plug-ins and viewers are available; you just have to know where to find them. A good starting point for plug-ins is the Netscape Navigator Components page, at **http://home.netscape.com/comprod/mirror/ navcomponents_download.html**. You can find links to viewers and plug-ins that will work in Internet Explorer at **http://www.microsoft.com/ie/addons/**. You can also find many viewers at the sites discussed in Appendix A.

About now, you're probably wondering whether you should use a plug-in or a viewer. In general you'll probably prefer working with plug-ins because they allow the browser itself to display or play the file. Effectively, a plug-in extends the capabilities of the browser, allowing it to work with a file type that it couldn't use before. A viewer, on the other hand, is a completely separate program; the Web browser remains at the previous Web page, while the multimedia file is sent to the viewer.

Of course, there may be cases in which a viewer is actually a better program and has more features than the equivalent plug-in. You may want to experiment and find the most capable of the two.

Which Do You Need? Which Do You Want?

You really don't need all the viewers and plug-ins available. There are literally hundreds already, and more are being added all the time. So unless you are independently wealthy and don't need to waste time working, you probably won't have time to install them all (and you probably don't have the disk space you'd need). To help you determine which plug-ins and viewers you should get, I've broken them down into a few categories and the most common file formats.

Music and Voice (Very Useful)

Some of the most useful plug-ins and viewers are those for music and voice. In particular, you'll want RealAudio, TrueSpeech, and StreamWorks, three different systems that allow a sound file to play as it is being transferred. Most sound formats can't play until they have been completely transferred to your disk drive (you twiddle your thumbs for ten minutes—and then listen).

The RealAudio viewer playing the newscast from NPR.

The RealAudio, TrueSpeech, and StreamWorks formats are the most popular systems of those that play sounds as they are being transferring. They're used by radio stations and music libraries, for example, so you can listen to the news from National Public Radio (**http://www.npr.org**) or music from the Internet Underground Music Archives (**http://www.iuma.com**). The figure on the previous page shows the Internet Explorer screen as it looks while RealAudio plays a file from the NPR site.

During your Internet travels, you are likely to come across these other sound formats:

Check This Out...

You Already Have Viewers
In many cases, you may already have viewers for certain file formats. For instance, if you use Windows, you can use the Windows Media Player as a viewer for MIDI files. If you use the Macintosh and have Word, you can use Word as the viewer for Word .DOC files.

.AU, .AIF, .AIFF, .AIFC, and .SND   A variety of common sound formats, used on UNIX and on the Mac. Your browser can probably play these without an additional plug-in or viewer.

.WAV   The Windows sound format. Your browser can probably play these without an additional plug-in or viewer.

.MID, .RMI   These are MIDI (Musical Instrument Digital Interface) formats. You may need to add a plug-in or viewer for these. (Netscape 3 comes with a pre-installed plug-in that will work with MIDI files.)

The MIDI formats are not common, but they are of interest to people who, well, are interested in MIDI. Many MIDI sites on the Web have sound clips. (MIDI is a system used to create music using computers and other electronic toys.)

Other Document Formats (Also Very Useful)

Viewers and plug-ins are also available for a number of document formats that you'll find on the Web. In particular, the Adobe Acrobat Reader is useful. Adobe Acrobat is a hypertext format that actually predates the Web. It allows an author to create a multipage hypertext document that is contained in a single file, and which can be read by any Acrobat reader, regardless of the operating system it is running on. Many authors like to use Acrobat because it gives them more control over the layout than they get when creating Web pages. You'll often find documents in Acrobat format linked to Web pages. You can see an example of an Acrobat file in the following figure.

An Adobe Acrobat file from the New York Times, displayed in the Adobe Acrobat viewer.

You'll also find viewers and plug-ins that display Microsoft Word, Envoy, and PostScript documents.

3-D Worlds (Greatly Overrated!)

Netscape Navigator has a plug-in called Live3D that you can use to view 3-D images on the Web (see the next figure). Live3D may have been installed when you installed Netscape, depending on which version you have. You can download other 3-D plug-ins or viewers, too.

Do you really want a 3-D plug-in or viewer? Probably not. Once you've see a couple of 3-D sites, the novelty will quickly wear off. This is another of those much-touted technologies that hasn't yet lived up to the hype. 3-D images load slowly and move slowly. They are, in my opinion, an unnecessary gimmick. Perhaps one day they'll be an integral part of the Web, but for now they're little more than a toy.

VRML These 3-D images are in a format known as VRML: Virtual Reality Modeling Language.

85

These Netscape cubes
are spinning, thanks
to the magic of
Live3D.

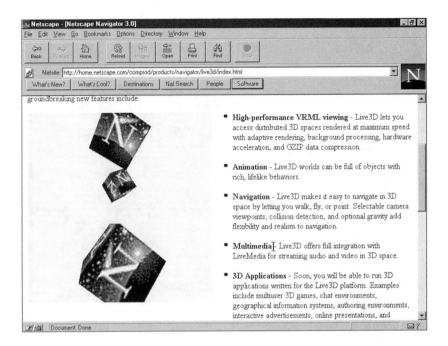

Video (If You Can Wait)

Video is fairly popular on the Web, but it has serious drawbacks. The main problem is speed. It can take literally hours for anything big to transfer, and if it's small, well, what's the point? After watching a five-second cut from a movie, I was left with the question "was that really worth it?" ringing in my head.

Video is another of those things that really requires a fast connection. If you are on a corporate network you are probably okay, but if you are using a modem to connect to a service provider, you'll find it rather sluggish. (This just in...Microsoft Founder Bill Gates, in a recent interview, claims that most people will be stuck with slow modem connections for another five years or so. Hey, I've been saying that for a long time, but would anyone listen to *me*?)

Still, if you want to try it, you can find many viewers and plug-ins for video. The most common formats are the Windows .AVI format (which may be built into your browser already), QuickTime, and MPEG. A new format, .VIV, is a compressed .AVI file that provides streaming video. The following figure shows Netscape's simple plug-in. Netscape 3.0 comes with a built-in .AVI plug-in, but other .AVI plug-ins and viewers actually have more features.

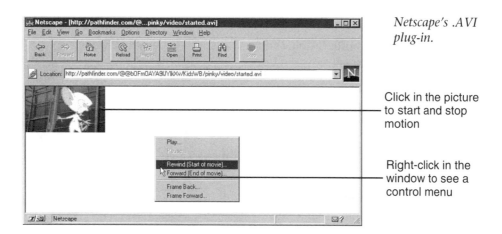

Netscape's .AVI plug-in.

Click in the picture to start and stop motion

Right-click in the window to see a control menu

Streaming Video

I mentioned RealAudio earlier. RealAudio is a "streaming" audio format, which means it plays as it transmits. That's the new thing in video, too. Not too long ago you'd have to wait for a video file to transfer completely before you could play it. Now streaming video viewers and plug-ins are turning up; these play the video as it transmits.

Animations (Here and There)

You'll find many animation plug-ins and viewers ...but only a few different formats are commonly used on the Web. It's popular these days for any software company with a proprietary file format to create a plug-in for it. Netscape predicts that there will be more than 100 plug-ins by the end of 1996. But very few Web authors are actually using animation, and only a few of the available formats are commonly used. Probably the most common animation formats are Macromedia's Authorware and Directory animations, which can be viewed using the Shockwave plug-in. (What do I mean by animation, as opposed to video? Think of video as a film; think of animation as a cartoon.)

Other Weird File Formats

You'll find plug-ins and viewers available for all sorts of unusual file formats. And some plug-ins are not really programs designed for handling particular file formats that you may come across while cruising the Web; they are more like special utilities designed to extend the features of the Web browser. For instance, there are Netscape plug-ins available for these:

➤ **Carbon Copy**   A Netscape plug-in that lets you control a PC across the Internet.

➤ **Chemscape Chime**   A plug-in for 2-D and 3-D chemical models.

➤ **EarthTime**   A plug-in that displays eight different times from cities around the world.

➤ **ISYS Hindsight**   A plug-in that keeps a record of every Web page you've seen and even allows you to search the text of pages you've seen.

➤ **Look@Me**   Allows you to view another user's computer screen across the Web and see what's going on.

➤ **Net-Install**   A plug-in designed to automate the transfer and installation of software across the Internet.

Looking for Samples?   A good place to find samples of these various multimedia formats is the Netscape page that I mentioned earlier. For each plug-in or viewer, you'll find links to Web sites using the file format handled by that program.

As I mentioned earlier, though, any file type can be sent to a viewer of some kind. However, you will rarely run across these file types on the Web. There are only a handful that are commonly used (the ones I mentioned earlier as the common formats). You'll only want to install other plug-ins and viewers if the particular file type happens to be used at the Web sites that you frequent.

You don't necessarily need to install these plug-ins or viewers right away. You can wait until you stumble across a link to one of the file formats. If your browser doesn't recognize the format, it will ask you what to do with the file. We'll look at installing viewers and plug-ins next.

Installing a Plug-In

Installing a plug-in is very easy. Simply transfer the installation file from the Web and place it in a download directory (see Chapter 17). Then run the file (double-click it, for instance) to run the installation program. The installation program may run immediately, or you may find that a series of files are extracted from the one you downloaded, in which case you have to run a setup.exe file to start the installation program.

Follow the instructions to install the file. When it's finished, your browser will be able to automatically call the plug-in anytime it needs it.

By the way, your browser may sometimes tell you when you need a plug-in. For instance, if you see the dialog box shown in the following figure, you have displayed a Web page with an embedded file format that requires a plug-in. You can simply click the **Get the**

Plugin button, and the browser will open another window and take you to a page with information about plug-ins.

This Netscape dialog box opens when you click a link that loads a file requiring a plug-in you don't have.

Installing a Viewer

Installing a viewer is a little more complicated than installing a plug-in, but it's still not rocket science. There are actually two different types of viewer installations. One is the type that Netscape uses, where you tell the browser which viewer to work with for each file type. The other is the type used by the Windows versions of Internet Explorer. These use the Windows file associations to set up viewers. For instance, by default Windows associates .WAV files with the Sound Recorder program. That means if you double-click a .WAV file in File Manager, Sound Recorder opens and plays the file. Internet Explorer uses the same system-wide file association system to determine which program should be used when it comes across a file type.

The next section gives you a look at installing a viewer in Netscape (which is very similar to the system used in many other browsers). The section after that covers installing a viewer in Internet Explorer.

Installing a Viewer in Netscape

We're going to take a look at how to configure a viewer in the Windows version of Netscape. (The process is similar in other versions of Netscape, and even in some other browsers.) Let's say you've came across a link that looked interesting, and you clicked it. Netscape displayed the Unknown File Type dialog box, shown here. This means that Netscape doesn't recognize the file...so you have to tell it what to do.

The Unknown File Type dialog box opens if you click a link to a file that Netscape doesn't recognize.

If you want, you can click the **More Info** button. Netscape will open another browser window and display an information document with a link to a page from which you can download a plug-in. Let's assume that you already know there is no plug-in for this particular file type, or that for some other reason you want to configure a viewer. Click the **Pick App** button, and you'll see the dialog box in the following figure.

The Configure External Viewer dialog box lets you define which viewer should handle the file type.

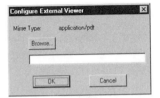

Click the **Browse** button and then find the program that you know can handle this type of file. (Remember, you can find viewers at the sites listed in Appendix A.) Double-click the program, and it is placed into the Configure External Viewer dialog box. Then click **OK**. That's it! You've just configured the viewer.

The file referenced by the link you clicked will now be transferred to your computer and sent to the program you defined as the viewer. The viewer will then display the file (assuming, of course, that you picked the right viewer).

Setting Up Netscape Beforehand

You can also set up Netscape's viewers before you ever get to a site that uses unusual file formats. Choose **Options, General Preferences,** and then click the **Helpers** tab. You'll see the dialog box shown here.

You can preconfigure viewers in Netscape's Preferences dialog box.

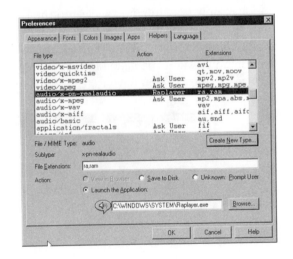

The big list shows all of the different file types (well, most of them; you can add more using the **Create New Type** button). To configure a viewer for one, click it in the list, and then click one of the **Actions**. You can tell Netscape to **Save to Disk** if you want, but if you intend to configure a viewer, click **Launch the Application** instead. Then click the **Browse** button to find the application you want to use as the viewer.

What's That Button For?

In case you're wondering, the Unknown: Prompt User option button is the default setting for formats that haven't been set up with a viewer. If you click a file for which you've configured this setting, Netscape will ask you what to do with the file.

Installing a Viewer in Internet Explorer

Internet Explorer uses a similar system, but instead of simply modifying Internet Explorer's settings, you are actually modifying the Windows 95 settings.

When you click a file type that Explorer doesn't recognize, it opens the dialog box shown in the following figure. (This is similar to what you saw from Netscape.) Because Explorer doesn't recognize the file type, you have to tell it what to do. Click the **Open it using an application on your computer** option button, and then click **OK**. Explorer transfers the file and then tries to open it.

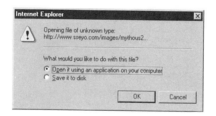

If Explorer doesn't recognize a file, you will see this dialog box.

You'll then see the Open With dialog box, shown next. Type a name for this type of file into the text box at the top. Then, if you can find the viewer you want to use in this list, click it and click **OK**. If you can't find it, click the **Other** button. In the Open dialog box that appears, select the viewer you want to use.

Enter a name for the file type, and then choose the application you want to use as a viewer.

As with Netscape, you can always install an Internet Explorer viewer before you need it. You do this using the File Types system, which you can access from the Windows Explorer file management utility or from within Internet Explorer itself. Within Internet Explorer, choose **View**, **Options**, and then click the **File Types** tab. You'll see the Options dialog box shown in the following figure.

You can add viewers to Internet Explorer using the Options dialog box.

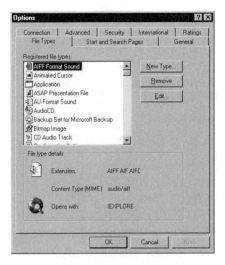

To add a new viewer, click the **New Type** button, and then fill in all the information in the dialog box that appears. Enter the description (whatever you want to call it), the file extensions used by that file type, and the MIME type. Click the **New** button and type **open** in the first text box you see. Then click the **Browse** button and find the application you want to use as the viewer.

What's MIME?

MIME stands for Multipurpose Internet Mail Extensions. Though originally intended for e-mail transmission of files, it's used on the Web to identify file formats. You can find detailed information about MIME and a large list of MIME types at **http://sd-www.jsc.nasa.gov/mime-types/** or at **http://home.netscape.com/assist/helper_apps/mime.html**.

The Least You Need to Know

➤ A browser can handle many file formats: HTML, text, graphics and sounds of various kinds. If it encounters a file format that it can't handle, it tries to pass the file to a viewer or plug-in.

➤ Viewers and plug-ins are designed to play or display file types that browsers can't handle. The difference between the two is that a plug-in temporarily converts the browser window into a viewer, while a viewer is a completely separate program that opens without changing the browser window in any way.

➤ There are literally hundreds of viewers and plug-ins, for scores of file types. Most of these file types are rarely used, however.

➤ Plug-ins are more convenient than viewers are. However, if you find a viewer that has more features than the plug-in, use it.

➤ If your browser comes across a file type that it can't recognize, it asks what to do. You can then install a plug-in or specify a viewer.

Your Very Own Web Page

When we first sat down to discuss what should go in the third edition of this book, someone mentioned that people were asking for information about creating their own Web pages. Quite frankly, I was skeptical. "This is an introduction to the Internet," I said. "That's a bit advanced, isn't it?" Indeed, it may seem a bit advanced to you, too. After all, you've barely learned how to get onto the Internet, and all of a sudden you can *contribute* to the Internet? Not likely!

Well, actually it's very likely. And more importantly, it's very easy. Creating a Web page is quite simple (...so simple that I'm betting I can teach you to create a simple Web page in, oh, one chapter). No, I take that back! I'll bet you can create a very simple customized Web page in about 10 minutes. I'll cheat a little, though by giving you a template, in which you can fill in the "blanks."

My Fill-in-the-Blanks Web Page

I've created a Web page for you and put it on the CD. It's a file called OWNWEB.HTM, and you can find it on the CD in the back of this book.

Copy the file from the CD into a directory on your hard drive. Then open the file in any kind of text editor, such as SimpleText (on the Mac) or Notepad (in Windows). You could use a word processor just as easily, but when you finish, you'll have to remember to save the file as a text file instead of as a normal word processing file. As you'll learn later in this chapter, Web pages are simple ASCII text files. And although you can use a word processor, in many cases it's not a great idea because they often automatically insert special characters such as curly quotation marks and em dashes that can't be converted to ASCII. Therefore, you're better using a text editor.

Of course, you might not have a CD-ROM drive, but you might not want to wait for e-mail to arrive either. For those of you who are that impatient, I've included the text from that file here. You can type the following lines into your text editor if you want, but you must make sure you type it exactly the same as it appears here.

```
<HTML>
<HEAD>
<TITLE>My Very Own Web Page--Replace if You Want</TITLE>
</HEAD>
<BODY>
<H1>Replace This Title With Whatever You Want</H1>
Put whatever text you want here.<P>
This is another paragraph; use whatever text you want.
<H2>First Subcategory: Replace this With Whatever Title You Want</H2>
<A HREF="http://www.mcp.com">The Macmillan Web Site</A><P>
<A HREF="url_here">Another link: replace this text</A><P>
<A HREF="url_here">Another link: replace this text</A><P>
<A HREF="url_here">Another link: replace this text</A><P>
<A HREF="url_here">Another link: replace this text</A>
<H2>Second Subcategory: Replace this With Whatever Title You Want</H2>
Put more text and links here.
<H2>Third Subcategory: Replace this With Whatever Title You Want</H2>
Put more text and links here.
<H2>Fourth Subcategory: Replace this With Whatever Title You Want</H2>
Put more text and links here.
</BODY>
</HTML>
```

Don't Have a CD-ROM Drive?

If you don't have a CD-ROM drive, you can get this Web page file by sending an e-mail message to **ciginternet@mcp.com**, with **ownweb** in the subject line of the message. Then save the message as a text file and open it in a text editor. Remove all of the text *before* the <HTML> text. (*Don't* remove the <HTML> part; just remove all of the text prior to it.) For more information about using the mail responder, see Appendix C.

The following figure shows you what this file looks like when displayed in a Web browser.

This is what the Web page template looks like in a Web browser.

For now, don't worry if you don't *understand* what is going on here; you're trying to break a speed record, not actually learn right now. In a few moments, I'll explain how this whole Web-creation thing works.

Before I get to that, though, I want you to replace some things. You can start with the text between the <TITLE> and </TITLE> *tags*. Whatever text you type between those tags will appear in the browser's title bar (as you can see in the figure), so replace the text that's there by typing your name, or **My Home Page**, or whatever you want. When you finish doing that, replace the text between the <H1> and </H1> tags. The text you type here will be a heading—the *top level* heading, as a matter of fact. You can use the same text that you entered as the title if you want (that's what Web authors often do).

What's a Tag?
Text that has a less than symbol (<) in front of it and a greater than symbol (>) after it is known as a *tag*. The tags tell your Web browser how to display the text in an HTML file.

Next, add some text if you want. Replace the text immediately below the <H1></H1> heading, or simply remove it if you don't want it. Notice, by the way, that you must end each paragraph with the <P> tag. After that, replace the next headings with names of categories that describe the sort of links you want in your page. If you have favorite music sites that you visit, you might make the first heading **Music**. Another heading might be **Financial**, and another might be **Goofing Around**. It's your page. Use whatever categories you want.

Before you change the "Another link…" lines, take a close look at the links I've created. The first one is a link to the Macmillan Web site. (This book is published by Que, a division of Macmillan.)

```
<A HREF="http://www.mcp.com">The Macmillan Web Site</A><P>
```

The words *The Macmillan Web Site* appear on the Web page as the actual link text; you can see those words in the figure. The URL for the linked page goes between the quotation marks, as in "**http://www.mcp.com**". Keeping that in mind, go ahead and modify the links I've provided. For instance, you might change this:

```
<A HREF="url_here">Another link: replace this text</A><P>
```

to this:

```
<A HREF="http://www.iuma.com">Internet Underground Music Archive</A><P>
```

Be Careful
Make sure that you don't remove any of the < or > symbols. If you do, it can really mess up your page.

Replace all the generic links with links to Web sites you like to visit. As a shortcut, you can copy a link, paste it a few times below each category heading, and then modify each of the copied links so that they point to more Web sites. When you finish making your changes, save the page, and then open it in your Web browser using the **File**, **Open** command. Right before your very eyes, you'll see your brand new 10-minute Web page. Didn't I tell you it was easy?

Make It Your Home Page

Once you've created a home page, you need to tell your browser to use it as the home page. In Internet Explorer, begin by displaying your new page in the browser window. Then choose **View**, **Options** and click the **Start and Search Pages** tab (see the following figure). Choose **Start Page** from the drop-down list box. (Internet Explorer uses the term *Start Page* instead of home page.) Then click the **Use Current** button.

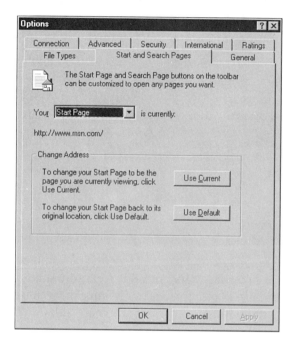

In Internet Explorer, you can click the Use Current button to select the currently displayed page as the home (start) page.

To make your Web page the home page in Netscape, choose **Options**, **General Preferences**, and click the **Appearance** tab. Look for the **Browser Starts With** text box. You have to type the path and file name of the page you want to open. (For instance, in Windows 95 you would type c:\program files\netscape\navigator\ownweb.htm for a file named ownweb.htm that's in the \program files\netscape\navigator\ directory on drive C:.) Then click the **OK** button.

The next time you start your browser, you'll see your very own home page. And the next time you click the **Home** button, up pops your home page.

Your Web Page—What's It Good For?

Why bother creating your own page? There are a few reasons. First, telling your browser to view a home page on your hard drive will speed up loading the program. Most browsers these days are configured to use a home page at the browser publisher's Web site, but it's much quicker to load from a "local" drive than to transfer it from across the Internet. However, if that were the only reason, you could just copy an HTML document from the Web somewhere and put it on your hard drive.

The second reason has to do with the fact that everyone uses the Internet in a different way. The home page someone else has created won't have all the links you want and will contain plenty of links that you don't want. So you might as well customize your home page to work the way you want it to work and include links to sites you want to go to. You can also create a home page that has a series of documents linked to it (such as one for work, one for music, one for newsgroups, and so on).

And another reason (if you still need coaxing) is that you might want to put information about yourself or your business on the World Wide Web. You're not limited to creating a Web page for your own use and saving it on your hard drive. You can create a Web page that the world can read, saving it on your service provider's system so that it's available to the Internet at large.

First, the Basics

You've already seen how simple Web authoring can be. Now you're going to learn a bit more theory about *HTML* (Hypertext Markup Language). HTML is the "language" of the Web, and all those <xxx> tags you looked at are HTML tags.

HTML files are really not very complicated. They're in a simple text format known as ASCII. ASCII, short for American Standard Code for Information Interchange, is a standard system computers use to recognize text. The nice thing about ASCII is that it's widely recognized by thousands of programs and many different types of computers.

It's important to understand that while text editors (such as Notepad and SimpleText) create ASCII text files, word processors do not. A word processor is like an advanced text editor. It formats the text in many ways that pure ASCII text cannot. It adds character formatting (italic, bold, underlines, and so on), adds special characters (curly quotation marks, copyright symbols, em and en dashes, and many others), and formats paragraph spacing, for example. That's why you have to be careful when creating HTML files in a word processor; you must save the file as ASCII text instead of in the word processor's file format.

HTML files are special text files that have been specially designed to be read by Web browsers. They use the same characters as any other ASCII file, but they use a special convention that all Web browsers understand. That convention is this: "if you see anything in brackets like these < >, you know it's a special code." So when Web browsers are rendering the HTML document into normal text so that they can display the document on the screen, they look for these brackets and follow the instructions inside them.

You've already created a Web page, so you know what tags look like. But take a minute to go back and examine the tags you used.

<TITLE> </TITLE> The text between these tags is the title of the document. You won't see this text in the document itself; it's simply an identifier that the browsers use. For instance, Netscape and Internet Explorer would put the text in the title bar. In addition, this title is used in bookmark and history lists.

<H1> </H1> These particular tags mark the first level heading. You can include up to six different levels using the tags <H2>, <H3>, <H4>, <H5>, and <H6>. Experiment with these in your own Web page.

<P> This tag is used at the end of a paragraph. Simply typing a carriage return in your HTML file will *not* create a new paragraph in the final document that appears in the browser. You must use the <P> tag instead. Without the tag, you will find that the paragraphs run together.

Techno Talk

Rendering This term is used to describe the action carried out by the browser when it looks at the HTML codes and formats the text according to the instructions within those codes. It strips the codes out of the text and displays the resulting text in the browser.

Check This Out...

Does It Have to Be Upper-case? Don't worry about the case of the tags. You can type **title, TITLE, Title, TItlE,** or **TiTlE**—whatever tickles your fancy.

Notice that, in most cases, tags are paired. There's an opening and a closing tag, and the closing tag is the same as the opening tag with the exception of the forward slash after the left angle bracket. <H1> and </H1> form a pair, for instance. The <P> tag is one exception to this. You use only one <P> tag, and it appears after the paragraph.

Finally, there's an *anchor* tag, which is used to create a link:

```
<A HREF="http://www.mcp.com">The Macmillan Web Site</A><P>
```

This is simple enough. Notice that the URL is included within the angle brackets and within quotation marks. A *link tag* (a tag that you use to create a hypertext link in your document) consists of <A, followed by a space, followed by HREF=". After that tag, you enter the URL. You've looked at URLs before; these are the same URLs that you can use to tell a browser to go to a particular Web site. At the end of the URL, you add ">, followed by some kind of text—anything you want. (That text is going to appear on the finished Web page as the link text.) Following the text, you use the closing tag </A>. In the example above, I also used the <P> tag to start a new paragraph; I wanted to make sure that the link would appear on its own line.

101

Anchors The `<A HREF="url">` tags are often called anchors. For this reason, many people refer to the actual links in the Web documents as anchors.

A Word About Paragraphs

Web browsers don't deal with paragraphs in the same way that word processors do. If the browser finds several spaces, including blank lines, it will compress all the space into a single paragraph unless it sees the `<P>` tag somewhere. When it finds the `<P>` tag, it ends that paragraph and starts a new one below it, generally leaving a blank line between the two.

If for some reason you want to move text down to the next line but you don't want a blank line between the two lines of text, you can use the `<BR>` tag instead of `<P>`. The `<BR>` tag inserts a line break without starting a new paragraph.

`<P>` and `</P>` You've already learned that the `<P>` tag doesn't have to have a matching code to make a pair. Actually, you can use `<P>` and `</P>` as a pair if you want. `<P>` marks the beginning of a paragraph, and `</P>` marks the end. However, this is not necessary, and few Web authors do so.

Don't Stop at One: Multiple Pages

You can easily create a hierarchy of documents. Why not have a document that appears when you open the browser, with a table of contents linked to several other documents? In each of those documents, you can then have links related to a particular subject.

Say, for instance, you want to set up a document for the music sites you are interested in. Call it RNR.HTM, or MUSIC.HTM, or whatever you want. Create that document in the same way you did the first one, and put it in the same directory. You can then create a link from your home page to the Rock n' Roll document, like this:

```
<A HREF="RNR.HTM">Rock n' Roll</A>
```

Although RNR.HTM is a file name, you can use it in place of the URL. In fact, RNR.HTM is a URL: it's what's known as a *relative URL*. This link tells a Web browser to "look for the RNR.HTM file." Although it doesn't tell the browser where to look for the file, the browser makes a basic assumption. Because the URL doesn't include the host name or directory, the only place the browser can look is in the same directory as the original file. (And that's just fine because you are going to place the RNR.HTM file in the same directory, right?)

This is really simple, isn't it? You create a home page (called HOME.HTM) with links to any number of other documents in the same directory. You might have links to Rock n' Roll, art, music, conspiracy theories, or whatever sort of information you are interested in and can find on the Web. Then you fill those documents up with more links to all those interesting sites. Whad'ya know! You're a Web publisher!

Finding URLs

There are shortcuts to creating home pages. Who wants to type all those URLs, after all? Well, one way to grab the URLs is to visit the Web page you are interested in and copy the text from the Location or Address text box at the top of the browser window. To do that, you can highlight the text, and then press **Ctrl+C** or select **Edit, Copy**. (Most browsers have some method for copying the URL.) Then you can just paste it into your home page.

You can also grab URLs from links on a document. Point at a link and right-click to see a pop-up menu. Click the **Copy Shortcut** option in Internet Explorer, or click the **Copy Link Location** option in Netscape.

You can also grab information from the bookmark or, in some cases, the history list. In Internet Explorer, you can open Favorites (that's the name it uses for its bookmark system). Choose **Favorites, Open Favorites Folder**, right-click an item, and choose **Properties.** Then click the **Internet Shortcut** tab and copy the URL from the **Target URL** text box.

In Netscape, you can open the Bookmarks window (**Window, Bookmarks**) and do much the same thing. Right-click an item, select **Properties**, and then copy the URL from the box that appears. You can also choose **File, Save As** to save the entire bookmark system in an HTML file. Then you can open that file in a text editor and pick and choose which URLs you want.

You and Your Service Provider

If you actually want to publish on the Web, you have a two-step process to go through. First, you create the page. But then, you have to place it somewhere that is accessible to the Internet. It has to be put on a Web server.

Most online services and Internet service providers allow their subscribers to post their own Web pages. Some of these services even allow each subscriber to post a megabyte or two of Web pages, graphics, and so on. Check with your service to find out how much data you can post and where to put it.

How do you get it where it needs to go? Generally, you'll have to use FTP, which you'll learn about in Chapter 12. This is a system that allows you to transfer files from your computer to another computer on the Internet. Some of the online services use a different system, though; check with your online service for more information.

Just a Little Help

The online services have Web-authoring programs to help you create Web pages and automatically post them to the service's Web site. Dig around a little in your online service to see what's available.

So You Like This, Eh?

You want more? Okay, you get more. Look on the CD bundled with this book to find a complete copy of *The Complete Idiot's Guide to Creating an HTML Web Page*. It's in HTML format, so you can read it from within your Web browser. That book explains how to use more advanced tags and how to insert graphics, modify text styles, and so on. In addition, it talks about the different HTML editing tools available.

The Least You Need to Know

➤ Creating a home page is very simple; you can use the template provided to create one in as few as 10 minutes.

➤ Enclose HTML tags within brackets < >.

➤ In most cases, you need an opening tag and a closing tag, such as `<TITLE>My Home Page</TITLE>`.

➤ You use tags to tell your browser which text you want displayed as titles, headings, links, and so on.

➤ To create a link, type `<A HREF="URL">Your Link Text</A>`, replacing "URL" and "Your Link Text" with those you actually want to use.

➤ If you use a file name in place of the URL in the link, the browser will look in the same directory as the current document.

➤ You can replace your browser's default home page with your new one.

➤ Once you've created a page, you can post it at your service provider's site so the whole world can see it!

Part 2
There's Plenty More

The Internet is far more than just the Web, although you might not be able to tell that from the media coverage. The Internet offers tens of thousands of discussion groups (newsgroups and mailing lists), a file-library system called FTP, a "librarian" called Archie, and a once-popular menu system known as Gopher. And, of course, there's chat. No, it's not really chat—instead of talking, you type—but many people find it to be a great way to while away an hour or ten. And how about Voice on the Net? You'll learn about a system that enables you to make international phone calls for just pennies an hour!

You might even use Telnet, a relatively little-used system that allows you to log on to computers around the world—to play games, for instance. Even if you don't use all of the services covered in this part of the book, you're almost certain to find something useful.

 EXTRA! EXTRA!

Chapter 9

Newsgroups: The Source of All Wisdom

In This Chapter

➤ What is a newsgroup?

➤ What you can find in newsgroups

➤ Finding out what newsgroups exist

➤ What is UseNet?

➤ Choosing a newsreader

In this chapter, I'm going to introduce you to one of the Internet's most dangerous services: newsgroups. Many people find these discussion groups to be addictive. Get involved in a few groups, and if you have an addictive personality, you'll soon find that the rest of your life is falling apart, as you spend hours each day swapping messages with people all over the world, on subjects such as bushwalking in Australia, soap operas, very tall women, or very short men.

But don't let me put you off. If you don't have an addictive personality, newsgroups can be interesting, stimulating, and extremely useful. And anyway, it's better than being addicted to booze or drugs. So read on, and in this chapter you'll find out what newsgroups are; in the next chapter, you'll find out how to use them.

What's a Newsgroup?

Let's start with the basics: *what is a newsgroup?* Well, are you familiar with bulletin board systems (BBSs)? Electronic BBSs work much like the real corkboard-and-thumbtack type of bulletin board. They're computerized systems for leaving both public and private messages. Other computer users can read your messages, and you can read theirs. There are tens of thousands of small BBSs around the world, each of which has its own area of interest. In addition, many computer companies have BBSs through which their customers get technical support, and many professional associations have BBSs so their members can leave messages for each other and take part in discussions.

An information service such as CompuServe is essentially a collection of many bulletin boards (called *forums* in CompuServe-speak). CompuServe has a few thousand such BBSs. Instead of having to remember several thousand telephone numbers (one for each BBS), you can dial one phone number and access any number of BBSs in the series.

As you've already seen, the Internet is a collection of networks hooked together. It's huge, and consequently it has an enormous number of discussion groups. In Internet-speak, these are called *newsgroups*, and there are thousands of them on all conceivable subjects. Each Internet service provider subscribes to a selection of newsgroups—sometimes a selection as large as 3,000, 6,000, or even 15,000.

What do I mean by "subscribe?" Well, these newsgroups are distributed around the Internet by a service called UseNet; consequently, they're often referred to as UseNet groups. UseNet distributes somewhere around 17,000 groups. (The number keeps changing.) But not all service providers get all of the groups. A service provider can choose which groups it wants to receive, in essence *subscribing* to just the ones it wants. Although 17,000 exist, most providers get only a few thousand of them.

If your service provider subscribes to a newsgroup, you can read that group's messages and post your own messages to the group. In other words, you can work only with groups to which your service provider has subscribed. As you'll see, you read newsgroup messages by using a *newsreader*, a program that retrieves messages from your service provider's *news server*.

If you've never used a newsgroup (or another system's forum, BBS, or whatever), you may not be aware of the power of such communications. This sort of messaging system really brings computer networking to life, and it's not all computer nerds sitting around with nothing better to do. (Check out the Internet's "alt" newsgroups; these people are not your average introverted propeller-heads!) In my Internet travels, I've found work, made friends, found answers to research questions (much quicker and more cheaply than I could have by going to a library), and read people's "reviews" of tools I can use in my business. I've never found a lover or spouse online, but I know people who have (and anyway, I'm already married). Just be careful not to get addicted and start spending all your time online.

Public News Servers

If your service provider doesn't subscribe to a newsgroup you want, ask the management there to subscribe to it. If they won't, you *might* be able to find and read it at a public news server. Try looking at these sites for information about public servers:

http://www.yahoo.com/News/Usenet/Public_Access_Usenet_Sites/

http://www.lipsia.de/~michael/lists/pubservers.html

http://www.geocities.com/Athens/2694/freenews.html

So What's Out There?

You can use newsgroups for fun or for work. You can use them to spend time "talking" with other people who share your interests—whether that happens to be algebra (see the alt.algebra.help group) or antique collecting (rec.antiques). You can even do serious work online, such as finding a job at a nuclear physics research site (hepnet.jobs), tracking down a piece of software for a biology project (bionet.software), or finding good stories about what's going on in South Africa for an article you are writing (za.events).

The following newsgroups represent just a tiny fraction of what is available:

News? True to its UNIX heritage, the Internet uses the word "news" ambiguously. Often, when you see a reference to news in a message or an Internet document, it refers to the messages left in newsgroups (not, as most people imagine, to journalists' reports on current affairs).

alt.ascii-art Pictures (such as Spock and the Simpsons) created with ASCII text characters.

alt.comedy.british Discussions on British comedy in all its wonderful forms.

alt.current-events.russia News of what's going on in Russia right now. (Some messages are in broken English, and some are in Russian, but that just adds romance.)

alt.missing-kids Information about missing kids.

bit.listserv.down-syn Discussions about Down's syndrome.

comp.research.japan   Information about computer research in Japan.

misc.forsale   Lists of goods for sale.

rec.skydiving   A group for skydivers.

sci.anthropology   A group for people interested in anthropology.

sci.military   Discussions on science and the military.

soc.couples.intercultural   A group for interracial couples.

If you are looking for information on just about any subject, the question is not "Is there a newsgroup about this?" The questions you should ask are "What is the newsgroup's name?" and "Does my service provider subscribe to it?"

Can You Read It?

There are so many newsgroups out there that they take up a lot of room. A service provider getting the messages of just 3,000 newsgroups may have to set aside tens of megabytes of hard disk space to keep up with it all. So service providers have to decide which ones they will subscribe to. Nobody subscribes to all the world's newsgroups because many are simply of no interest to most Internet users, and many are not widely distributed. (Some are of regional interest only; some are of interest only to a specific organization.) So system administrators have to pick the ones they want and omit the ones they don't want. Undoubtedly some system administrators censor newsgroups, omitting those they believe have no place online.

I Want to Start One! Do you have a subject about which you want to start a newsgroup? Spend some time in the news.groups newsgroup to find out about starting a UseNet newsgroup, or talk to your service provider about starting a local newsgroup.

I've given you an idea of what is available in general, but I can't specify what is available to *you*. You'll have to check with your service provider to find out what they offer. If they don't have what you want, ask them to get it. They have no way of knowing what people want unless someone tells them.

Okay, Gimme a List!

The first thing you may want to do is find out what newsgroups your service provider subscribes to. You can do that by telling your newsreader to obtain a list of groups from the news server; we'll talk more about newsreaders in a little while.

What if you don't find what you are looking for? How can you find out what's available that your provider does not subscribe to? There are lots of places to go these days to track down newsgroups. I like Tile.Net, which is shown in the following figure. At **http://www.tile.net/** you can find lists of newsgroups, mailing lists (see Chapter 11), and FTP sites (see Chapter 12). In addition to Tile.Net, you can try the UseNet Info Center (**http://sunsite.unc.edu/usenet-i/**) or the Finding Newsgroups and Mailing Lists page (**http://www.synapse.net/~radio/finding.htm**). And of course you can search at any Web search site (which you'll learn about in Chapter 19). For instance, try Yahoo (**http://www.yahoo.com/News/Usenet/Newsgroup_Listings/**).

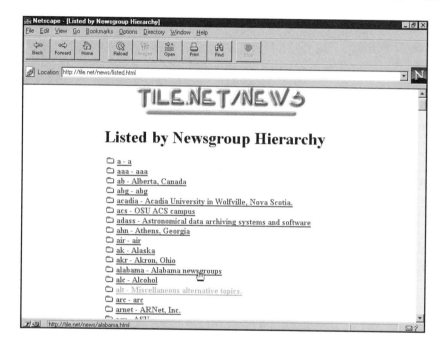

Tile.Net is a good place to find out what's available on UseNet.

Where Does It All Come From?

Where do all these newsgroups come from? People create newsgroups from their computers all over the world. Any system administrator can create a newsgroup, and many do. Each host has newsgroups of local interest—about the service provider's services, local politics, local events, and so on.

A large number of newsgroups—though not all of them—are part of the UseNet system. Like the Internet, UseNet is intangible—a network of networks. No one owns it, and it doesn't own anything itself. It is independent of any network, including the Internet (in fact, it's older than the Internet). UseNet is simply a series of voluntary agreements to swap information.

Techno Talk
blah blah
blah bla

Moderated Groups As you'll see from the lists, some newsgroups are *moderated*, which means someone reads all the messages and decides which ones to post. The purpose is to keep the newsgroup focused and to prevent the discussions from "going astray." Of course, it may look a little like censorship—depending on what you want to say.

What's in a Name?

Now let's take a quick look at how newsgroups get their names. Newsgroup names look much like host addresses: a series of words separated by periods. This is because, like host names, they are set up in a hierarchical system (though instead of going right-to-left, they go left-to-right). The first name is the top level. These are the primary top-level UseNet groups:

comp Computer-related subjects.

news Information about newsgroups themselves, including software you can use to read newsgroup messages, and information about finding and using newsgroups.

rec Recreational topics, including hobbies, sports, the arts, and so on.

sci Discussions about research in the "hard" sciences, as well as some social sciences.

soc A wide range of social issues, such as discussions about different types of societies and subcultures, as well as sociopolitical subjects.

talk Debates about politics, religion, and anything else that's controversial.

misc Stuff. Job searches, things for sale, a forum for paramedics. You know, *stuff*.

Not all newsgroups are true UseNet groups. Many are local groups that UseNet distributes internationally (don't worry about it, it doesn't matter). Such newsgroups are known as Alternative Newsgroup Hierarchies. They comprise other top-level groups, such as these:

alt "Alternative" subjects. These are often subjects that many people consider inappropriate, pornographic, or just weird. In some cases, however, it's simply interesting reading, but someone created the newsgroup in an "unauthorized" manner to save time and hassle.

bionet Biological subjects.

bit A variety of newsgroups from BITNET.

biz Business subjects, including advertisements.

clari Clarinet's newsgroups from "official" and commercial sources; mainly UPI news stories and various syndicated columns.

courts   Related to law and lawyers.

de   Various German-language newsgroups.

fj   Various Japanese-language newsgroups.

gnu   The Free Software Foundation's newsgroups.

hepnet   Discussions about high energy and nuclear physics.

ieee   The Institute of Electrical and Electronics Engineers' newsgroups.

info   A collection of mailing lists formed into newsgroups at the University of Illinois.

k12   Discussions about kindergarten through 12th-grade education.

relcom   Russian-language newsgroups, mainly distributed in the former Soviet Union.

vmsnet   Subjects of interest to VAX/VMS computer users.

You'll see other groups, too, such as the following:

brasil   Groups from Brazil (Brazil is spelled with an "s" in Portuguese).

Birmingham   Groups from Birmingham, England.

podunk   A local interest newsgroup for the town of Podunk.

thisu   This university's newsgroup.

Okay, I made up the last two, but you get the idea. Seriously, though, if you'd like to see a list of virtually all of the top-level group names in both UseNet and "Alternative" newsgroups, go to the page at http://www.magmacom.com/~leisen/master_list.html.

Reaching the Next Level

The groups listed in the previous section make up the top-level groups. Below each of those groups are groups on another level. For instance, under the alt. category is a newsgroup called alt.3d that contains messages about three-dimensional imaging. It's part of the alt hierarchy because, presumably, it was put together in an unauthorized way. The people who started it didn't want to go through the hassle of setting up a UseNet group, so they created an alt group instead—where anything goes.

Another alt group is **alt.animals**, where people gather to talk about their favorite beasties. This group serves as a good example of how newsgroups can have more levels. Because it's such a diverse subject, one newsgroup isn't really enough. So instead of posting messages to the alt.animals group, you choose your particular interest. The specific areas include:

> alt.animals.dolphins
>
> alt.animals.felines.lions
>
> alt.animals.felines.lynxes
>
> alt.animals.felines.snowleopards
>
> alt.animals.horses.icelandic
>
> alt.animals.humans

And there are many more. If you're into it, chances are good there's a newsgroup for it.

All areas use the same sort of hierarchical system. For example, under the bionet first level, you can find such newsgroups as **bionet.genome.arabidopsis** (information about the Arabidopsis genome project), **bionet.genome.chrom22** (a discussion of Chromosome 22), and **bionet.genome.chromosomes** (for those interested in the eucaryote chromosomes).

I'm Ready; Let's Read

Now that you know what newsgroups are, you'll probably want to get in and read a few? Newsgroups store the news messages in text files—lots of text files. You'll read the messages using a *newsreader* to help you sort and filter your way through all the garbage.

If you are with an online service, you already have a built-in newsreader. These range from the good (MSN's newsreader is pretty capable), to the absolutely awful (CompuServe's was horrible last time I looked; maybe their next software upgrade will fix that). If you are with a service provider, they may give you a newsreader. For example, Netscape and Internet Explorer have built-in newsreaders (see the following figure). Or you may have one of the other newsgroup programs, such as WinVN, Gravity, Free Agent, or OUI (on Windows), or NewsWatcher and Nuntius (on the Mac). There are also *loads* of commercial newsreaders around, many of which are included with products such as Internet Chameleon, SuperHighway Access, and Internet in a Box.

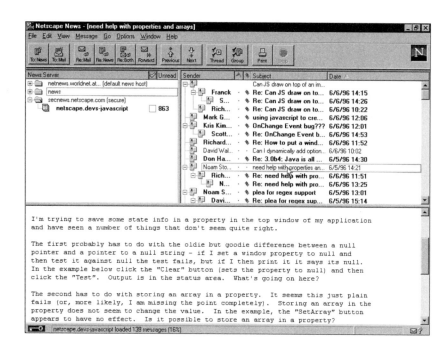

Netscape's built-in newsreader.

I'm trying to save some state info in a property in the top window of my application and have seen a number of things that don't seem quite right.

The first probably has to do with the oldie but goodie difference between a null pointer and a pointer to a null string - if I set a window property to null and then test it against null the test fails, but if I then print it it says its null. In the example below click the "Clear" button (sets the property to null) and then click the "Test". Output is in the status area. What's going on here?

The second has to do with storing an array in a property. It seems this just plain fails (or, more likely, I am missing the point completely). Storing an array in the property does not seem to change the value. In the example, the "SetArray" button appears to have no effect. Is it possible to store an array in a property?

Still Using UNIX?

If you are using a command-line interface, send e-mail to **ciginternet@mcp.com**, with **news** in the Subject line to receive the newsgroup chapters (Chapters 15 and 16) from the first edition of *The Complete Idiot's Guide to the Internet*, which explain how to use a UNIX-based newsreader. Or, find those same chapters on the CD in the back of this book (see Appendix C for more information).

I'm going to use the Gravity newsreader for my examples in the next chapter. If you have something different, the actual commands you use will vary, but the basic principles will remain the same. Of course, different programs have different features, so you might want to try out a few programs to see what you like (see Appendix A for information about finding software).

The Least You Need to Know

➤ A newsgroup is an area in which people with similar interests leave public messages—a sort of online public debate or discussion.

➤ There's a newsgroup on just about every subject you can imagine. If there isn't, there probably will be soon.

➤ Newsgroup names use a hierarchical system, and each group may have subgroups within it.

➤ The major online services have built-in newsreaders. If you are with a service provider, it may have given you a newsreader. If for any reason you're looking for a newsreader, try the software "libraries" listed in Appendix A.

➤ Some available newsreaders include Gravity, Free Agent, WinVN, and OUI on Windows, or NewsWatcher and Nuntius for the Mac.

Chapter 10

Your Daily News Delivery

In This Chapter

➤ Starting your newsreader

➤ Reading and responding to messages

➤ Marking messages as read

➤ ROT13: encoded messages

➤ Sending and receiving binary files

➤ Special newsreader features

It's time to see how to work in the newsgroups. As I mentioned in the previous chapter, I'm going to use the Gravity newsreader for my examples. (If you'd like to try this program, go to **http://www.microplanet.com/**.) Of course, if you are using an online service, you may be using that service's system. For instance, in MSN, you'll see icons all over the place representing collections of newsgroups. Many of MSN's BBSs—the term MSN uses for forums or subject areas—contain icons that represent links to newsgroups. Double-click the icon to go to the newsgroups, or use the Go To word **Internet** to go to the Internet BBS. In CompuServe, **GO INTERNET**, or in AOL, use the keyword **Internet** to find more information about starting the newsreaders.

There are many available newsgroup programs. Although each is a little different, they all share certain characteristics. Check your program's documentation for the specific details and to learn about any extra features it includes. Even if you don't have Gravity, I suggest that you read this information because it provides a good overview of the functions available in most newsreaders.

A Quick Word on Setup

I want to quickly discuss setup and subscribing. If you are with an online service, there's nothing to set up; it's all done for you. If you are with a service provider, though, you *may* have to set up the newsreader.

First, your newsreader must know the location of your news server. Ask your service provider the host name of the news server (remember, the news server is the system used by the service provider to send messages to your newsreader), and check your newsreader's documentation to see where to enter this information. For instance, it may be news.big.internet.service.com, or news.zip.com, or something like that.

The other thing you may have to do is *subscribe* to the newsgroups you are interested in. I've already said that your service provider has to subscribe to newsgroups; that means that the provider makes sure the newsgroups are available to its members. However, the term subscribe has another meaning in relation to newsgroups. You may also have to subscribe to the newsgroup to make sure that the newsgroup you want to read is available to your newsreader. Not all newsreaders make you subscribe in order to read a newsgroup. For instance, you don't have to worry about this if you use MSN's newsreaders. Many newsreaders, however, require you to fetch a list of newsgroups from your service provider (the newsreader has a command you'll use to fetch and display the list) and then "subscribe" to the ones you want to read. This is no big deal, you simply choose which ones you want. Until you subscribe, though, you can't see the messages.

Check This Out...

Pick Your Own Newsreader

Some of the online services have rather weak newsreaders. But if your online service allows you to get to the Internet through a TCP/IP connection, you may be able to install another newsreader, such as Gravity, Free Agent, OUI, NewsWatcher, and Nuntius. However, in order to do so you may have to connect to one of the public news servers that we mentioned in Chapter 9. The online services often have special news servers that are not designed to be accessed by TCP/IP; they're designed to be accessed with the service's own program. Check with your service's technical support staff.

Starting and Subscribing

The figure below shows the newsreader called Gravity, which I'm using for my examples. The first time you use the program, a dialog box opens, asking for certain information.

To connect to the news server using Gravity, select **File**, **Connect** (or click the **Connect/ Disconnect** toolbar button). Then select **Newsgroup**, **Get New Groups** to get the latest list of groups from your service provider's news server. The dialog box in the next figure appears, showing the newsgroups that are available on your news server. Remember that this is a list of only the newsgroups that your service provider has subscribed to, not a full list of all the groups distributed by UseNet. (For information about finding such a list, see Chapter 9.) Double-click a newsgroup name to subscribe to it, and then click **Done** to continue. (You can also use the **Search** box to search for a particular name.)

Where Are the Alt. Groups?

If you are with an online service, you may find that you can't initially read the alt. groups, and perhaps some others as well. Your online service may regard these as a trifle "naughty," in which case you have to apply for permission to read them. Go to your online service's Internet forum or BBS to find out how to activate these groups, or refer to the parental-control information.

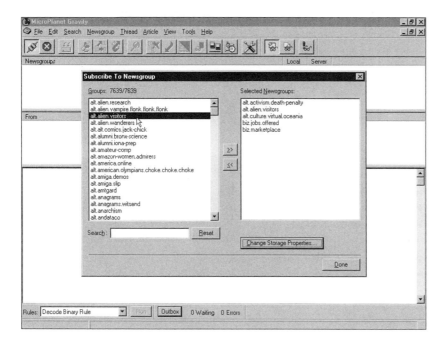

Gravity's Subscribe To Newsgroup dialog box.

119

When the dialog box closes, you'll see a list of the newsgroups you subscribed to. You can subscribe to more later. You just have to select **Newsgroup**, **Subscribe** to see the dialog box again. You can also select **Newsgroup**, **Get New Groups** to see only those newsgroups that have been added very recently (service providers are continually adding new ones). Or you can select **Newsgroup**, **Re-Read All Groups** to get the full list again and then display the dialog box.

Double-click one of the subscribed newsgroups, and you'll get a list of messages in that newsgroup (see the next figure). However, many newsgroups are empty, so you won't always see these message "headers." Notice, for instance, that alt.culture.virtual.oceania shows a zero in the Server column.

Double-click on a newsgroup, and the newsreader retrieves a list of message headers.

The list of subscribed newsgroups

Messages in the selected newsgroup

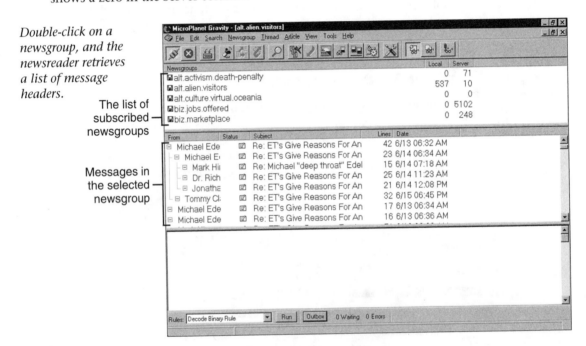

Not All the Messages

You may not see all of the messages listed at once. Some newsreaders allow you to specify a number to retrieve each time (in the program's Options or Preferences). So if it's a very busy newsgroup, you may see only a portion of the messages listed; you'll have to use another command to retrieve the rest.

Taking a Look

Notice that some messages are indented below others, and that there's a small – icon next to the messages. This indicates that the message is part of a *thread* (known as a *conversation* in some newsreaders). So what's a *thread*? Let's say you post a message to a newsgroup that isn't a response to anyone, it's just a new message. Then, a little later, someone else reads your message and replies. That message, because it's a reply, is part of the thread you began. Later, someone else sends a response to *that* message, and it becomes part of the thread. (Note, however, that there's generally a *long* lag time—a day or more—between the time someone sends a message to a newsgroup and the time that message turns up in everyone's newsreader.)

If you click the little – icon, the thread closes up, and you see only the message at the "top" of the thread. The icon changes to a + icon. Click the + icon to open the thread up again. (A message that has a – icon but does not have messages indented below it is not part of a message thread.) Most newsreaders (but not all) support threading and many other functions in a very similar manner.

To read a message, simply double-click the message's header. The newsreader retrieves the message and places it in the bottom pane of the window as you can see in the following figure.

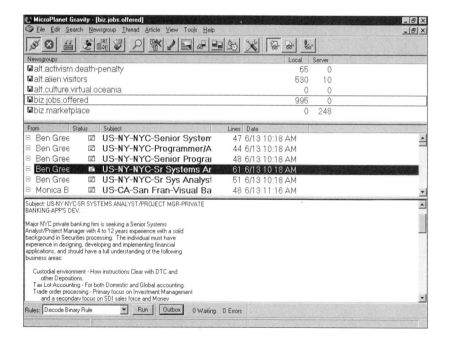

This message is from the biz.jobs.offered newsgroup.

The Messages Are Gone!

The first time you open a newsgroup, you see all the messages from the newsgroup your service provider currently holds. How long a message stays in the newsgroup depends on how busy that newsgroup is and how much hard-disk space the service provider allows for the newsgroup messages. Eventually all messages disappear.

You don't necessarily see all the newsgroup's messages the next time, though. When you return to the newsgroup later, you may see all the messages *except* those marked as read.

Why didn't I just say "messages that you haven't read?" Well, there's a slight difference. The newsreader has no way of knowing which messages you've read—it can't see what you are doing. Instead it has a way of marking messages that it thinks you've read, and it generally provides you with a way to mark messages as "Read," even if you haven't read them (in effect, providing a way for you to tell it that you don't want to see the messages).

Marking Your Messages

Most newsreaders mark a message as "Read" when you open the message. They often also allow you to mark the messages as Read even if you have not read them. This might come in handy to tell the newsreader that you don't want to see certain messages when you come back to the newsgroup in a later session. For instance, say you get a couple of messages into a conversation and realize it's pure rubbish (you'll find a lot of messages that have virtually no usefulness to anyone!). Mark the entire thread as Read, and you won't see the rest of the messages the next time you open the newsgroup window. Or maybe the messages are worthwhile, but you quickly read all the messages' Subject lines and find that nothing interests you. Mark them *all* as Read so you see only new messages the next time.

You can generally also mark messages several other ways. Here's what you can do in Gravity, for instance:

➤ Click a message header and select **Article**, **Mark as Read**.

➤ Click a message header and select **Thread**, **Kill**. This marks the entire thread as read.

➤ Right-click a message header and select **Mark As Read** or **Mark Thread As Read** from the shortcut menu.

➤ Choose **Newsgroup**, **Mark As Read (Catchup)** to mark all the current newsgroup's messages as read.

Different newsreaders handle "Read" messages differently. Gravity actually removes them from the list. However, if you don't want the newsreader to remove them, you can change the view by choosing **Newsgroup**, **Filter Display**, **Read**; then Gravity shows the message header in gray text. Other newsreaders might use special icons or gray text to indicate messages that you've read.

Articles In keeping with the "news" metaphor, newsgroup messages are often known as *articles*.

I Want the Message Back!

If you need to bring a message back, you'll generally find that your newsreader has some kind of command that enables you to do so. Gravity has the **Newsgroup**, **Filter Display**, **Read** command that you just looked at, for instance. But if your service provider no longer holds the message you want to see—that is, if the message has been removed from the service provider's hard disk to make more space for new messages—you're out of luck. So if you think there's a chance you may want a message later, save it using the **File**, **Save As** or equivalent command.

Some newsreaders even have commands for marking messages as Unread. Perhaps you've read a message, but want to make sure it appears the next time you open the newsgroup. You can mark it as Unread so that it will appear in the list next time you open the newsgroup.

Moving Among the Messages

You'll find a variety of ways to move around in your messages. As you already know, you can double-click the ones you want (some newsreaders use a single click). In addition, you'll find commands for moving to the next or previous message, the next or previous thread, and perhaps, the next or previous unread message or thread.

Many newsreaders also provide a way for you to search for a particular message. In Gravity, for example, select **Search**, **Search**, and you'll get a dialog box in which you can do a fairly sophisticated search. You can look for text in the From or Subject lines, or even within the text of the messages themselves; you can specify whether to search the selected newsgroup or all of the subscribed newsgroups; and you can even tell it whether to search only those messages already transferred to the newsreader or to search messages still held by the news server.

Saving and Printing

If you run across a message that you think might be useful later, you can save it or print it. Simply marking it as Unread isn't good enough because newsgroups eventually drop all messages. So sooner or later it won't be available.

Most newsreaders have a File, Save As (or simply File, Save) command and toolbar button. Most also have a File, Print command and button. And, of course, you can always high-light the text, copy it to the Clipboard, and then paste it into another application such as a word processing or e-mail program.

Your Turn: Sending and Responding

There are several ways to send messages or to respond to messages. For example, you can use any of the techniques listed here in Gravity. (Although Gravity is very typical, the commands might be different in other newsreaders.)

➤ You can send a message that isn't a response (that is, you can start a new thread). In Gravity, for instance, select **Article**, **Post** or click the **Post** toolbar button.

➤ You can reply to someone else's message (the reply is often known as a follow-up). In Gravity, you choose **Article**, **Follow Up** or click the **Follow Up** button. Other newsreaders use something like Reply to Group.

➤ You can reply to someone privately via e-mail (that is, send a message that *doesn't* appear in the newsgroup). To do so in Gravity, select **Article**, **Reply** or click the **E-mail Author** button. Other newsreaders use something like Reply by E-mail.

➤ You can send a copy of the message to someone else. In Gravity, select **Newsgroup**, **Forward via E-mail**.

Sending messages to a newsgroup—or via e-mail in response to a message—is much the same as working with an e-mail window. You type the message and click some kind of **Send** button.

What's This Gibberish? ROT13

Now and again, especially in the more contentious newsgroups, you'll run into messages that seem to be gibberish. Everything's messed up, each word seems to be a jumbled mix of characters, almost as if the message is encrypted. It is.

What you are seeing is *ROT13*, a very simple substitution cipher (one in which a character is substituted for another). It's actually very easy to read. ROT13 means rotated 13. In other words, each character in the alphabet is replaced by the character 13 places further along. Instead of A you see N, instead of B you see O, instead of C you see P, and so on. Got it? So to read the message, all you need to do is substitute the correct characters. Easy. (Or *Rnfl*, as I should say.)

For those of you in a hurry, there is an easier way. Most newsreaders have a command that quickly does the ROT13 for you. For instance, in Gravity, select **Article**, **Unscramble (ROT13)** and, like magic, the message changes into real words. If you don't run across any ROT13 messages, and want to see what ROT13 looks like, simply use the command to take a normal message and convert it to ROT13 message (which is what I did for the following figure). How do you actually create one of these messages when sending one to a newsgroup? You'll often find a ROT13 command in the window in which you create a message. For instance, in Gravity's message composition window, there's an Options, Unscramble (ROT13) command.

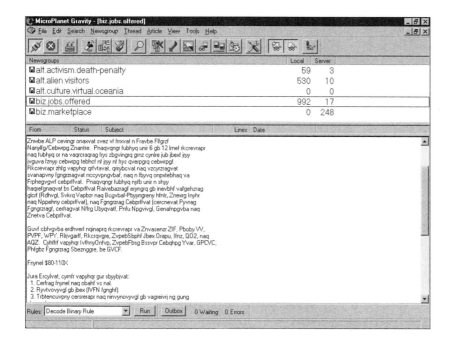

An example of a ROT13 message.

You might be wondering why a person would encode a message with a system that is so ridiculously easy to break. People don't ROT13 their messages as a security measure that's intended to make them unreadable to anyone who doesn't have the "secret key." After all, anyone with a decent newsreader has the key. No, ROT13ing (if you'll excuse my use of the term as a verb) is a way of saying "if you read this message, you may be offended; so if you are easily offended, *don't read it!*" ROT13 messages are often crude, lewd, or just plain rude. Offensive. Nasty. When a message is encoded with ROT13, the reader can decide whether or not he wants to risk being offended.

Pictures (and Sounds) from Words

The newsgroups contain simple ASCII text messages. You can't place any character into a message that is not in the standard ASCII character set. So if you want to send a computer file in a newsgroup message—maybe you want to send a picture, a sound, or a word processing document—you must convert it to ASCII. Some of the newer newsreaders will help you do this, either by automating the process of attaching MIME-formatted files to your messages, or by uuencoding files and inserting them into your messages. Some newsreaders will even convert such files "on the fly" and display pictures inside the message when they read the newsgroup messages; others will automatically convert the file to its original format.

For the moment, most newsreaders are at a fairly basic, non-sophisticated stage, and they require that you manually uuencode computer files that you want to send or manually uudecode those that you receive. You learned about both UUENCODE and MIME back in Chapter 3.

If you were using Gravity, for example, you could follow these steps to send a file.

1. Open the message composition window using the **Post** command or the **Follow** command.

2. Choose **Options**, **Add Attachment** or click the **Attach a file** toolbar button. You'll see a typical File Open dialog box, from which you can choose the file you want to send.

3. Select the file and click **OK**. The name of the attached file appears in the Attachments list of the message composition window (see the following figure).

Most newsreaders let you send uuencoded or MIME files to a newsgroup.

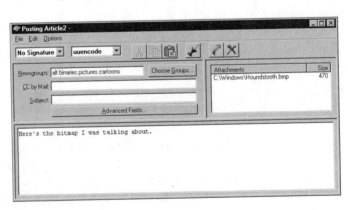

4. From the drop-down list at the top of the window, choose the form of encoding you want to use (**uuencode** or **MIME**). That's it.

5. Send the message and the attached file. The name of the file appears in the message header when you view the messages in that particular newsgroup.

The following figure shows how one newsreader displays a newsgroup message with an attachment. It is an example of what the file looks like if your newsreader *doesn't* convert the file to its correct format.

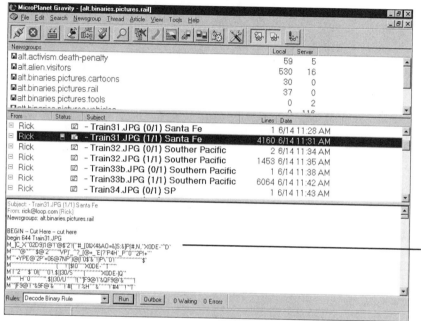

This message contains an attached file.

The encoded file

However, many newsreaders can convert files. In particular, they will convert .GIF, .JPEG, and perhaps .BMP files to their original formats. So if someone puts a picture in a message, that picture will actually appear in the window. In the case of Gravity, you can click the **View Image** button or select **Article**, **View**, and it converts the file for you and then places it in a viewer window, as shown in this figure.

No Built-In Converter?

If you are using a newsreader that doesn't have a built-in conversion system, you can save the message on your hard disk and then use a conversion program such as Wincode (a Windows program that converts UUENCODE), munpack (a DOS program that converts MIME), or Yet Another Base64 Decoder (a Macintosh program that converts both UUENCODE and MIME).

The same message after the attachment has been converted to its original format.

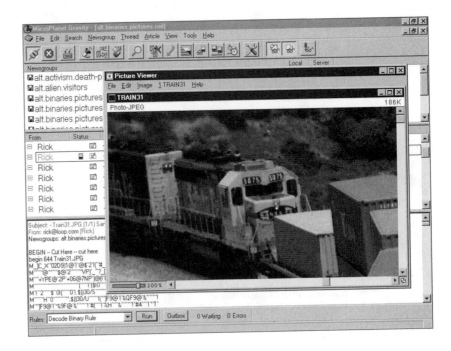

The Fancy Stuff

Some newsreaders might have nice extra features. You may be able to get the newsreader to automatically "flag" messages if the header contains a particular word. Or perhaps you can automatically remove a message if the header contains a particular word. Gravity also has a sophisticated "rules" system by which you can automatically carry out a variety of actions—throw the message away, display a special alert message, save the message in a text file, and so on—according to what appears in the header or body text. Some newsreaders let you click e-mail addresses or Web URLs that appear in messages to automatically open the mail window or your browser.

Some newsreaders will display the picture in the message window; Netscape's newsreader can do this, for instance. Some newsreaders can decode several messages together. If someone posts a large picture split into several pieces, for instance (as people often do), the newsreader may automatically retrieve all the pieces and paste them together. There are a lot of different things that newsreaders can do, so you may want to experiment to find the best for you.

A Word of Warning

Newsgroups can be *very* addictive. You can find messages about anything that interests you, angers you, or turns you on. If you are not careful, you can spend half your life in the newsgroups. You sit down in the morning to check your favorite newsgroups, and the next thing you know you haven't bathed, eaten, or picked up the kids from school.

Hang around the newsgroups, and you'll find people who are obviously spending a significant amount of time writing messages. These people are usually independently wealthy (that is, they work for large corporations who don't mind paying for them to talk politics over the Internet or who don't know that they are paying for them to do so). If you have a job, a family, and a life, be careful.

The Least You Need to Know

> ➤ Start your newsreader, and then download a list of newsgroups from the server. You may also have to subscribe to the groups you want to read; each newsreader does this a little differently.

> ➤ A good newsreader lets you view a "thread" or "conversation," which shows how messages relate to each other.

> ➤ ROT13 is a special encoding system that stops people from accidentally stumbling across offensive messages. Many newsreaders have a ROT13 command that converts the message to normal text.

> ➤ You can include binary files in messages using UUENCODE or MIME.

> ➤ Many newsreaders these days can decode UUENCODE and MIME attachments. If your newsreader doesn't, you'll need a utility such as Wincode or munpack (for Windows and DOS) or Yet Another Base64 Decoder (for the Macintosh). Or you can get another newsreader!

Chapter 11

Yet More Discussion Groups: Mailing Lists

In This Chapter

➤ More discussion groups?

➤ How mailing lists work

➤ Manual and automated lists

➤ LISTSERV mailing lists

➤ Finding lists of interesting groups

➤ Subscribing to mailing lists

Are you getting enough sleep? Are you socializing, meeting with friends and family? Do you have time to eat and bathe? Yes? Then you're clearly not spending enough time on the Internet. I've already shown you how to work with thousands of *newsgroups*, discussion groups on almost any subject (see Chapter 9). But obviously, that's not enough. So here are thousands more discussion groups: the *mailing lists*.

Mailing lists are another form of discussion group. The difference between a mailing list and a newsgroup is simply the manner in which messages are distributed. While newsgroups are distributed through a system specifically set up for their distribution, mailing lists are distributed via e-mail.

How Do Mailing Lists Work?

Each mailing list discussion group has an e-mail address. You begin by subscribing to the group you are interested in (I'll explain how in a moment). The e-mail address acts as a mail "reflector," a system that receives mail and then sends it on to a list of addresses. So every time someone sends a message to a group of which you are a member, you get a copy of the mail. And every time you send a message to a group address, everyone else on the list gets a copy.

You learned in Chapter 10 that you read newsgroups using special programs called newsreaders. However, you don't need any special program to work with a mailing list; all you need is whatever program you use for reading your e-mail. You send e-mail messages to the list in the same way that you send messages to anyone else: you enter the mailing list's address in the To box of your mail program's Compose window, type your message, and send it. And incoming messages are placed in your Inbox right along with messages from your friends and colleagues.

There are thousands of mailing lists on the Internet. Here are some suggestions of how you can go about finding the ones that interest you.

➤ Use your Web browser to go to the **http://www.tile.net** Web page. You'll find a big list of mailing lists, sorted by subject and name. You can also search the list.

➤ Send an e-mail message to **listserv@bitnic.educom.edu**. In the message text, type **list global**. You get an e-mail message back that contains a list of thousands of LISTSERV mailing lists. (I'll explain what these are later in this chapter.)

➤ Search for **mailing list** at one of the Web search sites (covered in Chapter 19), or try the **http://www.yahoo.com/ /Computers_and_Internet/Internet/ Mailing_Lists/** Web page.

Check This Out...

Peered Groups
Some LISTSERV mailing lists are shown on the list as "peered." A peered LISTSERV group is the same as a "moderated" newsgroup: someone is checking the mail and deciding what stays and what gets trashed.

➤ Go to the **news.announce.newusers** newsgroup. Sometimes you can find a list of mailing lists posted there. (See Chapters 9 and 10 for information about working with newsgroups.)

➤ Send an e-mail message to **listserv@vm1.nodak.edu** with the command **GET NEW-LIST WOUTERS** in the body of the message. In response, you'll receive Arno Wouter's text file entitled *How to Find an Interesting Mailinglist*.

➤ FTP to the **pit-manager.mit.edu** FTP site, change to the **/pub/usenet-by-group/news.lists/**

directory, and find the **Publicly_Accessible_Mailing_Lists,_Part_*n*** files. These are non-LISTSERV mailing lists.(For information about using FTP, see Chapter 12.)

➤ At the FTP site mentioned above, take a look in the **/pub/usenet/ news.announce.newsusers/** directory. You can find a variety of lists there.

➤ Learn by word of mouth. Hang around in some newsgroups and mailing lists, and you'll hear about private mailing lists that you may be able to join by invitation.

It's a Busy FTP Site

The pit-manager.mit.edu site is often very busy. If you can't get through, you can try again later. In addition, if you look carefully at the message you receive when you are unable to log on, you'll find FTP addresses of other sites that should contain the same files, as well as an e-mail address you can use to find out how to get files sent to you by e-mail. Note also that some of these directories are very large and can take a long time to load.

The Types of Lists

There are two basic types of mailing lists:

➤ Manually administered

➤ Automated

Some very small mailing lists are set up to be administered by a person who will add your name to the list. Such lists are often private, with subscription by invitation only. Other lists use special programs (mailservers) to automatically add your name to the list when you subscribe. These are often, although not always, public lists that are open to anyone.

Perhaps the most common form of automated list is the LISTSERV list. These are named after the LISTSERV mailing list program and are distributed through the Internet by the BITNET computer network. (Just to confuse the issue, I should state that there are now LISTSERV programs for a variety of different computer systems, which are used to run mailings lists that are *not* distributed by the BITNET computer network.)

There are other mailing list programs, too; Majordomo is one of the most common. But you don't need any fancy mailing list software to set up a small mailing list. It's actually quite easy to set up a manually administered mailing list.

Some mailing lists are run from UNIX Internet accounts using a few very simple utilities to make the work easier. For instance, a UNIX user can set up a forwarding utility to automatically forward incoming e-mail to a list of e-mail addresses.

Using a LISTSERV Group

Many people think that mailing lists and LISTSERV groups are one and the same. Not quite. Although LISTSERV groups are a type of mailing list (perhaps the largest category), not all mailing lists are LISTSERV groups. The term "LISTSERV" refers to one popular mailserver program; so mailing lists administered by the LISTSERV program are known as LISTSERV groups, LISTSERV lists, or just LISTSERVs. LISTSERV originates on the BITNET network. However, many LISTSERV groups are now based on the Internet, on various UNIX hosts. There are well over 4,000 BITNET LISTSERV groups, covering subjects such as those listed in the following table:

A Sampling of BITNET LISTSERV Groups

Mailing List	Description
9NOV89-L@DB0TUI11.BITNET	Events around the Berlin Wall
AAAE@VM.CC.PURDUE.EDU	American Association for Agricultural Education
AAPOR50@USCVM.BITNET	American Association for Public Opinion Research
AATG@INDYCMS.BITNET	American Association of Teachers of German
ABSLST-L@CMUVM.BITNET	Association of Black Sociologists
ACADEMIA@TECHNION.BITNET	Academia—Forum on Higher Education in Israel
ACADEMIA@USACHVM1.BITNET	Grupo Selecto de Matematicos Chilenos
ACCESS-L@PEACH.EASE.LSOFT.COM	Microsoft Access Database Discussion List
ACCI-CHI@URIACC.BITNET	Consumer Economics and Chinese Scholars
ADA-LAW@NDSUVM1.BITNET	Americans with Disabilities Act Law
ADD-L@HUMBER.BITNET	Forum for discussion of concerns of drinking and driving
AE@SJSUVM1.BITNET	Alternative Energy Discussion List
CHRISTIA@FINHUTC	A Christian discussion group
H-RUSSIA@MSU.EDU	H-Net Russian History list
H-SHGAPE@MSU.EDU	H-Net Gilded Age and Progressive Era List
HESSE-L@UCSBVM.UCSB.EDU	The Works of Hermann Hesse
ISO8859@JHUVM	A group that discusses ASCII/EBCDIC-character set issues (what fun!)

Mailing List	Description
L-HCAP@NDSUVM1	A group for people interested in issues related to handicapped people in education
OHA-L@UKCC.BITNET	Oral History Association Discussion List
ONO-NET@UMINN1.BITNET	Resource for those interested in the works of Yoko Ono
PALCLIME@SIVM.BITNET	Paleoclimate, Paleoecology for late Mesozoic & early Cenozoic
PFTFI-L@ICNUCEVM.BITNET	Progetto Finalizzato Telecomunicazioni–UO Firenze
PHILOSOP@YORKVM1	The Philosophy Discussion forum
SCAN-L@UAFSYSB.BITNET	Radio Scanner Discussion forum
SCR-L@MIZZOU1.BITNET	Study of Cognitive Rehabilitation, Traumatic Brain Injury
SCREEN-L@UA1VM.UA.EDU	Film and TV Studies Discussion List
SEMLA-L@UGA.BITNET	Southeast Music Library Association Mailing List
SEXADD-L@KENTVM.BITNET	Exchange forum for sexual addiction, dependency, or compulsion
SFER-L@UCF1VM.BITNET	South Florida Environmental Reader
SHAMANS@UAFSYSB.BITNET	Shamans Impact of the Internet on Religion
SHEEP-L@LISTSERV.UU.SE	This is a list for people interested in sheep
SIEGE@MORGAN.UCS.MUN.CA	Medieval Siege Weaponry List
SKATE-IT@ULKYVM.BITNET	Skating discussion group
SKEPTIC@JHUVM.BITNET	SKEPTIC Discussion Group
SLAVERY@UHUPVM1.UH.EDU	The history of slavery, the slave trade, abolition, and emancipation
SLDRTY-L@LISTSERV.SYR.EDU	Members of Solidarity, a socialist organization, Detroit
SLLING-L@YALEVM.BITNET	Sign Language Linguistics List
SPACESCI@UGA.BITNET	sci.space.science digest
SS-L@UIUCVMD.BITNET	SS-L Sjogren's Syndrome
SWL-TR@TRITU.BITNET	Short Wave Listening in Turkiye
TECTONIC@MSU.EDU	Geology 351 Class

continues

A Sampling of BITNET LISTSERV Groups   Continued

Mailing List	Description
TEX-D-L@DEARN.BITNET	German TeX Users Communication List
TFTD-L@TAMVM1.TAMU.EDU	Thought for the day
TGIS-L@UBVM.BITNET	Temporal Topics on GIS List
THEATRE@PUCC.BITNET	The Theatre Discussion List
THYST-L@BROWNVM.BITNET	Thistle Discussion List
TIBET-L@IUBVM.BITNET	Tibet Interest List
TN-L@UAFSYSB.BITNET	Discussion of Cranial Neurolgia Disorders
TNT-L@UMAB.BITNET	TNT Discussion Group
TRANSY-L@UKCC.BITNET	Transylvania University Alumni
TREPAN-L@BROWNVM.BITNET	Weird News List
TVDIRECT@ARIZVM1.BITNET	Professional TV Directors and Producers
UBTKD-L@UBVM.BITNET	UB TaeKwonDo
UIWAGE-L@ECUVM1.BITNET	Unemployment Insurance Wage List
UNCJIN-L@ALBNYVM1.BITNET	United Nations Criminal Justice Information Network
UNIX-WIZ@NDSUVM1.BITNET	UNIX-Wizards Mailing List
UNLBIO-L@UNLVM.BITNET	UNL Center for Biotechnology List
UTOPIA-L@UBVM.BITNET	Utopias and Utopianism
VAMPYRES@GUVM.BITNET	Vampiric lore, fact and fiction.
VEGAN-L@TEMPLEVM.BITNET	Vegan Discussion Group
VETTE-L@EMUVM1.BITNET	Corvette Discussion—Service Info, Shows, etc.
VOEGLN-L@LSUVM.BITNET	Discussion list on Eric Voegelin's writing and philosophy
VOICES-L@ORACLE.WIZARDS.COM	Voices In My Head List
VWAR-L@UBVM.BITNET	Vietnam War Discussion List
WCENTR-L@MIZZOU1.BITNET	Moderated Writing Center forum
WEIMING@ULKYVM.BITNET	Chinese Newsletter Distribution List
WHITESOX@MITVMA.BITNET	Chicago White Sox Mailing List
WHR-L@PSUVM.BITNET	Women's History in Rhetoric
WORCIV-L@UBVM.BITNET	World Civilization Committee

Mailing List	Description
WVMS-L@WVNVM.BITNET	NASA Classroom of the Future: WV Mathematics and Science List
XTROPY-L@UBVM.BITNET	Extropians—discussion and development of Extropian ideas
YACHT-L@HEARN.BITNET	The Sailing and Amateur Boat Building List

Does this list give you an idea of the wild, wacky, and well-worth-reading mailing lists available to you? (I'm planning to check out the Voices in My Head List.) This is just a tiny portion of what's out there. And this is just the LISTSERV groups; there are many non-LISTSERV groups that cover a similarly eclectic subject matter.

The LISTSERV Address

Let's take a look at the LISTSERV address. It's made up of three parts: the group name itself, the LISTSERV site, and (usually) **.bitnet**. For instance, the address of the group College Activism/Information List is actnow-l@brownvm.bitnet. Actnow-l is the name of the group, and brownvm is the name of the site. (As you can see in the previous table, some of these LISTSERV groups—such as SLAVERY@UHUPVM1.UH.EDU—don't have the .bitnet bit at the end.)

A *site* is a computer that has the LISTSERV program, and it handles one or more LISTSERV groups. In fact, a site may have dozens of groups. The brownvm site, for instance, also maintains the ACH-EC-L, AFRICA-L, and AGING-L forums, among about 70 others.

Let's Do It—Subscribing

Once you've found a LISTSERV group to which you want to subscribe, you must send an e-mail message to the LISTSERV site (not to the group itself), asking to subscribe to the list. Don't worry, you are not going to have to pay; the vast majority of mailing lists are completely free. Send a message with the following text in the body (not the subject) of the message.

SUBSCRIBE *group firstname lastname*

For instance, if I wanted to subscribe to the actnow-l list at the brownvm LISTSERV site, I would send a message to listserv@brownvm.bitnet, and in the body of the message, I'd write SUBSCRIBE actnow-l Peter Kent.

As you can see in the following figure, you send the message to **listserv@*sitename*** (in this case to listserv@brownvm.bitnet), and the SUBSCRIBE message contains only the name of the group (not the entire group address).

137

Don't Forget These Details

Note that you might have to put something in the Subject line; some e-mail programs won't let you send e-mail unless you do so. In such a case, just type something—anything (1, for instance)—in the Subject line. And if your e-mail program automatically inserts a signature (information such as your name, street address, and so on that is inserted at the end of the message), turn the signature off before sending the message.

You may (or may not) receive some kind of confirmation message from the group. Such a message would tell you that you have subscribed, and would provide background information about the group and the different commands you can use. You may receive a message telling you how to confirm your subscription. If so, follow the instructions in the message. You may also receive instructions about working with the mailing list; read this carefully, as it will contain important information. Once you've subscribed, you can either sit back and wait for the messages to arrive, or you can send your own messages. To send messages, address mail to the full group address (to actnow-l@brownvm.bitnet, for example).

In NavCIS CompuServe Navigator, this is all it takes to subscribe to a LISTSERV mailing list.

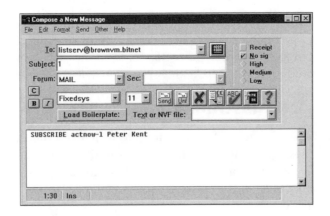

Enough Already!—Unsubscribing

When you're tired of receiving all these messages (and the volume may very well be overwhelming), you'll have to unsubscribe, which you do by sending another message to the LISTSERV address. You still send the message to **listserv@*sitename*** (such as listserv@brownvm.bitnet), but this time type **SIGNOFF actnow-l** in the body of the message.

The next figure shows the SIGNOFF message you use to unsubscribe. Again, make sure you address it to **listserv@sitename**, not to the group name. And make sure the group name—but not the entire group address—appears after **SIGNOFF**.

Message Digests

Here's a way to make your mailing lists easier to handle: get message digests. With message digests, you'll receive one large message at the end of the day that contains all the messages the mailing list has received during the day—instead of receiving dozens of messages throughout the day. To request message digests, send a message to the LISTSERV server at **listserv@*sitename*** and type the message **set *listname* digest** (such as **set actnow-1 digest**).

The message you receive at the end of the day has a list of Subjects at the top. You can use your e-mail program's Find command (or save the message in a text file and use your word processor's Find command) to quickly get to the messages that interest you. If you want to turn the digest off, use the command **set *listname* nodig**. Note, however, that not all mailing lists can provide message digests.

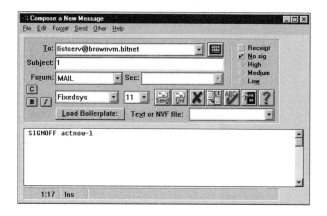

Unsubscribing to a LISTSERV mailing list is also easy.

Getting Fancy with LISTSERV

You can do a few neat things with LISTSERV. By sending e-mail messages to the LISTSERV site, you can tell the LISTSERV software how you want to handle your messages. You can ask LISTSERV to send you an acknowledgment each time you send a message (by default, most groups won't do this). You can find information about another group member, or you can tell LISTSERV not to provide information about you to other users. You can tell LISTSERV to stop sending you messages temporarily (perhaps when you go on vacation),

139

or you can tell it to send only the message subjects instead of the entire messages. You can request a specific message, and you can even search the archives for old messages.

When you first subscribe to a mailing list, it's a good idea to send the **info** command to the **listserv@***sitename* address (not the group itself). Put the word **info** in the body of the message. A document containing important information about working with the list will be returned to you.

Remember This!
Remember that when you want to send a message to be read by other group members, you must address it to the groupname@sitename. For all other purposes (to subscribe, unsubscribe, change user options, get more information, and so on), send the message to listserv@sitename. Send these messages to the group itself, and you may get complaints. But hey, you wouldn't be alone. Many of us (me included, several times), forget to change the address and send these commands to the wrong address! Actually, these days, some LISTSERV servers recognize a message that contains commands, intercepts it before it gets to the mailing-list group, and sends it back to you.

In addition, you can combine these commands. For instance, you can send an e-mail message to **listserv@brownvm.bitnet** with these lines in the body of the message:

> **list**
>
> **query** *groupname*
>
> **info ?**

This tells LISTSERV to send you a list of the groups handled by this site (**list**), to tell you which options you have set (**query** *groupname*), and to send you a list of information guides (**info ?**). It's a good idea to use this last command to find out about user documentation they have available, and then to use the **info** *documentname* command to have specific documents sent to you. (At some sites, sending e-mail to the LISTSERV address with the message **INFO REFCARD** will get you a document outlining the commands.)

Using Majordomo

The other common mailing list program is Majordomo. Here's how to subscribe to a Majordomo list. It's very similar to working with LISTSERV.

To subscribe, send a message to **majordomo@***sitename*. For instance, majordomo@usa.net, majordomo@big.host.com, and so on. In the body of the message type **subscribe** *group firstname lastname*.

The same as with LISTSERV, eh? When you unsubscribe, though, you'll use a different command. Instead of SIGNOFF, use:

> **unsubscribe** *group*

Finally, when sending messages to the group, remember to send them to *group@sitename*.

Using Manually Administered Lists

Some lists are administered manually. That means there is no computer running the list; instead, some person actually reads the subscription requests and adds people to the list manually.

This can be administered in many ways. You may simply send e-mail to the person who administers the list and say, "hey, add me to the list please." Often, however, there's a special address associated with the list. You may have to send your subscription list to *listname*-**request@***hostname*. For instance, if the list is called goodbeer, and it's at the bighost.com hostname, you would send your subscription request to goodbeer-request@bighost.com. Once you had subscribed, you would send your actual correspondence to the list to goodbeer@bighost.com.

Handling Mailing List Correspondence

Working with a mailing list is quite simple. When a message arrives, you find it in your e-mail inbox along with all your normal e-mail. If you read a message to which you want to reply, simply use the reply function of your e-mail program (see Chapter 3 for more information), and the new message is addressed to the correct place. At least, in most cases it is addressed correctly. Check the return address that your e-mail program enters for you. With some mailing lists, you'll find that the Return address in the header of the message you received is not the address to which you are supposed to send messages.

To send a message about a new subject, simply write a new message, address it to the mailing-list address, and send it off.

In some ways, working with mailing lists is not as convenient as working with newsgroups. The newsgroup programs have a lot of features for dealing with discussions. Of course, your e-mail program will almost certainly let you print and save messages just as a newsgroup program would. What's missing, though, are the threading functions that you get in newsgroup messages (which enable you to quickly see which messages are part of a series of responses). You may also find that messages are sent to you out of order, in which case you may end up reading a response to a message that appears lower down in your e-mail inbox before you read the original message. This is all the more reason you should use the message digest (discussed earlier) to get the messages in the most convenient form possible.

The Least You Need to Know

➤ A mailing list is a discussion group in which messages are exchanged through the e-mail system.

➤ Mailing lists may be administered manually or run by a program such as LISTERV or Majordomo.

➤ Subscribe to a LISTSERV group by including the command **SUBSCRIBE** *groupname firstname lastname* in the body of a message and sending the message to **listserv@*sitename***.

➤ To unsubscribe from a LISTSERV list, send the command **SIGNOFF** *groupname* in the body of a message.

➤ To subscribe to a Majordomo list, you normally send a message saying **SUBSCRIBE** *groupname firstname lastname* in the body. The message goes to the major-domo address (such as majordomo@bighost), not the list name address.

➤ To unsubscribe from a Majordomo list use the **UNSUBSCRIBE** command (not SIGNOFF).

➤ To subscribe to a manually administered list, write to the person running the list and ask to join. Or you may need to e-mail to ***listname*-request@*hostname***.

➤ When you join a list, send a message with the command **info** in the body to find out important information about working with the list.

Chapter 12

The Giant Software Store: FTP

In This Chapter

➤ What is FTP?

➤ FTP can be difficult, but it can be easy

➤ Ftping with your Web browser

➤ Clues that will help you find files

➤ Ftping with true FTP programs

➤ Dealing with compressed files

➤ Protecting yourself from viruses

The Internet is a vast computer library. Virtually any type of computer file imaginable is available somewhere on the Internet. You'll find freeware (programs you can use for free) and shareware (programs you must pay a small fee to use) in almost all types of files: music, pictures, video, 3-D images, and many types of hypertext documents. You'll probably find every file type you can possibly name on the Internet.

Where are these files? You looked at the World Wide Web in Chapters 4–8, and you know that you can download plenty of files from the Web. But there's another system that predates the Web: FTP.

To give you a little bit of history, FTP is one of those quaint old UNIX-geek terms. It stands for *file transfer protocol*, and it's an old UNIX system for transferring files from one computer to another. In fact, FTP is really the original core of the Internet: the whole purpose of the Internet was to allow the transfer of computer files between research institutions. Even e-mail came later; it was reportedly slipped into the Internet by geeks who didn't keep the bureaucrats fully apprised. (The geeks feared that the managers would think e-mail would be misused; from what I've seen of electronic communications, the managers would have been right!)

Using the Command Line?

Command-line users can refer to Chapters 18 and 19 of the first edition of *The Complete Idiot's Guide to the Internet* for more information. You can get those chapters from the CD in the back of this book (described in Appendix C), or you can send e-mail to **ciginternet@mcp.com** with **allftp** in the Subject line to have the chapters mailed to you. See Appendix C for more information on using the mail responder.

There are FTP sites all over the Internet, containing literally millions of computer files. And although some of these sites are private, many are open to the public. With FTP, it's very possible that you might discover a fascinating file on a computer in Austria (or Australia, or Alabama, or anywhere). You might have checked it out because someone told you where it was, or because you saw it mentioned in an Internet directory of some kind, or because you saw a message in a newsgroup about it. The file itself could be a public domain or shareware program, a document containing information you want for some research you're working on, a picture, a book you want to read, or just about anything else.

Suppose then that you're searching for one of the files described above. You might be told to "ftp to such and such a computer to find this file." That simply means "use the FTP system to grab the file." Of course, you don't know what that means either, so you find yourself asking, "how do I get the file from that computer to my computer?"

In some cases, you may have specific permission to get onto another computer and grab files. A researcher, for instance, may have been given permission to access files on a computer owned by an organization involved in the same sort of research—another university or government department, perhaps. (I have private FTP directories on various publishers' FTP sites, so I can upload Web pages, or chapters for a book, or whatever.) To get into a directory that requires special permission, you need to use a login name and a password.

In other cases, though, you'll just be rooting around on other systems without specific permission. Some systems are open to the public; anyone can get on and grab files that the system administrator has decided should be publicly accessible. This type of access is known as *anonymous ftp* because you don't need a unique login name to get onto the computer; you simply log in as *anonymous*, and you normally enter your e-mail address for the password. If you are working at the UNIX command line, as many unfortunate people still do, you have to type this information. However, the rest of you are using a program that will enter this information for you.

Before you start, let me give you a word of advice about *when* you should use FTP. Many systems don't like people digging around during business hours. They would rather you come in during evenings and weekends. In fact, you may have trouble getting into many FTP sites during the day because they are so busy. You may see a message asking you to restrict your use to after-hours, or the FTP site may not let you in at all during certain hours. Of course your day may be the site's night, so you need to consider where (geographically) the site is located.

Tracking Down a File with Archie What if you know the file you want, but you have no idea where to look for it? A quick way to track down a file is using Archie. You'll learn about Archie in Chapter 13.

Different Flavors of FTP

FTP was originally a command-line program in which you had to type commands at a prompt and press the Enter key. Information would then scroll past on your screen, perhaps too fast for you to read (unless you knew the secret command to make it slow down or stop). You'd have to read this information and then type another command. Although UNIX geeks got some sort of strange masochistic pleasure out of that sort of thing, real people found early FTP to be a painful experience—and most people avoided it. If you want to see an example of command-line FTP, take a look at Chapters 15 and 16 in the first edition of *The Complete Idiot's Guide to the Internet* (on the CD at the back of this book).

In the early 1990s (a year or two before the Internet boom), FTP became automated to some extent. This automation made it possible to get to some FTP sites using *Gopher*, a system covered in Chapter 14. With Gopher, you selected files from a menu system instead of by typing commands. Yet even this was inconvenient for a number of reasons, the most important being that you could access only FTP sites for which some kindly Gopher author had created menus.

Next came graphical FTP programs. There are plenty around, but the best I've seen are WS_FTP, a Windows freeware program, and Fetch, a Macintosh shareware program (see Appendix A for information about finding these). I also like CuteFTP, a Windows shareware program and Anarchie, a Macintosh shareware program (one that you'll learn more about in Chapter 13). Many others are available, particularly for Windows. Most of the graphical FTP programs allow you to see lists of files and to use your mouse to carry out the operations. Using FTP with these systems was a pleasure; FTP became easy.

Finally, FTP was incorporated into Web browsers. You can now go to an FTP site using your Web browser—and usually without a special FTP program. Because the FTP site appears as a document with links in it, you can click a link to view the contents of a directory, to read a text file, or to transfer a computer file to your computer.

In this chapter, you're going to look at running FTP sessions with a Web browser—for a couple of reasons. First, it's a very easy way to work with FTP. Second, you probably already have a Web browser. However, you may run into FTP sites that won't work well through a Web browser, or you may need to upload files to an FTP site, which (as of the time of writing of this book) most browsers won't let you do. In these cases, you'll want to use a true FTP program, which you'll read about near the end of this chapter.

Hitting the FTP Trail

To work through an FTP example, go to **ftp://ftp.dartmouth.edu/**. This is where you can find the Fetch program. (If you prefer to visit another FTP site, you can follow along and do so; the principles are the same.) I've given you the FTP site names, but not the directories holding the files; you can track them down when you get there.

Techno Talk

What's in a Name?

Take a minute to analyze a site name. First there's the **ftp://** part. This simply tells your browser that you want to go to an FTP site. Then there's the FTP site name (or host name): **ftp.dartmouth.edu**. It identifies the computer that contains the files you are after. That might be followed by a directory name. I haven't given you a directory name in this example, but I could have told you to go to ftp.dartmouth.edu/pub/software/mac. The **/pub/software/mac** bit tells the browser which directory it must change to in order to find the files you want.

To start, open your Web browser. Click inside the **Address** text box, type **ftp://ftp.dartmouth.edu** (or **ftp://** and the address of another site you want to visit), and press **Enter**. Actually, in most browsers these days, you can omit the ftp:// as long as the FTP site name begins with ftp. In other words, instead of typing out **ftp://ftp.dartmouth.edu**, you can generally get away with typing only **ftp.dartmouth.edu**.

In a few moments, with luck, you'll see something like the screen shown in the following figure. Without luck, you'll probably get a message telling you that you cannot connect to the FTP site. If that happens, check to see if you typed the name correctly. If you did, you'll have to wait and try again later; the site may be closed, or it may be very busy.

Name or Number The FTP site or host name could even be a name (leo.nmc.edu) or a number (192.88.242.239).

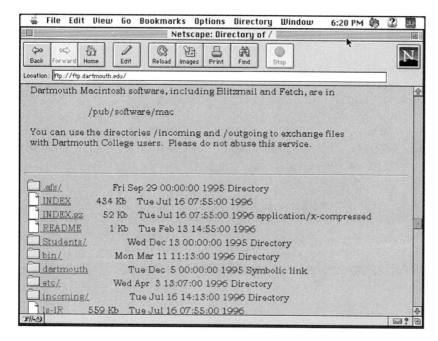

If you've used command-line FTP, you'll love working in a browser.

Notice, by the way, that you didn't have to enter the anonymous login name or your e-mail address as a password. The browser handled all of that for you.

There's another way to get to an FTP site. Many Web authors create links from their Web pages to an FTP site. Click the link, and you'll go to that site.

Files and Links—What Is All This?

What can you see at the FTP site? Each file and directory is shown as a link. Depending on the browser you are using, you might see information about the file or directory (refer to the previous figure). You might see a description of each item—file or directory, for instance—and the file size, so you'll know how big a file is before you transfer it. You'll often see the file date and little icons that represent the directory or file type. In the previous figure, you can see that there are both files and directories.

Private FTP Sites

If you want to enter a private FTP site, you will have to enter a login ID and a password. You can often enter the FTP site information in the format ftp://*username:password@hostname/directory/*. For example, if you enter **ftp://joeb:1234tyu@ftp.microsoft.com/t1/home/joeb**, your browser connects to the ftp.microsoft.com FTP site and displays the /t1/home/joeb directory; it uses the username **joeb** and the password **1234tyu** to gain access. However, in some browsers, using that method causes the browser to save your password in a drop-down list box associated with the Location text box. Therefore, if you want to be really safe, use the format ftp://*username@hostname/directory*. When the browser connects to the FTP site, it opens a dialog box into which you can type your password.

Click a directory link to see the contents of that directory. The browser displays another Web document, showing the contents of that directory. In most browsers, you'll also find a link back to the parent directory: in Netscape you'll see an "Up to a higher level directory" link, for instance. The following figure shows what you will find if you click the **pub** link at the **ftp.dartmouth.edu** site. Why pub? Because that's commonly used to hold publicly available files. This time, you can see that there's a file in this directory, along with three more subdirectories.

The contents of the pub directory at the FTP site. This time you're looking at a Windows version of Netscape.

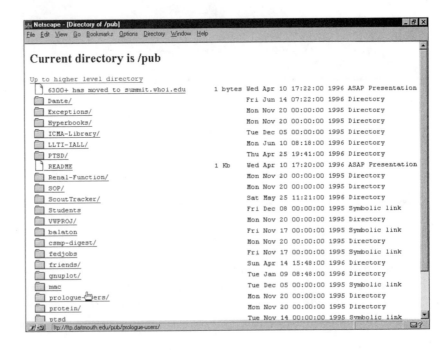

What happens when you click a link to a file? The same thing that would happen if you did so from a true Web document. If the browser can display or play the file type, it will. If it can't, it will try to send it to the associated application. If there is no associated application, it will ask you what to do with it, allowing you to save it on the hard disk. This all works in the same way as it does when you are at a Web site—the browser looks at the file type and acts accordingly. (See Chapters 5 and 7 for more information.)

How Do I Find Files?
Don't forget Archie! Archie is a system that lets you search an index of FTP sites throughout the world for just the file you need. See Chapter 13 for more information.

Finding That Pot o' Gold

Now that you're on, you want to find the file that you know lies somewhere on this system. (In my example, you're looking for Fetch, the Macintosh FTP program.) Where do you start? Well, finding files at an FTP site is often a little difficult. There are no conventions for how such sites should be set up, so you often have to dig through directories that look like they might contain what you want, until you find what you want.

Remember, though, that your Web browser can display text files. When you first get to an FTP site, look for files called INDEX, README, DIRECTORY, and so on. These often contain information that will help you find what you need. The more organized sites even contain text files with full indexes of their contents, or at least lists of the directories and the types of files you'll find. Click one of these files to transfer the document to your Web browser, read the file, and then click the **Back** button to return to the directory.

Look for Clues

You'll often find that directories have names that describe their contents: **slip** will probably contain SLIP software, **mac** will have Macintosh software, **xwindow** will have X Window software, **windows** will have Microsoft Windows software, **gif** will contain GIF-format graphics, and so on. If you know what you are looking for, you can often figure out what the directory names mean. In the example, you knew where to go because, when you first arrived at the site, you saw a message saying that Fetch was in /pub/software/mac. So you clicked on **pub**, and then on **software**, and then on **mac**.

FTP Connections Through Web Pages Many FTP sites are now accessible directly through Web documents. For instance, instead of going to ftp:// ftp.winsite.com/ (a well-known shareware archive), you could go to http://www.winsite.com/. It's often easier to connect to and search the Web sites than it is the FTP sites.

It Looks a Little Strange

You'll often see full FTP site and path information, which takes you straight to the directory you want (such as ftp.usma.edu/msdos/). If you're used to working in DOS and Windows, FTP site directory names may seem strange for two reasons. First, you'll see a forward slash (/) instead of a backslash (\), separating the directories in the path. In the DOS world, you use a backslash (\), but in the UNIX world, you use the forward slash character (/) instead—and most Internet host computers still run on UNIX. Second, the directory names are often long. In DOS, you can't have directories with more than 12 characters in the name (including a period and an extension). In Windows 95, however, you can. This new operating system *and* UNIX computers allow long file and directory names.

Getting the File

When you find the file you want, simply click it, and save it in the same way you would save a file from a Web document (see Chapter 5). The following figure shows Fetch being saved from FTP.

You can save files from FTP sites with a few clicks.

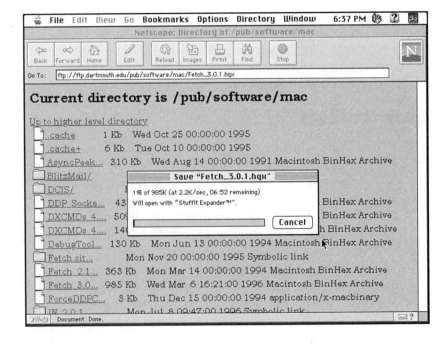

Many files on FTP sites are *compressed*. That is, a special program has been used to "squeeze" the information into a smaller area. You can't use a file in its compressed state, but if you store it and transmit it in that state, you'll save disk space and transmission time. You can read more about these compressed formats in Chapter 15.

In this case, we are transferring a .hqx file that contains a .sit file. A program such as StuffIt Expander can extract the .sit file (a compressed file) from within the BinHex .hqx file (a common format for transferring Mac files across the Internet).

It's the Real Thing: Using a Real FTP Program

There may be times when you try to connect to an FTP site with your Web browser, and it just won't work. Of course, it may be that the FTP site is simply too busy to let you on (most limit the number of people using them). But sometimes your browser simply can't manage the site.

It might be a private site, and even if you have a password to enter the site, some browsers won't be able to use it. (Most probably can these days, though; both Internet Explorer and Netscape can.) Your browser may not be able to take that password and pass it on. Also, FTP sites come in many "flavors"— many different computer types and operating systems. Your browser may simply have trouble communicating. And if you want to *upload* files (transfer files *from* your computer to the FTP site), you won't be able to do so through your browser. (At least, at the time of this writing, this was true; however, this feature will be added to browsers soon.)

So you may run into cases in which the browser FTP features are not enough. For those times, you need to get a real FTP program.

> **Check This Out...**
>
> **Same Name, Different Extension** While digging around in an FTP site, you might notice that files often have the same name except for the last few characters; you might find **thisdoc.txt** and **thisdoc.zip**, for instance. The first is a simple ASCII text file, and the second is a ZIP file, which (if you notice) is much smaller than the first. If you know you can decompress the file once you have it, download the compressed version. It'll save you time and money.

Which and Where

There are lots of good FTP programs around. If you use the Mac, try Fetch or Anarchie. For Windows, start with WS_FTP (my personal favorite) or try CuteFTP. Many good Windows FTP programs are available as freeware or shareware on the Internet. See Appendix A for ideas on where to look for the software you want.

Let's take a quick look at WS_FTP. You don't need to go into great detail about working with this program, but it will give you an idea of what's going on. When you get an FTP

151

program, go through that old familiar routine: read the documentation carefully to make sure you understand how to use it. (FTP programs are generally fairly easy to deal with.)

WS_FTP is actually very easy to use. If you've ever used UNIX FTP, you'll think that using it was like eating soup with a fork—not particularly satisfying. WS_FTP, on the other hand, is what FTP should be. You have all the commands at your fingertips, plus a library of FTP sites to select from. No more mistyping FTP host names!

Installing WS_FTP is simple. Just run the installation program. Then start WS_FTP by going through the Start menu, or double-click its Program Manager icon. You'll see the Session Profile dialog box shown in the following figure. This is where you can select an FTP site from the list (WS_FTP comes with a bunch already configured), or you can enter information about a particular site you want to visit. Click **New** to clear the boxes, and then follow these steps:

1. Type a **Profile Name** (anything that helps you remember what the site contains).

2. Enter the actual FTP site Host Name.

3. If you know it, enter the **Host Type**. (If you are not sure, ignore this setting and let WS_FTP pick it for you.)

Set up your session profile before connecting.

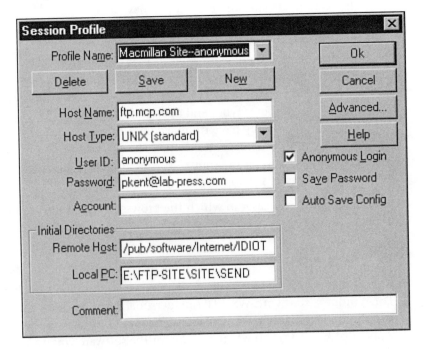

4. If you are going to an "anonymous" FTP site, click the **Anonymous Login** check box. If you are going to a private site, type your **User ID**.

5. If this is a private site, enter your **Password**.

6. If you know which directory you want to go to when you get to the FTP site, enter it in the **Initial Directories: Remote Host** text box.

7. (Optional) Enter the Local PC directory—the directory on your computer that should be displayed and into which transferred files will be placed.

8. Click the **Save** button to save the information.

9. Click **OK** to begin the session.

When you click OK, WS_FTP tries to connect to the FTP site. Once it's connected, you'll see the FTP site's directories listed on the right, and the directories on your computer's hard disk listed on the left (see the following figure).

You can move around in the directories by double-clicking or by using the ChgDir button. This is really handy because if you know where you want to go, it's a lot quicker to type it in and go directly than to go through each directory in the path to get there.

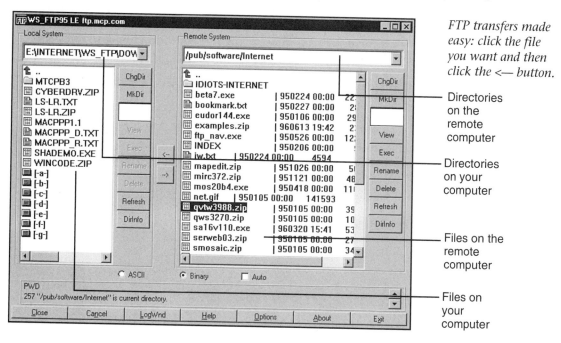

FTP transfers made easy: click the file you want and then click the <— button.

Directories on the remote computer

Directories on your computer

Files on the remote computer

Files on your computer

The two buttons you'll use most are the View and <— buttons. Say you find an index file you want to read. Click it and click the **View** button on the right side of the window, and the index file is placed into the Windows Notepad program so you can read it. And when you find the files you want, press and hold **Ctrl**, click each one, and then click the <— button to transfer them to your hard disk.

Select the File Type Notice the little ASCII and Binary option buttons below the file list windows? Make sure you select the correct one before transferring a file. Select **ASCII** for files you know to be ASCII text files; select **Binary** for anything else. And remember, word processing files are not ASCII, they're binary; they contains special codes that are used to define the character formatting.

You probably won't use some of the buttons much, at least not on the FTP site. You can create a new directory and delete a directory (ChgDir and RmDir). If you are using an anonymous login, you won't be able to do this on the FTP site, but you can use the buttons to add and remove directories on your own hard disk. You can also rename and delete files, and even automatically transfer a file and load it into the program the file's extension is associated with in Windows (using the Exec button).

Sometimes WS_FTP is unable to figure out what type of host it's connecting to. It can usually do it, but now and again you'll notice strange occurrences, such as no directories appearing in the directories list, or file dates appearing instead of file names, or partial file names appearing. When you try to transfer one of these strange files to your system, you'll get a message saying that it doesn't exist. Follow these steps for an easy solution to that problem:

1. Click the **LogWnd** button to see the session log. You'll see a log showing the entire FTP session from the command-line point of view.

2. Go back to the start of the session log and see if you can find the type of host mentioned; usually an FTP site will identify its type.

3. Click the **Options** button.

4. In the dialog box that appears, click the **Session Options** button.

5. Select the host type from the drop-down list.

6. Click **Save**.

It's Alive! Viruses and Other Nasties

If you haven't been in a cave for the past six or seven years, you've probably heard about computer viruses. A *virus* is a computer program that can reproduce itself and even convince unknowing users to help spread it. It spreads far and wide and can do incredible amounts of damage.

As is true of real viruses, the effects of a virus on your system can range from almost-unnoticeable to fatal. A virus can do something as harmless as display a Christmas tree on your screen, or it can destroy everything on your hard disk. Viruses are real—but the threat is overstated. We'll be talking more about viruses in Chapter 20.

Where Now?

There are thousands of FTP sites all over the world. Generally, however, FTP is a service of last resort. These days, people go to the Web first and only use FTP if they know exactly where to go to get what they are looking for. Perhaps you've read in a newsgroup message or a magazine article that a particular file is available at a particular FTP site. You *can* go directly to the site to find it, but most people don't go looking for things at FTP sites. The Web sites are far more convenient.

However, you might want to see the http://hoohoo.ncsa.uiuc.edu/ftp/ Web site—the Monster FTP Sites list—where you can find thousands of FTP sites. If you are searching for a particular file and can't find it at the sources mentioned in Appendix A, you can try Archie, a friendly (but slow, as you'll learn in Chapter 13) little fellow who'll help you dig around in FTP.

The Least You Need to Know

➤ FTP stands for file transfer protocol and refers to a system of file libraries.

➤ Anonymous FTP refers to a system that allows the public to transfer files.

➤ Start an FTP session in your Web browser using the format **ftp://*hostname*** in the Address text box (replacing *hostname* with the appropriate URL) and pressing **Enter**.

➤ Each directory and file at an FTP site is represented by a link; click the link to view the directory or transfer the file.

➤ If your browser can't connect to a particular site, try an FTP program such as WS_FTP (Windows) or Fetch (Macintosh).

➤ Protect yourself against viruses, but don't be paranoid. They're not as common as the antivirus companies want you to think.

Chapter 13

Archie, the Friendly File Librarian

In This Chapter

➤ What does Archie do?

➤ Four ways to use Archie

➤ Finding an Archie gateway on the Web

➤ Searching for files using your Web browser

➤ Using an Archie client

➤ Using Archie mail (if you don't want to wait)

➤ Doing descriptive (whatis) searches

Using FTP is okay—if you know where to go to find the file you want. And granted, you might find out about the FTP site by reading it in an e-mail message or in a document you find somewhere. However, that's just not helpful when you know the name of the file you are looking for you but have no idea where to go to find it.

Archie to the rescue!! Designed by a few guys at McGill University in Canada, Archie is a system that indexes FTP sites, listing the files that are available at each site. Archie lists several million files at FTP sites throughout the world and provides a very useful way to find out where to go to grab a file in which you are interested. There's just one problem: Archie's extremely busy these days and can be very slow.

Try Archie Mail

Archie has a descriptive-index search. That means you can search for a particular subject and find files related to that subject. You can't do this using a Web browser; try using Archie mail, instead. You can read more about Archie Mail later in this chapter.

Archie's Client/Server Stuff

Like certain other Internet systems, Archie is set up using a *client/server* system. An Archie server is a computer that periodically takes a look at all the Internet FTP sites around the world and builds a list of all their available files. Each server builds a database of those files. An Archie client program can then come along and search the server's database, using it as an index.

It's generally believed in Internet-land that it doesn't matter much which Archie server you use because they all do much the same thing; some are simply a few days more recent than others. This isn't always true. Sometimes, you may get very different results from two different servers.

For example, one server might find two *hits* (matches to your search request), and another might find seven.

Getting to Archie

To use Archie, you access an Archie server. No matter which Archie server you access, you can choose from several methods of connecting with it:

➤ You can use Archie through the *command line*. This is unwieldy and difficult, though, and you *don't* want to do it this way if you can help it! If you absolutely can't help it, see Chapter 20 in the first edition of *The Complete Idiot's Guide to the Internet*, which is on the CD in the back of this book. Or send e-mail to **ciginternet@mcp.com**, with **archie** in the Subject line to have the chapter mailed to you. (See Appendix C for more information about working with the CD or mail responder.)

➤ You can use your Web browser to go to an Archie *gateway*, a Web page containing a form that will help you search an Archie index. You enter information into the form, the information is sent to the Archie server, and the response from the server appears in another Web page.

➤ You can use a special Archie client program, such as WS_Archie (Windows) or Anarchie (Macintosh).

➤ You can use e-mail to send questions to an Archie server.

We'll start with the easiest way to use Archie: through your Web browser. Then we'll take a look at the last two methods listed above.

Archie on the Web

Your Web browser is not a true Archie client. That is, there is no archie:// URL! Therefore, you'll have to use a "gateway" to an Archie client, of which there are dozens on the Web. Open your Web browser and go to **http://web.nexor.co.uk/archie.html** to find a list. Just in case that Web site's busy, here are several Archie sites you can try:

> **http://www.lerc.nasa.gov/archieplex/**
>
> **http://hoohoo.ncsa.uiuc.edu/archie.html**
>
> **http://src.doc.ic.ac.uk/archieplexform.html**

Archie? What does Archie mean? It's not an acronym (unlike Veronica and Jughead, whom you'll meet in Chapter 14). Instead it comes from the word *archive* (as in file archive). Remove the *v* and what have you got? Archie.

Most Archie sites offer both forms and nonforms search methods. Internet Explorer and Netscape are forms-capable browsers, which means that they can display such forms components as text boxes, command buttons, option buttons, and so on. If you are using one of these browsers or another forms-capable browser, select the forms search. (Most browsers can work with forms these days.)

Searching Archie

The following figure shows an example of an Archie form, specifically, one at Imperial College in London (located at http://src.doc.ic.ac.uk/archieplexform.html). The simplest way to search is to type a file name or part of a file name into the **What would you like to search for?** text box and press **Enter** (or click the **Start Search** button). For instance, if you want to find the WS_Archie program you're going to look at later

Different Gateways, Different Options These Archie forms vary. Each Archie gateway is a little different, so if you use a different one from the one you're about to look at, you may find the options vary slightly.

in this chapter, type **wsarchie** and press **Enter**. Why not WS_ARCHIE? Because even though the program name is WS_Archie, the file you need is actually called WSARCHIE.ZIP or WSARCHIE.EXE. Of course there's no way for you to know that if I hadn't told you…. If you are using a Macintosh, you might search for **anarchie** (as shown).

Archie gateways provide a link from the Web to Archie servers around the world.

Type what you're looking for.

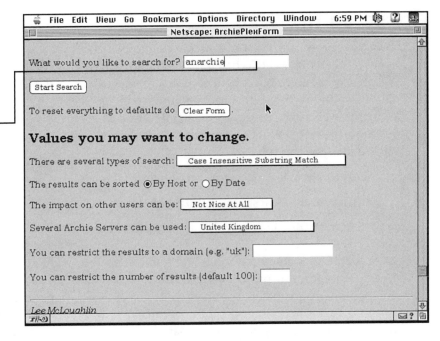

Archie searches are often very slow; often, they simply don't work because the Archie server you are working with is busy. (I'll show you how to choose another server in a moment.) If you are lucky, though, you'll eventually see a screen like the one shown next. This shows what the Archie server found: links to the WSARCHIE files. You can see that there are links to the host (the computer that contains the file you are looking for), the directory on the host that contains the file you want, and in some cases, directly to the file you want. If you click one of the wsarchie.zip links, the browser begins transferring the file; if you click a link to a directory, your browser begins an FTP session in that directory.

Stop! To cancel a search, click the browser's **Stop** toolbar button.

Notice in the next figure that the pointer in the illustration is pointing at a directory. If you click it, you'll go to that directory on the oslo-nntp.eunet.no server, which happens to be a computer in Norway. (That directory was created in 1995.) There is, of course, a copy of the wsarchie.zip file on the ftp.cac.washington.edu host. If you look closely, though, it was created in 1994; it might not be the most recent version.

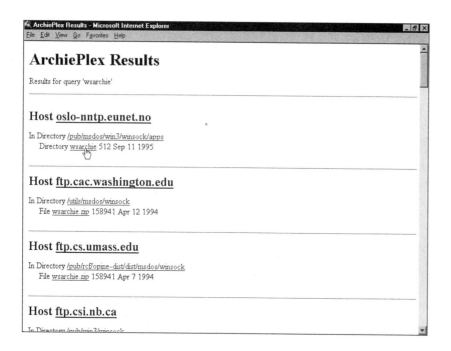

ArchiePlex Results

Results for query 'wsarchie'

Host oslo-nntp.eunet.no

In Directory /pub/msdos/win3/winsock/apps
   Directory wsarchie 512 Sep 11 1995

Host ftp.cac.washington.edu

In Directory /utils/msdos/winsock
   File wsarchie.zip 158941 Apr 12 1994

Host ftp.cs.umass.edu

In Directory /pub/rcf/opine-dist/dist/msdos/winsock
   File wsarchie.zip 158941 Apr 7 1994

Host ftp.csi.nb.ca

In Directory /pub/win3/winsock

When (or if) Archie returns the result, it will be in a Web document containing links to the files.

Search the Document

Remember that you can use your browser's Find function to search the list of files once it's on-screen (in both Internet Explorer and Netscape, it's **Edit**, **Find** or **Ctrl+F**). For instance, let's say you want to download an EXE file (a self-extracting archive) instead of a ZIP file. Search for **.exe** to go directly to the file you need.

Archie's Options

Below the text box where you type what you want to search for are some more options you can use to narrow your search. Here's what you'll find:

➤ **Search type** There are four types of searches, which I'll explain in a moment.

➤ **Sort by** The list of files that is returned to you might be sorted by file date or according to the host containing the file. The file-date search is a good idea, as it will help you pick the latest version of the file.

➤ **Impact on other users** You can tell Archie that you are not in a hurry (so other users can go first), or that you want the results right away. Difficult choice, huh?

➤ **Archie servers** Of all the Archie servers all over the world, you can select the one you want to use from a list. If you find that the Archie server you tried is busy, or if it can't find what you want, try another one. You might want to try servers in countries in which the people are currently asleep; obviously, the servers are likely to be less busy at night than during the day.

➤ **Restrict the results to a domain**   You can tell the Archie server that you only want to see files in a particular domain (a particular host-computer type) such as UK (FTP sites in the United Kingdom), COM (commercial FTP sites), EDU (educational FTP sites) and so on.

➤ **Number of results**   You can tell the Archie server how many results you want to see, but note that this setting is not always accurate.

Impact on Users

A couple of years ago, people were talking seriously about how you should work on the Internet in a way that wouldn't slow down the network. For example, you should access sites that are close to you, access sites at night, and so on. However, it's hard to take that sort of thinking seriously anymore, as altruistic as it may be. What with video, multimedia, Java, and so on, you're working on a whole new Internet with completely different data-transfer needs and capabilities.

The Search Types

Before you begin searching for a file name, you should determine which type of search you want to use. You have the following choices:

➤ **Exact** or **Exact Match**   You must type the exact name of the file for which you are looking.

➤ **Regex** or **Regular Expression Match**   You will type a UNIX regular expression. That means that Archie will regard some of the characters in the word you type as wild cards. If you don't understand regular expressions, you should probably just avoid this type of search altogether. (Everyone except UNIX geeks should probably avoid this option.)

➤ **Sub** or **Case Insensitive Substring Match**   This tells Archie to search among file names for whatever you type. That is, it will look for all names that match what you type, as well as all names that *include* the characters you type. If you are searching for "wsarch," for example, archie finds "wsarch" and "wsarchie." Also, when you use a sub search, you don't need to worry about the case of the characters; Archie finds both "wsarch" and "WSARCH."

➤ **Subcase** or **Case Sensitive Substring Match** This is like the sub search, except that you need to enter the case of the word correctly. If you enter "wsarch," Archie finds "wsarch" but not "WSARCH." You should generally avoid this type of search.

More often than not, you'll want to use the sub search (Case Insensitive Substring Match), and you'll probably find that sub has been set up as the default. It takes a little longer than the other types, but it's most likely to find what you are looking for.

It Doesn't Seem to Work

The Substring Matches won't always find file names that contain what you typed. For instance, if you search for "ws_ftp" (which you looked at in Chapter 12), it might not find ws_ftp32 at all, or it might find only one or two matches—even though you know there are many files named ws_ftp32 at many FTP sites. Why does this happen? Archie shows you the ws_ftp matches before it shows you the ws_ftp32 matches; therefore, a lot of ws_ftp matches might exceed the find limit (controlled by the Number Of Results option). You can increase the number of results and run the search again to see if there are any ws_ftp32 files, or you can make the search more specific, changing the search string to ws_ftp32.

You should realize, however, that file names are not always set in stone. With thousands of people posting millions of different files on thousands of different computers, file names sometimes get changed a little. If you have trouble finding something, try a variety of possible combinations.

Getting an Archie Client

If you use Archie a lot, you may want to get hold of a true Archie client: WS_Archie (Windows) or Anarchie (Macintosh). Actually, even if you don't like working with Archie through a Web site, you might want to give it another chance. Whereas you might often find that Archie is busy when you access via the Web, or that the Web site that contains the gateway is busy, you'll probably come to find that a true Archie client provides the information in a way you prefer.

Looking for Shareware

Before you spend a lot of time with Archie, remember that you can often find files (particularly shareware programs) more easily at one of the Web libraries. Appendix A gives you all the details on finding software.

Of course, the Web method is very convenient in the way it creates links to the file you need. But an Archie client can also automate getting the files you want by interacting with an FTP program. For instance, WS_Archie can interact with WS_FTP, ordering WS_FTP to go and get the file you select. Anarchie has a built-in FTP program, so you can search and retrieve with the same program.

You can find an Archie client at one of the software libraries mentioned in Appendix A. You also saw how to search at an Archie gateway for WS_Archie a few moments ago. Go ahead and download the client, and then install it according to the instructions you get with the program.

The following figure shows the WS_Archie screen. For this example, I searched for the Anarchie program for the Mac. I typed **anarchie** into the **Search for** text box, and then clicked **Search**—and off it went. Of course, it may take a while, and sometimes it appears as if nothing is happening. But the program is really just waiting. (Read the Help file for an explanation of what the status bar messages mean.) If WS_Archie finds what I want, I can simply click the file I want to retrieve and select **File**, **Retrieve**. WS_Archie then launches WS_FTP, which downloads the file and then closes.

WS_Archie links to WS_FTP to automate downloads.

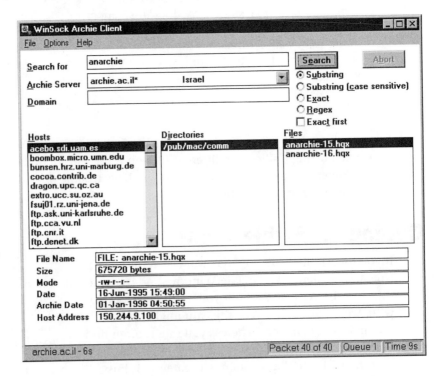

Mail-Order Archie

Archie's real downfall is time. It can take a long time to do an Archie search, and sometimes you find that you can't even get started because the Archie server is too busy to deal with your request.

For those times when you don't want to wait for Archie or spend time trying different Archies, you can use your e-mail program to send an e-mail message to an Archie server and wait for the response. You'll eventually receive a list of files and where you can find them. You then have to use your Web browser or FTP program to go to the FTP site and download the file.

How Soon Will I Get a Response?

Some responses take just a few minutes, but others (even responses to commands in the same e-mail message) can take hours. Archie says that if you wait two days without any response, there's probably a problem, and you may want to try the **set mailto** *emailaddress* command (where *emailaddress* is your e-mail address) to make sure that Archie has your correct e-mail address.

Using Archie by mail is actually quite simple. You send a message to **archie@***archieserver* (where *archieserver* is the address of the Archie server you choose). You can choose any Archie server you want. The following table lists some possibilities.

Available Archie Servers

Archie Server Address	Location
archie.ans.net	USA, ANS
archie.internic.net	USA, AT&T (NY)
archie.rutgers.edu	USA, Rutgers U.
archie.au	Australia
archie.th-darmstadt.de	Germany
archie.wide.ad.jp	Japan
archie.sogang.ac.kr	Korea

Archie List To find the latest list of Archie servers, send an e-mail message to an Archie server with the address **archie@*archieserver*** (such as archie@archie.rutgers.edu). In the body of the message, type *servers* on the first line. See Chapter 3 for more information about using e-mail.

Having chosen the server, you're ready to create an e-mail message to the server. You can leave the Subject line blank if you want and put all the commands in the body of the message. However, note that some e-mail systems don't allow blank Subject lines; if yours doesn't, you can put the first command in the Subject line.

Put the Archie commands (or the rest of them, if you put the first in the Subject line) in the body of the message. You can put as many commands as you want in a message, but each command must be on a separate line, and the first character of each command must be the first character on its line. For example, you might enter these commands:

> **servers**
> **find wsarchie**
> **whatis encryption**

The **servers** command asks Archie to send you a list of Archie servers. (This list may not be complete; you may want to try several different servers to get a complete picture.) The **find** command tells Archie to search for wsarchie. The **whatis** command enables you to do a descriptive search (in this case I'm searching for information about encryption). I'll explain **whatis** in the next section. Finally, when you finish all of this, send the e-mail message.

"Whatis" the Descriptive Index?

Archie has a **whatis** search that you might want to try. Unfortunately, this command is not currently available through the Web gateways or WS_Archie. You can use it with Archie mail, though. This command searches a *descriptive index*, an index of file descriptions.

Not all files indexed by Archie have a description, but many do. It may be worth a try if you are having trouble finding what you need. For example, you might use this command:

> **whatis encryption**

Archie searches, and returns a list of files that meet your criteria. You may get a list of descriptions like this, for example:

codon	Simple encryption algorithm
des	Data encryption system (DES) routines and a login front-end
des-no-usa	Data encryption system (DES) code free of US restrictions

Sometimes you won't be able to figure out why the keyword you used matched some of the files listed, but that doesn't matter as long as some of them look like what you want.

Notice the word at the left end of each line. If you want to find out where the listed file is located, send e-mail back to the server with the command **find** *name* (where *name* is the word at the left end of the line in the preceding list). For example, if you type **find des-no-usa**, Archie will list the DES encryption files that you can download without worrying about U.S. export restrictions.

More E-Mail Commands

Here are other commands that you can use to configure your e-mail search:

➤ **set search** *type*   You learned about the different search types earlier. You can send the **set search** command followed by **exact**, **regex**, **sub**, or **subcase** to tell Archie what type of search you want to do. If you don't specify a search type, the system will use **sub**.

➤ **help**   Sends a Mail Archie user's guide.

➤ **site** *host*   You can enter a host IP address (the numbers that describe a host's location) or domain name, and Archie will send a list of all the files held at that FTP site.

➤ **quit**   This tells Archie to ignore everything that follows in the message. If you have a mail system that inserts a signature file automatically at the end of each message, you can use **quit** to make sure Archie doesn't think this signature information is another command. If Archie sees any command it doesn't understand, it automatically sends the help information—and you don't want to receive the help information every time you send an Archie request.

➤ **set mailto** *mailaddress*   If you find that your Archie requests often go unanswered, it may be because your mail program is not inserting enough information in the From line. You can use this command (replacing *mailaddress* with your e-mail address) to enter the path to which you want Archie's response sent.

If you like the idea of working with Archie through the mail, send the **help** command to get the user's guide. There are plenty of little tricks you can use with this system.

The Least You Need to Know

➤ Archie servers index available files at thousands of FTP sites periodically. Archie clients can read the indexes.

➤ The easiest way to use Archie is through a Web page gateway on the Web. See **http://web.nexor.co.uk/archie.html** for a list of gateways.

➤ It's important to pick the correct type of search. The simplest is the **sub** search, which lets you enter part of the file name without worrying about the case you use.

➤ You may want to try WS_Archie (for Windows) or Anarchie (for the Mac). These are Archie client programs. WS_Archie works with WS_FTP to download a file you find. Anarchie has its own built-in FTP program.

➤ Using Archie by mail can be easy and convenient. You send messages to **archie@*archieserver*** (where *archieserver* is the name of the server you choose) and put the commands in the body of the message.

➤ Use the **whatis** command to search for a file description.

Chapter 14

Digging Through the Internet with Gopher

In This Chapter

➤ A bit of Gopher and Web history

➤ Why bother with Gopher?

➤ Starting a Gopher session

➤ Finding your way around Gopherspace

➤ Saving text documents and computer files

➤ Using Jughead to search a Gopher server

➤ Using Veronica to search in Gopherspace

The World Wide Web is what's "hot" on the Internet right now. Most of the growth in the Internet is occurring on the Web, and it's supposedly doubling in size every few weeks. True, that's another of those dubious Internet statistics, but regardless of the actual figures, it's certainly growing fast.

However, the Web is really quite new. At the end of 1993, even well into 1994, the World Wide Web was a sideshow on the Internet. Few people knew how to use it, and fewer still bothered. It wasn't hard to use, but there wasn't much incentive. For most Internet users, there was no way to display pictures, listen to sounds, play video, or do any of the neat things you've learned to do with Internet Explorer, Netscape Navigator, or other browsers. It wasn't just that the Web was primarily text and little else; it was because the software simply wasn't available. (In fact it wasn't until the fourth quarter of 1994, soon after Netscape was released, that the Web boom really took off.)

Knowing that, you're probably wondering how Internet users got around back in the distant past (okay, a couple of years ago). What was the hot "navigation" system on the Internet in the days before Web? *Gopher.*

If you never used the Internet in the old command-line days, if Netscape and Internet Explorer and the other graphical user interface systems that abound are your only taste of the Internet, then you don't know how difficult the Internet could be. (Actually, millions of people are *still* using the Internet through a command-line interface—that is, typing complicated commands to get things done.) Many people who tried to use the Internet just a year or two ago, when the cyberhype all began, were so turned off by the experience that they went away and never came back. FTP (which you learned about in Chapter 12) was extremely difficult. Telnet (Chapter 18) was pretty clunky—and still is. E-mail was just about bearable. All in all, the Internet was *not* a user-friendly place.

Let There Be Gopher

Check This Out...

Command-Line Users
If you are one of the unfortunate souls still using the command-line interface, send an e-mail message to **ciginternet@mcp.com** and put the word **gopher** in the subject line. In return, you'll get the Gopher chapter from the first edition of the *Complete Idiot's Guide to the Internet.* This explains how to use Gopher if you're working from a dumb terminal.

Then along came Gopher. This tool was a revolution in simplicity, providing a nice menu system from which users could select options. Instead of remembering a variety of rather obscure and arcane commands to find what they needed, users could use the arrow keys to select options from the menu. Those options could take the user to other menus or to documents of some kind. The Gopher system is, in some ways, similar to the World Wide Web. It's a worldwide network of menu systems. Options in the menus linked to menus or other documents all over the world. These Gopher menus made the Internet much easier to use and much more accessible to people who weren't long-term cybergeeks.

For a while, Gopher looked like the future of the Internet—at least to a number of people who invested time and money in Internet software. A variety of "graphical point-and-click" Gopher programs were published commercially and were distributed as shareware and freeware. (You may have heard of WinGopher, for instance, an excellent Windows program for navigating through the Gopher system.)

Then along came the Web. Or rather, along came the graphical Web browsers, which all of a sudden made the Web not only easy to use, but exciting, too. Interest in Gopher subsided rapidly, and everyone rushed off to learn how to create Web documents. And just where did that leave Gopher? Still alive and well, actually, for a couple of good reasons. First, there were already many Gopher systems set up. Second, there are still millions of Internet users who don't have access to graphical Web browsers, and for them, Gopher is the easiest tool available.

There's a lot of interesting information on Gopher servers around the world. Fortunately, you can get to it with your Web browser. That's right: your Web browser may be designed to work on the World Wide Web, but you can use the Web to access Gopher.

Enough History—What Is Gopher?

The Gopher system is based on hundreds of Gopher *servers* (computers that contain the indexes) and millions of Gopher *clients* (computers that are running the Gopher menu software that accesses the server's indexes). Gopher servers are generally public, so any client can access the information from any server. And your Web browser is, in effect, a Gopher client.

Both commercial and shareware versions of graphical Gopher programs are available. You'll probably never use one, though. Working with Gopher through your Web browser works extremely well. Unlike FTP, which works well most (but not all) of the time, you'll find that your browser handles Gopher sites just fine *all* of the time. (Okay, to be honest, there are a *few* geek things you can do with a true Gopher program that you can't do with a Web browser—such as see details about a menu option—but few people will miss these features.) So we're going to take a look at gophering through the Web.

Gopher? Why Is It Called Gopher? For three reasons. First, it was originally developed at the University of Minnesota, home of the Golden Gophers. Second, "gofer" is slang for someone who "goes fer" things—and Gopher's job is to "go fer" files and stuff. And third, the system digs its way through the Internet, like a gopher digs through a burrow. By the way, when you use Gopher, you are traveling through Gopherspace.

Gopher It!

How do you get to a Gopher server? You can start a Gopher session in two ways: by clicking a link in a Web document that some kindly Web author has provided, or by typing the **gopher://** URL into the Address text box and pressing **Enter**. For instance, **gopher:// wiretap.spies.com/** will take you to Internet Wiretap Gopher server, which you can see in the following figure.

The Internet Wiretap Gopher is worth a visit; you'll find loads of interesting documents here.

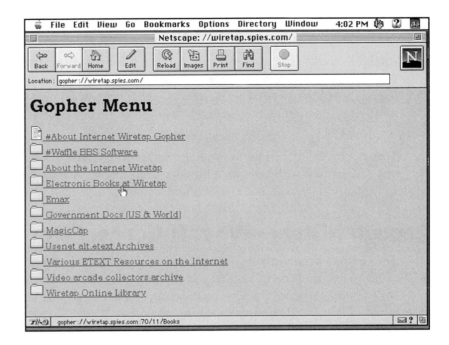

By the way, if you are using Internet Explorer or Netscape (and probably a number of other browsers), you can often ignore the gopher:// bit. If the gopher address starts with the word *gopher*, you can type the address and forget the gopher:// part. For instance, you can type **gopher.usa.net** instead of **gopher://gopher.usa.net**.

Where Can I Start?

For a list of links to Gopher servers, go to **gopher://gopher.micro.umn.edu/ 11/Other%20Gopher%20and%20Information%20Servers**. Or if you don't want to type all that, go to **http://www.w3.org/hypertext/DataSources/ ByAccess.html** and click the **Gopher** link.

You can also include *directories* in the URL. For instance, if you type **gopher:// earth.usa.net/00/News%20and%20Information/Ski%20Information/ A%20List%20of%20Today%27s%20SKI%20CONDITIONS** into the Address box and press Enter, you'll go to the Internet Express Gopher server. Then automatically select the Colorado Ski Information and Ski Conditions menu options.

How, then, do you use a Gopher server with a Web browser? The Gopher menu options are represented by links; click the link to select that option. If the option leads to another menu, that menu appears in the window. If the option leads to a file of some kind, the file is transferred in the normal way, and your browser displays it or plays it (if it can). Files are treated just the same as they would be if you were working on a Web site.

You'll find that most of the documents at Gopher sites are text documents. But as you'll remember from Chapter 7, Web browsers can display text documents within their own windows. Of course, you won't find any links to other documents within these text documents—they're not true Web documents, after all. So when you finish, you click the **Back** toolbar button to return to the Gopher menu you were just viewing. In the following figure, you can see a text document that I ran across at the Wiretap site. I selected the "Electronic Books at Wiretap" menu option and then the "Aesop: Fables, Paperless Edition" link.

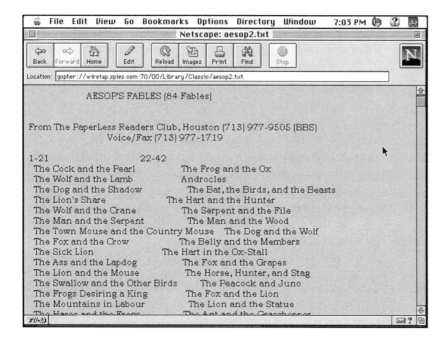

Aesop's fables, from the Wiretap site.

Searching Gopher Menus

Some Gopher menus are very long. The original Gopher system had a special / command that allowed you to search a menu. Although you can't use that command, remember that your browser has a Find command. In Internet Explorer and Netscape you can use Edit, Find to perform the same function.

Archie's Friends: Veronica and Jughead

Gopher servers have two types of search tools: Veronica (Very Easy Rodent-Oriented Net-wide Index to Computerized Archives) and Jughead (Jonzy's Universal Gopher Hierarchy Excavation And Display). Do these acronyms mean much? No, but *you* try to create an acronym from a cartoon character's name!

Cartoon Characters

Why Veronica and Jughead? They are characters in the famous Archie cartoon strip. Remember Archie, the Internet system you learned about in Chapter 13? Archie arrived on the Internet first. Then the people who created the Gopher search systems figured Archie needed company, so they named their systems Veronica and Jughead.

Veronica lets you search Gopher servers all over the world. Jughead lets you search the Gopher server you are currently working with (though many Gopher servers don't yet have Jugheads).

If you want to search Gopherspace—this giant system of Gopher menus that spreads across the Internet—find a Veronica or Jughead menu option somewhere. For instance, at the **gopher://gopher.cc.utah.edu/** Gopher site, you'll find menu options that say "Search titles in Gopherspace using veronica" and "Search menu titles using jughead." You might have to dig around to find menus on some sites; sometimes, they are several levels down the menu system. (I couldn't find Veronica or Jughead at the Wiretap site.) Although many sites don't have Jughead, virtually all have a link to Veronica.

Jughead

When you select the Jughead option, you'll see a few more links. You'll often find links to other Jughead servers at other sites, and you'll probably find a link to information telling you how to work with Jughead.

Of course, there's also a link to the actual search. For instance, go to the **gopher://gopher.cc.utah.edu** site, and you can choose **Search menu titles using jughead** and then click **Search University of Utah Menus Using Jughead**. When you click this link, you'll go to an index-server form like the one shown here. Type a word (such as **elec-tronic books**) into the form and press **Enter**. The Gopher system searches for all menu options containing that word.

Type the word you want to search for and press Enter.

Soon you'll see another Gopher menu, one that was created especially for your search and that contains a list of all the items Jughead found for you. (When you are working with Jughead, the response will probably be fairly quick. Veronica is much slower.) Click an item to see what it is, or point at it and look in your browser's status bar to see what the link "points" to.

If you don't find what you are looking for, you can click the **Back** toolbar button to return to the form and try again. This time, you might enter **book or publication**, for instance, and press **Enter** to search again.

> **Check This Out...**
>
> **Case Doesn't Matter** You can enter the search statement in uppercase or lower-case letters; Jughead doesn't care. It considers "BOOK" to be the same as "book."

The Boolean Operators

A search in which you enter more than one term is known as a *Boolean* search. When typing your search term, you can use the Boolean operators **or**, **and**, and **not** as described here:

> **a and b**   This tells the system to search for a menu item that contains both word **a** *and* word **b**.
>
> **a or b**   This tells the system to search for a menu item that contains either word **a** *or* word **b**.

a not b   This tells the system to search for a menu item that contains the word **a** but does *not* contain the word **b**.

When I searched for **book or publication**, I got a few more menu options. When I searched for **book or publication or publications**, I got even more.

Any Wild Card You Want, As Long As It's *

You can also use *wild cards* in your search text. A wild card is a character that takes the place of another character. So, for example, if you enter **pub*** as your search term, you're telling Jughead to search for any word beginning with "pub." The asterisk simply means "some other stuff here."

You can also combine wild cards and Boolean operators in your search. If you were to type the search term **book or pub***, Jughead would search for the word "book" *or* any words beginning with "pub." This search might find such words as "publication," "publications," "publicity," "public," and "publican."

Check This Out...

Wild Card Rules

Jughead has only one wild card: the * character. You cannot use the ? character, which is a common wild card in many other computer programs. Also, remember these basic rules: you can't start a word with the asterisk, and you can't put an asterisk within a word (it's ignored if you do).

So you can search for "book or pub*" instead of typing out "book or publication or publications." Searching like this will increase your "hit" rate dramatically—you may end up with hundreds of items. Of course, you might ask yourself, "Do I want all this extra stuff?" Well, the "publishers" and "publishing" entries that are found may be useful, but "public" and "pubs" gives you a lot of extra stuff you didn't want (like "Title 53A - State System of Public Education, Chapter 11—Students in Public Schools, Part 3—Immunization of Students").

More Boolean Stuff

Let's take a quick look at the Boolean operators again. If you enter several words on a line without one of the Boolean operators (**and**, **or**, or **not**) between the words, Jughead assumes you mean **and**. For example, Jughead interprets the search terms **book and pub*** and **book pub*** to mean exactly the same thing: "find entries that contain both the word **book** and a word beginning with **pub**."

There are a few other things you also need to be aware of. If Jughead sees any special characters (!"#$%&'()+,-./:;<=>?@[\]^_'{|}~) in the search statement, it treats them as if they were spaces and replaces them with the Boolean operator **and**. For instance, if you enter the search term **This.file**, Jughead searches for **this and file**. That's not necessarily a problem, though. If I search for **Pubs_by SCERP_Researchers**, I will still find the correct menu item, because Jughead will still search for the words **Pubs**, **by**, **SCERP**, and **Researchers**.

Every One Is Different
Remember that each Gopher site is different. What you find at one site when searching with Jughead is not the same as what you'd find at another site.

Also, because you are using the words **and**, **or**, and **not** as Boolean operators, you can't actually search for these words. But then again, you'll probably never need to do so anyway.

Special Commands—Maybe

Jughead currently has four special commands you can include in a search string. Well, you *may* be able to, but some browsers won't work with these commands for some reason. Try them, and if you get a blank page returned to you, you'll know the browser can't handle them. The four special commands include:

➤ **?all [*what*]**   This tells Jughead to include *all* of the hits it finds. Usually, it limits the hits to 1,024, so if it finds 2,000 matching entries, you won't see 976 of them. Mind you, 1,024 is a lot—more than you are likely to need. For instance, if you search for **?all book or pub***, Jughead will search for the words **book** and **pub***, and if it finds more than 1,024 matches (it probably won't), it will display them all.

➤ **?help [*what*]**   This tells Jughead to create a menu option that lets you get to the Jughead Help file. You can use the **?help** command by itself, if you want, or you can do a search at the same time (for example, **?help book or pub***).

➤ **?limit=*n* [*what*]**   This tells Jughead to limit the number of menu items it gives you. For instance, if you used the command **?limit=10 book or pub***, Jughead would display only the first 10 items it finds.

➤ **?version [*what*]**   This gives you the Jughead version number. When you use this command, you'll see a menu option that reads

1. **This version of jughead is 1.0.4** (or whatever the actual version number is)

You can then click that menu option to read the Jughead Help file. You can use the **?version** command by itself, if you want, or you can do a search at the same time (for example, **?version book or pub***).

You cannot combine these commands, by the way; you can use only one for each search.

Veronica

Working with Veronica is very similar to working with Jughead, with a couple of important differences. First, when you select a Veronica menu option, you'll get the choice of servers. Veronica searches *all* of Gopherspace—Gopher servers all over the world. Something called a *Veronica server* stores an index of menu options at all of these Gopher servers, so you are actually searching one of these indexes; you get to pick which one.

At the same time, you have to decide whether you want to limit your search. You can search all menu options, or only menu options that lead to other menus. Assume, for instance, that you went to **gopher://gopher.cc.utah.edu** and then chose the **Search titles in Gopherspace using Veronica** option. If you now select **Find GOPHER DIREC-TORIES by Title Word(s) (via U of Manitoba)**, you will be looking for menu options that lead to other menus (often called *directories* in Gopherspeak) using the University of Manitoba Veronica server. If you select the **Search GopherSpace by Title Word(s) (via University of Pisa)**, you will be searching all menu options, both directories and options leading to files and documents, at the University of Pisa Veronica server.

When you make your selection, you'll see the same Index Search dialog box that you see when doing a Jughead search. Type the word you want to search for and press **Enter**. What happens then? Well, there's a good chance you'll get a message saying ***** Too many connections - Try_again soon. ***** (or something similar). Try another server. If you don't get such a message, it may seem like your browser just waits and waits; the clouds keep moving across the busy icon's background, but nothing seems to happen. These servers are very busy, so it often takes a long time to get a result. When you finally do get a result, though, you'll get a much bigger list than you did from the Jughead search. After all, you are searching the world's Gopher servers, not just one.

Veronica Search Details

Veronica searches are very similar to Jughead searches, but again there are a few differences. As with Jughead, you can use Boolean operators and the * wild card, which still must appear at the end of the word—not at the beginning or within the word. With Veronica, however, if you put the * inside the word, Veronica aborts the search (whereas Jughead just ignores the asterisk).

Veronica also has a special -t command. This is placed within the search string (at the beginning, middle, or end—it doesn't matter) and is followed by a number that defines the *type* of item you are looking for. For instance, **book -t0** means "search for the word 'book,' but only find text documents that contain that word." Similarly, **book -t01** means "search for the word 'book,' but only find text documents and Gopher menu items that match." This list shows the numbers you can use with the -t command:

Read the Help! For detailed information about Jughead and Veronica searches, read the Help files that you'll find in the Gopher menus near the Jughead and Veronica menu options.

Number or Letter	Description
0	Text file
1	Directory (Gopher menu)
2	CSO name server (a searchable database used to track down other Internet users)
4	Macintosh HQX file
5	PC binary file
7	A searchable index
8	Telnet session (see Chapter 18)
9	Binary file
s	Sound file
e	Event file
I	Image file (other than GIF)
M	MIME multipart/mixed message (MIME is a system used by Internet e-mail systems to transfer binary files)
T	TN3270 Session (a similar system to Telnet)
c	Calendar
g	GIF image
h	HTML Web document

179

You can also use the **-m** command to specify a maximum number of items to find. For instance, the search term **-m300 book** tells the Veronica server to show up to 300 items that it finds that contain the word "book." If you don't use the **-m** command, the Veronica server searches only until it finds the default limit of 200 items. Use **-m** to tell the server to find more than the default number.

The Least You Need to Know

➤ Gopher is a text-based menu system, a real boon to Internet users working with text-based software.

➤ You can easily work with Gopher through a Web browser.

➤ Travel through Gopherspace by clicking menu options.

➤ To save a text document or file, click the link. Your browser will treat it the same way it treats any file on the World Wide Web.

➤ Use your Web browser's Bookmark system to add a bookmark to any Gopher menu you want to return to later.

➤ Many Gopher systems now use Jughead, a special search mechanism that enables you to find things on that server.

➤ Veronica is a powerful tool you can use to search through thousands of miles of Gopherspace at once. Look for a Veronica menu option somewhere in the Gopher menu.

Chapter 15

Yak, Yak, Yak: "Chatting" in Cyberspace

In This Chapter

➤ What are chat and talk?

➤ Chat sessions and public auditoriums

➤ Using the online service chat rooms

➤ Using a graphical chat program—pick your avatar

➤ Working with IRC (Internet Relay Chat)

➤ Real uses for chat

One of the most important—yet least discussed—systems in cyberspace is *chat*. It's important because its immense popularity has been a significant factor in the growth of online systems (not so much the Internet, but more the online services). It is, perhaps, the least discussed because the fact is that many people use the chat systems as a way to talk about sex and even to contact potential sexual partners.

In this chapter, you'll take a look at chatting in cyberspace—in Internet Relay Chat (the Internet's largest chat system) as well as in the online services. And you'll also learn that there's plenty more than sex-related chat.

Chatting and Talking

What is chat? Well, here's what it's *not:* a system that allows you to talk out loud to people across the Internet or an online service. That sort of system does exist (see Chapter 16), but a chat system does not use voice, it uses the typed word. Communications are carried out by typing messages to and fro.

What's the difference between chat and e-mail, then? With e-mail you send a message and then go away and do something else. You come back later—maybe later that day, maybe later that week—to see if you have a response. Chat is just the opposite: it takes place in *real-time*, to use a geek term. (What other kind of time is there but real-time, one wonders.) In other words, you type a message, and the other party in the chat session sees the message almost instantly. He can then respond right away, and you see the response right away. It's just like in, yes, a chat—only you are typing instead of talking.

Check This Out...

Chat *Can* Have Voice

That's the problem about the Internet: you make a statement today, and tomorrow it's wrong. Right now the use of voice in chat sessions is rare. Voice *is* being added to chat, though, and you can expect chat sessions to gradually come to resemble the real thing, as people type less and talk more. However, as wonderful as that may sound it presents a problem. Many IRC (Internet Relay Chat) users are working at big companies, sitting in their little cubicles, typing away and looking busy. Their bosses may think they are working hard, but they are actually gabbing on IRC, and *voices would just give away the game!*

There's also something known as *talk,* which also isn't talking. Talk is a system in which one person can "call" another on the Internet and, once a connection has been made, can type messages to the other person. It's very similar to chat, once the two parties are connected. But the manner in which you connect is different. With chat you have to go to a chat "room" to chat with people; with talk, you simply open the talk program, enter the e-mail address of the person you want to connect to, and click a button to call that person (who may not be available, of course). To further complicate the issue, some Voice on the Net programs (discussed in Chapter 16) incorporate these talk programs—though they sometimes call them *chat* systems! For instance, CoolTalk has a little program that you can use to type messages to another person, but it's called the *Chat Tool*.

Chat is one of those "love it or hate it" kind of things. Obviously many people just love it; they even find it addictive, spending hours online each night. Personally, I can do without it. It's an awkward way to communicate. I can type faster than most people, yet I find it rather clunky. Quite frankly, my experiences with chat question-and-answer sessions have not been exactly the high points of my life. I've been the guest in chat sessions in both MSN and CompuServe; the sessions tend to be chaotic at worst, simply slow at best. You run into too many people trying to ask questions at once (though MSN has an excellent system for controlling the flow of questions, and CompuServe should have a new improved chat system soon), lots of typos, long pauses while you wait for people to type and they wait for you, and so on. No, I'm no chat fan, but I guess millions of people can't be wrong; and it certainly holds an appeal for many.

Two Types of Sessions

Chat sessions are categorized into two types: private and group. Generally, what happens is that you join a chat "room," in which a lot of people are talking (okay, typing) at once. Then someone may invite you to a private room, where just the two of you can talk without the babble of the public room. These private rooms are often used for "cybersex" sessions, though of course they can also be used for more innocent purposes, such as catching up on the latest news with your brother-in-law in Paris, discussing a project with a colleague, or talking about a good scuba-diving spot in Mexico.

Often public chat rooms are used as sort of auditoriums or lecture halls. A famous or knowledgeable person responds to questions from the crowd. Michael Jackson and Buzz Aldrin, for instance, have been guest "speakers" in chat forums, as has Peter Kent and many other world famous people.

> *Check This Out...*
>
> **Sex?** Should I be talking about sex in this book? It's been suggested by my editors that I should avoid sexual subjects for fear of offending people. Chat, however, is a case in which it's hard to avoid the sexual. Certainly many people go to chat rooms for nonsexual purposes. But be warned that many (possibly most?) are there to meet members of the opposite sex...or the same sex in some cases...for sexual purposes. Cybersex may not be as much fun as the real thing, but it's very real in its own way.

Score 1 for the Online Services

I'm going to mostly discuss the online services in this chapter because they generally have the most popular, and in some ways the best, chat systems. Chat has been extremely important to the growth of the online services, so they've made an effort to provide good chat services. Chat on the Internet, though, is still relatively little used, and in many ways not as sophisticated. (That's changing, as many new chat programs designed for the Internet, often running through the Web, are introduced.)

If you use CompuServe or AOL, you can get to the chat rooms by using the Go or Key word **chat**. Most forums have conference rooms for chatting too, but they are often empty. If you use The Microsoft Network, you'll find chat rooms scattered all over the place; almost every forum (or BBS as they're known in MSN-speak) has a chat room. You can also go to a Chat BBS by using the Go To word **chat**. If you want to use Internet Relay Chat on the Internet, it's a little more complicated (I've covered this later in the chapter).

MSN's Chat System

While MSN's chat system is perfect for conferences in which one speaker is a guest answering questions from participants, it currently has some problems in relation to normal chatting. At the time of writing of this book, MSN's chat system makes private conversations difficult. A new chat program in which this will be possible *is* on the way, but right now if you want a private chat, you have to go to one of the private rooms already set up for two people. You'll find rooms labeled *Table B for 2, Table C for 2*, and so on. You have to open one and then invite the other person to come to that room...but someone else might get there first, which prevents the invitee from getting in. It's not a good setup, but the new software should fix that.

The following figure shows the new MSN chat window. It allows you to send e-mail or chat messages to participants and invite them to private rooms directly. You can leave an Away From Keyboard message when you leave temporarily, you can view information about other people, you can turn off the display of messages coming from other people, and so on. There's even a way to launch the Web browser directly from the chat window so that you can view a Web site people are talking about.

MSN's chat system is still a work in progress.

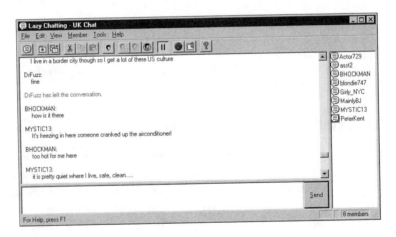

Latest Chat Rooms

You may have to upgrade your MSN software to get the latest chat room features, including the ability to go to private rooms. Currently, one way to do this is by using the Go To word **ukchat**. If you don't have the latest chat program, it will be automatically upgraded.

CompuServe's Conference Rooms and CB

To use a CompuServe chat room you can go to just about any forum or to the Chat forum, where you'll find loads of chat sessions. Most forums have a number of conference rooms, but unless some kind of presentation has been scheduled, they may all be empty.

You can be sure to find people to chat with in the Chat forum, though (GO **CHAT**). You have to select a *Band*. Although they're called conference rooms in most forums, the Chat forum uses a CB radio analogy. Instead of rooms, it has channels, and a group of channels are bundled together within a band.

So you start by selecting a band, and then you see the Channel selector window (shown in the following figure). Click a channel to see the channel title, and then double-click to join the channel—that is, to join in the chat session. (In fact there are two ways to join a session: you can *Tune* in and take part fully, or you can *Monitor*, which means you listen in but do not chat.) Click the channel, and then click the **Monitor** button.

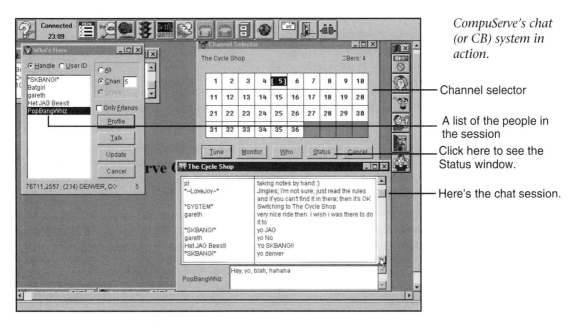

CompuServe's chat (or CB) system in action.

Channel selector

A list of the people in the session

Click here to see the Status window.

Here's the chat session.

There's also a useful Status window that uses a bar chart to show the number of people in each channel. This might be helpful if you want to pick a quiet one or get right into the action. As you can see in the figure, you can "listen" by reading other people's messages. Whenever you want to jump in, you can type your own message in the lower panel of the window.

Chatting in AOL

In AOL, use the keyword **chat**, or click the **People Connection** button in the Welcome window, and you go straight to a chat window (see the next figure). Use the **List Rooms** button to see all the available chat rooms. There are about a dozen categories and hundreds of individual rooms.

AOL's chat room system: lots of glitz, very busy.

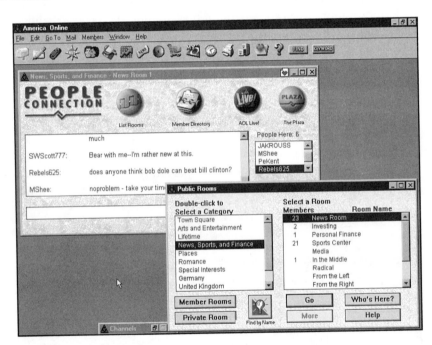

AOL's system allows you to create private rooms so that you and your friends (or family or colleagues) can use that room without interference. If you just want to talk to only one person, you just double-click the person's name in the People Here box and click the **Message** button. If the person responds, you get your own private message window for just the two of you. You can see in the following figure that this message box has special buttons that allow you to modify the text format.

AOL provides you with a little message window in which you can carry on private conversations.

Commands to Look For

While the details for using each chat system differ, a number of features are the same from one system to another. For example, these features are generally similar (even though the names may vary between systems):

Who or **People Here** shows a list of people currently participating in the chat session.

Invite enables you to invite a participant in the current chat to a private chat room. (On AOL you send the Person an Instant Message.)

Ignore or **Squelch** enables you to tell the program to stop displaying messages from a particular user. This is very useful for getting rid of obnoxious chat-room members (you'll find a lot of them!).

Profile allows you to view information about a particular participant, including whatever information they decided to make public. Some systems allow more information than others, but the information might include a person's e-mail address, interests, real name, and even phone number and address in some systems (although most participants choose *not* to include these). Some systems let you change your profile from within the Chat program, but on others you may have to select a menu option or command elsewhere.

Change Profile or **Handle** gives you access to the place where you'll change your own information.

Record or **Log** or **Capture** usually lets you record a session. (Of course, in most cases you'll want to forget the drivel.... Oh, there I go again!)

Preferences enables you to set up how the system works: whether to tell you when people enter or leave the room, for example.

No matter which chat system you use, read the documentation carefully so you can figure out exactly how to get the most out of it.

Pick Your Avatar

The latest thing in chat is the use of graphical systems in which you select an *avatar*, an image that represents you in the chat session. The following figure shows an avatar from MSN's V-Chat. The dialog box on top is where you select an avatar. You can choose from a list or even create your own.

So far, I've heard mixed reactions to these graphical chat systems. Some people say they are awful, some say they're nothing special; some say it's just stuff to get in the way of the chat. Others really like them. Experiment and decide for yourself!

Other Avatar chats are available, including some that are available to the public on the Web. For instance, you might try one of these:

MTV's Tikki Land (http://www.mtv.com)

Time Warner's Palace (http://www.thepalace.com/)

Worlds Chat (http://www.kaworlds.com)

Although you can reach these sites on the Web, you have to download a special Chat program and then reconnect using that program.

MSN's V-Chat, one of the new visual chat systems in which each person selects an avatar.

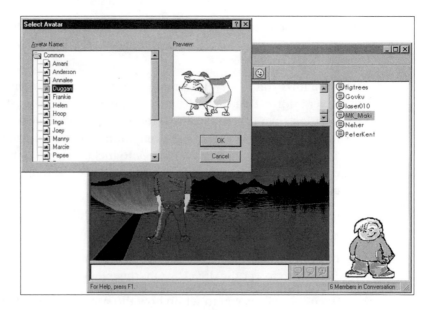

188

They're Everywhere!

These avatar chats are now sprouting on the Internet like weeds in my backyard. The Palace software, for instance, allows people to set up their own chats at their own Web sites—and many people have done so already. For more information, see the Palace site (address above) or look at Yahoo's 3D Worlds information (**http://www.yahoo.com/Recreation/Games/ Internet_Games/Virtual_Worlds/3D_Worlds/**).

Internet Relay Chat—Productivity Sink Hole?

I'll admit I haven't spent a lot of time in Internet Relay Chat. That's mainly because I've found that what few visits I *have* made have been so uninspiring that I can't think of a good reason to return. But there I go again, slamming a chat system. Actually many thousands of people really *do* like IRC (as it's known). So let's take a look at how to use it.

Command-Line User?

If you don't have a graphical user interface, you cannot use these fancy IRC programs of course. You'll have to use a command-line interface to IRC, which is very awkward ...but hey, thousands of other people have managed, and you can too. For help doing this, you can get the IRC chapter from my out-of-print book *The Complete Idiot's Next Step with the Internet* by sending e-mail to **ciginternet@mcp.com** and putting the word **irc** in the Subject line (leave the message body blank). For more information, see Appendix C.

Step 1: Get the Software

The first thing you'll need is an IRC "client" program. That's the program you'll use to send and receive IRC communications. If you are using a Mac, you might try Ircle, a well-known IRC program for that operating system. On Windows, you might try mIRC or PIRCH. (There's also Netscape Chat, which is designed to integrate with the browser, but it's not quite as good as the other two.)

So go to the software archives I discuss in Appendix A and download a copy of some kind of IRC program. Then follow the documentation's instructions to set up the program, and spend some time reading everything there is to read. Unfortunately, IRC can be a little complicated, if only because it has so many features.

Step 2: Connect to a Server

Check This Out...

Nicknames
Your nick-
name is the
name by
which you will
be identified in
the chat sessions. Notice that
you can remain anonymous
in a chat session by entering
incorrect information into the
Real Name and e-mail address
boxes.

The next thing you have to do is connect to an IRC server somewhere. These are programs that run on someone's computer out on the Internet and act as "conduits," carrying information between IRC participants. These servers are the equivalent of the online services chat forums. At a server, you'll find hundreds of different IRC channels that you can choose from.

Find the command that you must use to connect to a server. With mIRC, for instance, the dialog box in the following figure opens automatically when you start the program. You can get back to it later (to select a different server, for example) by choosing **File**, **Setup**.

Here's where you choose a server to connect to and enter your personal information in mIRC.

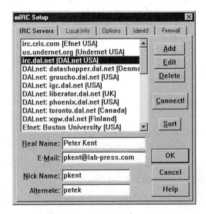

Select the server you want to use, click the **Connect** button, and away you go. You're connected to the server, and a dialog box appears, listing some of the channels (see the next figure). This is by no means all of the channels; most servers have literally hundreds. This box holds a list of the ones you are interested in (actually it's initially a list of channels that the programmer thought you might like to start with, but you can add more). To get into one of these channels, simply double-click it.

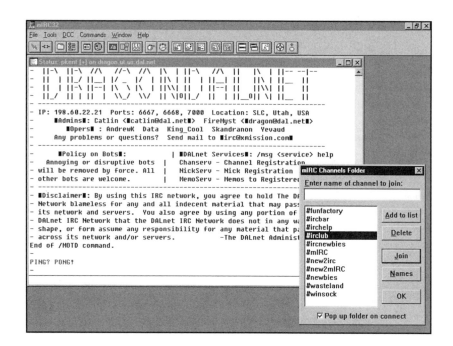

You've connected, and you're ready to join a channel.

If you'd like to see a complete listing of all the channels, close the dialog box, type /**list** in the text box at the bottom of the main window (which is where you type your messages and any IRC commands), and press **Enter.**

Know the Commands

IRC commands begin with a slash (/). There are loads of them, and most of these IRC programs hide the commands from you to some degree, providing menu commands instead. But they don't replace all of them. Some things can only be done using the original typed IRC command.

In mIRC, the /**list** command opens a window in which all the channels are listed. This may take a while because there are so many channels. As you can see in the title bar in the following figure, this server has 744 channels! If you want to enter one of these channels, all you have to do is double-click it.

mIRC's channel listing: Are 744 channels enough for you?

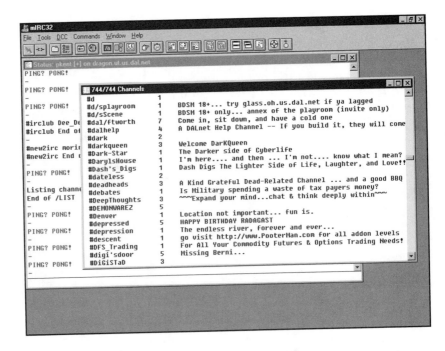

Once you are into a channel, just start typing; it's much like chatting in any other chat system. In the next figure, you can see a chat in progress. As usual, you type your message in the little box at the bottom, and you view what's going on in the big panel.

The participants are listed on the right side. You can invite one to a private chat by simply double-clicking a name. You can right-click to see a pop-up menu with a series of commands such as Whois (which displays information about the user in another window).

Here's where you chat in mIRC.

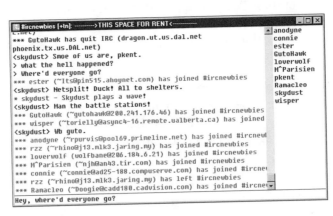

There's a lot to learn about IRC. These programs are a little complicated because IRC has so many features. For example, you can transmit computer files to other users; people often send pictures to each other. You can also add a special program that reads incoming messages from other chat members or that bans, kicks, and ignores users. (If you open a channel, you have some control over who you let in.) And there's much more!

Spend some time playing around with the program you choose to see what it can do, and read the documentation or help files carefully. It's complicated stuff, but once you have the feel for what one program can do, you can quickly pick up on how to use one of the others.

How Many Conversations Can You Keep Going?

IRC is almost a game. People get into multiple chat sessions at once. They chat in the main window, and then they have a few private chat sessions in other windows. That's why it takes them so long to respond sometimes!

What Is It Good For? Real Uses for Chat

It could be argued that chat systems are a complete waste of perfectly good electrons. (*I* wouldn't claim that, of course, but I'm sure many people would.) The chat is often little better than gibberish. "Hey, dude, how goes it? ...Cool man, you? ...Yeah, doing well; you chatted with that babe CoolChick, yet? ...No, she cute?" ...blah ...blah ...blah.) This is neither educational nor particularly interesting.

However, I know I'm going to upset people with these comments, so I should note that not all chats are quite so inane. Chats allow people of like interests to get together in cyberspace, literally reaching across continents, across the entire globe, to discuss issues that interest them in a way that would be prohibitively expensive using any other technology. (Actually, I've proposed a *stupidity-tax* to make the totally stupid chats prohibitively expensive again.)

There are other worthwhile uses, too. This list points out a few such scenarios:

➤ Technical support can be given using chat rooms. This will become more important as more software is distributed across the Internet. For instance, a small company that, in the past, might have provided support only within the U.S.A. can now provide support to any nation with an Internet account.

➤ Companies can use chat systems for keeping in touch. An international company with sales people throughout the world can arrange weekly "meetings" in a chat room. Families can do the same so that family members can keep in touch even when they're separated by thousands of miles.

➤ Groups that are planning international trips might want to try chat rooms. For instance, if a scout group is traveling to another country to spend the summer with another group, a chat room could provide a way for the leaders to "get together" beforehand to iron out final details.

➤ Colleges can use chat. Many colleges already provide courses over the Internet, using the Web to post lessons and using e-mail to send in completed assignments. In addition, teachers can use chat to talk with students, regardless of the geographic distance between them.

However, having said all that …I'll cue you to read Chapter 16. Chat may soon become superseded by what's known as Voice On the Net, a system that allows you to place "phone calls" across the Internet and even have conference calls.

The Least You Need to Know

➤ A *chat* system allows participants to take part in public discussions or to move to private "rooms" if they prefer. A *talk* system is a direct link between participants in a conversation, without the need for a public chat room.

➤ Neither chat nor talk uses actual voices; you type messages and send them to and fro.

➤ Chat sessions are often very crude and sexually orientated; so if you're easily offended, pick your chat room carefully.

➤ All the online services have popular chat systems.

➤ If you want to use Internet Relay Chat, you'll have to download an IRC program from a shareware site and then connect across the Internet to a server.

➤ You can use chat rooms to keep in touch with friends, family, or colleagues— or to meet new people.

Chapter 16

Voice on the Net—Talking on the Internet

In This Chapter

➤ International calls for 5 cents/minute...

➤ Calls routed to domestic phone systems

➤ Where do you get phone software?

➤ Connecting to a "server" and finding someone to talk to

➤ Text transmission, white boards, conferencing, and more

➤ Video conferencing and other weird stuff

This chapter covers a new Internet technology that very few people are using, but that you're going to hear a *lot* about very soon: the ability to make "phone calls" on the Internet.

In the past, the word *talk* was a euphemism on the Internet. As you saw in Chapter 15, there is actually a service called *talk* that has been around for years. As you saw in that chapter, it might be more appropriately called *type*. Today, however, technology has advanced to the point that you can actually talk—yes, use your voice—across the Internet. Voice on the Net (VON) is the next big Internet application.

The Incredible Potential of Voice on the Net

I recently co-authored a book with my brother. Because he's in England and I'm in the U.S. of A., I knew we'd be spending a lot of time on the phone—and that worried me. If I had to pay 80 cents a minute, my phone bill was going to skyrocket. Luckily, I found out about Voice on the Net.

Even though you pay for online time, talking across the Internet is still much cheaper. For example, if I used one of the major online services and paid for extra hours at, say, $2.90 per hour, an Internet "phone" call would cost me 4.8 cents a minute. I wouldn't do that, though. Through a service provider, I can get Internet time for $1 an hour …which breaks down to 1.7 cents a minute. I also have an "unlimited access for $19.95" account. Therefore, any additional time I would spend talking on the Internet (over and above the time I would be on the Internet anyway), costs me 0 cents per minute! Beat that, AT&T!

Unlike with real phone calls, though, both parties pay for an Internet phone call. So in my case, my brother would also have to connect to his service provider and pay whatever rates he pays. But hey, that's his problem. And anyway, even if you combine what we would pay, the total's going to be much lower than the 80 cents I would pay for a traditional phone call (or even the 35 to 45 cents I might be able to get through cut-price phone services).

I can see it happening. You're starting to see the potential. Have any relatives in Russia, Australia, or France? You can cut your costs to the bone, or you can spend the same amount of money but talk for a much longer time than you ever really wanted to. Similarly, if you run a business with offices around the world, you can connect the offices' networks to the Internet, get everyone a sound card and a mike, and spend the money you save on a new Mercedes.

It Gets Better: Link to the Real World

Oh, but it gets better than that. Imagine that someone created a special program that would allow phone calls across the Internet to be connected to real phone lines. A computer hooked up to the phone lines in, say, London, could accept Internet calls from anywhere in the world, connect them to the phone system, and allow Internet users to make *domestic* calls within the United Kingdom.

Such a system already exists. Although very few of these "servers" (systems that connect from the Internet to the phone system) are running, many more will soon be up and running. Imagine the potential. New telecommunications companies that are set up on a shoestring could be offering international phone service at domestic rates (plus a small fee, of course). Or international companies could be setting up phone "servers" in cities that their employees often call, virtually slashing the corporate phone bill.

And Internet phones carry more than just voice. They can also carry text and even doodles. So, while you are talking to someone, you can be transmitting the text of a memo or sketching something. Internet phones are a very powerful tool you're going to be seeing a lot of very soon.

Phone Companies—No Imminent Danger

The phone companies are not in imminent danger of going out of business, though. First, many people simply don't have computers. Fewer still have the sort of equipment required to use a system like this (you'll learn about the hardware requirements in a moment). And even fewer people want to call someone who *also* has the necessary equipment. Then consider these other problems.

➤ The calls don't provide high-quality sound. No doubt, you will *not* hear a pin dropping the other end of one of these lines!

➤ They are inconvenient. Because few people spend all day connected to the Internet, in many cases, you'd have to arrange a call. (Still, in the early days of the telephone, that's just what people did. They arranged a time to go to the drugstore and rent time on the phone, and their relatives on the other side of the country, or the world, did the same. In fact, in many parts of the world, that's still how people use telephones.)

➤ Currently, you can only talk to people who are using the same software you are (though this might change).

Check This Out...

Can You Hold Back Technology?

Although the phone companies will not be going out of business anytime soon, some are still worried enough to try to ban Internet phones. At the time of writing of this book, a small group of telecommunications companies was trying to get the U.S. Government to ban the use of Internet phones. Apart from the fact that this is similar to a group of horse-drawn carriage manufacturers trying to ban the newfangled automobile, it's hard to see how you can ban this kind of technology. Even if you ban it in the U.S., foreign companies will still sell it across the Internet. If we're going to do that, perhaps we should ban international credit card transactions or close our cyberborders. (For more discussion on this issue, see Chapter 23.)

Do You Have the Hardware You Need?

This might sound interesting, but there's a small hurdle you have to leap first. Do you have the right equipment?

To even consider using Internet phones, you'll need a fairly new computer. Not necessarily top of the line, but not an old piece of junk either. If you have a PC, it generally has to be a 486SX or better, perhaps even a 486DX (actual requirements will vary depending on the software you are using). If you have a Mac, you'll probably need a Quadra, Performa, or Power PC (some only run on the Power PC). On any platform, you'll also need a fair amount of RAM—probably a minimum of 8MB. But as I always say, you can never have too much money, too much time off, or too much RAM.

Next you'll need a connection to the Internet, and it should be either a fast network connection (the ideal, of course) or a dial-in direct connection (SLIP or PPP). If you have a dial-in connection, you'll want at least a 14,400bps modem; but your calls will undoubtedly sound better with a 28,800bps modem.

You need a sound card, of course. Make sure it's a 16-bit card or better, and that it also allows you to record (some don't). Ideally, you need a *full-duplex* card. Check the card's specifications (on the box) when you buy it to see if it's full-duplex.

Full-Duplex vs. Half-Duplex
If you have a full-duplex card, both you and the other person can talk at the same time. The card can record your voice at the same time it's playing incoming sounds. On the other hand, if you have only a half-duplex card, you'll have to take turns talking (like the men who talked over the radios in those old war movies: "Joe, you there? Over").

You also need a microphone and speakers, or perhaps a headset. And finally, you need the software. That's easy enough to come by, but the big catch is that you must have the same software as the person you want to call. As a result, you may end up using two or three programs. That should change soon, though (perhaps by the end of 1996), as the software companies start to create standards.

Which Program Should I Use?

The use of VON software is about to increase exponentially because the major online services plan to provide it to their subscribers in 1996. Therefore, if you are a member of CompuServe, AOL, or MSN, you might soon find that your service is bringing the software to you.

If you can't wait or if you use an Internet service provider, you'll have to find your own software. That's easy, but you might have to pay. The three "biggies" among the available products are Internet Phone, WebTalk, and CoolTalk. Internet Phone and WebTalk have reputations as being the best products. CoolTalk has only recently been introduced by Netscape Communications; it can be downloaded along with the Netscape Navigator Web browser. Follow these directions to get your hands on one or all of these products:

>**CoolTalk:** You can download CoolTalk (with Netscape Navigator 3.0 or by itself) from **http://www.netscape.com**.

>**WebTalk:** Download this Quarterdeck product from **http://www.qdeck.com**.

>**Internet Phone:** Available from an Israeli company called VocalTec, this is available for download from **http://www.vocaltec.com**.

>**NetMeeting:** This is Microsoft's Internet phone system, available for download from **http://www.microsoft.com/ie/conf/**.

You can find other products by going to Yahoo and searching for *internet voice*. Or go to the Voice on the Net page at **http://www.von.com/**. Many such products are available as shareware, commercial products, and give-it-away-ware. You'll find WebPhone (NetSpeak), FreeTel, DigiPhone (Third Planet Publishing), PowWow (Tribal Voice), and so on.

Check This Out...

Give-It-Away-Ware?

The Internet is full of stuff that is simply given away. CoolTalk, for instance, is given away with Netscape Navigator, which is also given away. Yes, you're supposed to register Navigator, but Netscape Communications really doesn't expect many people to do so. Microsoft is currently giving the beta version (a sort of test version) of NetMeeting, even though the final release may be part of an "Internet add-on pack." But then again, Internet Explorer is part of an add-on pack, so it's also given away free on the Internet.

Working with Your Phone Program

Let's take a look at how to work with one of these systems. I'll assume that you have your sound card and microphone properly installed—that's one can of worms I'm *not* crawling into! I'll also assume that you've installed some sort of phone program and have run through the setup (so it already has all of your personal information that it needs, such as your name, Internet e-mail address, and so on).

The next question is, to quote Ghostbusters, *Who ya gonna call?* Yes, I know …you were so excited about the idea of making phone calls on the Internet that you went ahead and installed everything you need. But you haven't quite persuaded your siblings or your mad

Aunt Edna to do the same. So you actually have *nobody* to call. Don't worry, you'll find someone.

All the software companies have set up servers to which you can connect to find someone else, just like you, who is all dressed up with nowhere to go. For instance, if you are using VocalTec's Internet Phone, you can click the little plug button on the toolbar, or you can choose **Phone, Connect to Server**. Either way, you'll see a couple of dialog boxes, one of which lists all of the VocalTec servers. They have servers all over the place: in many U.S. sites, Australia, Japan, Germany, The Netherlands, Russia, and so on. Select the area that interests you from the **Domain** drop-down list box (see the following figure). Then select a server from the list box (you'll see where the server is). Click the **OK** button, and the server appears in the dialog box below. Click **OK**, and the program tries to connect to that server.

Here's how to connect to a server using VocalTec's Internet Phone.

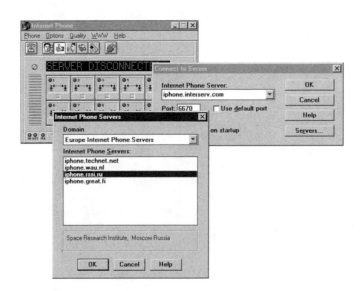

You might have to try a few servers, but eventually the dialog box will close, and you'll see a **SERVER CONNECTED** sign in the main window. At that point, you can connect to one of the other people using the server. Click the button showing someone talking on the phone, or choose **Phone, Call**, and the box you can see in the next figure opens. This lists all the people connected to the server. You can click a person's name in the list and then click **OK** to connect to that person. Go ahead, don't be shy.

Of course, someone else might try to connect to you first. You'll hear a beep to inform you that someone is trying to call you. You may have the program set up to accept all incoming calls automatically (in Internet Phone, you do that using the **Options, AutoAccept Calls** command), or you may have to click a button to accept a call. In

Internet phone, you'll see that the big buttons in the middle of the window flash when you have a call coming in.

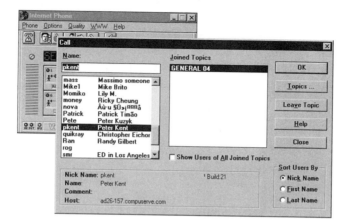

Once you've connected to a server, you can ask someone to join you in a conversation.

The CoolTalk and WebTalk Servers

These servers all work differently. CoolTalk has a directory available on a Web site (at **http://live.netscape.com**). Likewise, you can see an example in the following figure.

Find the person you want to talk to and click his name. The CoolTalk installation program automatically configures CoolTalk as a Netscape viewer (see Chapter 7). So when you click a name in the Web page, CoolTalk opens and tries to contact the other person.

You can also access this list from within CoolTalk. Click the **Start Conference** button or choose **Conference**, **Start**, and an Open Conference box appears. You can then click the **IS411 Directory** tab to see the people listed in the directory. The problem with CoolTalk's server, though, is that it shows all people who have set up CoolTalk—not just those people who are online and available at the moment. So it might still be difficult to find someone to talk to.

WebTalk has a similar system. You have to configure the program as a browser viewer, and for some odd reason, Quarterdeck seems to have gone out of its way to make the system hard to configure (by hiding critical information). Make sure you configure the WEBUDIR.EXE file as the viewer, not the WEBTALK.EXE program itself. Then you have to connect to WebTalk's server (at **http://webtalk.quarterdeck.com/**), log in, and click the **Launch WebTalk** button. WebTalk opens and displays the WebTalk user directory.

As of now, CoolTalk has a phone book, not a real server that lists people who are currently online.

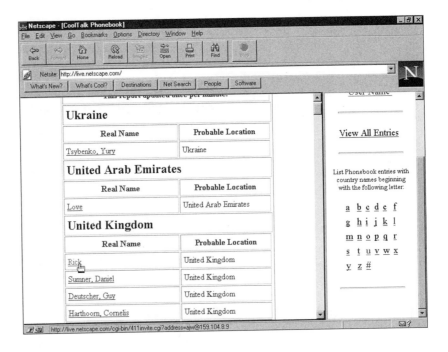

Ukraine

Real Name	Probable Location
Tsybenko, Yury	Ukraine

United Arab Emirates

Real Name	Probable Location
Love	United Arab Emirates

United Kingdom

Real Name	Probable Location
Rick	United Kingdom
Sumner, Daniel	United Kingdom
Deutscher, Guy	United Kingdom
Harthoorn, Cornelis	United Kingdom

View All Entries

List Phonebook entries with country names beginning with the following letter:

a b c d e f
g h i j k l
m n o p q r
s t u v w x
y z #

Nothing Better to Do? Connect to one of these servers (not the CoolTalk one, but one of the servers with people actually connected) and just wait. Every now and then, you'll get a call. It's a kind of a magical mystery phone session, not knowing who's going to call next. Where does he live? What does she do? Can she get her microphone working?

Now You Get to Talk

Some of these servers enable you to create new "rooms." You can create private rooms and use these as sort of meeting rooms for your friends and colleagues. Or perhaps, you have to just click a person and then a **Call** button or something similar to connect to that person. You'll have to read the program's documentation to figure this out; there are as many different ways to do it as there are programs.

Once you are talking, you might find that the sound is a bit warbly. That's okay, though. You might be speaking with someone on the other side of the world for a tiny fraction of what you'd pay your friendly phone company. What do you want? Low cost *and* quality?

If you are both using full-duplex modems, you can probably just talk as if you are on the phone. Otherwise, you may have to take turns speaking, clicking a button to turn your mike on and off. (The button is the equivalent of saying "over.")

It's Not Always the Same

Most dial-in users don't have permanent TCP/IP host addresses. When you connect to your service provider you are assigned a temporary host address, so the next time you connect you may get a different address. That means it's difficult to configure voice programs to call other users directly. Instead you can use these private rooms as meeting places; you can arrange to call someone at a particular time and use the room as a way to make the connection.

The Bells and Whistles

These products offer more than just voice connections. You might want to look for some of the following features in an Internet phone system.

➤ **An answering machine.** Some products, such as CoolTalk, have built-in answering machines. If someone tries to contact you while you are not there, your "answering machine" takes a message. Of course, this works only if your computer is online. Although it's very useful for people with permanent network connections, it's not nearly as useful for people who dial into a service provider.

➤ **Type while you talk capability.** This can be a very handy feature. You can send text messages at the same time you are talking. You can send small memos or copy parts of an e-mail message you're discussing. If you are working on a project with the other person, you may find it convenient to send to-do lists or schedules back and forth. Authors working together can send materials to each other, programmers can send bits of the code they are discussing, and so on. The following figure shows one system in which you can write as you talk.

➤ **Business card.** CoolTalk will soon have a Business Card feature that will enable you to attach a photo and transmit your business card when you talk to someone.

➤ **Image transmission.** Related to the business-card feature, and to the white board feature (discussed in a moment), is the capability to send a picture while you're talking. If you haven't seen Aunt Natasha in Siberia for a while, she can send a picture of the kids while you are chatting.

➤ **Conferencing.** Why speak to just one person, when you can talk to a whole crowd? Some of these programs let you set up conferences, so a whole bunch of you can gab at once.

WebTalk's "Chat" window lets you type messages while you talk.

➤ **Group Web surfing.** This is an odd one, and I only know of one program that currently does it: PowWow (**http://www.tribal.com/powwow/**). A whole bunch of people, a tribe even (well, okay, six people), can go on group Web surfs together. When one person clicks a Web link, the other participants' Web browsers update to show the new page.

➤ **Web-page indicator.** You can automatically add an icon to your Web page showing whether you are online and able to accept calls (another neat PowWow feature).

➤ **White Boards.** A white board is one of those big white chalkboard-type things you see in conference rooms. A white board feature functions similarly to the image transmission feature previously mentioned. Instead of typing something, though, you are using a sort of doodle pad thing. You can sketch something, and it's transmitted to the person at the other end. You can even use this to send graphic files, and you can open the file in the white board so the person at the other end can see it. CoolTalk's white board appears in the next figure.

➤ **Connecting voice to your Web page.** You can put links in your Web pages that, when clicked, open the user's Voice program so he can talk with you. This is for *real* geeks who rarely leave their computers. (You *do* have Web pages, don't you? See Chapter 8 to find out how to create them.)

Unfortunately, it's not a perfect world, so not all voice programs have all these neat features. You'll just have to find the feature that's most important to you and go with the program that has that feature.

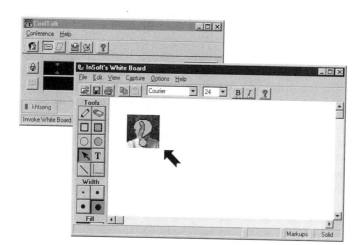

A white board feature lets you send a picture while talking.

Internet-to-Phone Connections

One of the most intriguing uses of this technology is the ability to connect to a computer across the Internet and route onto the local phone service. So, you might connect across the Internet from New York to Sydney and be connected to the Australian phone system—which means you can make international calls at Australian domestic rates.

A few companies are working on these products, and there are servers currently operating in Guam; Jakarta, Indonesia; Melbourne, Australia; Moscow, Russia; Vancouver, Canada; Norwalk, CT, USA; Phoenix, AZ, USA; and Los Angeles, CA, USA. Perhaps there will be many more by the time you read this. Check the Voice on the Net page (**http://www.von.com/**) for the latest information, or see the Free World Dialup site (**http://www.pulver.com/fwd/**) as this is planned as a free service for noncommercial calls.

The Future Is Video—and Other Weird Stuff

It doesn't stop here, of course. The next step is to add video to the "phone" conversations. Finally, a true video phone; the phone companies have been talking about it for 40 years, but it took the Internet to bring it about.

Mind you, this step is a much bigger one than simply putting voice on the Internet. Voice is fairly simple. There is not too much data involved in transmitting sounds, relatively speaking. The problem with video, though, is bandwidth. The term *bandwidth* refers to the amount of information that can be transmitted across a connection. A 28,800bps connection has greater bandwidth than does a 14,400bps connection, for instance. Video images contain a lot of information, and you want the information right away. After all, video only makes sense if it's in motion. So many compromises have to be made. The images are small, are low resolution, and have few individual images each second. Thus, video transmitted across the Internet can often be blurry and shaky. Unless you really need it, you may find that the novelty soon wears off.

Personally, I don't think video on the Internet will really catch on for a few more years—not until very high-speed connections are cheap and easily available. You also need a fast computer, of course. For now, it's limited to companies with network connections. However, that hasn't stopped a variety of companies from selling video software for use on the Internet. Actually, these products are generally thought of as video-conferencing products, but the principle is the same: real-time communications across the Internet between two or more people. Go back to the Voice on the Net site (**http://www.von.com**), and you'll find information about this, too.

The best-known product is Cu-SeeMe ("see you, see me," get it? Yeah, yeah). In fact, this product is so well known in the computer business that it's becoming a generic term, in the same way that *Hoover* is a generic term for vacuum cleaners. You can see a demo of this product at work at **http://www.wpine.com/**.

Other telecommunication systems will be added to the Internet soon. How about this idea? Have your faxes and voice mail connected to your e-mail system. If you live in the U.S. but do business in the UK, you can have a phone line set up in London. Your customers can call and leave voice mail for you or can fax you at that number, and your messages can then be compressed and attached to an e-mail message that is sent to you! In fact, you can have a number in New York, London, or Atlanta, or you can have a U.S. Toll Free number. And you'll even get the graphics in your faxes sent to you. See JFAX at **http://www.jfax.net/** for more information about this. And keep your eyes open for other weird and wonderful telecommunication/Internet hybrid services.

The Least You Need to Know

➤ You can connect to other users and actually talk on the Internet at a fraction of the cost of long distance or international calls.

➤ New Internet-to-phone system servers are being set up, which will enable you to connect across the world on the Internet, and then call someone using another country's domestic phone system.

➤ The software is plentiful and often cheap. Check out the Web site **http://www.von.com** for sources.

➤ Most companies have set up servers to which you can connect and find someone to talk to; test the system before you make the rest of your family use it.

➤ Many useful features are available in some products. You can send text or pictures while you talk, talk to a group of people, or even go on group Web trips.

➤ Video phones are available, but they require fast connections to the Internet.

Chapter 17

What on Earth Are All Those File Types?

In This Chapter

➤ About the directory (folder) system

➤ Picking a download directory

➤ File extensions and file types

➤ File types you'll run into

➤ What are compressed files?

➤ Working with compressed and archive files

➤ Avoiding viruses

It's possible to work with a computer for years without really understanding directories and file types. I know people who simply save files from their word processor (the only program they ever use) "on the disk." *Where on the disk?* Well ... you know ... on the hard disk. *Yes, but where? Which directory?* Well ... you know ... where the program saves the files.

You can get away with this lack of knowledge if you use only one program and don't use it too much. But if you plan to spend any time on the Internet and plan to make the most of your time there, you'll need to understand a bit more about files and directories.

You'll come across a plethora of file types, and it helps if you understand what you are looking at.

About Download Directories

I don't want to spend a lot of time explaining what a directory is. This is very basic computing stuff, and if you don't understand it, you should probably read an introduction to computing (such as *The Complete Idiot's Guide to PCs*) by Joe Kraynak. However, I'll quickly explain it, and that may be enough.

You can think of a directory as an area on your hard disk that stores computer files. You might think of it as a file folder in a filing cabinet. The hard disk is the filing cabinet, holding dozens, maybe hundreds, of folders (directories). In some graphical user interfaces, such as Windows 95 and the Macintosh, directories are called *folders*. (But I've been using the term *directory* too long to give it up now.)

If you look inside a filing cabinet and open a file folder, what do you find? Documents—those are the individual files. And you may also find another folder within the first folder. That's what we call a subdirectory. So directories can contain files and other directories, and those directories can contain more files and more directories (more subdirectories), and so on. Thus you have what is known as the directory tree. (The following figure shows what this "tree" looks like.) The point of this system is to help you organize your files. It's not uncommon for today's computers to have thousands of files, tens of thousands even. If you don't organize this lot logically, you'll end up with a mess that will make the Gordian Knot look simple.

Directories Are *Not* Areas of the Hard Disk!

Before you e-mail me saying that a directory is *not* an area on your hard disk, let me say *I know that!* It just *appears* to be an area on your hard disk. Actually, computer files are spread across the disk in an apparently illogical and disorganized manner—a piece of a file here, a piece there. The directory system is simply a visual way to organize the files, to make the hard disk easier to use.

The disk says, "I have a directory here that contains these files." But that's a lie, really, as the files are actually scattered willy-nilly all over the place. But it doesn't matter. It's rather like a child who *swears* that he has tidied up his room, that his socks are in the dresser and his shoes are in the closet. They're not, of course; everything's scattered over the floor. But you really don't want to look inside because it will just upset you. So you accept it and think in terms of where things *should be* within the room, without wanting to see the truth.

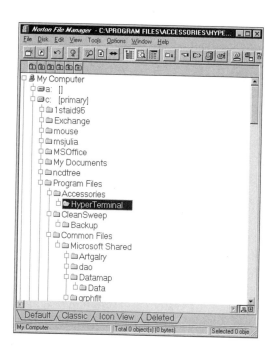

Folders, within folders, within folders make up the directory tree, shown here in the Norton File Manager program.

A *download directory* is a directory into which you download a file. For instance, let's say that you are using your Web browser to download a shareware program from one of the libraries listed in Appendix A. Where is that file saved? By definition, it's downloaded into the download directory. However, no directory is called the download directory; the download directory is whichever directory you say to put the file in.

I think it's important for you to understand that the directory chosen by the browser as the download directory is not always the best place to put the file. In many cases it's a lousy choice. Internet Explorer, for instance, wants to place downloaded files on the Windows 95 *desktop*. (In Windows 95, the desktop is actually a special subdirectory of the WINDOWS directory; anything placed inside that directory will appear on the desktop—the area of your computer screen that is visible when all the programs have been closed.) That's often a bad place to put it; if you download a lot of things, your desktop will soon be as cluttered as my office. (And believe me, that's not pleasant.) Of course you can always move the file to another directory later, but in that case, why not put it where you want it in the first place?

Also, many of the files that you will download are archive files; these are sort of file containers. Although an archive file is a single file, it has other files within it, perhaps hundreds of them. When you extract those files from inside, they are generally placed in the same directory. After you extract those files, you no longer have one easily recognized file on your desktop (or in whichever download directory the program chose). You now have dozens or more new files there. Do this with several download files and you'll soon become confused; which file came from which archive?

Pick a Download Directory Sensibly

When you download files from the Web, FTP, Gopher, your online service, or wherever, think sensibly about where you place the downloaded file. Many users create a special directory called DOWNLOAD. Some programs even do this automatically: WS_FTP, for instance, creates a DOWNLOAD directory to be used as the default location for downloaded files. You can place all the files you download directly into that directory. Later you can decide what you want to do with the files.

I prefer to go one step further. When I download a file, I think about where I'll eventually want the file. For instance, if it's a document file related to a book I'm working on, I save it directly into one of the directories I've created to hold the book. If it's a program file, I'll have to create a directory to hold the program at some point, so why not create a directory for the program right now and download the file directly into that directory? (Depending on which operating system and program you are using, you may be able to create the directory while you are telling the program where to save the file; or you may have to use some kind of file-management program to create the directory and *then* save the file.)

Learn about directories. Make sure you understand how to find your way around the directory tree (or folder system as it's known in some operating systems). And make sure you save files in the right places, in such a manner that you can find them when you need them.

A Cornucopia of File Formats

Many computer users don't understand the concept of file formats because they never really see any files. They open their word processors, do some work, and then save the file. They may notice that when they give the file a name, the program adds a few letters such as .DOC or .WPD at the end, but they don't think much about it. If you're going to be playing on the Net, though, you need to understand just a little about file formats because you'll have to pick and choose the ones you want.

All computer files have one thing in common. They all save information in the form of zeros and ones. The difference between a file created by one word processor and another, or between a file created by a word processor and one created by a graphics program, is in what those zeros and ones actually *mean*. Just as two languages can use the same basic sounds and string them together to create different words, different programs use the zeros and ones to mean different things. One program uses zeros and ones to create words, another to create sounds, another to create pictures, and so on.

The File Extension

How, then, can a computer program identify one file from another? Well, they can often look for a familiar sequence of zeros and ones at the beginning of a file; if they find it, they know they've got the right file. But there's also something called *file extensions* that identifies files, and it has the added advantage of being visible to mere mortals. An extension is a piece of text at the end of a file name, preceded by a period, that is used to identify the file type. For example, look at this sample file name:

THISDOC.TXT

The extension is the .TXT bit. This means the file is a plain text file; any program that can read what is known as ASCII text can open this file and read it.

Now, in most operating systems (including DOS and Windows), file extensions are typically three characters long, in some cases four. And normally each file has only one file extension. Some operating systems, such as UNIX and Windows 95, for example, allow multiple extensions and extensions with more than three characters such as THISDOC.NEWONE.TEXT. However, this sort of thing is becoming rare on the Internet these days, and you'll generally only run into simple three- and four-character extensions.

You might be thinking that there are probably three or four file formats you need to know about. No, not quite. Try four or five dozen. The following table gives a list to keep you going.

Check This Out...

Different Extensions, Same Format

Some files are identified by two or more different file extensions. For instance, the .JPEG extension was used on UNIX computers to identify a form of graphics file commonly used on the Web. But because Windows 3.1 and DOS can't display four-character extensions, the file is often seen with the .JPG extension; different extension, but exactly the same file format. You'll also find .HTM and .HTML files, .TXT and .TEXT files, and .AIF and .AIFF files (sound files).

File Formats You Should Know

File Format	Type of File It Identifies
.ARC	A PKARC file (a DOS compression file).
.AU, .AIF, .AIFF, .AIFC, .SND	Sound files often used on Macintosh systems; Netscape and Internet Explorer can play these sounds.
.AVI	Video for Windows.
.BMP, .PCX,	Common bitmap graphics formats.

continues

File Formats You Should Know   Continued

File Format	Type of File It Identifies
.DOC	Microsoft Word files, from Word for the Macintosh, Word for Windows, and Windows 95's WordPad.
.EPS	A PostScript image.
.EXE	A program file or a self-extracting archive file.
.FLC, .FLI, .AAS	Autodesk Animator files.
.GIF	These are graphics files. They share one thing in common: they are the formats used for graphics images on the Web.
.gzip and .gz	A UNIX compressed file.
.HLP	Windows Help files.
.HTM, .HTML	The basic Web-document format.
.hqx	A BinHex file, a format often used to archive Macintosh files. Programs such as StuffIt Expander can open these.
.JPG, .JPEG, .JPE,	JPEG graphics files that most Web browsers can display.
.JFIF, .PJPEG, .PJP	A few more variations of the JPEG format that Netscape can display.
.MID, .RMI	MIDI (Musical Instrument Digital Interface) sounds.
.MMM	Microsoft Multimedia Movie Player files.
.MOV .QT	The QuickTime video format.
.MP2	An MPEG audio format.
.MPEG, .MPG, .MPE, .M1V	The MPEG (Motion Pictures Expert Group) video formats.
.PDF	The Portable Document Format, an Adobe Acrobat hypertext file. This format is becoming a very popular means of distributing electronic documents.
.pit	The Macintosh Packit archive format.
.PS	A PostScript document.
.RAM, .RA	RealAudio. This is a sound format that plays while it's being transmitted. Click a link to a RealAudio file, and it begins playing within a few seconds (you don't have to wait until the entire file is transferred).
.RTF	Rich Text Format, word processing files that work in a variety of Windows word processors.

File Format	Type of File It Identifies
.sea	A Macintosh self-extracting archive.
.SGML	A document format.
.shar	A UNIX shell archive file.
.sit	The Macintosh StuffIt archive format.
.tar	A UNIX tar archive file.
.TIF	A common graphics format.
.TSP	TrueSpeech, a sound format similar to RealAudio, though of a higher quality.
.TXT, .TEXT	A text file. These are displayed in the Netscape window.
.WAV	The standard Windows wave file sound format.
.WRI	Windows Write word processing files.
.WRL	A VRML (Virtual Reality Modeling Language) 3-D object.
.XBM	Another graphics file that can be displayed by Web browsers.
.XDM	The StreamWorks webTV and webRadio format. This is similar to RealAudio, but it allows the real-time playing of video in addition to sound.
.Z	A UNIX compressed file.
.z	A UNIX packed file.
.ZIP	A PKZIP archive file (a DOS and Windows compression file).
.zoo	A zoo210 archive format available on various systems.

Is that all? By no means! Remember that Netscape claims it will have 100 plug-ins by the end of 1996, each with a different file format. There are all sorts of file formats out there; to be honest, though, you'll only run across a few of them. You may never even run across a few of the ones I included in the table; for instance, the .ARC format, which used to be very common, is quite rare now.

File Compression Basics

As you can see from the preceding table, a number of these file formats are archive or compressed formats. These are files containing other files within them. You can use a special program to extract those files; or, in the case of a "self-extracting archive," the file can automatically extract the file.

Is It Possible?
This is similar to Dr. Who's Tardis, which has much more space *inside* than would be allowed within a box of that size according to normal physics. And no, I don't plan to explain how it's done. Suffice it to say that, thanks to a little magic and nifty computing tricks, these programs make files smaller.

Why do people bother to put files inside archive files? Or even, in some cases, a single file within an archive file? Two reasons. First, the programs that create these files compress the files being placed inside. So the single file is much smaller than the combined size of all the files inside.

You can reduce files down to as little as 2% of their normal size, depending on the type of file and the program you use (though 40% to 75% is probably a more normal range). Bitmap graphics, for instance, often compress to a very small size, while program files and Windows Help files can't be compressed so far. If you want to transfer a file across the Internet, it's a lot quicker to transfer a compressed file than an uncompressed file.

And the other reason to use these systems is that you can place files inside another file as a sort of packaging or container. If a shareware program has, say, 20 different files that it needs in order to run, it's better to "wrap" all these into one file than to expect people to transfer all 20 files one at a time.

Which Format?

You'll find that most of the compressed DOS and Windows files are in .ZIP format, a format often created by a program called PKZIP (though as the file format is not owned by anyone, other programs create .ZIP files, too). There are other programs, though; you may also see .ARJ (created by a program called ARJ) and .LZH (created by LHARC) now and again, but probably not very often. PKZIP won the compression war.

Archive versus Compressed
What's the difference between an archive file and a compressed file? Well, they're often the same thing, and people (including me) tend to use the terms interchangeably. Originally, however, an archive file was a file that stored lots of other files: it archived them. An archive file doesn't have to be a compressed file, it's just a convenient place to put files that you are not using. A compressed file must, of course, be compressed. These days, archive files *are* usually compressed files, and compressed files are often used for archiving files. So there's not a lot of difference between the two anymore.

In the UNIX world, .Z and .tar files are common archive formats. And on the Macintosh, you'll find .sit (StuffIt) and .pit (Packit) compressed formats, as well as .hqx (BinHex) archive files. This table gives you a quick rundown of the compressed formats you'll see.

Common Compressed File Formats

Extension	Program That Compressed It
.arc	DOS, PKARC (an older method, predating PKZIP)
.exe	A DOS or Windows self-extracting archive
.hqx	Macintosh BinHex
.pit	Macintosh Packit
.sea	A Macintosh self-extracting archive
.shar	UNIX shell archive
.sit	Macintosh StuffIt
.tar	UNIX tar
.Z	UNIX compress
.z	UNIX pack
.ZIP	PKZIP and others
.zoo	zoo210 (available on various systems)

It goes without saying (but I'll say it anyway, just in case) that if you see a file with an extension that is common on an operating system other than yours, it may contain files that won't be any good on your system. Macintosh and UNIX software won't run on Windows, for instance. However, that's not always true. The file may contain text files, for instance, which can be read on any system. So there are cross-platform utilities; for example, Macintosh utilities can uncompress archive files that are not common in the Macintosh world.

Those Self-Extracting Archives

Finally, there's something called self-extracting archives. Various programs, such as PKZIP and ARJ, can create files that can be executed (run) to extract the archived files automatically. This is very useful for sending a compressed file to someone when you're not sure if he has the program to decompress the file (or would know how to use it). For instance, PKZIP can create a file with an .EXE extension; you can run such a file directly from the

Check This Out...

In the Meantime...
How can you download and extract one of these programs before you have a program that will extract an archive file? Don't worry, the programmers thought of that! These utilities are generally stored in self-extracting format, so you can download them and automatically extract them by running them.

DOS prompt just by typing its name and pressing Enter, or by double-clicking the file in Windows 95's Windows Explorer file-management program. When you do so, all of the compressed files pop out. In the Macintosh world .sea—Self Extracting Archive—files do the same thing. Double-click an .sea file, and the contents are automatically extracted.

If you find a file in two formats, .ZIP and .EXE for instance, you may want to take the .EXE format. The .EXE files are not much larger than the .ZIP files, and you don't need to worry about finding a program to extract the files. In such a case, you must have a program that can read the .ZIP file and extract the archived files from within.

You may already have such a program. Some Windows and Windows 95 file-management programs, for instance, can work with .ZIP files. Otherwise you'll need a program that can extract from the compressed format. See Appendix A for information about file libraries where you can download freeware and shareware that will do the job.

Your Computer Can Get Sick, Too

Downloading all these computer files can lead to problems: computer viruses. File viruses hide out in program files and copy themselves to other program files when someone runs that program. Viruses and other malevolent computer bugs are real, and they do real damage. In 1988, 6,000 computers connected to the Internet were infected with a "worm." (The Internet has grown tremendously since then; the numbers would surely be higher today.) Now and then you'll hear of service providers having to close down temporarily after their systems become infected.

Unfortunately, security on the Internet is lax. The major online services have strict regulations about virus checks. Members generally cannot post directly to public areas, for instance; they post to an area in which the file can be checked for viruses before it's available to the public. But on the Internet, it's up to each system administrator (and there are thousands of them) to keep his own system clean. If just one administrator does a bad job, a virus can get through and be carried by FTP, the Web, or e-mail all over the world.

Viruses Under the Microscope

The term virus has become a "catch-all" for a variety of different digital organisms, such as

➤ **Bacteria**, which reproduce and do no direct damage except using up disk space and memory.

➤ **Rabbits**, which get their name because they reproduce very quickly.

➤ **Trojan horses**, which are viruses embedded in otherwise-useful programs.

➤ **Bombs**, which are programs that just sit and wait for a particular date or event (at which time they wreak destruction); these are often left deep inside programs by disgruntled employees.

➤ **Worms**, which are programs that copy themselves from one computer to another, independent of other executable files, and "clog" the computers by taking over memory and disk space.

However, having said all that, I've also got to say that the virus threat is also overstated—probably by companies selling antivirus software. We've reached a stage where almost any confusing computer problem is blamed on computer viruses, and technical support lines are using it as an excuse not to talk with people. "Your computer can't read your hard disk? You've been downloading files from the Internet? You must have a virus!"

Most computer users have never been "hit" by a computer virus. Many who think they have probably haven't; a lot of problems are blamed on viruses these days. So don't get overly worried about it. Take some sensible precautions, and you'll be okay.

Tips for Safe Computing

If you are just working with basic ASCII text e-mail and perhaps ftping documents, you're okay. The problem of viruses arises when you transfer programs—including self-extracting archive files—or files that contain mini "programs." (For instance, many word processing files can now contain macros, special little programs that may run when you open the file.)

Check This Out...

Rule of Thumb

Here's a rule of thumb to figure out if a file is dangerous. "If it does something, it can carry a virus; if it has things done to it, it's safe." Only files that can actually carry out actions (such as script files, program files, and word processing files from the fancy word processors that have built-in macro systems) can pose a threat. If a file can't do anything—it just sits waiting until a program displays or plays it—it's safe. Pictures and sounds, for instance, may offend you personally, but they won't do your computer any harm. (Can self-extracting archives carry viruses? Absolutely. They're programs, and they run—you don't know that they're self-extracting archives until they've extracted, after all.)

If you do plan to transfer programs, perhaps the best advice is to get a good antivirus program. They're available for all computer types. Each time you transmit an executable file, use your antivirus program to check it. Also, make sure you keep good backups of your data. Although backups can also become infected with viruses, if a virus hits, at least you can reload your backup data and use an antivirus program to clean the files (some backup programs check for viruses while backing up).

The Least You Need to Know

➤ Don't transfer files to your computer without thinking about *where* on your hard disk they should be. Create a download directory in a sensible place.

➤ Files are identified by the file extension, typically a three-character (sometimes four-character) "code" preceded by a period.

➤ Compressed and archive files are files containing other files within. They provide a convenient way to distribute files across the Internet.

➤ Self-extracting archives are files that don't require a special utility to extract the files from within. Just "run" the file, and the files within are extracted.

➤ Viruses are real, but the threat is exaggerated. Use an antivirus program, and then relax.

➤ The virus rule of thumb is this: "If it does something, it can carry a virus; if it has things done to it, it's safe."

Chapter 18

Telnet: Inviting Yourself onto Other Systems

In This Chapter

➤ Finding a Telnet program

➤ Four ways to start Telnet

➤ Using HYTELNET

➤ Running your Telnet session

➤ IBM tn3270 Telnet sites

➤ MUDs, MOOs, and other role-playing games

Millions of computers are connected to the Internet, and some of them contain some pretty interesting stuff. Wouldn't it be great if you could "reach out" and get onto those computers (well, some of them) to take a look at the games and databases and programs on computers around the world?

Well, you can. At least, you can get onto computers whose administrators want you to get on them, and there's a surprisingly high number of those who do. A special program called Telnet lets you turn your computer into a Telnet *client* to access data and programs on some Telnet *server*.

Many Internet users have private Telnet accounts. A researcher, for example, might have several computers he works on regularly, and he might have been given a special login name and password by the administrators of those computers. But many computers also allow "strangers" into their systems. This is completely voluntary, depending on the good will of the people who own or operate a particular computer. If a Telnet server is open to the public, anyone can get on the system and see what's available.

Step 1: Find a Telnet Program

First, you'll need a Telnet program. The selection and quality of Telnet programs are among the weakest features of the Internet. There are wonderful Web browsers around, as well as excellent e-mail and FTP programs, for instance, but the Telnet programs I've run across all seem a bit weak.

Part of the problem is that there's a limit to how much a Telnet program can help you. When telnetting, your computer becomes a terminal of the computer you've just connected to, so it has to follow the "rules" used by that computer. Because there are thousands of systems out there on the Internet, each using slightly different menu systems, command systems, and so on, it's hard to create a really good Telnet program. All the average Telnet program does is provide a window into which you can type commands and in which will appear responses. Also, because Telnet isn't a terribly exciting subject (when was the last time you saw a *TIME* or *Newsweek* article on the wonders of Telnet?), it's been ignored by most software developers.

Now I know what you're thinking…. You're thinking, "he'll probably explain how to use Telnet through the browser, and then how to use a real Telnet program." Well, you're wrong. You *can't* Telnet through your browser. Although you can *start* a Telnet program from your browser, the browser itself can't run the session. At least, none of the most popular browsers have built-in Telnet capabilities. So if you want to use Telnet, you'll need a Telnet program.

You may already have one. If you are working with CompuServe, you'll find a Telnet program built into the KIM program. AOL does not have a built-in Telnet program, but you can use the keyword **telnet** to find information about Telnet as well as a library of Telnet programs you can download. MSN does not have a built-in Telnet program either, but you probably have Microsoft Telnet, which is usually installed when you install your Windows 95 TCP/IP network software. If you are with an Internet service provider, you might have received a Telnet program with the software they gave you—but there's a good chance you didn't.

If you have to find your own Telnet program, you can do so at the software archives listed in Appendix A. You might use something like CRT for Windows or NetTerm for Windows; if you are a Macintosh user, try NCSA Telnet or dataComet.

Making the Connection

You have a number of choices of how to begin a Telnet session.

➤ In your Web browser, click a **telnet://** link. In Web documents, you'll sometimes run across links that use the telnet:// URL. When you click the link, your Telnet program opens and starts the session with the referenced Telnet site. (You'll have to tell your Web browser which Telnet program to use; you enter that as the browser's **Options** or **Preferences**.)

➤ In your Web browser, type the **telnet://** URL. If your Web browser is open, you can also start a Telnet session by typing **telnet://** followed by a Telnet host address and pressing **Enter**. For instance, if you type **telnet://pac.carl.org** into Internet Explorer's Address text box and press **Enter**, Windows Telnet launches and connects to the Denver Public Library's site. (Type **PAC** and press **Enter** to log on.)

➤ Open a Telnet program. You can also open Telnet directly. For instance, if you are using Windows 95, you can look in the Windows directory in Windows Explorer and double-click **telnet.exe**.

➤ Open a Telnet program from the Start menu. In Windows 95, you can also open the Windows **Start** menu, click **Run**, type **telnet://***hostname* (such as **telnet://pac.carl.org**), and press **Enter**. The Telnet program starts automatically.

A Telnet site name looks something like this: **pac.carl.org**, **freenet.sfn.saskatoon.sk.ca**, **fdabbs.fda.gov**, or sometimes a number, such as **150.148.8.48**. If you are opening a Telnet site from within your Telnet program, you'll enter the Telnet site or host name into the appropriate dialog box. For instance, to get a Telnet program to connect to a Telnet site, you might have to select **File**, **Connect** (or something similar), enter the Telnet site, and press **Enter**. If you are using CompuServe, use the **TELNET** GO word, choose **Access a Specific Site**, type the Telnet host name, and press **Enter**. You can see CompuServe's Telnet window in the following figure.

Configuring Your Browser You must tell your browser which Telnet program you plan to use. In Netscape, for instance, choose **Options**, **General Preferences**, and then click the **Apps** tab to find where you must enter the Telnet program.

CompuServe has a built-in Telnet window that you can access using the TELNET GO word.

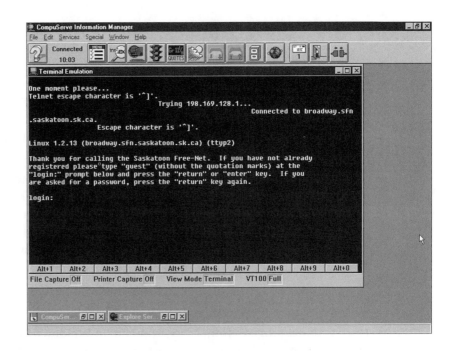

HYTELNET: Your Guide to the World of Telnet

To get a taste of what's available in the world of Telnet, take a look at HYTELNET, the Telnet directory. This used to be available only through Telnet itself, but now you can view the directory at a World Wide Web site, which is much more convenient. Open your Web browser and go to **http://library.usask.ca/hytelnet/**. (Alternatively, you can find other HYTELNET services at **http://radon.gas.uug.arizona.edu/~shunter/hytel.html** and **http://www.cc.ukans.edu/hytelnet_html/START.TXT.html**.)

From this document, you can launch Telnet sessions on computers all over the place. In the next figure, you see the first page of HYTELNET. The most important links in this page are the Library Catalogs and Other Resources links. They take you to directories of Telnet sites (the other links just take you to information about working with Telnet).

Click the **Other Resources** link, for instance, and you'll be taken to another page with links to Databases and bibliographies, Fee-Based Services, NASA databases, and more. Travel further down the hierarchy of documents, and you'll come to information about individual Telnet services (see the next figure). This shows information about the FDA (Food & Drug Administration) Electronic Bulletin Board Telnet site, where you can find news releases, import alerts, information on AIDS, and plenty more. This page shows the Telnet address (fdabbs.fda.gov or 150.148.8.48), and the name you must use to log in once connected (BBS). It also shows a list of commands you can use once connected. Note that it also has a link; the Telnet addresses are links that you can click to launch your Telnet program and begin the Telnet session.

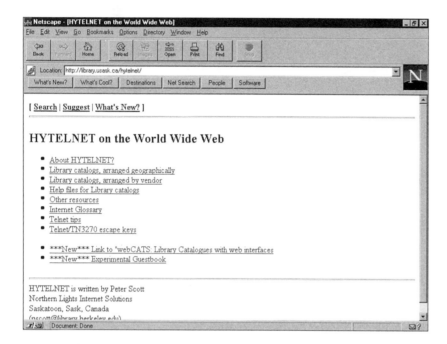

HYTELNET provides the best way to find Telnet sites.

More Directories

Here are two more Web directories that will help you find Telnet and other resources:

http://www.w3.org/hypertext/DataSources/ByAccess.html
http://www.ncsa.uiuc.edu/SDG/Software/Mosaic/MetaIndex.html

You can also search for the word "telnet" at Web search sites; see Chapter 19.

223

HYTELNET provides
information about
each Telnet site (so
you'll know what
login name to use to
work with the
system, for example).

Click one of these
links to start a Telnet
session with the
FDA's computer.

This is the login
name you will use
after you connect.

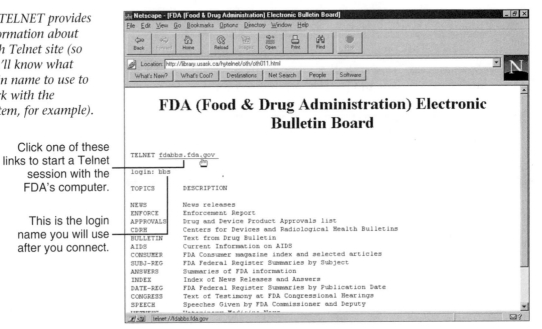

You're In. Now What?

After your Telnet program has connected to the Telnet site, you may have to log in. To do so, you'll need to know the account name you should use. HYTELNET describes Telnet sites, including the required account names. And when you find a Telnet site described in a book or magazine, the account name is often included. In some cases, you *won't* have to log in; the computer will let you right in without asking for further information. And in other cases, the introductory screen you see when you first connect may tell you what to use. The site shown in the following figure (Saskatoon Free-Net) explains how to log on.

When you connect to a Telnet session, you often have to identify the type of computer terminal you are using. Of course, you are using a PC, but your Telnet program can *emulate* (pretend to be) a standard terminal program. By default, it's probably set to emulate a VT-100 terminal, which is good because the VT-100 setting works in most cases you'll run into. If you run into a site that doesn't like the VT-100 setting—perhaps the text on your screen isn't displayed properly during the session—you can try changing the emulation. But you don't always have many choices.

```
CRT - freenet.sfn.saskatoon.sk.ca                          _ □ X
File  Edit  Preferences  Transfer  Help

Linux 1.2.13 (broadway.sfn.saskatoon.sk.ca) (ttyp3)

Thank you for calling the Saskatoon Free-Net. If you have not already
registered please type "guest" (without the quotation marks) at the
"login:" prompt below and press the "return" or "enter" key. If you
are asked for a password, press the "return" key again.

login: guest

****************************************************************
NEED SOME HELP?  Check out our information/help sessions on May 15,
June 19, July 17, and August 21.  Volunteers will be available to answer
questions and show people how to use the Saskatoon Free-Net.  All
sessions are held in Room #3 of the Frances Morrison Public Library
(downtown branch) on the lower floor starting at 7:00pm.

For more information type `ginfo_session` (go info_session).

****************************************************************
Last login: Tue Jun 18 16:47:19 on tty09
No mail.
Time Limit for this session is 60 minutes.
Welcome to the Saskatoon Free-Net.

Once you have registered, you will have access to mail and news and you
won't have to read all this everytime you sign on! Explore the system
and when you are ready to register, type:    go register

For our records, please enter your name here:

Ready                              81 Cols, 36 Rows  VT100
```

You can log on to the Saskatoon Free-Net as a guest.

Terminal Emulations

When you connect to a Telnet site you are, in effect, turning your computer into a "dumb terminal." The programs at the Telnet site will run on that site's computer, not yours. All you are using your computer for is to send text (commands) to the Telnet site and to view the results. And that's just what a computer "terminal" does. But there are many different kinds of terminals. Your Telnet program is pretending to be a computer terminal, but it has to be told which one to imitate (or *emulate*, in computer jargon). The VT-100 terminal is one of the most common types, and it is recognized by most Telnet sites.

Working in a Telnet Session

Every Telnet system is different. Your Telnet program functions as a means of transferring what you type on your computer to the computer you are connected to, and for that computer to send text back to you. In effect, you've turned your computer into a dumb terminal connected to another computer, so you have to follow the rules of that system.

What you see depends on what sort of system is set up on that computer. It might be a series of menus from which you select options, or it might be a prompt at which you type. Each system varies a little.

225

Let me warn you about one thing: Telnet can be slow—*very* slow—sometimes. On occasion, you may type something and not see what you have typed for several seconds or even several minutes. It depends on the amount of network traffic going that way as well as the number of people working on that machine at that time. If you find a particular task to be too slow, you should probably try again later. If it's always slow at that Telnet site, maybe you can find another site with the same services.

Special Features

Telnet programs vary from the absolutely awful to the quite reasonable. Many simple programs do very little but connect you to the Telnet site; once there, you're on your own. Others let you create login scripts (to speed up connecting to the site), program function keys to carry out certain actions at a particular site, modify text and background colors, and so on. Figure out what your Telnet program can do *because you're going to need all the help you can get!* Telnet is not an easy system to use; if you like the Web, you just might hate Telnet.

Keeping a Record

Many Telnet programs let you keep a record of your session. For instance, in Windows Telnet (the Telnet program that comes with Windows 95's networking software), you can select **Terminal, Start Logging**. In CRT, you can choose **File, Log Session**. You'll generally see a dialog box, into which you can enter a file name, and everything that happens in the session is saved in the named file.

You can also usually copy text from the session. Drag the mouse pointer across the text (or choose **Edit, Select All** in some Telnet programs), and then choose **Edit, Copy**. You can then go to another program—your word processor or e-mail program, for instance—and paste in that text. CRT has a useful feature: it copies the selected text and then sends the text as if you typed it. Thus, it allows you to respond to a prompt by typing in something that appeared earlier in the session.

Waving Good-Bye to the Telnet Site

Once you log on to a Telnet site, you're in that computer's system. Because you log off differently in each system, you'll have to try a number of commands to see which one works for you. Try **quit, exit, Ctrl+d, bye**, and **done**, in that order. One of those will probably end the session. If none of them does the trick, look for some kind of prompt that tells you what you need to type to get out.

It's polite to end a Telnet session using the correct method. However, as a last resort, you can close the connection by closing the Telnet window or by using the program's disconnect command (**Connect, Disconnect**, perhaps).

Telnet's Ugly Sister: tn3270

Some Telnet sites are on IBM mainframes running "3270" software. If you try to telnet to a site and find that the connection is instantly closed (even before you get to the login prompt), that particular site *might* be a 3270 site (though there's no guarantee of it).

On the other hand, if you log in and see this

```
VM/XA SP ONLINE-PRESS ENTER KEY TO BEGIN SESSION
```

you've definitely reached a 3270 site. For example, if you telneted with the command **telnet vmd.cso.uiuc.edu**, you'd probably see this:

```
Trying 128.174.5.98 ...
Connected to vmd.cso.uiuc.edu.
Escape character is '^]'.
VM/XA SP ONLINE-PRESS ENTER KEY TO BEGIN SESSION.
```

Your Telnet program probably won't be able to handle a tn3270 session. You're welcome to try it and see, but there's a good chance it won't.

These 3270 sessions are not that common, so you may never run into them. But if you really do have to use a tn3270 site, you'll need to find a tn3270 emulator. You might try QWS3270 (a Windows tn3270 emulator), dataComet (a Macintosh program that can run both Telnet and tn3270 sessions), or tn3270 (a Mac tn3270 program). See Appendix A for information on software sites at which you can find these programs.

MUDs, MOOs, and MUCKs

Telnet is not a very popular system right now. It's been eclipsed by the World Wide Web, and many new Internet users don't have the slightest idea what it is. However, there's one very popular use for Telnet: role-playing games. These are games known by such bizarre names as MUDs (Multi-User Dimensions, or maybe Multi-User Dungeons), MOOs, and MUCKs, Tiny MUDs, Teeny MUDs, UnterMUDS, and so on.

In these games, you type responses to a program running in a Telnet session. The program may describe where you are: You're in a room with a door on the West wall, a window on the East wall, and steps going down. You then tell it what to do: You might type **door** to go through the door. If this sounds exciting, these games are for you. (If it doesn't, you're not alone.)

If you are interested, check out one or more of the following options:

➤ Go to the Multi-User Dungeons page at **http://www.teleport.com/~morpheus/ muds.shtml** for more information.

➤ Try searching for MUD at Yahoo or another search site (see Chapter 19).

➤ Try **gopher://gopher.micro.umn.edu.** When you get to the Gopher menu, choose **Fun & Games** and then **Games**.

➤ If you use AOL, you can find quite a bit of information about MUDS using the **telnet** keyword. You'll find that while these games have predominantly been Telnet games in the past, they are now moving onto the Web. In addition, there are special client/server programs designed for role-playing games.

I'm told that these games are extremely addictive—that people log on and get stuck for days at a time. Personally I don't see the excitement. But there again, I don't understand why some people become addicted to collecting string or hubcaps. Who am I to judge?

The Least You Need to Know

➤ You may already have a Telnet program; if not, you can find them in the software libraries mentioned in Appendix A.

➤ You can start your Telnet program by entering a **telnet://** URL in your Web browser or by clicking a Web link that references a Telnet site.

➤ You can also start the Telnet program and then enter the Telnet site name.

➤ Try the HYTELNET site (**http://library.usask.ca/hytelnet/**); it has links to hundreds of Telnet sites.

➤ When you connect to a Telnet site, you may have to enter a login name and password; HYTELNET tells you what to use.

➤ Once you are in, you are on your own. Each Telnet site has its own rules.

➤ Telnet sessions are often very slow.

➤ If you can't view a site, you may have entered a tn3270 site. You should get hold of a tn3270 program.

➤ If you are into role-playing games, Telnet to a MUD site. For more information, try **http://www.teleport.com/~morpheus/muds.shtml** or **gopher://gopher.micro.umn.edu** (**Fun & Games, Games**).

Part 3
Getting Things Done

Now that you've learned how to use the Internet's services, it's time to learn some important general information about working on the Net. This place is so huge, you might have trouble finding what you need. And you'll also need to learn how to stay safe on the Internet. You've heard about the problems that go along with using credit cards on the Internet, about kids finding pornography, and so on.

In addition to covering all of those issues, I'll answer all sorts of questions I've heard from Internet users, from how to get rich on the Internet to why those $500 Internet boxes may not be such a great buy. In this part, I'll also tell you about a couple of dozen different ways that people use the Internet. Maybe, you'll find something worth pursuing or you'll think of an idea of your own. And you'll even find out where the Internet is going in the future.

Finding Stuff

By now you must have realized that the Internet is rather large: tens of millions of users, millions of files in FTP sites, millions and millions of Web pages, Telnet sites, Gopher servers, newsgroups, mailing lists.... This thing is huge. How on earth are you ever going to find your way around?

Finding what you need on the Internet is surprisingly easy these days. Dozens of services are available to you to find your way around. And that's what this chapter is about, finding what you need and where you need to go.

Finding People

You might as well start with the most complicated task: finding people on the Internet. There are millions of Internet users ...and no single Internet directory. That's right.

Still Working at a Command Line? If you are using the command-line interface, send an e-mail message to **ciginternet@mcp.com** and type **who** in the Subject line of the message (leave the body blank). In return, you'll receive the chapters on finding people from the first edition of *The Complete Idiot's Guide to the Internet*. For more information, see Appendix C.

Unlike the online services, which have directories you can search to find someone you want to contact, there's no one place to search on the Internet. But that's not so surprising, really. After all, there's no single directory for the world's telephone system, and the Internet is comparable—it's thousands of connected networks that span the world. So how are you going to find someone?

Quite frankly, the easiest way to find someone is, if possible, to talk to (or e-mail) a mutual acquaintance. You can spend hours looking for someone in the Internet's various directories. If you know of someone else who might have the information, you can save yourself some time and trouble by tracking the person down that way. If you can't think of someone else who knows the person you're after, you'll have to dig a little deeper.

Directories, Directories, and More Directories

There are a lot of directories on the Web. (No, I don't mean directories on a computer's hard disk this time; now when I say "directories," I mean it as in "the telephone directory" or "directory assistance.") A good place to start is at Netscape's People page. Go to **http://home.netscape.com/home/internet-white-pages.html**, or if you are using the Netscape browser, click the **People** button in the Directory Buttons bar. Each time you go to this page, Netscape displays one of five directories (WhoWhere?, Four11, IAF, Bigfoot, and Switchboard). The first figure on the next page shows the WhoWhere? directory. You can search the directory Netscape displays, or you can choose one of the other four.

Another good directory to use is Yahoo (go to **http://www.yahoo.com/search/people/**). This is Yahoo's directory of people on the Internet, and it's surprisingly good. I searched for my own name and found myself ...along with about 90 other Peter Kents. (I hadn't realized there were so many of us.) You can see the Yahoo search form in the second figure on the next page. You can search for a name and narrow the search by including a city and state, or you can search for a telephone number.

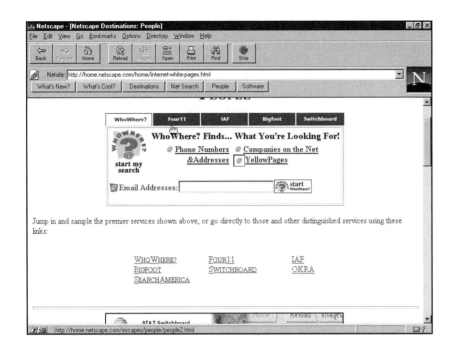

Netscape's People page automatically picks a directory for you.

Yahoo's People Search form.

Other Search Engines, Too
Yahoo is not the only *search engine* you can use to find directories. We'll look at more search engines later in this chapter, and you'll find that many of them will have links to directories you can use to find people, too.

If you don't find the person you need in Yahoo's People Search, don't worry; there's still a chance you'll find him or her. There are links to literally dozens more directories at Yahoo's **http://www.yahoo.com/Reference/White_Pages/** page; when I looked a moment ago I found links to 75 different directories, some of which had links to dozens more, including directories at colleges.

I'm not going to go into more detail about these directories. A year or two ago it was quite difficult to find people on the Internet (when I searched for myself for the first edition of this book, I had a lot of trouble finding myself—and I knew where I was!). These days there are so many of these things that, with a bit of time and trouble, you have a good chance of finding the person you need (assuming he or she has Internet access, of course).

Before you begin your search, here are a couple of other useful Web pages to start you off:

➤ **The Directory of Directories (http://www.procd.com/hl/direct.htm)**

Links to all sorts of directories: museums, local government, universities, and companies. This may be useful if you are trying to track someone down in a specific institution.

➤ **Flip's Search Resources (http://aa.net/~flip/search.html)**

A Web page set up by someone who did an adoption search, with links to useful sites he found, such as databases of Vietnam War casualties, genealogy records, and so on.

Finding "Stuff"

Now for the more general "stuff" category. You want to find information about, well, something or other, but you don't know where to start? The best place is probably on the Web at the Web search sites. There are dozens of these sites, and I'm always surprised what I can turn up in just a few minutes of searching. There are basically three ways to use these search sites:

➤ View a directory from which you can select a subject category and subcategories; then you'll see a list of links to related pages.

➤ Search an index of subjects, type a keyword into a form, and then click a Search button to carry out a search. You'll see a list of links to Web pages related to the subjects you typed into the search form.

➤ Search an index of pages. Some search engines let you search for words within Web pages. AltaVista, for example, claims that it has an index of most of the words on *30 million* Web pages! You'll see a list of pages that contain the words you typed into the form.

Which type of search should you use? The first or second method should normally be your first choice. Services such as AltaVista are very useful, but because they don't categorize the pages—they search for words within the pages instead of searching the subjects of the pages—they often give you more information than you can ever handle. The other services categorize pages (and sometimes even describe or review pages), so they are generally easier to use.

Finding the Search Sites

Getting started is easy. Most Web browsers these days have a button that takes you straight to a search page of some kind (generally a form that lets you search a choice of search sites). For example, Netscape offers the Net Search button, America Online's Windows 3.1 browser and Internet Explorer 3.0 have a Search button, and so on.

The Best?

Which is the best Web search site? There is no "best." Even though I really like Yahoo, I sometimes use others. Each one is different and works in a different way, which means each one will give you a different result. Try a few and see which you like, or check to see how others rate them. For instance, you might try one of these pages:

http://www.si.umich.edu/~fprefect/matrix/matrix.shtml

http://www.yahoo.com/Computers_and_Internet/Internet/World_Wide_Web/ Searching_the_Web/Comparing_Search_Engines/.

This list contains a few more URLs you can use. I've started with Yahoo because that's where I prefer to start. Of course, after you've used a few search sites, you may find that you have a different preference.

Yahoo: http://www.yahoo.com

Lycos: http://www.lycos.com/ (The Yellow pages at the back of this are taken from reviews of Web sites done by Lycos.)

InfoSeek: http://www.infoseek.com/

HotBot: http://www.HotBot.com/

AltaVista: http://www.altavista.digital.com/

Inktomi: http://inktomi.berkeley.edu/

What's the difference between a Web directory and a search engine? A directory provides categorized lists of Web pages from which you can select a category, and then a subcategory, and then another subcategory, and so on until you find the site you want. A search engine lets you use a program with which you'll search a database of Web pages. With a search engine, you type a keyword and click a Search button or press Enter. The search engine then searches the database for you. Some sites such as Yahoo contain both directories and search engines.

Check This Out...

Netscape Tip

If you use Netscape, here's a really quick way to search for something. Enter two words into the Location box. For instance, if you want to search for information about hiking in Iceland, type "iceland hiking." (If you just want to search for one word, enter it twice, as in "iceland iceland.") Press Enter, and Netscape picks a search engine for you from it's selection of five—Yahoo, Magellan, InfoSeek, Lycos, and Excite—and sends the search keywords to the search engine.

How Do I Use the Search Engines?

Internet *search engines* allow you to search a database. Take a quick look at InfoSeek (http://www.infoseek.com/) in the following figure as an example.

Start by typing a search term into the text box. You can type as little as a single word, but you may want to get fancy—in which case you should read the instructions. You'll find a link at InfoSeek, currently labeled *Huh?*, that takes you to a document that describes exactly what you can type. Read this document; it gives you many suggestions and hints for using the search engine. (Most search engines will have a link like this to background information.)

As you will learn in the information document, you can enter these types of things at InfoSeek:

➤ **Words between quotation marks.** Tells InfoSeek to find the words in the exact order you type them: "the here and now."

➤ **Proper names.** Make sure these are capitalized correctly: Colorado, England, or Gore.

➤ **Words separated by hyphens.** Tells InfoSeek to find both words when they are close together in the document: diving-scuba.

➤ **Words in brackets.** Tells InfoSeek to find the search words when they appear together, but not necessarily in the order you've entered them: [diving scuba].

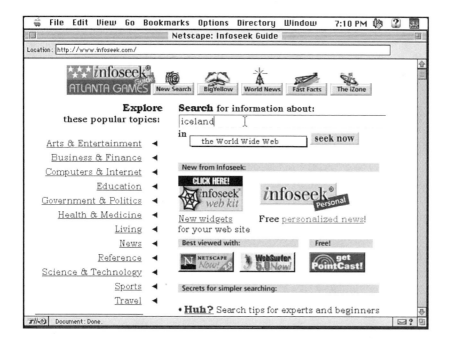

InfoSeek, a Web search engine.

Each search engine is a little different and allows you to use different sorts of search terms. You can always search by simply entering a single word, but the more you know about each search engine, the more efficiently you can search. When you first go to a search engine, look around for some kind of link to a Help document.

When you finish reading the Help information, click the **Back** button to return to InfoSeek, to the page with the text box. Enter the word or phrase you want to search for, and then press **Enter** or click the **Search** button. Netscape sends the information to InfoSeek, and with a little luck, you see a result page shortly thereafter (see the following figure). Of course, you may see a message telling you that the search engine is busy. If so, try again in a few moments.

InfoSeek found a few links to Icelandic subjects for me.

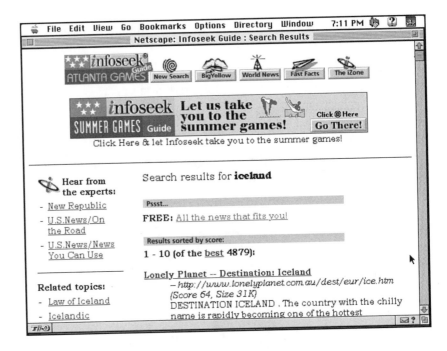

As you can see in the figure, when I searched for "iceland," InfoSeek found 4,879 links to Web sites that contain information about Iceland. The document I'm viewing doesn't show me all the links, of course. It shows me the first 10 and provides a link at the bottom of the page that I can click to see the next 10. It found links to things such as *Travel Guides to Iceland, History of Iceland, Books on Iceland, Airlines*, and plenty more. If one of these links interests me, all I have to do is click the link—and away I go, over the North Atlantic and into Iceland.

Browsing the Internet Directories

Now, let's look at the Internet directories. For a sample, we'll take a look at Yahoo. Go to **http://www.yahoo.com/**. Yahoo has a search engine, so you can type a word into the text box if you want. But notice the category links: *Art, Education, Health, Social Science*, and so on. Each of these links points deeper into the Yahoo system, a level lower down in the hierarchical system of document categories. To see how this works, click **Recreation**, and you see a document from Yahoo with a list of more categories: *Amusement/Theme Parks@, Aviation, Drugs@, Motorcycles*, and so on.

The @ sign at the end of some of these categories indicates that this entry is a sort of cross reference: you will be crossing over to another category if you select this link. For instance, click **Drugs@**, and you'll see a page from the *Health:Pharmacology:Drugs* category.

This page also contains links to other drug-related categories, along with links to Web pages that are related to recreational drugs (from alcohol to XTC), political and legal issues, pharmacology, and many other subjects.

You'll also notice that some links are shown with bold text and numbers in parentheses after them (such as *Nicotine (31)*), and links that are not bolded (such as *Psychiatric Drug Therapy*). The bold links take you farther down the hierarchy, displaying another document that contains more links. The number in parentheses after the link shows how many links you'll find in that document.

The regular-text links are links across the Internet to Web documents that contain the information you're looking for. Select **WWW Drug Links**, and you'll find yourself viewing a Web document with more links to drug pages.

Finding *Specific* Stuff

Now that you've seen how to search for general "stuff," you're ready to learn about searching for more *specific* stuff. Instead of going to a general search site, you can go to one of many sites that help you find specific things; you might want a site where you can search for stuff about museums and exhibits (**http://155.187.10.12/fun/exhibits.html**), boat stuff (**http://boatingyellowpages.com/**), or kid stuff (**http://www.yahooligans .com**), for example. You can find scores of these specialized search sites, with information about everything from lawyers to pets. A good place to find them is at **http:// www.yahoo.com/Computers_and_Internet/Internet/World_Wide_Web/ Searching_the_Web/**. You can also find them at any of the other big search sites.

Finding Out What People Are Saying

You shouldn't be paranoid, but people might be talking about you. How do you know what they are saying? It's possible to search newsgroup messages for particular words. So you can search for your own name to find out what your friends—or enemies—are saying about you. Or you can search for a subject if you are researching a particular topic.

There are a number of places you can search newsgroups. One of the best is DejaNews (**http://www.dejanews.com/**). For this example, however, try Yahoo. Go to **http:// www.yahoo.com**. At the search page, click the link—currently the **Options** link—that takes you to the advanced search. Then click the **Usenet** option button. (As another alternative, you can use InfoSeek and choose **Usenet Newsgroups** from the drop-down list before you search.) When the search site carries out the search, it displays a page of links to the matching messages. Click a link to read the message.

Set a Bookmark to Repeat the Search Later

Here's a handy little trick. If you've just done a search about a subject that you think you'll want to check back on later—to see what new information has appeared on the Internet—bookmark the search. I don't mean the search site, but the search itself. Here's how: go to the search site, carry out the search, and when you get the page displaying the search results, bookmark that page. The next time you want to search, all you have to do is select that bookmark. Your browser automatically sends the search statement to the search engine, which carries out the search and displays the result.

FTP, Gopher, Telnet, and More

No, you are not finished. You can search for much, much more. Go back to the earlier chapters on FTP, Gopher, Telnet, newsgroups, and mailing lists, and you'll see that I gave you information about how to find things on those services. For instance, you can use Archie to search FTP sites, and you can use Tile.Net and other similar services to find mailing lists and newsgroups related to subjects that interest you. You can also use Jughead and Veronica to search Gopherspace. So if you don't find what you need at any of the Web sites you learned about in this chapter, spend a little time searching the other services.

The Least You Need to Know

➤ There is no single directory of Internet users, so the easiest way to find someone is often to ask a mutual acquaintance.

➤ There are now lots of good directories. You may have to search a few, but there's a good chance that eventually you'll find the person you're looking for.

➤ A search engine is a program that searches for a word you enter.

➤ You can search indexes of keywords describing the contents of Web pages, or you can search the full text of the Web pages (millions of words in millions in pages).

➤ A directory is a categorized listing of Web links. Choose a category, then a subcategory, then another subcategory, and so on until you find what you want.

➤ Services such as DejaVu, Yahoo, and InfoSeek let you search newsgroup messages. The result is a list of matching messages. Click a link to read a message.

➤ You can set a bookmark on a page that displays search results; then, to repeat the search quickly at a later date, all you have to do is select that bookmark.

Chapter 20

Staying Safe on the Internet

In This Chapter

➤ Keeping kids "safe"

➤ Protecting your e-mail

➤ The identity problem

➤ Internet addiction

➤ Protecting your credit card

➤ Keeping out of trouble with your boss or spouse

There are many dangers on the Internet...most of them imagined or exaggerated. We're led to believe that our children will become corrupted or kidnapped, our credit cards will be stolen, and we'll be arrested for copyright infringement.

Well, okay, some of these dangers are real. But remember, you're sitting in front of a computer at the end of a long cable. Just how dangerous can that be? If you use a little common sense, it doesn't have to be very dangerous at all.

Your Kid Is Learning About Sex from Strangers

Sex, sex, sex. That's all some people can think of. The media's so obsessed with sex that sometimes the only thing that our journalists really notice are stories with a little spice in them. Consequently, the press has spent a lot of time over the last couple of years talking about how the Internet is awash in pornography. Well, it isn't.

I'll admit that there are pornographic images on the Internet, mostly in a handful of newsgroups and Web sites. Of course, what one person regards as pornographic someone else may regard as sensuous. So what do I mean by pornography? Well most of the publicly accessible sex-related Web sites are really quite "soft." If you are over 21, take a look at the *Hustler* site (**http://www.hustler.com**) or the *Playboy* site (**http://www.playboy.com**). Then run down to your local magazine store and take a look at them there. You'll find that the bookstore version is far more explicit than the Web version. (Believe me, I've done this little experiment—but only in the interest of research, you understand.)

Check This Out...

You Can Do Your Own Research
Because this is a family book, I'm not going to go much further on this topic. If you care to research the subject of sex on the Internet further, check out http://www.drv.com/hotline/hotlinx.html.

Although there is "nasty" stuff on the Internet, most of it is on *private* Web sites. To get in, you have to "subscribe" by providing a credit card number. In addition, some newsgroups carry very explicit sexual images and, in a few cases, images of violent sex. (Even though most things don't particularly shock me, I admit I have been disgusted by one or two things I've seen in newsgroups.)

Although the press would have you believe it's hard to get to the Smithsonian Web site or to read a newsgroup about cooking without somehow stumbling across some atrocious pornographic image, this is far from the truth. You really have to *go looking* for this stuff. The chance that you'll stumble across it is about as good as the chance that you'll run into Queen Elizabeth on your next trip to the supermarket. Of more concern, perhaps, is the access children have to explicit sites.

Don't Expect the Government to Help

If you have kids, you already know that they can be a big bundle of problems. The Internet is just one more thing to be concerned about. Still, you signed up for the job, and it's your responsibility.

Many people have suggested that somehow it's the *government's* responsibility to look after our kids. (These are often the same people who talk about "getting the government off our backs" when it comes to other issues.) The U.S. Congress recently passed the

Computer Decency Act, which bans certain forms of talk and images from the Internet. This law has definitely had an effect. Images at the public *Hustler* site, for instance, have become far less explicit (in fact, they're all but gone...or so I'm told). However, shortly before we went to print, this law was judged unconstitutional by a Federal court in Philadelphia; now it heads for the U.S. Supreme Court.

Does It Hold Water?

To put it bluntly, this law is a sloppy piece of work. Even some of the people who signed it into law said that it was probably unconstitutional. It's very vague. As Chief Judge Dolores Slovitzer said, "I was taught in law school that people are entitled to know what it is they may be prosecuted for." And one government witness was unable to say whether the famous *Vanity Fair* magazine cover of a nude Demi Moore would be legal on the Internet or not. Which raises another questionable point: what's perfectly legal in the "paper" press (such as discussing abortion) would be illegal on the Internet.

In its decision, the court stated that "Those responsible for minors undertake the primary obligation to prevent their exposure to such material." Hey, isn't that what I said? (I wrote most of this *before* the law was struck down. Looks like there could be a judicial career waiting for me!)

The bottom line is that the Computer Decency Act is history (and will probably remain so). And even if it's replaced by something else, remember that the Internet is an international system. How are we going to regulate Swedish, Finnish, German, or Japanese Web sites? We're not.

It's Up to You; Get a Nanny

If you want to protect your kids, I suggest you spend more time with them at the computer or get a nanny. You can't afford a nanny, you say? Of course, you can. There are now lots of programs available to help you restrict access to "inappropriate" sites. Programs such as Net Nanny (I'm not endorsing this one in particular, I just used it so I could put "Nanny" in the heading) contain a list of sites that are to be blocked; you can add sites from your own hate-that-site list, or you can periodically download updates from the Internet. Using these programs, you can block *anything* you want, not just pornography. As the Net Nanny site says, you can "screen and block anything you don't want running on your PC, like bomb-making formulas, designer drugs, hate literature, Neo-Nazi teachings, car theft tips—whatever you're concerned about."

You can find Net Nanny at **http://www.netnanny.com/**. To find other such programs, search for the word "blocking" at Yahoo or some other Web search site (or go directly to **http://msn.yahoo.com/msn/Business_and_Economy/Companies/Computers/ Software/Internet/Blocking_and_Filtering/**). You'll find programs such as SurfWatch, CyberPatrol, CYBERSitter, NetShepherd, TattleTale, Bess the Internet Retriever, and Snag. (I'm serious, all of these are names of real programs!)

If you use an online service, you'll also find that it probably offers some way of filtering out areas you don't want your kids to get to. America Online has had such filtering tools for a long time. And MSN allows you to block the Internet's alt. newsgroups and other "adult" areas.

You'll also soon find blocking tools built into most Web browsers. Internet Explorer 3.0 already has blocking tools. To use them, choose **View**, **Options** and click the **Ratings** tab. You'll find an area in which you can turn a filtering system on and off. This system is based on the Recreational Software Advisory Council's ratings (though you can add other systems when they become available), and you can turn it on and off using a password. You can set it up to completely block certain sites or to allow access with a password (just in case you don't practice what you preach!). The following figure shows a site that's blocked except for password entry.

With Internet Explorer 3.0's Ratings turned on, your kids can't get in—but you can!

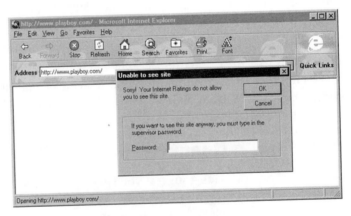

I've heard people criticize these blocking programs for two reasons: 1) because they're not perfect (of course, they're not) and 2) because they're an affront to the concept of free speech. Personally, I find them to be very useful and effective. I believe in supervising my kids, and these programs provide a supervision tool for a new era. They also provide a way for concerned parents to keep their kids away from sites they object to, without locking people up and forcing adults to read nothing more than sixth-grade materials on the Web.

What About *TIME*?

Oh, so you read *TIME* Magazine's exposé on Internet porn, did you? It was complete nonsense and widely criticized as sloppy and inaccurate. *TIME* based the story on a flawed study, which looked at pornographic images on BBSs (individual "adult" computer systems hooked up to the phone lines). It then used the findings to suggest that this proved somehow that the Internet was full of porn. *TIME* published a follow-up that didn't exactly apologize but that admitted the study was wrong. (It wasn't *TIME*'s fault, though; it was the fault of the "researcher," they said.) The author of the article has also publicly apologized. The original *TIME* article got front-page coverage; the follow-ups didn't, of course!

Your Private E-Mail Turned Up in the *National Enquirer*

E-mail can get you in a lot of trouble. It got Oliver North in hot water, and ordinary people have lost their jobs or been sued over things they've said in e-mail. Several things can go wrong when you use e-mail:

➤ The recipient might pass the e-mail on to someone else.

➤ The message can be backed up to a backup system and read by someone other than the recipient later.

➤ Someone could spy on you and read your e-mail looking for incriminating comments.

The most likely scenario is that the recipient intentionally or thoughtlessly passes on your message to someone who you didn't count on seeing it. The second problem—that the message could be copied to a backup system—is what got Oliver North (and others) into trouble. Even if you delete a message and the recipient deletes the message, it may still exist somewhere on the network if the system administrator happened to do a backup before it was deleted. So if you are ever the subject of some kind of investigation, that message could be revived. This is more of a problem on the Internet because a message goes from your computer, to your service provider's computer, to the recipient's service provider's computer, to the recipient's computer—at least four places from which it could be copied.

Finally, someone might be out to get you. Internet E-mail is basic text, and a knowledgeable hacker with access to your service provider's system (or the recipient's service provider's system) can grab your messages and read them.

What do you do, then? The simplest solution is to avoid putting things in e-mail that you would be embarrassed to have others read. The more complicated solution is to encrypt your e-mail. A number of encryption programs are available that scramble your message using a "public-key" encryption system. Here's how it works. You have two "keys," special codes that you type into the encryption program. One is the private key; the other is the public key. Now here's where it gets weird. Thanks to the magic of mathematics, these keys are related to each other. If you encrypt a file with one, you can decrypt it with the other. But you can't decrypt a file with the same key you encrypted it with.

So when you want to send a message to someone, you have to get hold of that person's public key. These keys are often posted—yes, publicly—on the Internet. There's no need to worry about who gets hold of the public key, as it can't be used to decrypt a secret message.

Using the recipient's public key, you encrypt a message and send it off. The recipient then uses his private key (also known as the secret key because that's just what it is) to decode the message.

Check This Out...

Digital Signatures You can also use this public-key encryption system to digitally sign documents. When you encrypt a message with the private key, it can only be decrypted with your public key. It's not safe; after all, your public key is public. But if it can be decrypted with your public key, it *must* have come from your private key. Therefore, it must have come from you.

These systems can be so safe that the U.S. Government is actually concerned. For instance, the best-known encryption program, PGP (Pretty Good Privacy), can create encrypted files that essentially *cannot be broken*. And there is no technology in the foreseeable future that can break them. Although it's illegal to export PGP, that is rather like banning the export of words. "No, we don't want other nations using the word 'hyperventilate'—we'll keep that one for ourselves. From now on, it's illegal to export the word 'hyperventilate'." Of course, you can't exactly ban the export of something that can be exported as easily as the word "hyperventilate" in e-mail or even across a phone line. Anyway, it's a case of closing the barn door after the horse has long gone. PGP is available throughout the world.

Where can you get these encryption systems? A good way to start is to search for the word "encryption" at any of the Web search sites (or try **http://msn.yahoo.com/msn/Computers_and_Internet/Security_and_Encryption/**). There's a problem with these systems, though. Right now, they're complicated to use. For example, PGP can be very complicated; if you want to use it, I suggest that you get one of the "front-end" programs that make it easier to use, such as WinPGP. In addition, because few people use encryption anyway, if you want to use it, you have to arrange to use it first.

That may change though as encryption becomes incorporated into e-mail systems. Although it's not included right now, Netscape keeps promising to add the feature. (Their press releases even claim that the browser *has* the feature; but the most recent version, Netscape 3.0 beta 4, *did not*.) When encryption is added to e-mail programs, you'll be able to download "certificates" containing the public keys of the people you want to communicate with, create your own public/private key pair, and distribute your public key. Until encryption is easy to use and widely available, it won't be widely used. And even when it is, remember that you're still trusting the recipient not to pass on the decrypted message to someone else.

Prince Charming Is a Toad!

I'm not sure why I should have to explain this, but I'll remind you that when you meet someone online, you *don't* know who that person is! There's something about electronic communications that allows people to quickly feel as if they know the person with whom they are communicating...but they don't!

There are two problems here. First, cyberspace is not the real world. People communicate in a different way online. As another author told me recently, "I know people who seem to be real jerks online, but who are really nice people offline. And I've met people who seemed to be great online, but were complete jerks offline."

Then there's the misrepresentation problem. Some people flat out lie. A man who claims to be single may be married. A woman who claims to look like Michelle Pfeiffer may actually look like Roseanne. A "35-year-old movie executive who graduated from Harvard" may actually be a 21-year-old unemployed graduate of Podunk Bartending School. It's easy to lie online when nobody can see you. Couple that with a natural tendency to feel like you know the people you meet online, and you have trouble.

Not everyone lies online though. As my friend Phyllis Phlegar wrote in *Love Online* (Addison Wesley), "Even though some individuals choose to be deceptive, many others see the online world as the ultimate place in which to be totally honest, because they feel safe enough to do so." (Phyllis actually met her husband online.) But she also recognizes the dangers: "As long as the person or people you are talking to can't trace you, free-flowing communication between strangers is very safe." But if you're not careful and you give out information that can be used to trace you, Prince Charming may turn out to be the Black Prince. And if you do choose to meet someone "live" after meeting them online, be cautious.

> **Check This Out...**
>
> **Profiles** If you are a member of an online service, be careful about what you put in your profile. Most services allow you to list information about yourself—information that is available to other members. Omit your address, phone number, and any other identifying information!

247

She's a He, and I'm Embarrassed!

Chapter 16 covers chat systems, which make for a great place to meet people. For many, they're a great place to meet people of the opposite sex (or of whatever sex you are interested in meeting). But you should know that sometimes people are not of the sex that they claim to be. I don't pretend to understand this, but some people evidently get a kick out of masquerading as a member of the opposite sex. Usually men masquerade as women, which could be construed as the ultimate compliment to womanhood or could simply be blamed on the perversity of men. Either way, there's a lot of it around, as the saying goes. (I recently heard chat systems described as being full of "14-year-old boys chatting with other 14-year-old boys claiming to be 21 year-old women." True, it's an exaggeration, but it illustrates the point well.)

If you hook up with someone online, bear in mind that she (or he) may not be quite who he (or she) says (s)he is.

You Logged on Last Night, and You're *Still* Online This Morning

The Internet can be addictive. I think three particular danger areas stand out: the chat systems, the Web, and the discussion groups (mailing lists and newsgroups).

Apparently, chat is extremely addictive for some people. I've heard stories of people getting stuck online for hours at a time, even until early in the morning. And I know of people who've met people online, spent hundreds of hours chatting, and finally abandoned their spouses for their new "loves."

The Web is not quite so compelling, but it's a distraction, nonetheless. There's just so much out there. If you go on a voyage of discovery, you *will* find something interesting. Start following the links, and next thing you know, you've been online for hours.

Discussion groups are also a problem. You can get so involved in the ongoing "conversations" that you can end up spending half your day just reading and responding.

What's the answer to net addiction? The same as it is for any other addiction: self discipline—along with some support. It also helps if you have a life in the real world that you enjoy. Fear probably helps, too (like fear of losing your job or kids). And if you need help, why not spend a bit more time online. Do a search for "addiction," and you'll find Web sites set up to help you beat your addiction. You might even try Addiction Manager, a Mac shareware program designed specifically for computer-related addictions (**http://www-personal.umich.edu/~gherrick/AddMan.html**).

Just Because You're Paranoid Doesn't Mean Someone *Isn't* Saying Nasty Things About You

A little while ago, someone started saying nasty things about me in a mailing list. What she didn't tell people was that she had a sort of vendetta going against me, and had for some time. (No, I'm not getting into details.) Anyway, I saw her comments in one mailing list and was struck by a thought: there are 15,000 internationally distributed newsgroups and thousands more mailing lists! What else is she saying? and where?!

Actually, there is a way to find out what's being said about you (or someone or something else) in newsgroups and Web pages. This is something that may be very useful for anyone who is in the public eye in any way (or for people involved in feuds).

You can read about a number of search "engines" in Chapter 19. You can search AltaVista to see what's being said about you in a Web page (this service lets you use a search engine that indexes all the words in a page, instead of just categorizing Web pages). To search a newsgroup, though, you'll need a program like Deja News (**http://www.dejanews.com/**). In Deja News, you type a name or word you want to search for, and the service searches thousands of newsgroups at once and shows you a list of matches (see the following figure). Click the message you are interested in to find out exactly what people are saying about you.

Deja News provides a great way to search newsgroup messages. (Looks like Elvis has been busy.)

When I did this little search, I was surprised at what I found. I discovered information about a science-fiction conference at which I was to be a guest, and I found messages in which people recommended a book I'd written about PGP. I also discovered that there's a stunt man called Peter Kent (I found that in alt.cult-movies).

Deja News is not the only such service; you can find a list of these services at **http://www.yahoo.com/News/Usenet/Searching_and_Filtering/**. How about mailing lists? Well, I haven't found a good mailing list search tool yet. There is one at **http://wais.sensei.com.au/**, but it catalogs only a few Macintosh-related lists. Still, I expect something like this to turn up on the Internet any day now.

I Was "Researching" at *Hustler* Online, and Now I'm Unemployed

It's Bugged!
You should know that with some new, special software programs, your boss can spy on your Internet activities whether you clear the cache and history list or not! So maybe you'd better just get back to work.

This title is more than a joke. Some people really have been fired for viewing "inappropriate" Web sites during work hours. Of course, you can avoid such problems by staying away from the sites in the first place. But, if you really *have* to go there, practice safe surfing by clearing the cache when you finish! (We discussed the cache in Chapter 5.) When you visit a site, a copy of the Web page is saved on your hard disk in case you want to view it again at a later time. In effect, this creates a history of where you've been. And speaking of history, some browsers (such as Internet Explorer) have excellent multisession history lists—which will also list every Web page you've seen!

To cover your tracks, clear the cache to remove the offending pages. Then clear the history list (either clear it completely, or remove just the offending entries).

I Think Kevin Mitnick Stole My Credit Card Number!

Here's another Internet myth: shopping on the Internet is dangerous because your credit card number can be stolen. The second part of the myth is correct. Yes, your number can be stolen. But the first part is nonsense. Using your credit card on the Internet is not unsafe. Let me give you a couple of reasons.

First, credit card number theft is quite rare on the Internet. It can be done, but only by a computer geek who really knows what he's doing. But why bother? Credit-card numbers are not very valuable because it's so easy to steal them in the real world. For example, I handed over my credit card to a supermarket clerk the other day and then started bagging my groceries. The clerk put my card down while I wasn't looking. The woman behind me in the line moved forward and set her bag down on the counter. When I went to look for my card, it was gone. It wasn't until I (politely) asked her to move her bag that I found the card underneath. And from the look on her face, I'm sure she knew where it was.

This sort of theft is very common. When you give your card to a waiter, a grocery-store clerk, or someone at a mail-order company, you don't think twice about it. But for some reason, people are paranoid about theft on the Internet. Banks know better, though. Internet-business author Jill Ellsworth found that credit card companies actually regard Internet transactions as safer than real-world transactions.

The second reason is that both Netscape and Internet Explorer, the two most-used browsers, have built-in data encryption. Many Web sites now use special Web servers that also have built-in encryption. When a credit card number is sent from one of these browsers to one of these secure servers, the data is encrypted and, therefore, unusable. The following figure shows a secure Web site. Notice the little lock in the lower-right corner of the window? This lock is Internet Explorer's way of indicating that a site is secure. Netscape displays a key image in the lower-left corner for the same purpose; if the key is broken, the site is not secure.

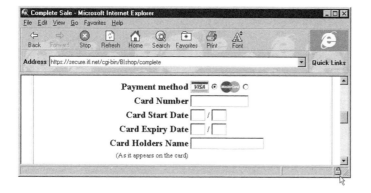

When you see the lock in the lower-right corner, you can send your credit card without worry.

As for Kevin Mitnick, cyber-thief extraordinaire, there's a lot of confusion about what he did. He broke into systems and stole information en masse. (He didn't steal individual numbers as they flew across the Internet.) And no matter how you pass your credit card number to a vendor, the most dangerous time is *after* they've received the number—and there's little you can do about that.

My Wife Found My Messages in alt.sex.wanted

There are a lot of people saying a lot of odd things on the Internet. Undoubtedly, each day thousands of people with very poor judgment make thousands of statements that could get them in trouble.

This little problem has long been recognized. And for some time now, there's been an (almost) perfect way around it: you post messages anonymously. One way to do that is to configure your e-mail or newsgroup program with incorrect information (with another name and e-mail address, for instance). When you send the message, the header contains that incorrect information instead of the true data. That will fool most list members, but it's not foolproof; the header also contains information that allows the message to be tracked by a system administrator (or the police).

Another method is to use an anonymous remailer, a system that posts the messages for you, stripping out all information that can be used to track you down. In other words, you send the message to the remailer with information about which newsgroup it should be posted to, and the remailer sends the message on, sans identity.

You can find these services by searching for remailers at a search site (or go to the list of remailers, at **http://electron.rutgers.edu/~gambino/anon_servers/anon.html**). They allow you to send both e-mail messages and newsgroup messages. But, note that they are not perfect. They depend on the reliability of the person running the service and, in some cases, on that person's willingness to go to prison. If the police come knocking at his door, the administrator might just hand over his records. Of course, if you are trying to avoid embarrassment more than the law, an anonymous remailer might be just what you need.

I "Borrowed" a Picture, and Now They're Suing Me!

As you've seen throughout this book, grabbing things from the Internet is as easy as stealing from a baby—but there's none of the guilt. It's so easy and so guilt free that many Internet users have come to believe in a sort of "finder's keepers" copyright morality. If it's there, and if you can take it, you can use it.

The law says otherwise, though. Here's a quick summary of copyright law: if you created it, it belongs to you (or to your boss if he paid you to create it). You can put it anywhere you want, but unless you actually sign a contract giving away rights to it, you still own the copyright. You don't have to register copyright, either.

Copyright law is quite complicated, however, and this summary misses many essential details. The important thing to understand is that it *doesn't* belong to you if you didn't create it! Unless something has been placed on the Internet with a notice explicitly stating that you can take and use it, you can take it for personal use but you can't use it publicly. You can't steal pictures to use at your Web site, for instance. (And even if there is a notice stating that the item is in the public domain, it may not be. After all, how do you know that the person giving it away really created it?)

Can I Take It for Personal Use?

In most cases, you probably can. When you connect to a Web site, all the things that are transferred to your computer end up in the cache anyway. However, some enthusiastic copyright lawyers claim that the use of a cache is in itself illegal—that even storing images and text on your hard drive goes against copyright law.

Copyright law even extends to newsgroups and mailing lists. You can't just steal someone's poetry, story, ruminations, or whatever from a message and distribute it in any way you want. It doesn't belong to you. And of course, if you are concerned that your work will be taken from a newsgroup or mailing list and distributed, don't put it there!

I Downloaded a File, and Now My Computer's Queasy

Yes, you know what I'm talking about: computer viruses. These are nasty little programs that get loose in your computer and do things they shouldn't, like wipe your hard drive or destroy the directory information that allows your computer to find files on the drive.

First, my role as contrarian dictates that I inform you that much of the fuss about viruses is exaggerated—greatly exaggerated. When something goes wrong with a computer, a virus usually gets the blame. An example of how the virus threat is exaggerated is the famous Good Times virus. This virus never actually existed; it was myth from the start. The story was that an e-mail message containing a virus was being passed around the Internet. The story was obviously wrong because a plain e-mail message without a file attached cannot contain a virus.

Only files that "do things" can contain viruses. That includes program files, as well as document files created by programs that have macro languages. For instance, a variety of Word for Windows macro viruses just appeared in the last year or so (what took them so long?). If a file can do nothing by itself—if it has to have another program to do something to it—it can't carry a virus. A plain text file (including text messages) can't do anything, and .GIF or .JPG image files cannot cause harm. (I'm just waiting for the next big hoax: someone will start a rumor that there's an image file used at many Web sites that contains a virus and that all you have to do is load the page with the image to infect your computer....)

Yes, viruses do exist. Yes, you should protect yourself. There are many good antivirus programs around, so if you plan to download software from the Web (not just images and documents from applications other than advanced word processors), you should get one. On the other hand, viruses are not worth losing sleep over.

The Least You Need to Know

➤ Yes, there's sex on the Internet, but not as much as the press claims. Get a filtering and blocking program if you want to keep the kids away.

➤ E-mail can easily be stolen or forwarded. Don't write anything that you could be embarrassed by later.

➤ People on the Internet sometimes lie (just like in the real world). They may not be who they say they are (or even the sex they claim to be).

➤ Internet addiction? Snap out of it!

➤ You can search thousands of newsgroups at once with systems such as Deja News to see what people are saying about you.

➤ Your boss can find out what Web sites you are visiting, so watch out!

➤ Credit card transactions made on the Internet are safer than those made in the real world.

➤ Anonymous remailers can protect your identity in e-mail and newsgroups.

➤ You don't own what you find on the Internet; it's copyright protected.

➤ Viruses are relatively few and far between; but it's a good idea to protect yourself with an antivirus program.

21 Questions: The Complete Internet FAQ

In This Chapter

➤ Shell accounts, finger, and winsocks

➤ Changing your password

➤ Why some programs won't run in Windows

➤ Getting rich on the Internet

➤ Slowdowns and connection problems

➤ Staying anonymous

In this chapter, you will find answers to some questions you may have and a few problems you may run into—everything from the meaning of certain terms to solutions for certain problems.

What's a Shell Account?

You may remember me telling you (back in Chapter 2) that a few years ago most people dialing into a service provider were using dial-in terminal accounts. These are often known as *shell* accounts. And if you have a PPP or SLIP Internet account with a service provider, you probably also have a shell account. So you have a choice: you can connect to the Internet via the fancy graphical software, or you can connect using the bland command-line interface. Why bother with the command line when you can have the splashy graphics? Well, the next question will provide an example of why you would want to, and when you look at the *finger* command later in this chapter, you'll see another example.

Most service providers give you a free shell account when you sign up for a PPP account. Others have the nerve to charge extra for the privilege. You really shouldn't have to pay extra for it.

How Do I Change My Password If I'm Using a PPP Connection?

The fact that this is even a problem strikes me as a little strange. Most service providers don't provide a convenient way for you to change your password with a PPP or SLIP connection, yet they'll tell you that you should change your password frequently for security's sake. They *could* provide a Web form, but most don't. So how *do* you change your password?

Not a Good Sign At least one major service provider, WorldNet, doesn't let you change your password at all. You have to call and ask them to do it for you, which is a *very* bad way to go about it!

If you are with an online service such as MSN, AOL, or CompuServe, there's probably some kind of menu option somewhere in the main program. But if you are with a service provider, you'll probably have to connect to their system with a terminal program. You need to get to the menu system used by people who are not fortunate enough to have a PPP or SLIP account. Find a menu option that says "Account Assistance" or something similar, and then look for one that says something like "Change Password." You can get to this menu in two ways.

One way is to connect using a simple serial-communications program (such as Windows 3.1's Terminal or Windows 95's HyperTerminal) or any commercial or shareware terminal program. You dial the phone number for your shell account and then log in; but you'll have to ask your service provider for information because the login instructions may be different. If you want more information about this, look at Chapter 7 of the first edition of this book (which is on the CD). Or you can send e-mail to **ciginternet@mcp.com**, type the word **first** in the Subject line, and leave the body of the message blank. You'll get Chapter 7 in an e-mail response message. (For more information about using the e-mail responder, see Appendix C.)

The other way is to connect in the manner you usually employ and then open a Telnet program (see Chapter 18). Connect to your service provider through Telnet, log on to your shell account, and then go to the change-password menu option. Call and ask your service provider which Telnet domain to use.

What's a Winsock?

Winsock is short for "Windows sockets," and it's the program used by Microsoft Windows to act as an interface between TCP/IP programs running on the computer and the Internet itself. Just as a printer needs a printer driver to interface between the programs and the printer, the Internet needs a "driver" to interface between the programs and the Internet. And in the Windows world, that's known as a Winsock.

In Windows 3.1, you have to acquire a Winsock program separately. The most commonly used one is Trumpet Winsock (which you can find at many software archives; see Appendix A). In Windows 95, Winsock is built in, so you don't need to get a separate program. (However, you may need an advanced degree in networking to figure out how to use it.) An easier way to handle all this is to get an installation program from a service provider or an online service that installs and configures the Winsock for you.

Why Won't Netscape Run in Windows 95?

This problem is all too common these days. Say, for instance, that you are using Windows 95 and have connected to CompuServe or some other online service, or perhaps to a service provider that gave you Windows software to install. Then you go to the Netscape Web site to download the latest version of that navigator, or maybe you download the latest version of Internet Explorer. Which version do you pick? Why, the Windows 95 version, of course! That's the operating system you are using, after all. You install the program, and try it...but it doesn't work. What's going on?

The problem is that, although you are using Windows 95 (what's known as a 32-bit operating system), the Winsock program you are using is a 16-bit program. Remember, the Winsock is the "driver" that connects your programs to the Internet. The Winsock is installed when you install the software needed to dial into the Internet. And, in order for a 32-bit program (such as the Windows 95 versions of Netscape or Internet Explorer) to run, you must use a 32-bit Winsock! Yet many online services and service providers are still handing out old Windows 3.1 Winsocks. Thanks, online services!

This problem will gradually disappear as the online services introduce 32-bit dial-in programs. In the meantime, your only options are to stick with 16-bit programs (those created for Windows 3.1), to find a service provider that will help you set up Windows

95's Dial-Up Networking software, or to install your own Winsock and configure it to work with the online service or service provider. (Unfortunately, not all online services will let you do that.) However, I have no intention of touching that in this book; unfortunately, the online services often don't provide much help either, and some service providers aren't much better.

Anytime you run a 16-bit Winsock, you are stuck with 16-bit Internet programs. If you are trying to install a Windows 95 or Windows NT program and can't get it to work, start by checking to see if you have a Winsock designed for Windows 95 or NT.

How Do I Get Rich on the Internet?

Oh, that's easy. First, start a business selling some kind of Internet service or software. Run it for a few months on a shoestring, and then go public. It doesn't really matter what the intrinsic value of the company is—as long as it has the word "Internet" attached to it somehow, you'll get rich.

At least, that has been the business model until recently, but it may be changing. *Newsweek* recently reported on the proposed *Wired* public offering. *Wired* is a well-known magazine about the cyberworld. It has some Internet services, too, such as *HotBot* (a Web search engine) and *HotWired*, an online magazine. As *Newsweek* pointed out, if *Wired* sells the stock they are planning to sell at the price they plan to sell it, the company will be valued at almost half a billion dollars. Not bad for a company that started with about $4.5 million, that has never made money, that doesn't appear to be anywhere *close* to making money, and that, according to *Newsweek*, could even be close to bankruptcy without the stock sale.

It remains to be seen whether *Wired* will make the money they hope to make. Judging from earlier Internet public offerings, though, there's probably plenty of Internet hysteria to get the stock onto the market at the price they want. Other Internet companies have used this get-rich-quick plan quite successfully. Best-selling author James Gleick (he wrote the NYT bestseller *Chaos*), for instance, is worth around $25 million according to the Internet Millionaires list (**http://www.pulver.com/million/**). Not bad for less than two years of work building a small service provider, *The Pipeline*, which he later sold to a large national service provider, *PSINet*.

However, you may be a bit too late to get into this game. The market currently seems to be flooded, and more people are losing money on the Internet than are making it. Wait for the next big wave, though, and try to catch it early!

How Can I Sell Stuff on the Internet?

The second way to make money on the Internet is by selling stuff—real stuff, not other Internet services. The editors took a poll and told me they'd seen salad dressing, teddy bears (see the following figure), model horses, live horses, legal services, picture-scanning devices, Internet tutoring, and real estate for sale. There are also books, CDs, and videos …as well as hot sauce, pizza, a newsletter for writers of children's stories, and all sorts of other stuff. Of course this doesn't mean that all these people are actually making *money* doing this.

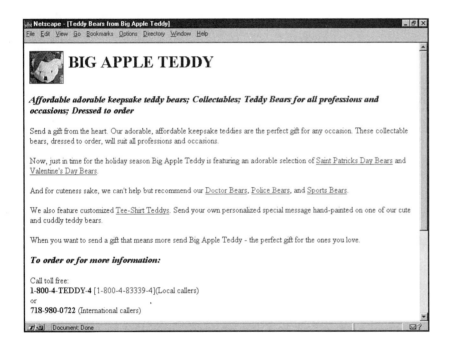

Yes, they really are selling teddy bears on the Internet.

Take heed of this warning though. Very few people are actually selling things on the Internet, and much of the talk about what a wonderful market the Internet provides is marketing hype. (In fact, the high failure rate in Internet businesses is a joke among Internet insiders; when I told an executive at a major Internet-software company that I wanted to write a book about companies that have actually figured out how to make money on the Internet, he said, "Is anyone making money; I mean, we are, but is anyone else?")

If you really want to try it, you've got a lot to learn about the Internet—far more than I can ever explain here. Don't think you can just put up a few Web pages and then start taking orders. You'll also have to promote your Web site in newsgroups, mailing lists, online service forums, and so on. The odds are against you, so be prepared.

If I Have a Fast Modem, Why Are Transfers So Slow?

You've just installed a fancy new 28,800 modem, and still some Web sites are about as speedy as molasses on a hot day in Iceland. What's going on here? Your information has to pass through many different computer systems, along lots of different lines; hey, it may be coming from halfway across the world, after all.

Think of this transfer across the Internet as a relay race. The information you want is passed from person to person, maybe dozens of times, between the Web site and you. The last person in the chain is that speedy 28,800 modem you bought. But when you look at the others involved in the race, you see that some are as athletic as Roseanne, and others are as fast as your grandmother. Still others may be very fast, but they've got other jobs to do, too. They are actually involved in hundreds of relay races at the same time! So if you are at a very popular Web site, for instance, hundreds of other people just like you are trying to get information at the same time, and that relay runner might be having serious problems keeping up.

If it's any consolation (it probably isn't), those people are sitting at their computers in Alberta, Arizona, Austria and other places beginning with different letters, saying, "I just bought this 28,800 modem. Why did I bother wasting my money?" Why would anyone bother to get a fast modem? Because with a slow one, you'll be even slower. (And not *all* Web sites are slow—just the ones that everyone wants to go to.)

Will the Internet Kill Television?

No way. Using the Internet is active; using the television is passive. If you remember, television was supposed to kill both movies and radio, but both seem healthy enough today. For that matter, movies were supposed to kill theater, and theater (if I remember right) was supposed to kill rock paintings.

Why Isn't Anyone Reading My Web Page?

I guess you heard the nonsense that "a Web page is a billboard that can be seen by millions," and you believed it. Well, let me put it this way. There are 250 million people in the United States. But if you put up a *real* billboard in the United States, will 250 million people see it? I won't bother answering that.

The Web is not a highway, and your page is not a billboard. If you want people to come to your Web page, you have to promote it. And don't believe all that "if you want people to come to your Web site it has to be compelling" nonsense either. A Web page has to serve a purpose; if it serves its purpose well and is well-promoted, it can do well (even if it doesn't use Java to display some pointless animation).

How Can I Remain Anonymous on the Internet?

Many people are concerned with keeping their privacy and anonymity on the Internet. In particular, women who like to spend time in chat rooms often feel the need to put up a protective wall between themselves and other members. If a relationship develops with someone online, they want to be in control of how much information about themselves they allow others to discover.

Well, there are degrees of anonymity on the Internet. The first level is easy to achieve.

➤ Get an account with an online service or service provider and obtain an account name that is nothing like your own name. If your name is Jane Doe, use an account name such as *HipChick* or *SusanSmith*.

➤ If you are with an online service, make sure your "profile" is empty; many online services allow you to enter information about yourself that others can view (in chat rooms, for instance).

➤ If you are with a service provider, you should also ask your provider to disable finger for your account. (finger is a service that other Internet users can employ to find information about you—see the next section.)

➤ Once you are actually on the Internet, be careful not to leave identifying information when you're leaving messages in newsgroups, working with mailing lists, and so on.

Although this doesn't ensure full anonymity, it's pretty good in most cases. In order to find out who HipChick or SusanSmith actually is, someone would have to persuade your service provider to divulge information. That's not impossible, but in most cases, it's unlikely (unless you're doing something to incite the interest of the police or the FBI).

Another form of anonymity is possible through *anonymous remailers*, systems that let you send anonymous messages to newsgroups via e-mail. You send a message to the remailer, and the remailer strips out identifying information and sends it on. (This is discussed in more detail in Chapter 20.)

You can also send anonymous messages from public e-mail connections. For instance, many libraries have Web browsers set up, and most Web browsers these days have e-mail programs. You can send messages from the browser and, in most cases, remain completely anonymous.

Getting a completely anonymous Internet account is probably more difficult. Most service providers require information that will identify you: a credit card, driver's license, and so on. With a little imagination, though, it's not impossible.

What's finger?

In the last section, I mentioned something called *finger*. This is a UNIX command that allows you to retrieve information about other people on the Internet if you have just a little bit of information. You can use this command in either of two ways:

➤ Log on to your shell account and get to the command line (you should find a menu option somewhere that will take you there; ask your service provider if you can't find it). At the command line, type **finger** and press **Enter** to run the command.

➤ Install an actual finger "client," a program that allows you to run finger from within your graphical user interface—from Windows or the Macintosh, for instance.

Here's how to use finger. Let's say you've seen the **HipChick@big.net** e-mail address and want to find out about HipChick. You use the finger command **finger HipChick@big.net** and press **Enter**. A request for information is sent to big.net. You *may* get such information as the account holder's real name, which is why I told you to make sure finger is disabled if you want to remain anonymous!

Check This Out...

Some You Win, Some You Lose

Many service providers completely disable finger requests. Others disable certain types of requests. For instance, if you were to try a command like **finger smith@big.net**, some service providers would send a list of all the account holders called Smith, but some providers simply wouldn't respond.

Can Someone Forge My E-Mail?

A few months ago, I saw a message in a mailing list containing complaints that an e-mail message that appeared to have been sent to the list from this person was actually forged. Someone else had sent a message using her e-mail address. Another member of the list wrote a message telling her that she should be more careful. He said (a little bluntly) that if she left her computer unattended she should expect trouble. Thinking I'd play a little game, I sent a forged message to the list in *his* name. (No, I didn't know him, and I definitely didn't have access to his computer.) "That'll teach him, I thought... He should be more careful."

It's actually very easy to forge e-mail messages—so easy, in fact, that I'm surprised it doesn't happen more often. (It probably happens more often to people who spend a lot of time in newsgroups, mailing lists, and chat rooms—where it's easy to get into fights—than to people who use other services.)

A person can forge a message simply by entering incorrect configuration information into a mail program or, better still, the mail program of a public Web browser. However, before you run out and play tricks on people, I should warn you that this mail can still be traced to some degree. (It might be difficult, though, for anyone other than a police officer with a warrant to get the service providers to do the tracing for him.)

How can you avoid this problem? There's not much you can do really, except keep your head down and stay out of "flame wars" (which we'll discuss next). You *could* digitally sign all your messages, as discussed in Chapter 20, but right now that's a bit of a hassle.

What's a Flame?

I've heard it said that the Internet will lead to world peace. As people use the Net to communicate with others around the world, a new era of understanding will come to pass ...blah, blah, blah....

The same was said about telegraph and the television, but so far, there hasn't been much of a peace spin-off from those technologies! But what makes me sure that the Internet will not lead to world peace (and may lead to world war) are the prevalence of flame wars in mailing lists and newsgroups.

A *flame* is a message that is intended as an assault on another person, an ad hominem attack. Such messages are common and lead to flame wars, as the victim responds and others get in on the act. In some discussion groups, flame wars are almost the purpose of the group. You'll find that the Internet is no haven of peace and goodwill—and I haven't even mentioned the obnoxious behavior of many in chat rooms.

I'm Leaving My Service Provider. How Can I Keep My E-Mail Address?

I currently have about eight Internet accounts. Over the past few years, I've had dozens, and that means I've had dozens of e-mail addresses. Although this is unusual, it's certainly not unusual for people to have a handful of different accounts as they search for the best one. Unfortunately, that means keeping your friends and colleagues up-to-date on your e-mail address is a hassle. If only there was a way to keep the same address, even when you changed providers....

Well, there just might be. It is possible to register your own "domain name." You do this through InterNIC, and you can find instructions for doing so at the **http://rs.internic.net** Web page. It costs $100 for the first two years and $50 a year after that to keep the domain name. Many service providers will actually register a domain for you, but they may charge you an additional fee to do so.

For example, I own a couple of domain names: lab-press.com and arundel.com. When you register a name you have to already have chosen a service provider because the provider has to set up its computers to recognize the name. InterNIC will check the domain to see that it "works." Your service provider can then set up an account for that domain. For instance, my service provider set up an account called pkent for my lab-press.com account. That means that I now have the e-mail address **pkent@lab-press.com**.

What if I decide to use a different service provider? I find the new provider and ask them to use my lab-press.com domain. They set up their computers to recognize the domain, and I contact InterNIC and ask them to change the domain to work with the new service provider. Then, even though I'm working with a different provider, I still have the same e-mail address. (At the time of this book's writing, InterNIC did not charge a fee for making a change.)

There's one big problem with this. The online services won't let you do this, nor will some of the large national service providers. They want you to use their domain names, and they don't want to mess with setting up special domains for individuals.

Another way to keep your e-mail address is to sign up with an e-mail service. This is something new, recently launched by USA.NET (other companies will probably follow). For a small fee, you can use an address they provide, and they'll forward all your mail to whatever Internet service provider you happen to be using. You can find out about this service at the **http://usa.net** Web page.

Why Can't I Get Through to That Site?

You'll often find that, all at once, you cannot connect to sites that you've used before or that you've seen or heard mentioned somewhere. You might find Web pages that you can't connect to, FTP sites that don't seem to work, and Telnet sites that seem to be out of commission. Why?

The first thing you should check is your spelling and case; if you type one wrong charac-ter or type something uppercase when it should be lowercase (or vice versa), you won't connect. (The following figure shows the dialog box Netscape shows when you've typed the name incorrectly.) Another possibility is that the service you are trying to connect to might just be very busy, with hundreds of other people trying to connect; depending on the software you are using, you might see a message to that effect. Likewise, it could be that the service is temporarily disconnected; the computer that holds the service might have broken or might have been disconnected for service. And finally, the service simply might not be there anymore.

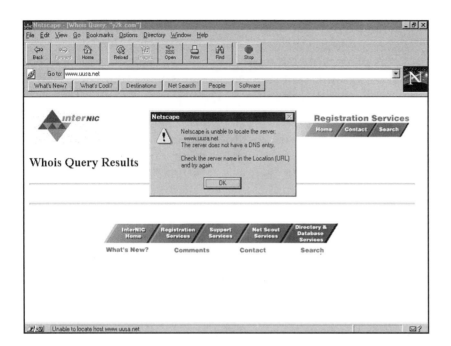

Oops! I mistyped the URL, and my browser can't find the host.

Trying again a few times often helps; you'll be surprised just how often you can get through to an apparently dead site just by trying again a few moments later. Also note that some software is a little buggy. For instance, some versions of Netscape seem to hang up and appear unable to transfer data from a site at times; but canceling the transfer and starting again often "jump starts" it.

Don't Place the Blame Too Quickly

Often it's your service provider, not the site you are trying to connect to, that's having problems. Try connecting to a variety of sites, and if you can't get through to any, it's probably a problem with your connection to the service provider or with the provider's system. Try disconnecting and logging back on.

Why Won't This URL Work?

URLs are a special case because even if they don't seem to work, you may be able to modify them and get them to work. First, make sure you are using the correct case. If a word in the URL was shown as uppercase, don't type lowercase (if the URL doesn't work with some words uppercase, though, you might try lowercase).

Check This Out...

Remove the Period When you type a URL, don't type a period at the end. You may find URLs in books and magazines that appear to end with a period because they are used at the ends of sentences. But real URLs don't end with periods, so make sure you don't include the periods when typing.

Second, make sure you are using the correct file extension if there is one. If the URL ends in *.htm*, make sure you are not typing *.html*, for instance. If it still doesn't work, start removing portions of the URL. For instance, let's say you have this URL:

http://www.big.net/public/software/macintosh/ internet/listing.html

You've tried using both "listing.html" and "listing.htm" at the end, and neither seems to work. So remove "listing.html" and try again. You may get a document with links to something you can use. If you still don't get anything, remove the "internet/" part (in other words, you are now typing just **http://www.big.net/public/software/macintosh/**). If that doesn't work, remove the next part, "macintosh/." Continue in this manner, removing piece after piece, and in most cases, you'll eventually find something useful.

Why Do So Many People Hate AOL?

It's an unfortunate truth that America Online members have a bad reputation on the Internet. You may run across rude messages in which people insult AOL members or treat them as if they are the scum of the earth.

Here's what happened. AOL, like all the online services, decided that it had better get Internet access in a hurry. So they started adding Internet services, and they added newsgroup access quite early. All of a sudden, about a gazillion AOL members flooded onto the Internet in a rush that would have the bulls at Pamplona running in the opposite direction. Millions of AOL members overwhelmed these discussion groups with questions such as "how do you download files from this group?" and "where are the pornographic pictures?" Of all the online services' members, AOL's members were probably the least computer literate. (AOL had targeted the "family" market, while CompuServe, for instance, had been a geek service for years.)

The Internet had been, until just a few months before, a secret kept from most of the world. All of a sudden, it was as busy as a shopping mall on a Saturday afternoon, and every bit as cultured. And there was an obvious scapegoat: all those people with @aol.com e-mail addresses! Unfortunately, you might still run across anti-AOL bias on the Internet.

My Download Crashed So I Have to Start Again. Why?

Most online services use file-transfer systems that can "recover" if the transfer is interrupted. For instance, if you are halfway through downloading a file from CompuServe when your three-year old kid decides he wants to see what happens when he presses the big red button on the front of your computer, all is not lost. After you reboot the computer and reconnect to CompuServe, you can begin the file transfer again. But you don't have to transfer the whole thing; instead the transfer begins in the middle.

However, that won't work on the Internet—at least not at the moment. Most file transfers use FTP (File Transfer Protocol), which can't restart interrupted downloads. That will eventually change, perhaps soon, as a protocol comes into use for file transfers across the Web. But for now, you'll have to keep your kid away from the computer while you are transferring files (or try covering the button with a piece of card).

Should I Start My Own Service Provider Company?

No.

Why Not?

One of the most common questions Internet writers get asked is, "how can I set up a business as an Internet service provider?" The easy answer is, "if you don't know, you shouldn't be trying." It's a very complicated—and currently very competitive—business. If you don't know what it takes, you probably don't know how little you know, and you shouldn't be trying. After all, over the next couple of years, thousands of Internet service providers will bite the dust as the big telecommunications companies get in on the act. Why add your blood, sweat, and tears to the pile? You can run many other businesses with a better chance of success.

Just One More Question...

You're going to come away from this book with lots of questions because the Internet is big, there are many different ways to connect, and there's a huge amount of strange stuff out there. I hope this book has helped you start, but I know you'll have many more questions.

Once you are on your own, what do you do? Try these suggestions:

➤ *Get the FAQs.* FAQ means "frequently asked questions," and it refers to a document with questions and answers about a particular subject. Many newsgroups and mailing lists have FAQs explaining how to use them, for example. Look for these FAQs and read them!

➤ *Continue your reading.* I've written about a dozen Internet books and really need to sell them, and you can continue buying and reading them. Well, okay, there are other writers putting out Internet books too (you may have noticed a few). Seriously, though, to become a real cybergeek, you'll need to learn much more. So check out a few of the books that are out there.

➤ *Read the documentation.* There are literally thousands of Internet programs, and each is a little different. Make sure you read all the documentation that comes with your programs so you know how to get the best out of them.

➤ *Ask your service provider!* I've said it before, and I'll say it again: if your service provider won't help you, get another service provider! The Internet is too complicated to travel around without help. Now and again you'll have to ask your service provider's staff for information. Don't be scared to ask—and don't be scared to find another provider if they won't or can't answer your questions.

The Least You Need to Know

➤ A shell account is a dial-in terminal account. You may have a free shell account, and you may need to use your shell account to change your password.

➤ If you are using Windows 95, make sure you have installed a 32-bit Winsock before you try to run 32-bit Internet software.

➤ Getting rich on the Internet is a lot harder than it's been made out to be.

➤ You may have a fast modem, but if the Internet itself is busy, things will still move slowly.

➤ You can be anonymous on the Internet—if you are careful.

➤ If your service provider won't answer your questions, you need another service provider!

Ideas

Throughout this book, I've explained many of the services the Internet can provide. But you might now be wondering "What good are these things?" Unfortunately, until you get onto the Internet, get hooked, and forget that you have responsibilities out in the "real" world, it's difficult to understand what the Internet can do for you. (Imagine, for a moment, the Neanderthal thawed out of the ice and introduced to modern technology. "Okay, so I can use this soap stuff to remove the smell from my armpits, right? But why?")

This chapter gives you a quick rundown on just a few of the ways in which ordinary (and some not-so-ordinary folks) are incorporating cyberspace into their daily lives.

The **O**bject Type list box displays a list of every OLE-supporting program on your computer by object type. If you select Microsoft Excel 5.0 Chart, for example, Excel starts when you exit the dialog box so you can create your object.

The Display as Icon option makes your linked or embedded object appear as an icon in the compound file, instead of as the object in its actual form.

The **Result** area in the bottom left corner of the dialog box describes what the results will be with all of the options you choose. You'll find this bit of information helpful while learning to use the linking and embedding features. It always tells you what's going to happen based on your selections.

To finally exit the Object dialog box, click **OK**.

If you have already created the object, and you know what file it's in, click on the Create from File tab to bring another set of options to the front of the Object dialog box.

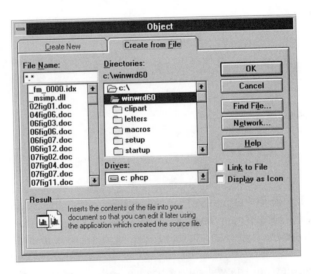

The Create from File tab of the Object dialog box.

The File Name list box is used to select the name of the file containing the object you want to link or embed. (Remember, the object can be text, a range of cells, a graphic, and more.)

The Directories box is used to select the directory where the file you want to link or embed is located.

The Drives box is used to select the drive where the file you want to link or embed is located.

The Link to File option will create a link between the selected object file and the document you're working in. Click on the Link to File check box to activate this option.

The Display as Icon option works the same way as in the Create New tab options. It makes your linked or embedded object appear as an icon in the compound file.

The **Result** area in the bottom left corner tells you what's going to happen based on your selections. Always stop and read it to make sure your task will be carried out as planned.

To exit the Object dialog box, click **OK**.

That's a brief introduction to the Paste Special and Insert Object commands. You'll get to use them more fully in the next chapters.

The Least You Need to Know

Linking and embedding can really make you more productive with your Office programs.

➤ OLE is a feature that enables programs to share data by linking or embedding.

➤ To link is to copy an object into a new file, yet still maintain an active connection with its original. When the original object is modified, the copied link object is also modified.

➤ To embed is to copy an object into a new file in such a way that the object will not reflect changes made to the original object. However, embedding does enable you to immediately access the program in which the object was originally created.

➤ You can link and embed objects with the Paste Special or the Insert Object commands.

Getting Software

We're back to instant gratification. You know that program you just saw advertised in *Internet Windows Computing World* magazine? Want to try it out? Go online and download a demo right now! There's no more waiting. Pretty soon everybody will be buying software and transferring it straight to his or her computer.

You can use one of the Internet's great shareware libraries, too. (See Appendix A for more information.) The following figure shows the TUCOWS site. TUCOWS, The Ultimate Collection Of Winsock Software, is a library of shareware Internet programs for Windows. You can find it on the Web at **http://www.tucows.com**.

TUCOWS: The Ultimate Collection Of Winsock Software.

Research

If you are writing a school paper, researching a book, or planning a vacation, the Internet contains a cornucopia of illuminating tidbits. It's *not* a library (contrary to the nonsense of those in the Internet community who got a little carried away with their predictions), and it will be a long time before it can replace one. Still, it does give you access to nearly unlimited amounts of useful information that's just waiting to be used.

For instance, suppose you are planning to visit, oh, I don't know, how about Iceland? Get onto the World Wide Web and search for Iceland (you learned how to search for stuff in

Chapter 19). What do you find? A hundred or more sites with information about Icelandic travel, sports, culture, media, real estate (there's no way *I'm* actually moving there), news, and more.

Visiting Museums

I suppose you can't afford to visit the Louvre *and* the Smithsonian this year. What a shame. Still, you can get online and see what you are missing (see the following figure). Actually, the potential here is greater than the reality. Maybe someday most of the masterpieces in the world's great museums will be online; but right now, many just provide one or two pictures and information about which subway to take to get there.

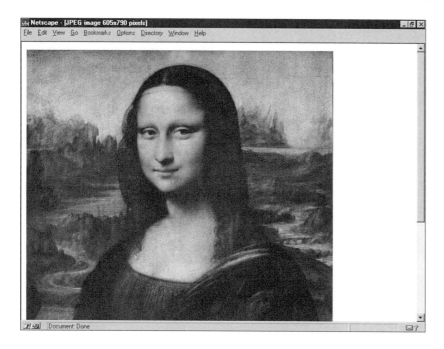

The Mona Lisa, *courtesy of the Louvre's Web site (http:// www.louvre.fr).*

Finding Financial Information

Want stock quotes? Information about competitors or about online banking services? You'll find it on the Internet. You can find links to great financial services at the search sites we discussed in Chapter 19. Or, you can try the Personal Finance page at GNN (**http://gnn.com/wic/wics/persfin.new.html**) or the Financial Web Information Network (**http://www.financial-web.com/**).

273

Music

If music is your passion, you'll be happy to know that you can hear some of the latest from the music world when you find it on the Internet. Try IUMA, the Internet Underground Music Archive (**http://www.iuma.com**). Would you prefer bagpipe music or film scores? Maybe you want to buy some CDs. Whatever you're looking for, you can find it on the Internet.

Magazines and 'Zines

You'll find thousands of magazines and 'zines online. (For the not-quite-so-hip among you, a *'zine* is a small magazine, usually published on a shoestring by someone with three or more pierced body parts.) You'll find underground books and comics, as well as newsletters on almost anything you can imagine (and probably a few things you can't imagine).

Hiding from the Real World

There's a wonderful cartoon that is legendary in the computer world. It shows a dog in front of a computer terminal, and it has the caption "Nobody knows you're a dog on the Internet." Well, it's unfortunate that the need exists, but quite frankly, there are people who use the Internet to hide from the real world. For one reason or another, although they have trouble with face-to-face relationships, on the Internet they can feel safe and like part of a community.

Shakespeare on the Net

I met a fellow computer-book writer recently who stages Shakespeare plays in IRC (Internet Relay Chat). This chap (yes, chap, he's English), takes a play, modifies it slightly to his taste (he recently staged an updated version of *Macbeth*), and breaks it down into its individual character parts. He sends each "actor" his lines *only*, no more. Each line has a cue number, so the person playing the character will know when to type the lines. Then they start, each person typing his or her lines at the appropriate cue position. It's an act of discovery for all the "actors" because they don't know what the other characters will say until they say it. Strange, but strangely fascinating.

If You Can't Get Out

There are those among us who would love to have more face-to-face relationships but for some reason can't get out. Perhaps they are elderly or disabled or are posted in the

Antarctic. The Internet provides a link to the rest of the world for those times when you can't physically get somewhere.

Joining a Community of People with Common Interests

Suppose you have some, er, let's say unusual interests. You believe the U.S. government has been chopping up aliens for years—or maybe that it's in cahoots with aliens. Or suppose that, by chance, you are consumed with a hatred of purple dinosaurs (one in particular, anyway) or that you feel compelled to tell others of your latest experience in the air.

> **Remember Your Old Friend, Chat?** As you learned in Chapter 15, IRC is a "chat" system. You type a message, and it's immediately transmitted to all the other people involved in the chat session. They respond, and you immediately see what they have typed.

Techno Talk

This one's not too hard: now suppose that, in your neighborhood, there are few people who share your interests. Who do you share your thoughts with? Where can you find a sense of community? On the Internet, of course, in the newsgroups and mailing lists (see Chapters 9–11). (And yes, the examples suggested above are real examples.) You may be surprised at the sort of people you find online. It's not all techno-chat. I have a friend who's a member of a discussion group on the subject of renovating antique tractors, for instance!

You Don't Trust Your Doctor, So ...

I must admit I don't have a lot of faith in doctors—and Grandma was probably right when she warned me to stay away from hospitals. (They're dangerous!) However, many people go to the Internet in search of the answers their doctors can't provide. Whether you have a repetitive-stress injury, cancer, or AIDS, you'll find information about it on the Internet. Want to try homeopathy, acupuncture, or just figure out what leeches can do for you? Try the Internet.

Shopping

Yes, yes, you *can* shop online, although statistically speaking you probably won't for at least a couple of years. The press seems to think that the raison d'être for the Internet is for K-Mart and Sears to find another way to sell merchandise. Really, though, the more interesting things are elsewhere on the Internet. So Internet shopping has been grotesquely overrated—but yes, it is there.

Cybersex

The Internet provides a wonderful form of communication for those who seem to have trouble finding others with similar sexual proclivities. This is by no means a minor part of cyberspace; some commentators even claim that the sexual use of online services played a major part in their growth. You can get online and talk about things that your parents or spouse might consider *very* weird, with people who consider them quite normal.

Political Activism

As they say, political activism infects every form of human communication. Well, the Internet is the latest frontier for political activities, providing militia groups a means of keeping in touch and providing Democrats and Republicans a place to seek votes.

Gore Vidal always did say it's a one-party system!

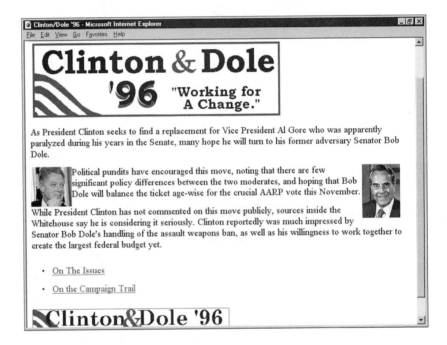

Subversion

The Internet provides a great way to subvert the political system in which you live. That's right, you too can publish information that your government doesn't want published, whether it's information about how Nutrasweet was created as part of a plot to take over our minds, or what was going on during the latest coup. Perhaps the most quoted such event was the last coup in Moscow, during which time much information was "exported" via the Internet. Closer to home, the Internet has become a thorn in the side of the U.S. Government as it makes the distribution of encryption software so easy.

Looking for Work (and Help)

Thousands of people are looking for work on the Internet, and thousands more are offering both full time and contract positions. I recently needed help with a project I was working on that I just didn't have time to finish. I sent a message asking for help, and within 20 minutes had found the ideal candidate.

Clubs and Professional-Association Information Servers

Are you running a large club or professional association? Why not set up a Web site? Your members can then check the Web site to find out when the next meeting is being held, search a database of fellow members, find out about the association's services, and more. Potential members can find out how to join, too.

Mating and Dating

Do people *really* meet online and get involved in romantic relationships of various kinds? Yes, they really do. I'd be inclined to make a joke about it, except that I have a friend who met a man online, and he eventually became her husband and the father of her child.

Long-Distance Computing

Being a computer geek comes with a real disadvantage: you always seem to be working. If you find yourself wishing you could get to the programs on your desktop computer while you are on vacation or are visiting relatives or clients, for example, you may have considered buying one of those remote control programs. You install the program on your laptop and then dial into your desktop machine. The program enables you to copy files between the computers and even run programs across the connection.

As you might guess, however, this can get very expensive. But now there's a new way to do it. Some of these programs actually let you make the connection across the Internet. So if you use a national service provider that has phone numbers throughout the U.S. (or even an international provider or an online service that has numbers throughout the world), you can dial into a local number and connect to your computer across the Internet and pay only a fraction of the long-distance charge.

Managing Your Links

Now that you've created a linked object, you need to know what you can do with it. After you link something, you may want to go back and update the original object. When you do, there are several ways you can manage the link itself.

Editing the Object at the Source

You can edit a linked object in two ways: in the source document from which it came, or in the destination document that leads back to the source document. We'll go over both ways. First, let's start with editing the object from the source document.

Open the application in which you created the object and open the file containing the object. Make any changes to the object, and then save the document. Then exit the source document and open the destination document. The changes should automatically show up in the destination document as well. If the changes don't appear in the object in the destination document, your program may not be set up properly to automatically update links. I'll tell you how to fix the update settings in a few.

Editing the Object from the Destination Document

If you edit a linked object from the destination document, you don't have to remember where it came from or its original filename. The link will trace you back to the source. From the destination document, just double-click on the object you want to edit. The server application opens and displays the source document.

 If double-clicking didn't work, open the Edit menu and choose Links. In the Links list dialog box, select the link you want to edit, and then click on the Open Source button. The server application should start, and you can make your changes.

Go ahead and make any necessary changes to the object. When you're done, save the file, and then exit the server application with the File Exit command. Pow! You're back in the destination document and your changes appear in this object as well.

Managing the Link's Update Settings

Pay attention now. You can control when changes to the linked object are updated in the destination document. You can control whether the link must be updated manually or whether it updates automatically. So far, we've been talking about automatic updates. If you change that to manual update, you'll have to go through the update steps each time you change the source document containing the linked object.

To set a link to manual update, open the destination document containing the linked object. Pull down the Edit menu and choose Links. The Links dialog box appears.

The list box lists all the linked objects in your document. Each link includes a name, the path name of the source document, and information about whether or not the link is manual or automatic. Select the link you want from the list and change the Update setting by clicking on the **Manual** option button at the bottom of the dialog box.

Click on the Update Now button at the right of the dialog box to update the object with any changes made to the source document. Click **OK** to exit the dialog box, and then save the destination file to save the new link settings.

You can also use the Links dialog box to lock a link to prevent the object from being updated with changes made in the source document. A locked link can't be updated until it is unlocked again.

The next time you make changes to the object's source document, you'll have to open the Links dialog box and click on the Update Now button to make those changes show up in the destination document.

Breaking the Link

There will come a time when you no longer want your linked object linked. If you want, you can leave the object in the destination document but break its link so that it is no longer associated with the source document. This turns the object into an ordinary Copy and Paste object, which has no ties to where the object came from.

To break a link, open the destination document. Pull down the Edit menu and select Links (or Link Options). The Links dialog box appears. Choose the link name for the object you want to break, and

➤ Lots of businesses are going to give up trying to make money on the Internet

➤ Eventually, the "let's get rich on the Internet" idiocy will subside; but we'll be left with plenty of good reasons to keep using it

Of all these things, I'm quite sure. However, in the rest of this chapter, I'm going to make some more predictions of which I'm, well, *pretty* sure. But as physicist Niehls Bohr once said, "Making predictions is very difficult, especially about the future."

Progress Will Slow Down

The rate of change on the Internet will slow down. Although the changes over the past two years have been phenomenal, this level of progress can't be maintained for two reasons.

First, most of the people who got on the Internet in the past couple of years were primed and ready to go. They were computer-literate, they had computers, and they had modems (or if they didn't, they could get them and install them). Few people went from being a complete neophyte who had never used or owned a computer to an Internet junkie. It will be difficult to continue the growth because newcomers to the Internet are likely to be new computer users as well as new Internet users, and therefore, they'll have bigger hurdles to jump. Getting the computerless and computer illiterate onto the Internet will be much more difficult than getting the already-computer-savvy up and running was.

Second, we appear to have seen great technological changes on the Internet in the past three years. But the changes have not been as dramatic as they first seemed. Most of the changes have come about as a result of companies taking existing technology and putting it together in a new way. For example, three years ago most people used some form of terminal account to access the Internet. Now they are using TCP/IP (SLIP and PPP) access, which allows them to use graphical-user-interface software. However, SLIP and PPP had been around for years; what made them popular was that a lot of companies wrote new software to take advantage of them. As another example, note that we've gone from considering the 14,400 modem the standard to the 28,800 modem being the standard. But the 28,800 modem was already in development, and anyway, it's just more of the same technology and not something radically different.

Further improvements will be more difficult. Wiring up the world with super high-speed connections will take years (at least five years for the United States, maybe more). And until these fast connections become available, the Internet can't live up to the hype and potential.

High Speed Connections (Not Quite Yet)

Much of the hype about the Internet depends on high-speed connections to the Internet. Some pundits claim that Web sites need multimedia to make them more compelling. (This seems to be rather insulting to the average Internet user, who supposedly values form over function; it indicates that he is so shallow that a bit of glitz keeps him happy.) Without high-speed connections, though, this multimedia stuff is more of a nuisance than a real benefit. Java, video, and animations are all very nice, but if you are getting the goodies over a phone line, even with a fast modem, the novelty soon wears off.

Although the Internet will eventually have high-speed connections, it won't come overnight. A lot of technological problems must be overcome before cable, for instance, can handle large numbers of Internet users. And there are a number of financial and logistical reasons why the phone companies won't be able to provide high-speed connections for everyone (at a reasonable price) anytime soon.

The Web Comes Alive—More Multimedia

It's a foregone conclusion that the amount of multimedia (video, sound, animations, and such) on the Internet will increase. With the new tools becoming available—tools that make multimedia easier to create—it's inevitable. But there is still the slow-connection problem that will hold back multimedia for some time to come. Take a look at the online services; have they incorporated multimedia? Yes, a little. But not much because the connections most people have are simply too slow for multimedia to work well.

Multimedia on the Internet gets much more attention right now than it deserves based on its actual level of use. Very few Web sites use multimedia (that is, sound and video). The vast majority of Web pages contain nothing more than text and pictures. For all the talk of multimedia and "cool" stuff, only a tiny fraction of Web sites—perhaps less than 1 percent—use sound, and that's probably the easiest "multimedia" format to work with. Very few Web sites have video or animation.

Check This Out...

It's Not All That Common I was recently paid to put together a list of 50 Web sites that don't use sound (don't ask why, it's a long story!). And you know, it was laughably easy. Very few Web sights have sound or video, though they are thought to be the most popular forms of multimedia and the easiest to work with.

Intercast PC/TV

Eventually, the Web browser and TV will merge. Web browsers will be built into TVs, and the "Intercast" PC/TV may be one way that this will happen.

The Intercast system will merge data from the Internet with television signals. While watching a show on the TV, for instance, you may decide you want more background information on what you're watching. No problem. If you were watching something on the Discovery Channel, you could open the TV's Web browser and view the Discovery Channel Web site. From there you could find information about the program currently showing, perhaps in the form of a bibliography, of links to other Web sites related to the show's topic, of links to the store where you can buy products related to the show, and so on.

The Web information transferred to your TV would be transmitted between the lines of television data in the same way that captions for deaf viewers are already transmitted to TV sets in the U.S. It is also the means by which information for TeleText systems is transmitted in Europe (for news, TV listings, sports scores, and so on). Of course, another component is needed for this to work as planned: transmissions *back* from the TV to the Web site asking for particular pages. For now you'll have to wait for Intercast PC/TV, which will be available when the Internet cable-connection problem has been sorted out.

The Internet Backlash

An Internet backlash is beginning as companies realize that making money on the Internet is not quite as simple as they were told. At the time of this writing, a well-known Web magazine called *WebReview* (**http://www.webreview.com/**) was preparing to go out of business, and other Web publications were in trouble. In addition, some publishers are reducing their Internet presence to some degree, after realizing that they can't sell enough books online to make it worthwhile. You'll soon begin to see more stories in the press about Internet failures, as the press looks for a new "angle."

Is this bad, you wonder? No, it's probably good. Let's get rid of the Internet hysteria—of all the inflated claims about what the Internet can do—and start to focus on what it can *really* do. We need fewer people running get-rich-quick schemes on the Internet, and more people using the Internet in a rational, reasoned manner.

The Internet Will Open Borders

The Internet *does* open borders. As more of the world runs on software, more of the software will become the focus of argument. Although it's rare these days for software to be banned, some software is now and again censored; violent games and encryption software are the targets of legislation in some countries.

The problem is that software can slip across borders quickly and undetected when one's borders are punctured by the Internet. A case in point, right now an organization of small telecommunications companies is trying to get the Federal Communications Commission to ban Voice on the Net programs (discussed in detail in Chapter 16). Let's say they are successful, and these programs are banned. Just how do you maintain such a ban? One of the best programs comes from Israel, and that company can continue to distribute the software across the Internet, perhaps without breaking any U.S. laws.

What can be done about this problem? The government could look for transmissions of this software and "bust" people who are caught using it. Or it could threaten Israel with sanctions if Israel didn't also ban the software. Or it could cut off the U.S. portion of the Internet from the outside world. In the next few years, you'll hear all three actions proposed in a variety of cases. The Internet crosses borders, and many people won't like that.

> **Something to Think About...**
>
> *check This Out...*
>
> The idea of one country distributing software to a country in which it's banned brings up another issue that has to be dealt with by the courts: if you distribute something on the Internet, can you be held liable for the actions of people who download the software in countries in which your product is banned?

The Internet and the Fight for Free Speech

Here's another aspect of the borders issue: free speech. Some of the things you might say in the United States are unacceptable in, say, Indonesia. And some of the things a person might say in Holland would be unacceptable in, say, the United States. Speech (and images) that are perfectly legal in some areas of the world are illegal in others. A few weeks before this book went to print, the Computer Decency Act in the U.S. was declared unconstitutional (and, therefore, unenforceable for the moment). Right now, what is considered acceptable speech on the Internet is unclear throughout the world.

Because the Internet is an international system, regulating it is very difficult. I think there are three possible paths.

> ➤ A few countries may simply cut their connections to the Internet (though in a world of satellite communications, they won't be able to do that completely).

> ➤ Others may declare the Internet to be a sort of no-man's land, where communications have to be unregulated (or at least they may turn a blind eye).

> ➤ Others may try to regulate it the best that they can—if only to realize eventually that it can't be done. (However, China already controls Internet access, "filtering" information before it can enter the country; other nations will probably follow suit.)

And all over the world we'll continue to hear what a dangerous and evil place the Internet is, for the very reason that it *can't* be fully regulated.

On the Web, these blue ribbons are the Electronic Freedom Foundation's symbol for the Free Speech Online Campaign.

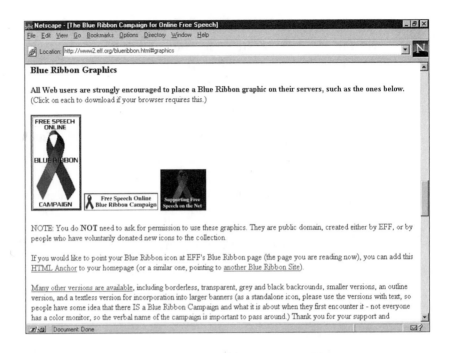

Schools Use the Internet; Test Scores Continue to Plummet

Some people say that the Internet will "save" our schools. Some go so far as to say that schools will no longer be *needed*, that our kids will learn at home through the TV.

To quote former Assistant Secretary of Education Dr. Diane Ravitch, "If Little Eva cannot sleep, she can learn algebra instead … she'll tune in to a series of interesting problems that are presented … much like video games." I don't know about your kids, but when mine can't sleep the last thing on their minds is algebra. Lewis Perleman (*School's Out*) says that we don't need schools anymore because information is plentiful outside schools (as if all that education is about is piping information into kids). Anyway, who's going to be looking after these kids? Oh, I forgot, we'll all be telecommuting by then, won't we?

Information is everything, these people think. All problems are a result of a lack of information, so if the information flows freely, all of our troubles will slip away. Put algebra on one channel and Power Rangers on another, and our children will make the "right" decision. If only life were so simple. Alan Kay, one of the founders of Apple Computer, says that problems schools cannot solve *without* computers won't be solved *with* them. He's dead right. Why *would* computers (and Internet connections) be a panacea? We've known how to educate kids well for centuries, so why would a sudden infusion of technology fix problems that have nothing to do with a lack of technology?

284

So my prediction is that computers with Internet connections will be found in greater numbers in schools. Yet, overall, it will make very little difference in whether or not kids succeed in school.

$500 Internet Boxes

Later in 1996 you'll be seeing a slew of cheap Internet boxes—the "$500" Internet boxes you may have heard about. The theory is this: produce a box that allows people to connect to the Internet at a really low cost. The problem is this: you get what you pay for.

What won't these boxes do or have? Just take a look:

➤ They won't allow you to download shareware (because they don't have hard disks).

➤ They won't have good screens (although some will connect to a television).

➤ They won't let you use the software you want to use; you'll be limited to what you are given or whatever software you can run from your service provider's system (a subject I'll cover next).

➤ You won't be able to use the box for anything but connecting to the Internet. For example, you won't be able to install games from your local software store or track your household expenses. You really won't be able to do much at all except "cruise" the Internet. (Again, we're coming back to the misconception of what sort of person cruises the Internet: a mindless idiot who simply wants to be entertained by "cool" and "compelling" Web sites, and who doesn't actually want to *do* much. So why connect to the Internet when you can watch TV?)

Proponents of the $500 Internet box claim that you will be able to run whatever software you need directly over the Internet—that you won't need a hard disk. The important word there is *will*. Right now this is a pipe dream.

Software Over the Internet

Eventually, a lot of software will be purchased from the Internet. Why take software, package it in hardware (disk, cardboard, plastic wrapper, etc.), put it in a store, and have someone buy it there, just so he or she can take it home and load it? Why not just sell it over the Internet as an electronic product delivered electronically. Software can already be bought across the Internet: some sites sell software online, but it's often "light" or demo software (see the following figure). One day, however, that may be a primary form of software distribution.

may want to go back and make some changes to it. When you do, there are a few things you need to know.

Editing Embedded Stuff

When you want to make some changes to an embedded object, all you have to do is double-click on it in the destination document. This immediately opens the server application and places the object in it. (If you prefer a more tedious route, you can open the Edit menu and select Object.)

When you double-click on an embedded object, a window to the server application opens automatically.

Make any necessary changes to the object. When you're ready to return to the destination document, click outside the server application window. Sometimes you may have to close the server application by using the File menu and the Exit command.

Converting Embedded File Formats

What do you do when you've got a destination document full of embedded objects, and you don't have access to the original application that created the objects? Maybe a friend gave you the destination document to work with, but you don't have the programs that created the objects loaded on your computer. Are you up the river without a paddle?

No sweat. You simply convert the embedded object into a different file format. Open the destination document and select the object with which you want to work. Then open the Edit menu and choose the Object command at the very bottom of the menu list (the name of this command may vary slightly, depending on what Office program you're using). In the submenu that appears, select Convert. The Convert dialog box opens.

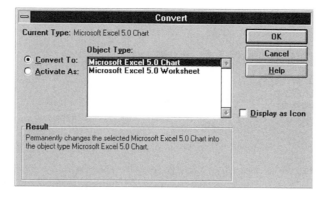

The Convert dialog box.

In the Object Type list, select the type of object to which you want to convert the embedded object. Click on the Convert To option button if you want to permanently change the object to the format you selected in the list box. Click on the Activate As option button if you want to temporarily change it to the selected object type. Click **OK**, and the conversion is completed. The next time you want to edit the embedded object, double-click on it, and it will open in the application you selected.

Here's my final prediction then: most of the predictions you hear about the Internet won't come to pass. (Not *my* predictions, of course; everything you read here is absolutely correct and most certainly *will* come to pass!) But all the wild predictions about how the Internet will create a new world—how "nothing will ever be the same," how it will bring about world peace (seriously, some people are predicting this) and a new form of electronic democracy, and so on—all this is nonsense.

How do I know that? Because all-encompassing, far-reaching predictions are *always* wrong. The Green Revolution was supposed to end world hunger, antibiotics were supposed to eradicate infectious diseases, and the PC was supposed to lead to fantastic increases in productivity. True, the Green Revolution *did* raise crop yields, we *did* eradicate smallpox, and the PC allows ordinary people to do things they wouldn't have been able to afford before (such as create professional-looking business documents). But we still have world hunger, infectious diseases seem to be making a comeback in the industrial world, and economists have been unable to find more than negligible gains in productivity that are attributable to the PC.

Me, a cynic? Why, yes!

The Least You Need to Know

➤ Progress on the Internet will slow down. Whereas most of the initial development was just waiting to happen, future gains will be more difficult.

➤ We're still at least five years away from widespread, low-cost fast Internet connections in North America.

➤ Intercast PC/TV is one way that the Internet (specifically the Web) can be merged with TV; but we're still waiting for high-speed connections.

➤ The Internet backlash is beginning: some businesses are no longer listening to the hype and are even, in some cases, "retreating" from the Internet.

➤ As the Internet opens borders, it will lead to fights over what may be distributed—and what may be said—across the Internet.

➤ Software will be more widely distributed across the Internet. However, we won't get rid of our hard disks and run programs over the Internet.

Part 4
Resources

Resources? You'll find reference information in this part of the book. I'll tell you where to find the software you need, which might include programs to help you on your travels around the Internet, games, print drivers, and unlimited other things. I'll also give you some background information about picking a service provider, in case you don't have Internet access yet or you want to find a new one.

You'll also find out what's on the CD that's bundled with this book and how to use the mail responder we've set up. And at the end of this part are a glossary of Internet terms and the Lycos Top 50 Yellow Pages, a directory of 50 interesting Web sites you should visit.

All the Software You'll Ever Need

In This Appendix

➤ Finding software at the online services

➤ Finding the browsers

➤ Macintosh, Windows, and UNIX software libraries

➤ Plug-ins and viewers

➤ Demos and drivers

You've read about a lot of software in this book, and there's much more that hasn't been mentioned. Literally thousands of shareware, freeware, and demoware programs for the Macintosh, Windows 3.1, Windows 95, Windows NT, and all flavors of UNIX are available for you to download and use. "Where are they?" you ask. "How do I find all these programs?" It's easy to find software once you know where to look.

Different Types of Software

Shareware is software that is given away for free, but which you are supposed to register (for a fee) if you decide to continue using it. *Freeware* is software that is given away with no fee required. *Demoware* is software that is generally free, but is intended to get you interested in buying the "full" program.

The Search Starts at Home

You can always begin looking at home. If you use one of the online services, you'll find stacks of software within the service itself; no need to go out onto the Internet. All the online services have Internet-related forums (or BBSs, or areas, or whatever they call them). They are good places to begin, and you can usually download the software more quickly from there than from the Internet. In addition, many online services have forums set up by software vendors and shareware forums. These are good places to get to know, too.

If you are with a true Internet service provider, you'll often find that your service has a file library somewhere. The library will have a smaller selection than the online services do, but it's a good place to start nonetheless.

The Software Mentioned

I've mentioned two programs in particular—Netscape Navigator and Internet Explorer—that you need to know how to find. You may already have one or the other of these. Many online services and service providers already provide one of them in the software package you get when you sign up. In addition, the Windows version of Internet Explorer is included on the CD at the back of this book (see Appendix C). But if you want to try Netscape or another version of Explorer, or if you simply want to get the very latest version, go to one of these sites:

> Netscape Navigator: **http://www.netscape.com/**

> Internet Explorer: **http://www.msn.com/ie/**

I've mentioned dozens of other programs throughout this book. Most of those programs can be found at the sites I discuss next.

The Internet's Software Libraries

The Internet is full of wonderful software libraries that are based on either FTP or Web servers. Check out some of the following sites, but remember that there are more, which you can find using the links mentioned in the section "Finding More," later in this appendix.

The University of Texas Mac Archive (Macintosh)

You can go to **http://wwwhost.ots.utexas.edu/mac/main.html** to find a good library of Macintosh software. It's not huge, but it's well-organized and helps you find the most important programs.

Info-Mac HyperArchive (Macintosh)

This is a large collection of Macintosh software at MIT (**http://hyperarchive.lcs.mit.edu/ HyperArchive.html**). It contains lots of files, but it's not very easy to work with.

The Ultimate Macintosh Site (Macintosh and Apple)

You'll find lots of information about the Mac, along with software, at the **http://www. velodrome.com/umac.html** Web site. You'll find links to Apple shareware sites, too.

TUCOWS (Windows)

TUCOWS, which stands for The Ultimate Collection of Winsock Software, is a large library of Windows software (for Windows 3.1, 95, and NT). Go to the **http:// www.tucows.com/** page (shown in the following figure).

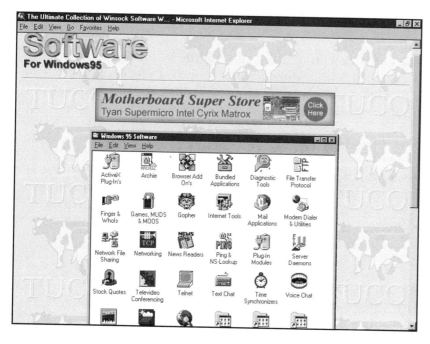

The TUCOWS site is an excellent place to find all sorts of useful Windows software.

The Consummate Winsock App Page (Windows)

Another excellent Windows software archive is at the **http://www.cwsapps.com/** Web site.

Winsite (Windows)

You can find another good Windows archive at the **http://www.winsite.com/** Web site or at the **ftp.winsite.com** FTP site.

Turning an Excel Range into a Word Table

Here's something interesting. When you copy a range of cells from Excel and paste them into a Word document, they automatically appear as a Word table. How about that? The text retains the formatting you gave it in Excel, but you can easily edit the data at any time when it's in Word.

To copy a range of cells from Excel, open the Excel worksheet containing the cells you want to copy. Select the range, and then click on the **Copy** button in the toolbar, or open the Edit menu and select Copy. Open the Word document to which you want to copy the cell data, and click in the place where you want the data to appear. Finally, open the Edit menu and select **Paste**, or click on the **Paste** button on the toolbar. The Excel range suddenly appears in your Word file as a table.

You can select the data for editing and use the Word calculation features to change it, but you cannot use the original Excel formulas any longer to change your data. Why? Because you used a regular copy and paste technique instead of a link.

Embedding and Linking an Excel Chart into Word

When you embed a chart into Word, you can still use the Excel features to control the way it looks, and you can still use its formulas and other calculations. To embed a chart, open the Excel file containing the chart you want to embed, select the chart, and select the Edit Copy command. (If you prefer, you can click on the **Copy** button on the toolbar.)

Then open the Word document and click where you want to embed the chart. Open the Edit menu and choose Paste Special. The Paste Special dialog box appears. Click on the Paste option. In the As list box, select the **Object** type, and then click **OK**. The chart appears in your Word document. To make changes to it, simply double-click on it. This opens the chart in an Excel window where you can apply all of the Excel tools.

If you link the range of cells into your Word document, you still have an active connection to the original formulas. To link the range of cells, open the Word document into which you want to paste the range, pull down the Edit menu, and choose Paste Special. The Paste Special dialog box appears. To link the range, just click on the Paste Link option button.

Inserting an Entire Worksheet into Word

You can insert an entire spreadsheet into your Word document if you want. To do so, open the Word document and click where you want to place the spreadsheet. Open the Insert menu and choose Object. In the Object dialog box, click on the Create from File tab to bring it to the front.

Using the **Directories** list box and the File **Name** list box, select the Excel file that you want to insert. Click **OK**, and the entire file is inserted into your Word document. To link the entire spreadsheet to Word, click on the Link to File check box in the Object dialog box.

Make a Worksheet Without Leaving Word

Hey, did you know you can create a spreadsheet without ever leaving your Word file? Want to know how? Use the OfficeLinks technology. First, in your Word document, click where you want to place the worksheet. Click on the **Insert Microsoft Excel Worksheet** button on the standard toolbar, and a drop-down diagram of columns and rows appears. In the diagram, drag over the number of columns and rows you want to use, and then release the mouse button.

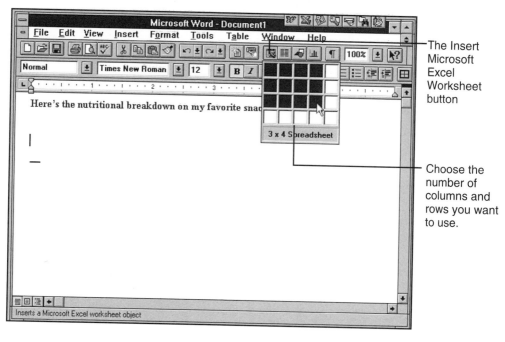

The Insert Microsoft Excel Worksheet button

Choose the number of columns and rows you want to use.

I'll bet you didn't know Word came with an automatic worksheet maker.

295

Looking for Something Strange?

If you're looking for a program that you simply can't find at the popular software libraries, remember that you can always search for it using the techniques discussed in Chapter 19. It's amazing what those search sites can turn up sometimes! So if you're looking for something really obscure that the average library doesn't hold, don't give up too soon. You can even try Archie (see Chapter 13) to search for a file at an FTP site if you have a good idea of the file name.

The Least You Need to Know

➤ You can find thousands of programs for Windows, the Mac, and UNIX, scattered around the Internet.

➤ If you use an online service, start there. It's generally quicker to download from "home."

➤ There are a number of good software archives, such as TUCOWS, shareware.com, Jumbo, The University of Texas Mac Archive, The Ultimate Macintosh Site, Winsite, and so on.

➤ A number of sites hold only plug-ins and viewers.

➤ Don't forget demos and drivers—commercial software that's often very useful.

➤ You can also search the Web search sites or Archie to find more.

Finding a Service Provider

If you are reading this, either you don't have a service provider, or you are considering changing the one you have. Let's deal with the first major question: which is the best Internet service provider?

I Want the Best! Where Do I Get It?

Ah, so you want the best Internet account you can get. Well, if that's the case, be prepared to empty your bank account. You're going to need a special high-speed line from the phone company, a fast computer with special hardware to connect it to that line, a system administrator to set it up and maintain it ...and on and on.

But for the rest of us, the ordinary Joe or Jane who wants to get hooked up to the Internet, what's the best way to do it? There's no easy answer to that, unfortunately. It's rather like asking "who makes the best spouse?" Needless to say, everyone has a different answer. A service that you think is good might prove to be a lousy choice for someone else.

Basically, what you need to do is pick a service provider that is cheap, helpful, and has a reliable and fast connection to the Internet and easy-to-install software. Of course, that's very difficult to find. I've had Internet accounts with a couple of dozen providers, and I haven't found one yet that I would rave about. They've ranged from pretty good to absolutely awful.

What's a Reasonable Cost?

Internet accounts vary quite a bit in cost. You might want to start out with an online service; there's no sign-up fee, and you'll probably get a trial period of 10 hours or so free. After that, it will cost approximately $10/month for the first five hours and $2.95 for each additional hour. Other plans might run, for example, $20 a month for 20 hours and $2.95 for each hour after that. Online service prices have dropped dramatically in the past year, partly because of the introduction of a new low-cost online service (The Microsoft Network) and partly in response to the low charges of the Internet service providers.

Check This Out...

It's Getting Better There's a trend toward flat-fee services right now. Although there are many "by-the-hour" services, as the flat-fee services become more reliable and promote their products more, there'll be a lot of pressure on the by-the-hour services to switch to flat fee.

Service providers are usually cheaper, but they might charge a sign-up fee ($25 to $50), and they generally don't offer a free trial period (though some do give a few hours away). Rates usually average approximately $1 an hour: $10.95 for the first ten hours and $1.25 per hour, for instance. Some offer "unlimited" access for a flat fee that might range from $19.95 to $24.95 a month. This enables you to use as many hours as you want for a set fee. (You're probably wary of the quotation marks around the word *unlimited*. In many cases, the service is unlimited only if you can actually get into it, and the busy signals may often thwart your attempts.)

Tips for Picking a Provider

Consider the following guidelines when you're trying to find an Internet service provider:

➤ The major online services often make it very easy to connect to the Internet: you just run the setup program, and away you go.

➤ On the other hand, the major online services are expensive (though their prices are dropping rapidly). Some of them also have a reputation for having very slow and unreliable connections to the Internet.

➤ There are a lot of low-priced Internet service providers (in Colorado, for example, there are about 70), and the competition is stiff!

➤ Unfortunately, many low-priced services have customer service that matches their prices: they are often not very helpful. To work on those services, you need more than a little of the geek gene inside you.

➤ On the other hand, some of these services are very good and will help you hook up to the Internet at a very good price.

➤ A number of large national Internet service providers—such as WorldNet (owned by AT&T), EarthLink, and PSINet—often have very good prices ($20–25 a month for unlimited usage, for instance). In addition, in some areas, they might even have good service.

➤ Many small service providers also advertise "unlimited" access to the Internet for a flat fee. They are less likely to live up to the unlimited promise than are the big networks.

➤ There are no hard and fast rules! A service that is very good in one area may be lousy in another.

If you don't have an Internet account yet, but you want to find one, I can help. I'm going to give you a few ideas for tracking down service providers. In addition to that, you should see Appendix C, in which you'll learn about what's on the CD at the back of this book.

Finding a Service Provider

Here are a few ways to track down service providers:

➤ Look in your local paper's computer section; local service provider's often advertise there.

➤ Look in your city's local computer publication for ads.

➤ Check the Yellow Pages' "Internet" category.

➤ Ask at your local computer store.

➤ Check for ads in one of the many new Internet-related magazines.

➤ Look in a general computer magazine (many of which *seem* to have turned into Internet magazines).

➤ Ask your friends and colleagues which local service providers are good (and which to avoid).

➤ If you know someone who has access to the World Wide Web, ask him to go to **http://www.yahoo.com/Business_and_Economy/Companies/Internet_Services/ Internet_Access_Providers/**. Or, better still, say "go to Yahoo and search for "**service provider**"; you may not know what that means, but the program probably will (check out Chapter 19 for more information). You'll find information about many service providers, and even some price comparisons.

Find a Free-Net

You might also want to look for a *Free-Net*. These are community computing systems. They might be based at a local library or college, and you can dial into the system from your home computer. And, as the name implies, they don't cost anything. (Well, some may have a small registration fee—$10, perhaps—but if it's not actually free, it's pretty close to it.)

Free-Nets offer a variety of local services, as well as access to the Internet. You may be able to find information about jobs in the area, or about local events and recreation. You may be able to search the local library's database, find course schedules for local colleges, or ask someone questions about social security and Medicare.

Free-Nets usually have a "menu" of options based on a simulated "town." There may be a Community Center, Teen Center, and Senior Center, for example. In addition, there might even be an Administration Building (where you can go to register your account on the Free-Net), a Social Services and Organizations Center (where you can find support groups and local chapters of national organizations such as the Red Cross), and a Home and Garden Center (where you can find out about pest control). There might even be a Special Interests Center, where you can chat about UFOs, movies, religion, travel, or anything else. And Free-Nets also have a system that lets you send messages to other users.

Free-Net or Freenet? You'll see the terms Free-Net, freenet, and FreeNet, and maybe even some other variations. All of these terms are service marks of NPTN (National Public Telecommuting Network), which prefers to use the term Free-Net. Note that some community computing systems, while not under the "umbrella" of the NPTN, still serve the same purpose as a true Free-Net.

Even without Internet links, Free-Nets are a great community resource, especially for home-bound people such as the elderly and handicapped. However, they have serious limitations. Not all Free-Nets will provide full access to the Internet. For security reasons, some may limit certain services. For instance, they may not want you to use FTP to bring possibly virus-laden files into their systems. And Free-Nets are often very busy and difficult to connect to.

Most importantly, they are generally dial-in terminal connections, or shell accounts. You probably won't be able to use the fancy graphical software that makes the Internet so easy to use.

If you still want to find a Free-Net or other form of free access in your area, e-mail **info@nptn.org** or call the NPTN (National Public Telecommuting Network) at 216-247-5800. Check the local computer paper, and ask at local computer stores (not the big chains, but the mom-and-pop type computer stores staffed by people who actually know what they are selling!).

Equipment You Will Need

You're going to need the following items to connect to the Internet:

➤ A computer

➤ A modem

➤ A phone line

➤ Software

Which computer? You know the story, the faster the better; the more RAM the better. Ideally, you need a computer that will run the nice graphical software, of which there are hundreds of programs for Windows and the Macintosh. If you don't have a computer that will run this sort of software, you can still access the Internet, but you'll have to use a dial-in terminal (shell) account.

A modem takes the digital signals from your computer and converts them to the analog signals that your phone line uses. You plug the phone line into the modem, and if it's an external modem, you plug the computer into the modem, too. (If it's an internal modem, you install it in a slot inside your computer, and the phone line connects to the edge of the card.)

When buying a modem, remember the rule of "the faster the better." Most service providers have 28,800bps connections these days, which is what you should go for also. You can buy a good 28,800bps modem for $150 to $200. If that's too much, consider a 14,400bps modem. You can get one of these for around $80.

Don't buy a modem from the *Acme Modem and Hiking Shoe Company* (or from any of the other hundreds of budget modem makers). Anyone can build and sell a modem; however, building a *good* modem is difficult. Modems are complicated things, and the cheap generic modems often do not connect reliably. Buy a modem from one of the well-known modem companies, such as US Robotics, Hayes, Practical Peripherals,

You Can Only Be So Tight
If you think $80(ish) for a 14,400bps modem is too much, you need to think long and hard before getting a slower modem. Even a 14,400bps modem will feel sluggish; anything less will be unbearable. (Actually, it's difficult to buy a *new* modem that is slower than 14,400, but you might find one second-hand—and you might regret your decision if you buy it.)

or MegaHertz. (Look in a computer magazine, and you'll soon see which modems are being sold by most of the mail-order companies.)

You Want Something Faster

Yes, there are faster connections …for some of us. The following sections give a quick rundown of other possible types of connection that might be available in your area.

ISDN

This is an old Botswanan acronym for "Yesterday's Technology Tomorrow—Perhaps." Okay, seriously, ISDN phone lines are fast digital phone lines. This technology has been around for years, but the U.S. phone companies, in their infinite wisdom, figured that we really didn't need it. Of course, now they are scrambling to provide it, spurred on by the increasing number of people that use the Internet. Still, in some areas, if you call the local phone company and ask if you can have an ISDN line, you might hear something like "Sure, move to Germany."

Don't bother to get an ISDN line until you find a service provider who also has an ISDN connection; currently most don't. You'll be charged at both ends, by the phone company (who will charge to install and maintain the line) and the service provider (who will charge extra for the privilege of connecting to the Internet with it).

Check This Out…

ISDN Modem An ISDN modem is not really a modem. The word "modem" is a contraction of two words "modulate" and "demodulate," which are the terms for the processes of converting digital signals to and from analog phone signals. Although they're called ISDN "modems," the signals are digital all the way; there's no modulating and demodulating there.

Not surprisingly, prices are all over the place. To use ISDN, you'll need a special *ISDN modem*, as they're known. That'll cost around $400–600, less soon. Then you pay the phone company to install the line (between $0 and $600—don't ask me how they figure out these prices), and you'll pay a monthly fee of $25 to $130.

T1 Line

You could install this special type of digital phone line. It would be about 10 times faster than ISDN, but it would cost you a couple of thousand dollars. Although this is okay for small businesses who really need fast access to the Internet (very few really do), it's out of the price range of most individuals.

Satellite

You can connect to the Internet through a satellite dish. It would cost around $1,100 to install and $30 a month to maintain. The connection should be about 3–4 times faster than ISDN.

Cable

The cable companies have been promising Internet access for some time, even running ads implying that they were *already* providing Internet access. And one day they just might. But for the moment, don't hold your breath, or you'll turn blue long before you connect to the Internet via cable. It will be several years before Internet access is widely available through cable.

When this does become available, it will probably be about four times faster than ISDN— perhaps faster later on. It will probably cost $300–500 to install and $30 a month or so to maintain.

ADSL

This may be our best hope. It's a new telephone technology due to be introduced in some areas late in 1996. It will be very fast—perhaps even faster than cable—at approximately 10 times the speed of an ISDN line. Costs should be comparable to cable. Let's keep our fingers crossed.

For now, however, most of us are stuck with modems. With luck, they're 28,800bps modems, which are slow but affordable.

What's on the CD?

You can find additional information related to this book in two forms: a CD and a mail responder.

As you've probably noticed, this book has a CD bundled with it. (You *haven't* noticed? Look in the insert at the back of the book.) There is also an e-mail responder that will automatically send you chapters from the first edition of *The Complete Idiot's Guide to the Internet* or a chapter from *The Complete Idiot's Next Step with the Internet*, in response to a special message from you. (I'll explain the details in a moment.)

The Compact Disc

The CD contains both books and software. Here's what you'll find on the disc:

Free MCI Internet Kit (for Windows 95)

The Complete Idiot's Guide to the Internet, First Edition

The Complete Idiot's Guide to Creating an HTML Web Page

The Complete Idiot's Guide to JavaScript

The Microsoft Internet Explorer 3.0 Web browser (for Windows 95)

The Microsoft Internet Explorer 2.0.1 (for the Macintosh)

About the First Edition

Why did we put the first edition of this book on the CD? The book you are reading is completely different from the first edition. Back in 1993 when the first edition was written, most people were using the command-line interface to work with the Internet. Now most are using some kind of graphical user interface. But because some people are still stuck at the command line, we've bundled the first edition so that these people can get to all the funky little UNIX commands they're going to need.

The Books

We've put three books on the CD: *The Complete Idiot's Guide to the Internet, First Edition, The Complete Idiot's Guide to Creating an HTML Web Page,* and *The Complete Idiot's Guide to JavaScript*. These are all in HTML format, which means you'll be able to read them using your Web browser. Here's how to open these books.

1. Insert the disk into the disk drive. (If you are using Windows 95 and your CD drive is set up to automatically run when a CD is installed, you'll see a screen asking if you want to install the internetMCI software. Click **No**.)

2. Open your Web browser, and select the command used to open files on your hard disk. (In Internet Explorer choose File, Open, then click on the Browse button. In Netscape choose File, Open File.)

3. On the CD drive, open the CIGBOOKS directory.

4. You'll find three directories within this directory: INTERNET (*The Complete Idiot's Guide to the Internet First Edition*), HTML (*The Complete Idiot's Guide to Creating an HTML Web Page*), and JSCRIPT (*The Complete Idiot's Guide to JavaScript*). Open the one you want.

5. Then open the INTERNET.HTM, HTML.HTM, or JSCRIPT.HTM file.

The Software

The software on the CD is in Windows 95 format. There's a single installation program that loads the internetMCI software and Internet Explorer.

The internetMCI service provides low-cost Internet access through more than 300 phone numbers across the U.S.A. (More numbers and access in other countries will be available soon, perhaps by the time you read this.) The service also has 800-number access, but be warned that there's a $5.95/hour fee for using the 800 numbers.

You'll get 30 days of free Internet access through internetMCI when you install the software on the CD. You'll be able to work on the Internet for a full 30 days. If you want to continue working with internetMCI after your free 30 days, you'll pay $19.95 a month for unlimited access; you can use as many hours as you want. And finally, if you pay for two full months at the end of your 30-day free trial period, you'll get another 30 days free. You can find more information about internetMCI at http://www.mci.com. Once you've installed the software you'll find a link to the MCI site in your Favorites folder.

When you install the internetMCI software, Internet Explorer 3.0 is also installed on your system. Note that the software will run only on a Windows 95 system. (Sorry, there's no Windows 3.1 or Macintosh software on the CD.)

To install the MCI Internet Kit and Internet Explorer software, follow these instructions:

> **No Strings Attached** The internetMCI service is operated by MCI, the well-known telecommunications company. Note, however, that you do *not* have to be an MCI telephone customer in order to use internetMCI.

1. Place the CD into the CD drive. In some cases, depending on the version of Windows you are using and how your CD drive is configured, the CD will automatically load and display a window with installation instructions. If so, follow the instructions. If you don't see that window, continue to step 2.

2. Choose **Start**, **Settings**, **Control Panel**.

3. In the Control Panel double-click the **Add/ Remove Programs** icon. Click the **Install** button, then click the **Next** button.

4. If the **Setup.exe** file is displayed in a text box, click **Finish** to run the installation program. If setup.exe does not appear in the text box, click **Browse**, select the CD drive, and double-click **Setup.exe**. Then click **Finish** and follow the instructions.

Finding OWNWEB

I've created a Web page for you and put it on the CD. (This page is used in Chapter 8, and serves as a template for your own customized Web page.) This page is in a file called OWNWEB.HTM, and you can find it in the OWNWEB directory on the CD. Simply copy it from the CD to a directory on your hard disk.

The E-Mail Responder

If you are working with the command-line interface and are logging into your organization's or your service provider's system with some kind of terminal access, you're going to run into a *little* problem. There's a good chance you don't have a CD-ROM drive. So how are you going to get to the information on the CD that helps you work with UNIX commands? You'll use our e-mail responder, a special system that will send you a chapter at your request. Here's how to use the mail responder.

1. Send an e-mail message to **ciginternet@mcp.com**.

2. In the Subject line of the message, enter the appropriate command from the list below. When the e-mail responder receives your message, it automatically sends a message back to you containing the requested chapter.

3. When you receive the message, save it to your hard disk, and then open the chapter in a word processor or text editor.

Don't bother to include any text in the message. Your message will be received by a computer—not an actual person—and whatever you write in the body of the message won't be read anyway. (If you want to contact QUE, see the contact information at the front of this book.)

With the e-mail responder, you can receive any of the following chapters from the first edition of *The Complete Idiot's Guide to the Internet* by typing the appropriate command.

Chapter	Command
5 Let's Get Physical: What You Need to Get Started	physical
7 Your First Trip to the Internet	first
8 Menus and Shells, Oh My!	shells
9 A UNIX Survival Guide	unix
10 Please Mr. Postman: An Intro to E-mail	email
11 UNIX Mail: Down to the Nitty Gritty	unixmail

Chapter	Command
12 Still More on Mail	moremail
13 Return to Sender, Address Unknown	sender
14 Finding Folks with Fred and Whois	fred
14 & 15 (Both chapters 14 and 15 together)	who
15 Newsgroups: The Source of All Wisdom	wisdom
16 More on Newsgroups and Mailing Lists	maillist
15 & 16 (Both chapters)	news
17 Telnet: Inviting Yourself onto Other Systems	telnet
18 Grabbing the Goodies: Downloading Files with FTP	ftp
19 More Neato FTP Stuff	moreftp
18 & 19 (Both chapters)	allftp
20 Archie the File Searcher	archie
21 Digging Through the Internet with Gopher	gopher
22 Finding Your WAIS Around	wais
23 Think Global: World Wide Web	web

Finally, the disc includes the following chapter from *The Complete Idiot's Next Step with the Internet*, which contains information about Internet Relay Chat:

    1 Yak, Yak, Yak, Talking on the Net   irc

Speak Like a Geek: The Complete Archive

ActiveX   A new multimedia-authoring system for the World Wide Web, from Microsoft.

alias   A name that is substituted for a more complicated name, usually in an e-mail program. For example, you can use a simple alias (peterk) instead of a more complicated mailing address (peterk@lab-press.com) for a mailing list.

America Online (AOL)   A popular online information system.

anchor   A techie word for an HTML tag used as a link from one document to another.

anonymous FTP   A system by which members of the Internet "public" can access files at certain FTP sites without needing a login name; they simply log in as *anonymous*.

Archie   An index system that helps you find files in more than 1,000 FTP sites.

archive file   A file that contains other files (usually compressed files). It is used to store files that are not used often, or files that may be downloaded by Internet users.

ARPAnet   Where the Internet began. The Advanced Research Projects Agency (of the U.S. Department of Defense) computer network, which was the forerunner of the Internet.

article   A message in an Internet newsgroup.

ASCII   Stands for American Standard Code for Information Interchange, which is a standard system used by computers to recognize text. An ASCII text file comprises the letters of the alphabet, the punctuation characters, and a few special characters. The nice thing about ASCII is that it's recognized by thousands of programs and many different types of computers.

backbone   A network through which other networks connect.

bandwidth   Widely used to mean the amount of information that can be sent through a particular communications channel.

baud rate   A measurement of how quickly a modem transfers data. Although, strictly speaking, this is not the same as bps (bits per second), the two terms are often used interchangeably.

BBS   See *bulletin board system.*

beta test   A program test based on the premise that "this program is virtually finished, but because we need a little help smoothing out the rough edges, we'll give it to a few more people."

BITNET   The "Because It's Time" network (really!). A large network connected to the Internet. Before the Internet became affordable to learning institutions, BITNET was the network of choice for communicating.

bits per second (bps)   A measure of the speed of data transmission; the number of bits of data that can be transmitted each second.

bookmark   A URL that has been saved in some way so that you can quickly and easily return to a particular Web document.

bounce   The action of an e-mail message being returned because of some kind of error.

bps   See *bits per second.*

browser   A program that lets you read HTML documents and navigate around the Web.

BTW   An abbreviation for By The Way; it's commonly used in e-mail and newsgroup messages.

bulletin board system (BBS)   A computer system to which other computers can connect so their users can read and leave messages or retrieve and leave files.

cache   A place where a browser stores Web documents that have been retrieved. The cache may be on the hard disk, in memory, or a combination of the two. Documents you "return to" are retrieved from the cache, which saves transmission time.

CERN   The European Particle Physics Laboratory (CERN) in Switzerland is the original home of the World Wide Web.

chat   A system in which people can communicate by typing messages. Unlike e-mail messages, chat messages are sent and received as you type (like a real chat—only without the voice). The most popular Internet chat system is Internet Relay Chat. The best and most popular chat systems, however, are on the online services.

CIX   The Commercial Internet Exchange, an organization of commercial Internet service providers.

client   A program or computer that is "serviced" by another program or computer (the server). For instance, a Gopher client program requests information from the indexes of a Gopher *server* program.

compressed files   Computer files that have been reduced in size by a compression program. Such programs are available for all computer systems (for example, PKZIP in DOS and Windows, tar and compress in UNIX, and StuffIt and PackIt for the Macintosh).

CompuServe   A large online information service.

cracker   Someone who tries to enter a computer system without permission. This is the correct term, though the term *hacker* is often mistakenly used in its place.

CSLIP (Compressed SLIP)   See *Serial Line Internet Protocol (SLIP)*.

cyberspace   The "area" in which computer users travel when "navigating" around on a network or the Internet.

DARPANET   The Defense Advanced Research Projects Agency network, which was created by combining ARPAnet and MILNET. The forerunner of the Internet.

DDN   The Defense Data Network is a U.S. military network that is part of the Internet. MILNET is part of the DDN.

dedicated line   A telephone line that is leased from the telephone company and used for one purpose only. On the Internet, dedicated lines connect organizations to service providers' computers, providing dedicated service.

dedicated service   See *permanent connection*.

dial-in direct connection   An Internet connection that you access by dialing into a computer through a telephone line. Once connected, your computer acts as if it were an Internet host. You can run client software (such as Web browsers and FTP programs). This type of service is often called SLIP, CSLIP, or PPP. Compare to *dial-in terminal connection*.

dial-in service   A networking service that you can use by dialing into a computer through a telephone line.

dial-in terminal connection   An Internet connection that you can access by dialing into a computer through a telephone line. Once connected, your computer acts as if it were a terminal connected to the service provider's computer. This type of service is often called Interactive or dial-up. Compare to *dial-in direct connection*.

dialup service   A common Internet term for a dial-in terminal connection.

direct connection   See *permanent connection*.

DNS   See *Domain Name System*.

domain name   A name given to a host computer on the Internet.

Domain Name System (DNS)   A system by which one Internet host can find another so it can send e-mail, connect FTP sessions, and so on. The hierarchical system of Internet host names (***hostname.hostname.hostname***) uses the Domain Name System. The DNS, in effect, translates words into numbers that the Internet's computers can understand. For instance, if you use the domain name firefly.prairienet.org, DNS translates it into 192.17.3.3.

dot address   A term for an IP address, which is in the form ***n.n.n.n***, where each ***n*** is a number (and each number is a byte).

download   The process of transferring information from one computer to another. You download a file from another computer to yours. See also *upload*.

e-mail or email   Short for electronic mail, the system that lets people send and receive messages with their computers. The system might be on a large network (such as the Internet), on a bulletin board or online service (such as CompuServe), or over a company's own office network.

EARN   The European network associated with BITNET.

EFF   See *Electronic Frontier Foundation*.

EFLA   Extended Four Letter Acronym. Acronyms are essential to the well-being of the Internet. See *TLA*.

Electronic Frontier Foundation (EFF)   An organization interested in social, legal, and political issues related to the use of computers. The EFF is particularly interested in fighting government restrictions on the use of computer technology.

emoticon   The techie name for small symbols created using typed characters, such as *smileys*— :)

encryption   The modification of data so that unauthorized recipients cannot use or understand it.

etext   Electronic text: a book or other document in electronic form, usually simple ASCII text.

Ethernet   A protocol, or standard, by which computers may be connected to one another to exchange information and messages.

FAQ (Frequently Asked Questions)   A document containing a list of common questions and corresponding answers. You'll often find FAQs at Gopher sites, in newsgroups, and at FTP and Web sites.

Favorites   The term used by Internet Explorer for its *bookmark* list.

Fidonet   An important network that is also connected to the Internet. Well-known in geek circles.

file transfer   The copying of files from one computer to another over a network or telephone line. See *File Transfer Protocol*.

File Transfer Protocol   A *protocol* defining how files transfer from one computer to another. FTP programs transfer files across the Internet. You can also use FTP as a verb (often in lowercase) to describe the procedure of using FTP as in, "ftp to ftp.demon.co.uk," or "I ftp'ed to their system and grabbed the file."

Finger   A program used to find information about a user on a host computer.

flame   An abusive newsgroup message. Things you can do to earn a flame are to ask dumb questions, offend people, not read the FAQ, or simply get on the wrong side of someone with an attitude. When these things get out of control, a flame war erupts.

flamer   Someone who wrote a flame.

form   A Web form is a sort of interactive document. The document can contain fields into which readers can type information. This information may be used as part of a survey, to purchase an item, to search a database, and so on.

forms support   A Web browser that has forms support can work with a Web form. Not all browsers can use forms (most recent ones can, though).

forum   The term used by CompuServe for its individual bulletin boards or discussion groups. In Internet-speak, the term is *newsgroups*.

frames   Some Web pages are split into different frames (or panes); in effect, they create two or more independent subwindows within the main browser window.

Free-Net   A community computer network, often based on the local library, which provides Internet access to citizens from the library or (sometimes) from their home computers. Free-Nets also have many local services, such as information about local events, local message areas, connections to local government departments, and so on.

freeware   Software provided free by its creator. (It's not the same as *public domain* software, for which the author retains copyright.) See *shareware*.

FTP   See *File Transfer Protocol*.

gateway   A system by which two incompatible networks or applications can communicate with each other.

geek   Someone who knows a lot about computers, but very little about communicating with his fellow man—and, perhaps more importantly, with his fellow woman. (Vice versa if the geek happens to be a woman, although the majority of geeks are men.) Geeks spend more time in front of their computers than talking with real people. The term "geek" may have started as a derogatory term, but many geeks are proud of their geekness—and many have become very

315

rich because of it. As Dave Barry (who got rich before becoming a computer geek) once said, "I'm a happy geek in cyberspace, where nobody can see my haircut."

GEnie   An online service owned by General Electric.

Gopher   A system using Gopher *clients* and *servers* to provide a menu system used for navigating around the Internet. Most Web browsers can act as Gopher clients. Gopher was started at the University of Minnesota, which has a gopher as its mascot.

gopherspace   Anywhere and everywhere you can get to using Gopher is known as gopherspace.

GUI (Graphical User Interface)   Pronounced "goo-ey," this is a program that provides a user with onscreen tools such as menus, buttons, dialog boxes, a mouse pointer, and so on.

hacker   Someone who enjoys spending most of his life with his head stuck inside a computer, either literally or metaphorically. See *geek* and *cracker*.

helper   See *viewer*.

history list   A list of Web documents that you've seen in the current session (some browsers' history lists also show documents from previous sessions). You can return to a document by selecting it in the history list.

home page   1. The Web document your browser displays when you start the program. 2. A sort of "main page" at a Web site. (Personally, I don't like this second definition, but there's not much I can do about it.)

host   A computer connected directly to the Internet. A service provider's computer is a host, as are computers with permanent connections. Computers with *dial-in terminal connections* are not; they are terminals connected to the service provider's host. Computers with *dial-in direct connections* can be thought of as "sort of" hosts: they act like hosts while connected.

host address   See *IP address*.

host name   The name given to a *host*. Computers connected to the Internet really have *host numbers*, but host names are easier to remember and work with. A host name provides a simpler way to address a host than using a number.

host number   See *IP address*.

hotlist   A synonym for *bookmarks*, URLs of Web documents you want to save for future use. You can return to a particular document by selecting its bookmark from the hotlist.

HTML (HyperText Markup Language)   The basic coding system used to create Web documents.

HTTP (HyperText Transfer Protocol)   The data-transmission *protocol* used to transfer Web documents across the Internet.

hyperlink   See *link*.

hypermedia   Loosely used to mean a hypertext document that contains, or has links to, other types of media such as pictures, sound, video, and so on.

hypertext   A system in which documents contain links that allow readers to move between areas of the document, following subjects of interest in a variety of different paths. With most browsers, you use the mouse to click a link to follow the link. The World Wide Web is a hypertext system.

HYTELNET   A directory of Telnet sites. A great way to find out what you can do on hundreds of computers around the world.

IAB   See *Internet Architecture Board*.

IAP   Internet Access Provider; another term for service provider.

IETF   See *Internet Engineering Task Force*.

IMHO   An abbreviation for In My Humble Opinion, which is used in e-mail and newsgroup messages.

index document   A Web document that lets you search some kind of database.

index server   A special program, accessed through an index document, that lets you search some kind of database.

inline images   A picture inside a Web document. These graphics must be .GIF, .JPG, or .XBM format files, because those are the formats browsers can display.

Integrated Services Digital Network (ISDN)   A digital telecommunications system that everyone's been waiting for but that the telephone companies seem unable to get installed in a decent time. ISDN allows voice and data to be transmitted on the same line in a digital format—instead of the normal analog—and at a relatively high speed (about four times the speed of a fast modem).

interactive service   See *dial-in terminal connection*.

internet   Spelled with a small i, this refers to networks connected to one another. "The Internet" is not the only internet.

internet address   See *IP address*.

Internet Architecture Board (IAB)   The "council of elders" elected by **ISOC**; they get together and figure out how the different components of the Internet will all connect together.

Internet Engineering Task Force   A group of engineers that makes technical recommendations concerning the Internet to the IAB.

Internet Explorer   A Web browser from Microsoft. It's one of the two best browsers around, giving Netscape Navigator a run for its money.

Internet Protocol (IP)   The standard protocol used by systems communicating across the Internet. Other protocols are used, but the Internet Protocol is the most important one.

Internet Relay Chat (IRC)   A popular *chat* program. Internet users around the world can chat with other users in their choice of IRC channels.

Internet Society   The society that, to some degree, governs the Internet; it elects the Internet Architecture Board, which decides on technical issues related to how the Internet works.

InterNIC   The Internet Network Information Center. Run by the National Science Foundation, this provides various administrative services for the Internet.

IP   See *Internet Protocol*.

IP address   A 32-bit address that defines the location of a host on the Internet. Such addresses are normally shown as four bytes, each one separated by a period (for example, 192.156.196.1). See *dot address*.

IRC   See *Internet Relay Chat*.

ISDN   See *Integrated Services Digital Network*.

ISOC   See *Internet Society*.

ISP   An abbreviation for Internet Service Provider that's much loved in geekdom. See *service provider*.

Java   A new programming language from Sun Microsystems. Programmers can create programs that will run in any Java "interpreter," so a single program can run in multiple operating systems. There are now two browsers with built-in interpreters: Netscape Navigator and Internet Explorer.

JavaScript   A sort of subset of Java; JavaScript is a scripting language that's simpler to use than Java. Both Netscape Navigator and Internet Explorer can run JavaScripts.

JPEG   A compressed graphic format often found on the World Wide Web. These files use the .JPG or .JPEG extension.

Jughead   Jonzy's Universal Gopher Hierarchy Excavation And Display tool. A Gopher search tool that's similar to Veronica. The main difference between Veronica and Jughead is that Jughead searches a specific Gopher server whereas Veronica searches all of gopherspace.

KIS   See *Knowbot Information Service*.

Knowbot   A program that can search the Internet for requested information. Knowbots are in an experimental stage.

Knowbot Information Service (KIS)   An experimental system that helps you search various directories for a person's information (such as an e-mail address).

LAN   See *Local Area Network*.

leased line   See *dedicated line*.

link   A connection between two Web documents. Links are generally pieces of text or pictures that, when clicked, make the browser request and display another Web document.

linked image   An image that is not in a Web document (that's an inline image), but is "connected" to a document by a link. Clicking the link displays the image.

LISTSERV lists   *Mailing lists* that act as newsgroups (using *mail reflectors*). Messages sent to a LISTSERV address are sent to everyone who has subscribed to the list. Responses are sent back to the LISTSERV address.

Local Area Network (LAN)   A computer network that covers only a small area (often a single office or building).

log in   The procedure of *logging on*. Also sometimes used as a noun to mean the ID and password you use to log on.

logging off   The opposite of *logging on*; telling the computer that you've finished work and no longer need to use its services. The procedure usually involves typing a simple command, such as **exit** or **bye**.

logging on   Computer jargon for getting permission from a computer to use its services. A "logon" procedure usually involves typing in a username (also known as an account name or user ID) and a password. This procedure makes sure that only authorized people can use the computer. Also known as *logging in*.

lurker   Someone involved in *lurking*.

lurking   Reading newsgroup or LISTSERV messages without responding to them. Nobody knows you are there.

mail reflector   A mail address that accepts e-mail messages and then sends them on to a predefined list of other e-mail addresses. Such systems provide a convenient way to distribute messages to a group of people.

mail robot   An e-mail system that automatically carries out some sort of procedure for you.

mail server   1. A program that distributes computer files or information in response to e-mail requests. 2. A program that handles incoming e-mail for a host (as in *POP3's* mail server).

mailing list   A list of e-mail addresses to which a single message can be sent by entering just one name as the To address. Also refers to discussion groups based on the mailing list. Each message sent to the group is sent out to everyone on the list. (*LISTSERV* groups are mailing list groups.)

MB   Abbreviation for *megabyte*.

MCImail   An e-mail system owned by MCI.

megabyte   A measure of the quantity of data. A megabyte is a lot when you are talking about files containing simple text messages, but it's not much when you are talking about files containing color photographs.

The Microsoft Network   A major online service (the fastest growing service in history); it was launched in 1995 when Windows 95 was released. Also known as MSN.

MILNET   A U.S. Department of Defense network connected to the Internet.

MIME (Multipurpose Internet Mail Extensions)   A system that lets you send computer files as e-mail. Also used to identify file types on the Web.

mirror site   An FTP site that is a "mirror image" of another FTP site. Every so often, the contents of the other FTP site are copied to the mirror site. The mirror site provides an alternative location, so that if you can't get into the original site, you can go to one of the mirror sites.

modem   A device that converts digital signals from your computer into analog signals for transmission through a phone line (modulation), and converts the phone line's analog signals into digital signals your computer can use (demodulation). (So-called "ISDN modems" are not true modems; they don't modulate and demodulate.)

Mosaic   The first popular *GUI Web browser*, from the *NCSA*. This was the first graphical browser; some of the original Mosaic programmers helped to found Netscape Communications, the publisher of Netscape Navigator.

MPEG   A computer video format. With the right software and, in some cases, hardware, you can play MPEG video files on your computer.

MUD   A type of game popular on the Internet. MUD means Multiple User Dimensions, Multiple User Dungeons, or Multiple User Dialogue. MUDs are text games. Each player has a character; characters communicate with each other by the users typing messages.

navigate   Refers to "moving around" on the Web using a browser. When you jump to a Web document, you are navigating.

navigator   A program that helps you find your way around a complicated online service. Several navigator programs are available for CompuServe, for instance. Navigators can save you money by letting you prepare for many operations (such as writing mail) offline, and then go online quickly to perform the operations automatically.

NCSA (National Center for Supercomputing Applications)   The people who make the *Mosaic* World Wide Web browser.

netiquette   Internet etiquette, the correct form of behavior to use while working on the Internet and in USENET newsgroups. These guidelines can be summarized as "Don't waste computer resources, and don't be rude."

Netnews   See *USENET.*

Netscape Navigator   The Web's most popular browser, created by some old NCSA programmers who started a company called Netscape Communications.

Network Information Center   A system providing support and information for a network.

Network News Transfer Protocol (NNTP)   A system used for the distribution of USENET newsgroup messages.

newbie   A new user. The term may be used to refer to a new Internet user, or a user who is new to a particular area of the Internet. Since everyone and his dog is getting onto the Internet, these loathsome creatures have brought the general tone of the Internet down a notch or two, upsetting long-term Internet users who thought the Internet was their own personal secret.

news server   A computer that collects newsgroup data and makes it available to *newsreaders.*

newsgroup   The Internet equivalent of a BBS or discussion group (or "forum" in CompuServe-speak) in which people leave messages for others to read. See *LISTSERV lists.*

newsreader   A program that helps you find your way through a newsgroup's messages.

NIC   See *Network Information Center.*

NNTP   See *Network News Transfer Protocol.*

NOC   Network Operations Center, a group that administers a network.

node   A computer "device" connected to a computer network. That device might be an actual computer, or something else—a printer or router, for instance.

NREN   The National Research and Education Network.

NSF   National Science Foundation; the U.S. government agency that runs the NSFNET.

NSFNET   The National Science Foundation network, a large network connected to the Internet.

online   Connected. You are online if you are working on your computer while it is connected to another computer. Your printer is online if it is connected to your computer and ready to accept data. (Online is often written "on-line," though the non-hyphenated version seems to be gaining acceptance these days.)

online service   A commercial service (such as *CompuServe, The Microsoft Network*, and *America Online*) that provides electronic communication services. Users can join discussion groups, exchange e-mail, download files, and so on. Most such services now have Internet access, too.

packet   A collection of data. See *packet switching*.

Packet InterNet Groper (PING)   A program that tests whether a particular host computer is accessible to you.

packet switching   A system that breaks transmitted data into small *packets* and transmits each packet (or package) independently. Each packet is individually addressed, and may even travel over a route different from that of other packets. The packets are combined by the receiving computer.

permanent connection   A connection to the Internet using a leased line. The computer with a permanent connection acts as a host on the Internet. This type of service is often called *direct, permanent direct*, or *dedicated service*, and is very expensive to set up and run. However, it provides a very fast high *bandwidth* connection. A company or organization can lease a single line and then allow multiple employees or members to use it to access the Internet at the same time.

permanent direct   See *permanent connection*.

PING   See *Packet InterNet Groper*.

plug-in   A special type of *viewer* for a *Web browser*. A plug-in plays or displays a particular file type within the browser's window. (A viewer is a completely separate program.)

point of presence   Jargon meaning a method of connecting to a service locally (without dialing long distance). If a service provider has a POP in, say, Podunk, Ohio, people in that city can connect to the service provider by making a local call.

Point-to-Point Protocol   A method for connecting computers to the Internet via telephone lines; similar to *SLIP*, though a preferred, and these days more common, method.

POP   See *point of presence* and *Post Office Protocol*.

port   Generally, "port" refers to the hardware through which computer data is transmitted; the plugs on the back of your computer are ports. On the Internet, "port" often refers to a particular application. For instance, you might telnet to a particular port on a particular host. The port is actually an application.

Post Office Protocol (POP)   A system for letting hosts get e-mail from a server. This is typically used when a dial-in direct host (which may only have one user and may only be connected to the Internet periodically) gets its e-mail from a service provider. The latest version of POP is POP3. Do not confuse this with point of presence (POP).

posting   A message (article) sent to a newsgroup, or the act of sending such a message.

postmaster   The person at a host who is responsible for managing the mail system. If you need information about a user at a particular host, you can send e-mail to **postmaster@hostname**.

PPP   See *Point-to-Point Protocol*.

Prodigy   An online service founded by Sears.

protocol   A set of rules that defines how computers transmit information to each other, allowing different types of computers and software to communicate with each other.

public domain software   Software that does not belong to anyone. You can use it without payment, and even modify it if the source code is available. See *shareware* and *freeware*.

RealAudio   A well-known streaming audio format.

reflector, mail   A kind of public mailing list. Messages sent to a mail reflector's address are then sent automatically to a list of other addresses.

reload (or refresh)   A command that tells your browser to retrieve a Web document even though you have it in the cache.

remote login   A BSD (Berkeley) UNIX command (rlogin) that is similar to Telnet.

rendered   An HTML document has been "rendered" when it is displayed in a Web browser. The browser renders it into a normal text document. You don't see the codes, just the text that the author wants you to see. An unrendered document is the source HTML document (with codes and all).

rlogin   See *remote login*.

rot13 (Rotation 13)   A method used to "encrypt" messages in newsgroups so that you can't stumble across an offensive message. If you want to read an offensive message, you'll have to decide to do so—and go out of your way to decode it.

router   A system used to transmit data between two computer systems or networks using the same protocol. For instance, a company that has a permanent connection to the Internet will use a router to connect its computer to a leased line. At the other end of the leased line, a router is used to connect it to the service provider's network.

RTFM   Abbreviation for (Read the F***ing Manual), which is often used in reaction to a stupid question (or in response to a question which, in the hierarchy of nebwies and long-term Internet users, is determined to be a stupid question).

Serial Line Internet Protocol (SLIP)   A method for connecting a computer to the Internet using a telephone line and modem. (See *dial-in direct connection*.) Once connected, the user has the same services provided to the user of a permanent connection. See *Point-to-Point Protocol*.

server   A program or computer that services another program or computer (the *client*). For instance, a Gopher server program sends information from its indexes to a Gopher client program.

service provider   A company that provides a connection to the Internet.

shareware   Software that is freely distributed, but for which the author expects payment from people who decide to keep and use it. See *freeware* and *public domain software*.

shell account   Another name for a simple *dial-in terminal* account.

signature   A short piece of text transmitted with an e-mail or newsgroup message. Some systems can attach text from a file to the end of a message automatically. Signature files typically contain detailed information on how to contact someone: name and address, telephone numbers, Internet address, CompuServe ID, and so on—or some strange little quote or poem.

Simple Mail Transfer Protocol (SMTP)   A *protocol* used to transfer e-mail between computers on a network.

SLIP   See *Serial Line Internet Protocol*.

smiley   A symbol in e-mail and newsgroup messages used to convey emotion or simply for amusement. Originally the term referred to a symbol that seems to "smile," but the term now seems to refer to just about any small symbol created with text characters. You create smileys by typing various keyboard characters. For example, **:-(** means sadness. Smileys are usually sideways: turn your head to view the smiley. The correct term for a smiley is *emoticon*.

SMTP   See *Simple Mail Transfer Protocol*.

source document   An HTML document; the basic ASCII file that is rendered by a browser.

stack   See *TCP/IP stack*.

streaming   In the old days, if you transferred an audio or video file, you had to wait for it to be transferred to your computer completely before you could play it. Streaming audio and video formats allow the file to play while it's being transferred.

tags   The codes inside an HTML file.

talk   A program that lets two or more Internet users type messages to each other. As a user types a character, that character is immediately transmitted to the other user. There are several common talk programs: talk, ntalk, and YTalk. Similar to *chat*, though chat systems are intended as "meeting places," while talk programs are "private."

tar files   Files *compressed* using the UNIX tape archive program. Such files usually have file names ending in .tar.

TCP/IP (Transmission Control Protocol/Internet Protocol)   A set of *protocols* (communications rules) that control how data transfers between computers on the Internet.

TCP/IP stack   The software you must install before you can run TCP/IP programs across a dial-in direct connection. You might think of the TCP/IP stack as an Internet driver. In the same way you need a printer driver to send something from your word processor to your printer, you need the TCP/IP stack to send information to (and receive information from) your dial-in direct programs.

Telnet   A program that lets Internet users log in to computers other than their own host computers, often on the other side of the world. Telnet is also used as a verb, as in "telnet to debra.doc.ca."

telneting   Internet-speak for using Telnet to access a computer on the network.

TLA (Three Letter Acronym)   An acronym for an acronym. What would we do without them? See *EFLA*.

tn3270   A Telnet-like program used for remote logins to IBM mainframes.

Trojan Horse   A computer program that appears to carry out a useful function but which is actually designed to do harm to the system on which it runs. See *virus*.

UNIX   A computer operating system. Many—probably most—hosts connected to the Internet run UNIX.

upload   The process of transferring information from one computer to another. You upload a file from your computer to another. See *download*.

URL (Universal Resource Locator)   A Web "address."

USENET   The "User's Network," a large network connected to the Internet. The term also refers to the *newsgroups* distributed by this network.

UUCP   UNIX to UNIX copy program, a system by which files can be transferred between UNIX computers. The Internet uses UUCP to provide a form of e-mail, in which the mail is placed in files and transferred to other computers.

UUCP network   A network of UNIX computers connected to the Internet.

UUDECODE   If you use UUENCODE to convert a file to ASCII and transmit it, you'll use UUDECODE to convert the ASCII file back to its original format.

UUENCODE   The name given a program used to convert a computer file of any kind (sound, spreadsheet, word processing, or whatever) into an ASCII file so that it can be transmitted as a text message. The term is also used as a verb, as in "uuencode this file." There are DOS, Windows, UNIX, and Macintosh UUENCODE programs. In Windows, there's a program called Wincode that can UUENCODE and UUDECODE files.

VBScript   A scripting language from Microsoft, which is similar in concept to *JavaScript*.

Veronica   The Very Easy Rodent-Oriented Net-wide Index to Computerized Archives, a very useful program for finding things in *gopherspace*.

viewer   A program that displays or plays computer files that you find on the Web. For instance, you need a viewer to play video files you find. These are sometimes known as *helpers*.

virus   A program that uses various techniques for duplicating itself and traveling between computers. Viruses vary from simple nuisances (they might display an unexpected message on your screen) to serious problems that can cause millions of dollars' worth of damage (such as crashing a computer system and erasing important data).

Voice-On-the-Net   Also known as VON, this is a new service by which you can talk to other Internet users. You need a sound card, microphone, speakers, and the right software; then you can make Internet "phone calls." They're warbly, but very cheap.

VT100   The product name of a Digital Equipment Corporation computer terminal (DEC). This terminal is a standard that is emulated (simulated) by many other manufacturers' terminals.

W3   See *World Wide Web*.

WAIS   See *Wide Area Information Server*.

Web   Pertaining to the *World Wide Web*.

Web server   A program that makes *Web* documents available to browsers. The browser asks the server for the document, and the server transmits it to the browser.

Web site   A collection of *Web* documents about a particular subject on a host.

Webspace   The area of cyberspace in which you are traveling when working on the *Web*.

White Pages   Lists of Internet users.

Whois   A UNIX program used for searching for information about Internet users.

Wide Area Information Server (WAIS)   A system that can search databases on the Internet for information in which you are interested.

Winsock   A *TCP/IP stack* for Microsoft Windows.

World Wide Web   A hypertext system that allows users to "travel through" linked documents, following any chosen route. World Wide Web documents contain topics that, when selected, lead to other documents.

WWW   See *World Wide Web*.

X.500   A standard for electronic directory services.

XBM   X Bitmap graphics format, a bitmap from the UNIX X Window system. These are simple images, one of only three types that can be used as inline graphics; the others are .GIF and .JPG.

The Lycos Top 50 Yellow Pages

The following is an excerpt from *Most Popular Web Sites: The Best of the Net from A2Z*, published by Lycos Press. Note that because of the ever-changing nature of the Internet and the World Wide Web, some of the Web pages mentioned in this section might no longer be available when you look for them.

ARTS & HUMANITIES

American Institute of Architects

http://www.aia.org/

The American Institute of Architects is a professional association that serves to foster communication between architects and the general public. This site offers information on the AIA's mission, history, and membership benefits. Find also tips on selecting an architect, careers in architecture, and K-12 classroom resources.

Ancient History Bulletin

http://137.122.12.15/Docs/
Directories/AHB/AHB.html

This quarterly publication contains scholarly articles covering ancient history and related topics such as the study of age-old manuscripts, currency, and inscriptions. This site offers access to indexed volumes, previews of pieces to be published, and information about submitting articles for consideration.

Architecture & Architectural Sculpture of the Mediterranean Basin

http://www.ncsa.uiuc.edu/SDG/
Experimental/anu-art-history/
architecture.html

Features classical and Hellenistic architecture of the Mediterranean basin in this collection of research images.

Visitors will find architecture and architectural sculpture from the preclassical period to the 19th century.

Bethany Christian Services

http://www.bethany.org/

The protection of the lives of children and families is the goal of this Christian organization. The site describes the group's mission and provides links to related Internet sites.

CLA Home Page

http://cla-net.cla.umn.edu/
noframe.htm

The home page of the College of Liberal Arts (CLA) at the University of Minnesota is maintained at this site. Visitors can obtain information about the College's academics, administration, departments and programs, read CLA and University of Minnesota publications, or link to the Colleges FTP site.

ExploraNet

http://www.exploratorium.edu/

San Francisco's Exploratorium houses a collection of interactive exhibits for teachers, students, and science enthusiasts. ExploraNet, its online museum, offers electronic tours and demonstrations.

FrameMakers Gallery and Framing

http://www.prairienet.org/arts/
framing/homepage.html

The home page of FrameMakers, a gallery and framing shop specializing in limited edition prints, offers online access to company products and services.

Visitors can also link to a handful of other art-related sites on the Web.

General Theory of Religion Page

http://world.std.com/~awolpert

This personal philosophy page, maintained by an independent religion scholar, offers "an introduction to a general theory of religion." Visit here to learn about one person's study of religion, based on "the cybernetic technique of Forrester-style system dynamics."

Guide to Early Church Documents

http://www.iclnet.org/

This guide, provided by the Institute of Christian Leadership, covers early canons and creeds, the writings of the Apostolic Fathers, and other historical works. Visit here for full text of many historically significant biblical passages.

Harvard University Faculty of Arts and Sciences

http://fas-www.harvard.edu/

The Faculty of Arts and Sciences at Harvard University maintains this informational site. Visit here to learn about its facilities, programs, resources, and student life. Links to local weather and community information are also available.

Honolulu Community College Dinosaur Exhibit

http://www.hcc.hawaii.edu/dinos/
dinos.1.html

Dinosaurs in Hawaii? You betcha. Honolulu Community College presents its permanent collection of "fossils"—replicas from the American Museum of Natural History, New York City. Visitors can browse fossil pictures and explanations or take the narrated tour.

HUMBUL Gateway
http://info.ox.ac.uk/departments/
humanities/international.html

Maintained at England's Oxford University, the HUMBUL Gateway points the way to humanities-related Web pages around the world. Begin with the general resources and search facilities, or move directly to the subject specific index.

Kassandra Project
http://www.reed.edu/~ccampbel/tkp/

The "Kassandra Project" offers a series of Web pages that feature German women writers, artists, and thinkers from the second half of the 1800s to the first decades of the 1900s. The project seeks to "clear the cultural shadows" cast by Goethe, Schiller, and Kant.

Kunsthochschule für Medien Köln—Titelseite
http://www.khm.de/

The Academy of Media Arts in Germany features its programs and current projects on this home page. Visitors also can check recent news about the school. Information in German and English.

Michigan Digital Historical Initiative in the Health Sciences
http://http2.sils.umich.edu/HCHS/

The Michigan Digital Historical Initiative in the Health Sciences (MDHI) serves as a guide to Web-based repositories of museum materials, photographs, artifacts, and online galleries, all containing objects of interest to medical historians. Visitors can view historical information about African-Americans' experiences with health care.

Mythtext
http://www.io.org/~untangle/
mythtext.html

Mythtext is an index to a large collection of mythological sites on the Net. The index includes pointers to Arthurian, Celtic, and classical texts and bibliographies. The page also promotes Godfiles 1.0, a commercial annotated index of over 3,000 gods and goddesses.

Oriental Institute
http://www-oi.uchicago.edu/OI/
default.html

The Oriental Institute at the University of Chicago is a museum and research body "devoted to the study of the ancient Near East." This site offers visitors a look at the institute's museum, its archives, archaeology and philology projects, plus related publications and databases.

Powersource Native American Art & Education Center

`http://www.powersource.com/`
`powersource/gallery/default.html`

Native American art graces the virtual walls of the Powersource Gallery. In addition to the art collection, access Native American cultural, historical, and political guides here.

Research Institute for the Humanities

`http://www.arts.cuhk.hk/`

This Chinese University of Hong Kong site presents an index of humanities resources. The site includes an extensive list of directories and libraries containing information on art, music, languages, literature, philosophy, and more.

Sean's One-Stop Philosophy Shop

`http://www.rpi.edu/~cearls/`
`phil.html`

Attempting to "create the ultimate philosophy link list." Categories of links include: university departments, gophers, real-life philosophers, famous works and discussions, various "isms," and more.

South Bank University Department of Architecture & Civil Engineering

`http://www.sbu.ac.uk/Architecture/`
`home.html`

South Bank University's Department of Architecture & Civil Engineering targets potential engineering students with access to architecture-related Internet sites. The site also includes a department catalog, admissions info, and course and project descriptions.

Stanford Electronic Humanities Review

`http://shr.stanford.edu/shreview/`

The Stanford Electronic Humanities Review opens up an intellectual landscape by providing a forum for scholarly dialogue. This page includes articles that deal with cognitive science, artificial intelligence, and similar topics. Includes a link to the Stanford University home page.

Stockholm University Department of Linguistics

`http://w3.ling.su.se/`

The home page for the Department of Linguistics at Stockholm University provides information on the department's staff, research projects, academic programs, and links to related sites in the Stockholm region.

The Genealogy Bulletin Board Systems

`http://genealogy.org/PAF/www/gbbs/`

The Genealogy Bulletin Board Systems (GBBS), published monthly, includes more than 1,000 computer bulletin board systems around the world. The GBBS appears in two formats: table-based pages and pages that do not use tables.

The Timothy Leary and Robert Anton Wilson Show

`http://www.intac.com/~dimitri/dh/`
`learywilson.html`

The Timothy Leary and Robert Anton Wilson Show contains information, writings, and interviews with these two outlaw intellectuals. The vast site includes links to publications, research, and philosophy.

Turkish Poetry Home Page

`http://www.cs.umd.edu/users/sibel/`
`poetry/poetry.html`

"Here we speak with a Turkish accent," the Webmasters write. They appear to do so in a variety of tongues. This page offers Turkish poetry in Turkish, English, Spanish, French, and Italian.

University of Chicago Philosophy Project

`http://csmaclab-www.uchicago.edu/`
`philosophyProject/philos.html`

The University of Chicago Philosophy Project is an electronically mediated forum for scholarly discussion. The site offers visitors a seat in the audience, or the option to suggest or join a discussion group. Includes links to current discussions, the sponsoring university, and a variety of related resources.

University of Toronto Centre for Landscape Research

`http://www.clr.toronto.edu:1080/`
`clr.html`

The Centre for Landscape Research, University of Toronto, states its purpose,

"as that of improving the overall spatial literacy of society." The center maintains this home page with information about the center's activities and projects, and links to related online libraries and organizations.

BUSINESS & INVESTING

American Society of Home Inspectors

`http://www1.mhv.net/~dfriedman/`
`ashihome.htm`

This unofficial guide to the American Society of Home Inspectors, certifying inspectors in the United States and Canada, is maintained by a local Internet service provider. Visitors will find an extensive index of trade resources, including online technical libraries, industry publications, and home buyer services.

Argus Associates Inc.

`http://argus-inc.com/`

Argus Associates Inc. specializes in design of large-scale information systems. Visitors to the company's home page will find information on its Web site design services, content-driven advertising, and Internet training sessions.

Ask Sherlock

`http://accnet.com/cgi-bin/`
`listings.pl`

This search engine, provided by ACCNET real estate services, allows visitors to scan the Internet for property listings. Includes instructions on running simple keyword searches.

Bank Public Information Center

http://www.worldbank.org/html/pic/PIC.html

The Public Information Center of the World Bank allows access to documents and publications not restricted to official users. Visit here for economic and sector reports, operations evaluations, sectoral policy papers, and other publicly available documents.

CCF

http://www.calvacom.fr/ccf/accueil.html

Paris, France-based financial institution CCF provides information on its corporate officers and latest service additions. Includes extensive index of finance-related World Wide Web links and publications. Information in French and English.

Closing Bell

http://www.merc.com/cbell2.html

Denver, Colorado-based Mercury Mail Inc. provides a variety of online subscription services, including stocks, sports, and weather reports. Visitors to its Closing Bell page will find out how to subscribe to its stock quote service, offering daily delivery of user-selected listings.

Computer Register

http://www.computerregister.com/

Browsers in the market for computer consultants or services can check out relevant advertisements, including employment. Classifieds are provided for job-seekers and employers.

Dartmouth University School of Business Administration

http://www.dartmouth.edu/pages/tuck/tuckhome.html

Dartmouth's Amos Tuck School of Business maintains this site to introduce its people and programs. Visit here for course offerings, alumni listings, and career services links.

Designlink

http://206.14.15.5/designlink/

Designlink is a San Francisco-based bulletin board system for artists and photographers. Visitors to its Web site can download shareware, browse through portfolios from graphic artists and photographers, and look for jobs. The site also posts information on Designlink's user group meetings.

Education, Training and Development Resource Center for Business and Industry

http://www.tasl.com/tasl/home.html

This page, maintained by Training and Seminar Locators Inc., provides help in finding business education resources. It includes an index of qualified training providers and information about products and services.

Frost Yellow Pages Inc.

http://www.frostyp.com/fyp/

Frost Yellow Pages Inc. features its twist on promoting effective "yellow pages" advertising on this page. Businesses can check out the consulting firm's services and preview the "90 Minute Guide to Yellow Pages Advertising (It'll Save You Money)."

Idea Factory

http://www.chiatday.com/factory/

Chiat/Day Inc. advertising presents its Idea Factory through this creative Web site. The advertising agency explains its vision, current projects, and the concept of a virtual office focusing on emerging media. Visitors can engage in a virtual focus group.

Institute for Fiscal Studies

http://www1.ifs.org.uk/

The Institute for Fiscal Studies provides information on its research, publications, and membership services. Visitors can access historical information about this European policy research institution.

Internet International

http://com.primenet.com/ssp/

This site, maintained by Internet access provider and Web page designer, SSP International Inc., features information for businesses interested in leasing space for commercial Web sites. Visitors also will find a list of current Internet International customers.

Intuit

http://www.careermosaic.com/cm/intuit/intuit1.html

Menlo Park, California-based Intuit, Inc., markets personal finance, small business accounting, and tax preparation software. Visitors to its home page can find out more about the company, its products, and customer services.

Market Beat

http://www.quote.com/newsletters/petruno/

Written for the do-it-yourself investor, Tom Petruno's thrice-weekly Los Angeles Times column features a "fresh off-Wall Street perspective on investing and financial markets." Visitors will find an electronic edition of the column, plus a host of market-related links.

Market ICI World Real Estate Network

http://www.iciworld.com/

The Market Industrial, Commercial, and Investment Real Estate Network, based in Toronto, Ontario, offers advertising and directory services to professional property buyers and sellers. Visit here for company news, subscription offers, and an extensive index of real estate resources.

Open Text Positions Available

http://www.opentext.com/docs/jobs.html

The Open Text Corporation, a developer of Internet search and directory services, provides this gateway to its current job listings page. Visitors are invited to learn more about the company and its employment opportunities.

Royal Bank of Canada

http://www.royalbank.com/

The Royal Bank of Canada offers details about its personal financial services, business banking, international services, and royal mutual funds. Visitors also will find corporate news and employment opportunities listings. Information in English and French.

TRW Inc.

http://www.trw.com/

Cleveland, Ohio-based TRW, a provider of high-tech products and services to the automotive, space, and defense industries, maintains this promotional site. Visit here for a company profile, plus information on the company's financial performance, products, and services.

Unigain Trading Co. Ltd.

http://www.pristine.com.tw/UNIGAIN/

The Unigain Trading Co. Ltd., a Taiwanese exporter to more than 30 countries worldwide, maintains this promotional page. Visitors can learn more about the company and its catalog of more than 1,200 products.

University of Tokyo Faculty of Economics

http://www.e.u-tokyo.ac.jp/

This page, from the University of Tokyo, provides information about the Faculty

of Economics and guides browsers to academics, staff, and coursework. Access the Economic Society 7th World Congress here.

U.S. Tax Code On-Line

http://www.fourmilab.ch/ustax/ ustax.html

Though not a site sponsored by the U.S. government, this page allows access to the complete text of the U.S. Internal Revenue Title 26 of the Code (26 U.S.C). For ease of cross-referencing, hyperlinks have been embedded in the text.

World Wide Trade Service

http://www.nas.com/~westg/ index.html

World Wide Trade Service provides information about its trade books, manuals, directories, and dealership services. Visitors to this site can browse pages about foreign and domestic wholesale products and import/export trade sources, read detailed company info, or obtain a price list and order form.

COMPUTERS

Apple Smorgasbord

http://www.info.apple.com/ web.pages.html

The Smorgasbord is an extension of Apple Computer's support and educational resources directory. It includes employment opportunity listings, links to personal home pages maintained by

Apple employees, and even a QuickTime movie archive.

British Computer Society

http://www.bcs.org.uk/

The home page of the British Computer Society provides information about the group's events, branches, members, and professional development.

Bugtraq Archives for July 1995—Present by Thread

http://www.eecs.nwu.edu/~jmyers/bugtraq/index.html

Bugtraq Archives, a personal collection of programming resources, exposes various UNIX security holes, what they are, and how to fix them. Find a mailing list designed to encourage discussion and create workable solutions.

Computer Shopper

http://www.zdnet.com/cshopper/

The online version of Ziff-Davis' *Computer Shopper* magazine includes feature stories, columns from industry pundits, and "review nuggets." Visitors can read the latest issue or review past selections.

Digi International

http://www.digibd.com/

Digi International is a producer of computer network and server products. Visitors to its site will find press releases, product and ordering information, and customer support.

Frontline Distribution Ltd.

http://www.frontline.co.uk/

Frontline Distribution, an England-based trade distributor of computer products and services, maintains this promotional site. Visit here to connect with its technical support department, vendors, and manufacturers.

Inside EDA: Mentor Graphics on the Web

http://www.mentorg.com/

Mentor Graphics, a professional design software developer, gives an overview of its services and products here. The site also contains trade show information, an online customer training page, and a Silicon Valley contest.

ITI Main Web Page

http://www.iti.gov.sg/

The Information Technology Institute site describes its research and development projects, general information about the Institute, and pointers to its various services. Includes job listings, staff directory, and links to related resources.

Jumbo! Official Web Shareware Site

http://www.jumbo.com/

This Jumbo! shareware site provides access to tens of thousands of programs. Features include instructions on downloading, access to descriptions and documentation, and indexing by subject classification.

337

Meta Virtual Environments

http://www.cc.gatech.edu/gvu/
people/Masters/Rob.Kooper/
Meta.VR.html

The Meta Virtual Environments page contains an annotated directory of virtual environment and virtual reality pages. Among the sites featured are universities, labs, and institutes in the U.S. and Europe.

MIPS Technologies, Inc.

http://www.mips.com/

MIPS Technologies, Inc. is a RISC microprocessor supplier. The company's home page hosts a glossy presentation combining product pitches, development tools, and company press releases.

More Details about DB2 Parallel Edition on SP2

http://www.austin.ibm.com/
developer/moved.html

This May 1994 article "describes IBM's plans for a parallel DB2/6000 database server using the shared-nothing hardware model and function shipping." According to the article, at the time of its writing, beta testing on the product was underway and availability was to be announced later that year.

Mortice Kern Systems Inc.

http://www.mks.com/

Mortice Kern Systems, Inc., a developer and international supplier of software, open systems, and communications applications, makes its Internet home at this site. Visitors can learn more about the company, its products, and its support services.

PC SoftDIR—The Automated DOS/ Windows Software Reference Guide

http://www.netusa.com/pcsoft/
softdir.htm

PC SoftDIR provides a comprehensive online resource for selecting software for DOS, Windows, and OS/2 computers.

Rockwell International Corp.

http://www.rockwell.com/

Global high-tech player Rockwell International packs its corporate home page with information on its many areas of expertise, which include avionics, defense electronics, and semiconductor systems. Visitors will find departmental information and more.

Rockwell Semiconductor Systems

http://www.nb.rockwell.com/

Rockwell Semiconductor Systems, a Newport Beach, California-based industrial supplier, maintains this promotional site for an overview of its operating divisions. Visitors will also find press releases, product briefs, help files, employment opportunities, and more.

Stollmann Entwicklungs und Vertriebs-GmbH

http://www.stollmann.de/

This promotional site (maintained by Stollmann, a computer products supplier in Hamburg, Germany) offers visitors to its home page information about the company, its hardware and software applications, and its customer services. Information in German and English.

StorageTek
http://www.stortek.com/

StorageTek, an information storage company, explains its services, corporate profile, and company background.

The CAVE: A Virtual Reality Theater
http://www.ncsa.uiuc.edu/EVL/docs/html/CAVE.html

The CAVE is a virtual reality system designed for scientists by the National Center for Supercomputing Applications (better known as NCSA) and the Argonne National Laboratory. Visitors will find a general overview, research applications, references, and acknowledgments for this visualization project.

The Connectix QuickCam
http://www.indstate.edu/msattler/sci-tech/comp/hardware/quickcam.html

Information about the Connectix QuickCam computer-mounted video camera is provided by a product beta tester. Visit here for unofficial software and platform compatibility information, product overviews, user instructions, and direct links to Connectix Corporation.

The Macintosh Advantage
http://www2.apple.com/whymac/

Apple Computer, Inc. presents this hypertext document on "why Macintosh computers are better than PCs running Windows 95." Visitors can read a wealth of Macintosh-related info and propaganda here, including a list of key Macintosh advantages and performance comparisons.

VSL: Master Site
http://www.shareware.com/

The Virtual Software Library, a powerful Internet-based software search tool, provides access to more than 130,000 software titles available online. Visit this site for a variety of search options to locate the Internet software resources you're looking for.

Welcome to Borland Online
http://www.borland.com/

Borland Online provides information on its products, services, and technical data. This page also includes press releases, company background, and a user feedback link.

Xicor Inc.
http://www.xicor.com/

Xicor, Inc. designs, manufactures, and markets "advanced nonvolatile memory products." The company's home page provides a corporate overview, information on products and services, investor info, pricing structures, and job listings.

Yggdrasil Computing, Incorporated

`http://www.yggdrasil.com/`

Named for the world tree of old Norse mythology, Yggdrasil Computing, Incorporated's stated mission is "to provide infrastructure to support the free software world." Find information on the company's products and technical support services, as well as links to freeware archives.

EDUCATION

Akatsukayama High School

`http://www.kobe-cufs.ac.jp/kobe-city/information/education/akatsuka/akatsuka.html`

Akatsukayama High School is located in Kobe, Japan. Visitors to the institution's home page will find general information about academics, students, and events. Links are provided to other Japanese high schools' Web sites.

CTI Centre for Economics Welcome Page

`http://savage.ecn.bris.ac.uk/cticce/Welcome.html`

The CTI Centre for Economics, based at the University of Bristol in the United Kingdom, encourages the employment of learning technologies in British higher education. The institution's home page lists its services and related news and provides links to similar resources.

Data Research Associates

`http://www.dra.com/`

Data Research Associates produces client/server automation systems and networking services for libraries and information providers. This site delivers background information on the company, its products, and clients.

ECU Home Page

`http://ecuvax.cis.ecu.edu/`

East Carolina University serves up a wealth of information about its academics, administration, computing services, student life, athletics, and campus organizations. Browsers can also access the school's telephone and e-mail directories.

fastWeb! (Financial Aid Search Through the Web)

`http://www.studentservices.com/fastweb/`

College-bound browsers will find a tool to help wade through the financial-aid morass, with fastWEB's scholarship search. A wealth of information about financial aid is provided for those on a scholarship search.

Flix Productions Animated Shareware

`http://www.eden.com/~flixprod/`

At this site, find shareware from Flix Productions, a company that specializes in animated educational software. Find descriptions, screenshots, and download options for such titles as Animated Old

Testament, Animated Mother Goose, and Animated Alphabet.

Indiana University Home Page

http://www-iub.ucs.indiana.edu/

Indiana University maintains this site to introduce its statewide campuses and programs. Visitors will find links to its system units and services, university mission statements, computer resources, and nine campus locations.

Information Booth

http://www.vpds.wsu.edu/sciforum/

A virtual science fair, complete with registration, judging, and prizes is held annually at this site. Browse the sample exhibits or obtain entry information at this educational site.

Insite

http://curry.edschool.Virginia.EDU/insite/

The Society for Information Technology and Teacher Education explores ways in which the Internet can benefit teacher education programs around the world. Read about the society's mission and its research findings.

Introducing the UC

http://www.reg.uci.edu/SANET/uc.html

The Registrar's Office of the University of California maintains this site for general information on admission, transfers, and tuition. Visit here to link with the university's many campuses, programs, and resources.

Minnesota New Country School

http://mncs.k12.mn.us/

At the Minnesota New Country School's site, visitors will get an overview of the school and staff, as well as a look at the students' artwork and home pages.

NEIRL: Northeast & Islands Regional Laboratory

http://www.neirl.org/

The Regional Laboratory for Educational Improvement of the Northeast and Islands profiles the multistate effort. Find out how a coalition of educators, policy makers, and parents is trying to ensure that all children learn and achieve.

ParentsPlace.com

http://www.parentsplace.com/

ParentsPlace.com, provides an online index of parenting resources on the Internet. Visitors can read articles and books, chat with other parents, or perform a keyword search of its data-bases. Links to a variety of parenting centers and related businesses are also available.

Provo City Library

http://www.provo.lib.ut.us/

The Provo City Library Web site features quick information through a reference section as well as information about the library's collection and children's programs. Includes links to community servers and the state of Utah. The site is searchable by keywords.

Special Education at the University of Kansas

http://www.sped.ukans.edu/
spedadmin/welcome.html

The Department of Special Education at the University of Kansas in Lawrence maintains this overview of its academic programs and research projects. Browsers can also meet the faculty, get an overview of its special technology lab, and link to related Internet resources.

STILE Project's WWW Server

http://indigo.stile.le.ac.uk/

The STILE Project (Students and Teachers Integrated Learning Environment) is a resource for students of the World Wide Web. Based out of the University of Leicester at Loughborough in the UK, the links include esoteric subjects ranging from Contemporary Crafts to Latin American Politics to images from various Archaeological Studies.

The Commonwealth of Learning

http://www.col.org/

The Commonwealth of Learning, an international organization comprised of 53 member countries, works to widen access to education and improve its quality through the use of communication technologies and distance learning. This site provides information about the COL, its publications, archives, and education programs.

The Medical Library Association Home Page

http://www.kumc.edu/MLA/

The Medical Library Association is an organization "of more than 5,000 individuals and institutions in the health information field." Explore membership options and association benefits at this site.

The Open University

http://www.open.ac.uk/

The Open University of the United Kingdom, founded in 1969, has no entry requirements for most of its courses. Included here is information about its degrees offered and academic departments. Studying at the Open University via the Internet is explained here.

The Student Guide 1995-96

http://www.ed.gov/prog_info/SFA/
StudentGuide/

This Student Guide details financial aid programs available from the U.S. Department of Education. Includes a general overview of programs, descriptions of specific grants, work-study opportunities, and loans.

The University of Dublin, Trinity College—Home Page

http://www.tcd.ie/

The home page for the University of Dublin, Trinity College in Dublin, Ireland provides information about the university, courses, and departments. Also available at this site is an index of

Irish World Wide Web servers and documentation on using the Internet.

The University of Sunderland, England

http://orac.sund.ac.uk/

The University of Sunderland, England provides information about its program and departments and also posts announcements for its staff and students. The site also contains detailed information on Northeast England.

UCI Financial Aid Office WWW Server[www.fao.uci.edu]

http://www.fao.uci.edu/

The Financial Aid Office of the University of California, Irving maintains this online guide for current and prospective students. Visit here to read its *Financial Aid Handbook* and link to other university information resources.

University of Sheffield, UK

http://www.shef.ac.uk/

The UK's University of Sheffield Information Service provides a window on academic activities and student life. Access the university's electronic resources, or tour the city of Sheffield and surrounding regions from this site.

UT Austin—Graduate School of Library and Information Science

http://fiat.gslis.utexas.edu/start.html

The graduate program for Library and Information Science at the University of Texas at Austin provides information

here on its courses, faculty, and students. The site also features a message board.

ENTERTAINMENT & LEISURE

Association of America's Public Television Stations

http://www.universe.digex.net/~apts/

The Association of America's Public Television Stations (APTS) is a professional organization for noncommercial television broadcasters. Find membership information as well as updates on the latest political developments affecting public broadcasting.

Bob Lafleur's Square Dancing Resource List

http://pages.map.com/~bobl/sdance.htm

An extensive index of square dancing resources has been compiled and posted to this page. Among the offerings, find links to Web sites, an alphabetical list of callers, and a list of clubs organized by state.

Cambridge University Press

http://www.cup.org/

The North American branch of Cambridge University Press calls this site its online home. Find a complete online catalog, along with a general overview of the press' history and publications.

CyberSleaze

http://metaverse.com/vibe/sleaze/
00latest.html

Consult the CyberSleaze page, an offering of *The Vibe*, an online entertainment magazine, for a daily dose of gossip about pop music stars and the entertainment industry.

Frontier Airlines

http://www.cuug.ab.ca:8001/~busew/
frontier.html

Denver, Colorado-based Frontier Airlines maintains this site for a glimpse of its more than 40-year history. Visitors can view old flight maps, read historical documents, and find current reservation information.

Heather Rose Busby

http://www.owlnet.rice.edu/
~busbyhea/

Heather Busby's personal home page features artwork, biographical notes, extensive lists of her favorite music and a résumé.

Joe Geigel's Favorite Theatre Related Resources

http://pscinfo.psc.edu/~geigel/
menus/Theatre.htm

Visitors to Joe Geigel's Favorite Theatre Related Resources will have a hard time choosing where to begin their exploration into the world of theatre. Stagecraft, publications, theatrical groups, shows, and performers headline the list of topics presented.

Kitty the Cat

http://www.dao.nrc.ca/DAO/STAFF/
kitty.html

Kitty, a resident guard cat, is the subject of this personal home page. Career and contact information for the cat is available here, as well as a list of research interests, which include small birds and mice.

KPIG Radio Online

http://www.kpig.com/

Oink, KPIG, oink, is a radio station based in Freedom, California, that broadcasts an eclectic mix of rock, blues, country, Hawaiian, Cajun, and a whole bunch of other stuff. Visitors to their sty—er, home page will find information on new music, related links and comedy, oink.

Nancy Drew Home Page

http://sunsite.unc.edu/cheryb/
nancy.drew/ktitle.html

The Nancy Drew home page contains information on the writers, central themes, and characteristics of the juvenile mystery series. Includes character sketches, plot summaries, and discussions of the evolution of the books since 1929.

Over the Coffee

http://www.cappuccino.com/

The Over the Coffee site, dedicated to coffee enthusiasts, contains general information about the stimulating bean. Includes a reference desk, business section, and related resource links.

Paulina Porizkova

http://darwin.clas.virginia.edu/
~mgk4e/paulina/paulina.html

This unofficial page is devoted to supermodel Paulina Porizkova. Visitors will find a variety of photos of the Polish beauty.

Photo Exhibitions and Archives

http://math.liu.se/~behal/photo/
exhibits.html

This vast collection of links pertaining to photos available on the Internet includes subjects such as alternative processes, stereoscopic and historical. Visitors can browse online galleries containing everything from pinhole to digital photography.

P.S. I Love You International

http://www.psiloveyou.com/

P.S. I Love You is the 1990s online version of mail order brides. This site features a roster of international female clients, with images and brief descriptions. Visitors who like what they see can order videos to find out more.

Publishers on the Internet

http://www.faxon.com/Internet/
publishers/pubs.html

Browsers after trades, journals, or books can use this comprehensive index to find publishers on the Net.

Rick's Scuba Page

http://sc.net/organizations/ribaum/
scuba/index.html

"Live Aboard Diving" and "Treasure Diving" are two of the featured articles found on this diver's page devoted to the sport he enjoys. Underwater photos and tips, equipment reviews, weather maps, a first aid kit, and links to other scuba pages are also featured.

Satellite Journal International Archives

http://itre.uncecs.edu/misc/sj/
sj.html

This site features the searchable archive of "Satellite Journal International," a trade journal for the television and radio industries. Find news and commentary on cable systems, network launches, and related telecommunications legislation.

TheatreWorks

http://none.coolware.com/tworks/

TheatreWorks is a professional theater located on the San Francisco peninsula. Its site includes general information, performance listings, season schedule, ticket information, and links to related resources.

The Daily Bikini

http://www.thedaily.com/bikini.html

The front page photo of "The Daily Bikini" changes every weekday, but it's always a beautiful bikini-clad babe. Other than that, this e-zine is full of links to an eclectic collection of resources, from entertainment to news to sports.

The Darmok Dictionary

http://www.wavefront.com/~raphael/darmok/darmok.html

The Darmok Dictionary, an unofficial "Star Trek: The Next Generation" trivia site, provides definitions of alien phrases used during the "Darmok" episode. Includes analytical discussion and sound files.

The Gigaplex!

http://www.gigaplex.com/

Gigaplex is a vast Web magazine with over 600 pages relating to arts and entertainment. Movies, theater, TV, books, art, and music are among the subject categories.

The Jihad to Destroy Barney

http://www.armory.com/~deadslug/Jihad/jihad.html

Join or simply monitor the nefarious activities of the Jihad to Destroy Barney at this site. Visitors will find propaganda mandating that the popular purple dinosaur that has captured the fancy of U.S. children must die.

The Simpsons Fan Site

http://turtle.ncsa.uiuc.edu/alan/simpsons.html

The creator of this "Simpsons" fan site claims it to be the first of its kind. Now all but abandoned, the site features links to other related fan resources on the Web.

The Terminator Movies Home Page

http://www.maths.tcd.ie/pub/films/terminator/

Learn more about the wildly popular science fiction adventure films that turned Ahh-nold into a superstar.

Zima.com

http://www.zima.com/zimag.html

From the folks who make Zima (Whatizit again?) comes this online fun 'zine offering answers to questions about the mysterious beverage. Also find movie reviews, audio clips, images, and more.

GOVERNMENT

1-800-TAX-LAWS

http://www.5010geary.com/

U.S. taxpayers can file online via this home page from a national network of tax professionals. Find a step-by-step set of forms, tax humor, and information about the company, including contact numbers.

Advocates for Self-Government

http://www.self-gov.org/

Take the world's smallest political quiz and find answers to Frequently Asked Questions (FAQ) about Libertarianism. Links to other Libertarian and related political sites are also featured.

Alabama's Secretary of State

`http://alsecst.jsu.edu:8000/`

Visit this page for information on Alabama's elections, voter registration, business regulations, and more. Links to related sites are also featured.

Althingi—The Icelandic Parliament

`http://www.althingi.is/`

The Althingi's home page contains basic information about the structure, procedures, and members of the Icelandic Parliament. Includes links to general information about Iceland. Information in Icelandic and English.

California Energy Commission

`http://www.energy.ca.gov/energy/`

The California Energy Commission is charged with establishing energy policy and planning to ensure a reliable and affordable energy supply. The agency's home page details the Commission's major responsibilities, describes its various divisions and programs, provides a topical index to Commission information, and posts an Internet site for educational resources.

Congressional Record—104th Congress

`http://thomas.loc.gov/home/`
`r104query.html`

Search the full text of the Congressional Record for the 104th Congress at this site. Find a variety of query options, including searches by keyword, speaker, and a range of dates.

Defense Acquisition University

`http://www.acq.osd.mil/dau/dau.html`

The U.S. Defense Acquisition University offers overviews of its courses and event schedule at this site. Created by Congress in 1990 to consolidate training for the Defense Acquisition Workforce, the DAU offers links to the Acquisition Reform Communications Center and other related sites.

Federal Rules of Evidence

`http://www.law.cornell.edu/rules/`
`fre/overview.html`

The Legal Information Institute presents a complete hypertext version of the U.S. Federal Rules of Evidence. The document includes a full-text search capability.

G7 Summit—Halifax, Nova Scotia

`http://fox.nstn.ca/~alfers/`
`AlfersG7.html`

Created for the June 1995 G7 Summit in Halifax, Nova Scotia, this site features an events calendar, news releases, and photos. The site continues to remain active as a record of the event.

Government Internet Index

`http://www.webcom.com/~piper/state/`
`states.html`

This index of state and local government Internet sites allows users to run quick keyword searches. Includes a Frequently Asked Questions (FAQ) file and state-specific links.

Immigration and Naturalization Service

http://gopher.usdoj.gov/offices/ins.html

An arm of the Department of Justice, the Immigration and Naturalization Service outlines its mission and duties on this page. A link to the INS information on the Justice Gopher is also included.

Internet Headquarters for Student Governments

http://www.umr.edu/~stuco/national.html

The University of Missouri-Rolla has compiled this catalog of university level student governments across the globe. Link to over 100 official student government organizations.

Libertarian Party

http://www.lp.org/lp/

The official site of the U.S. Libertarian Party provides an overview of the party's platform, information on membership, and access to member directories across the country. Official documents include By-Laws and Convention Rules, and Libertarian Programs from 1989 to the present.

Morris Campus Student Association (MCSA)

http://sci173x.mrs.umn.edu/~www/mcsa.html

This student government site contains general information on campus politics, resolutions, and links to University of Minnesota servers. Includes pointers to state and federal government organizations, related student government information, and student services.

Moscow Libertarium

http://feast.fe.msk.ru/libertarium/

The Moscow Libertarium is a project aimed at "the information support of social activity and scientific research on the problems of liberalism" in the emerging free-market system in Russia. The site provides articles, research materials, listings of organizations, and details on project management, and activities. Information in Russian with some English.

Naval Postgraduate School

http://www.nps.navy.mil/

The Naval Postgraduate School provides an overview of the U.S. Navy's advanced training institution, information on academic departments, and programs of study. Includes links to administrative departments, research groups, and the various campus-wide information systems.

Soldiers

http://www.redstone.army.mil/soldiers/home.html

Soldiers, the official U.S. Army magazine, is published to provide personnel with information about people, politics, operations, technical developments, and trends. Find the current and past issues, plus contact and submission information.

The International Political Economy Network

http://csf.colorado.edu/ipe/

The International Political Economy Network (IPENet) is a research site focusing on the global political economy. Includes an overview of the organization, discussion groups, access to IPENet archives, publications, and links to related resources.

The White House

http://www.whitehouse.gov/WH/ Welcome.html

Tour the White House and learn about its history, visit the First Family and find out what's new with the President, or search the virtual library for documents, speeches, and photos. Also find the *Interactive Citizens' Handbook* and a special area just for the children.

Twenty-Five Most Common Tax Preparation Errors

http://www.ey.com/us/tax/ 25error.htm

Visitors with an acute fear of taxes may find comfort here. The page lists the 25 most common tax preparation errors made by taxpayers when April 15 rolls around.

Uniform Commercial Code— Articles 1–9

http://www.law.cornell.edu/ucc/ ucc.table.html

Published by Cornell Law School's Legal Information Institute, this hypertext document offers access to Articles 1–9 of the Uniform Commercial Code. Articles are presented individually "for the limited purposes of study, teaching, and academic research."

U.S. Air Force Rome Laboratory

http://www.rl.af.mil:8001/

The U.S. Air Force's Rome Laboratory works to advance communications technology for the Air Force and assist in the creation of related applications for private industry. Visit this site for current events, information on technology transfers, and Internet resources.

U.S. Justice Department

http://justice2.usdoj.gov/

The U.S. Justice Department maintains this site for public informational resources. Visitors will find links to departmental indexes, issues-oriented materials, computer services, and other federal government and criminal justice information sources.

U.S. Patent Related Network Resources

http://town.hall.org/patent/ patent.html

Maintained by the Internet Multicasting Service, this site points to patent search services, the U.S. Patent and Trademark Office, and the Copyright Office gopher server. Also find links to the Global Network Navigator, the Legal Information Institute at Cornell Law School, and more.

World Wide Web Virtual Library: State Government Servers

http://www.law.indiana.edu/law/states.html

Organized alphabetically by state, this index points to official, state government information servers. Find state home pages, agency and departmental pages, and links to governors' offices, legislatures, and judicial systems.

HEALTH & MEDICINE

AIDS Information Newsletter

http://www.cmpharm.ucsf.edu/~troyer/safesex/vanews/

The AIDS Information Newsletter, a service of the U.S. Department of Veterans Affairs, offers biweekly updates on the critical health care issue. Visit here for important information about the prevention and treatment of AIDS.

Arizona Health Sciences Library Nutrition Guide

http://www.medlib.arizona.edu/educ/nutrition.htm

The Arizona Health Sciences Center provides this guide to selected nutrition resources on the Net. The site is specifically aimed at the educational, research, and health care needs of the center's community.

CancerNet Gopher

gopher://gopher.nih.gov/11/clin/cancernet/

CancerNet's Gopher menu provides information from the National Cancer Institute. Visitors can read information statements and view fact sheets, updates, and abstracts on various cancer-related topics.

The Chiropractic Page

http://www.mbnet.mb.ca/~jwiens/chiro.html

The Chiropractic Page corrals electronic resources for professional practitioners, students, prospective patients, and the health care provider community. Educational programs are outlined and research data is made available here.

Chrysalis Home Page

http://www.omix.com/sites/drSandy/home.html

This online brochure for Chrysalis Counseling Services in San Francisco provides a brief overview of its approach to counseling and invites clients to contact it via telephone, FAX, or e-mail.

Community Breast Health Project

http://www-med.stanford.edu/CBHP/

Sponsored by the Stanford Medical Center, the Community Breast Health Project is a public service dedicated to providing information and support for those with breast cancer and their loved ones. A fixed feature of the page is a section of links to relevant Web sites.

DeathNET

http://www.islandnet.com/~deathnet/

"Ask not for whom the bell tolls" is the greeting at DeathNET, "where the surfin' stops." This international archive specializes in all aspects of death, with a "sincere respect for every point of view."

Ebola Interview
```
http://outcast.gene.com/ae/WN/NM/
interview_murphy.html
```

A former director of the National Center for Infectious Diseases at the Centers for Disease Control is interviewed about new and emerging killer viruses. Read about the Ebola Virus in plain language, consult the bibliography, or look at electron micrographs of three viruses.

Family Explorer: Home Page
```
http://www.parentsplace.com/
readroom/explorer/index.html
```

The Family Explorer is a monthly print newsletter focused on science and nature activities that parents can do with their children. This Web page includes activities from the newsletter and offers information about how to subscribe.

Fam-Med
```
http://apollo.gac.edu/
```

Fam-Med is an e-mail discussion group for family physicians to help them stay current and obtain information that may not be available locally. Includes subscription and background information, descriptions of services, and instructions for obtaining files.

Health and Medical Informatics Digest
```
http://maddog.fammed.wisc.edu/hmid/
hmid.html
```

This e-zine focuses on the latest information in health and medical informatics and primary care research. Visit here to browse an index of back issues and find subscription information.

Impotence Information Page
```
http://www.demon.co.uk/herniaInfo/
mcd.html
```

Although the giant Impotence banner at the top of this page may put off some visitors, keep reading for the frank, myth-dispelling facts on this common problem.

Internet Medical and Health Care Resources
```
http://www.teleport.com/~amrta/
iway.html
```

The Internet Medical and Health Care Resources page features pointers to health care, nutrition, and alternative medicine resources. From acupuncture to yoga, with the Family Health and Medical Matrix pages in between, these resources cover a wide range of issues.

Michigan Digital Historical Initiative in the Health Sciences
```
http://http2.sils.umich.edu/HCHS/
```

The Michigan Digital Historical Initiative in the Health Sciences (MDHI) serves as a guide to Web-based repositories of museum materials, photographs, artifacts and online galleries, all containing objects of interest to medical historians. Visitors here can view historical information about African-Americans' experiences with health care.

National Institute of Mental Health (NIMH) Home Page

http://www.nimh.nih.gov/

This Web site includes general information about the Institute, current clinical studies and patient referral guidelines, grant information, and online brochures on a variety of mental health topics.

Office of Medical Informatics

http://www.med.ufl.edu/medinfo/

The College of Medicine at the University of Florida posts lecture slides, reports, and conference news. The extensive site also contains histology and radiological anatomy demos, project updates, and some of the college's publications.

Scientific and Medical Antiques

http://www.duke.edu/~tj/
sci.ant.html

The Scientific and Medical Antiques site provides information for enthusiasts and collectors of science and medicine antiques, including old telescopes, scales, and surgical equipment. Visitors can find out about online auctions and learn about rare and antiquarian books, among other services.

Sexuality

http://www.aus.xanadu.com/
GlassWings/sexual.htm

Mature visitors to this Web site can explore the variations and possibilities of sexuality. It features links to the alt.sex Frequently Asked Questions (FAQ) files, safe sex guidelines, and a queer resource directory. The women's link is broader in scope and includes information on activism, careers, and religion.

The Cute Kids Page

http://www.prgone.com/cutekids/

Summit Learning devotes a Web page to "cute kids." Visitors are treated to pictures and stories of exceptionally darling children, along with a quotes section titled "Kids say the darndest things."

Trace Research and Development Center

http://www.trace.wisc.edu/

The Trace Research and Development Center in Madison, Wisconsin, offers information on its research, resources, design guidelines, training, and direct services that make access to computer information systems easier for the disabled.

Vegetarian Resource Group

http://envirolink.org/arrs/VRG/
home.html

Vegetarianism and animal rights are the focus of the Vegetarian Resource Group home page. Resources include journals, nutrition information, recipes, travel guides, and links.

Virtual Anatomy Project

http://www.vis.colostate.edu/
library/gva/gva.html

This multimedia project aims to generate a three-dimensional database of the human body. The site contains links to information on the researchers at Colorado State University, the software they're using, and to anatomical MPEGS of the human body.

WebABLE
http://www.webable.com/

Computer users with disabilities can search a directory of accessibility resources, read about new products, and participate in online conferences at this site.

Web of Addictions
http://www.well.com/user/woa/

Developed to counteract pro-drug messages and provide a source of factual information, Web of Addictions offers sobering fact sheets and definition files on all types of substance abuse, a rolodex listing local and national support resources, and extensive links to related sites.

Welcome to Uptime's Web Site
http://www.up-time.com/

Uptime distributes Natural Cellular Nutrition, a high-energy vitamin supplement. Read the ingredients list, order a free sample, and check out its other products.

INTERNET

Alexandria: World Web
http://home.worldweb.net/www/

World Web, an Internet provider and new media publishing firm in the Washington, D.C. area, supplies information on its services and provides user support at this site. Find also a portfolio of World Web clients.

America Online FTP
ftp://mirror.aol.com/

Visitors to this America Online FTP site can access an array of archives. Find the AOL browser, Mac and PC software, games, musical resources, and much more.

America's Suggestion Box
http://www.asb.com/

America's Suggestion Box of Ronkonkoma, N.Y., provides BBS and Internet services. Its site presents company information, as well as details on its services. Commercial and member home pages are included.

BBN Planet
http://www.bbnplanet.com/

BBN Planet offers Internet service packages to business organizations worldwide. At the BBN Planet home page, visitors can read about the company's history, publications, profiles, services, and news.

Berkeley Internet Link
http://bilink.berkeley.edu:8000/net.html

Maintained by the University of California at Berkeley for its faculty, staff, and students, this online form allows visitors to open an Internet account. UC Berkeley ID is required.

BIX the Byte Information eXchange

`http://www.mcs.com/~jvwater/`
`bix.html`

The Byte Information eXchange home page offers links to full-text archives of *Byte* magazine, chat facilities, and online conferencing services.

Buffalo Free-Net

`http://freenet.buffalo.edu/`

The Buffalo Free-Net is an Internet community information service for western New York state. Includes links to governmental, cultural, professional, business, social, and educational info centers.

CA*net Networking, Inc.

`http://www.canet.ca/canet/`
`index.html`

Visitors to this page will find links to the Canadian IP Address Registry and the Canadian Domain Name Registry. Contact information for CA*net Networking, Inc. is also provided.

Capital Area Internet Service

`http://www.cais.com/`

Visitors to this promotional page will find the Web home of Capital Area Internet Service, a Washington, D.C., access provider. A company profile, services directory, and list of CAIS users' Web pages are featured.

Clark Internet Service

`http://www.clark.net/`

ClarkNet is an Internet access provider for the Metro Baltimore-Washington, D.C., area. The provider's resources and range of services for business and private use are detailed here. Includes a user directory.

Community Computer Networks and Free-Net Web Sites

`http://freenet.victoria.bc.ca/`
`freenets.html`

Victoria Free-Net member David Mattison's list of community computer networks and Free-Net Web sites around the globe makes its home on this page. The list features gateways in Canada and throughout the world.

CompuServe

`http://www.compuserve.com/`

The promotional page for CompuServe serves as the new home base for CompuServe's corporate lowdown, daily news reports, and membership information.

ConflictNet Home Page

`http://www.igc.apc.org/conflictnet/`

ConflictNet is a network of mediators "dedicated to promoting the constructive resolution of conflict." Visit here to learn how to join the network, which also provides Internet access, and to read about the professionals and organizations that already belong.

Crocker Communications

http://www.crocker.com/

Crocker Communications is an Internet access provider in Massachusetts. This site offers information about starting up an account, dial-up rates, and technical support. Includes links to corporate and user pages.

Ebone

http://www.ebone.net/

Ebone is a nonprofit European organization that connects over 40 regional networks in more than 20 countries to each other and the Internet. It gives an overview of its mission and work here, and lists what researchers and groups are part of its network.

Europe Online

http://www.eo.net/

Europe Online offers multilingual news, entertainment, and commercial information services to its European customers. Explore the company's corporate mission and a list of its products and online services, including Internet access.

GEnie Services

http://www.genie.com/

One of the giants among commercial online services, GEnie, introduces its products and rates at the GEnie Services home page. Check out the Internet guide here, or follow a link to receive information.

Grex

http://www.cyberspace.org/

Participate in conferencing on the Internet using the Ann Arbor public access system, Grex. Find out how to join Grex and who is currently logged onto the "electronic town hall."

HarvardNet

http://www.harvardnet.com/

HarvardNet, a dedicated Internet access provider, sponsors this promotional page with information about the company's products and services. A mix of utility, entertainment, and information links are also provided.

Internet Connection

http://cnct.com/

The Internet Connection, a New York-area Internet provider, presents information on its services and pricing. Subscription information is included, as are details on the Connection's Renegade Outpost MUD.

Japan Network Information Center

http://www.nic.ad.jp/index.html

The Japan Network Information Center offers a general overview of its domain registration functions and information provider services at this promotional site. Link to its corporate profile, or peruse company publications. Information in Japanese with limited English translations.

Pipeline New York

http://www.nyc.pipeline.com/

Pipeline New York provides Internet access to the city's metropolitan area and posts informative, useful links on its home page. Visit here to learn about the company's wide range of Internet access options or to read its Web publications.

RIPE Network Coordination Centre

http://www.ripe.net/

This business provides support to Internet access providers in Europe. Visit this page to learn more about the company and its support services, plus find practical how-to information of interest to current and would-be Internet hosts.

UUNET Canada

http://www.uunet.ca/

UUNET Canada, a Canadian Internet service provider, offers complete Internet access and custom network solutions to its clients. Order access or consulting services at the company's home page.

JUST FOR KIDS

Beakman's Electric Motor

http://fly.hiwaay.net:80/~palmer/motor.html

This Web site clearly explains, with diagrams, how to build a simple electric motor (like the one on TV's "Beakman's World") using just a few household items.

Berit's Best Sites for Children

http://www.cochran.com/theosite/ksites.html

Berit's Best Sites for Children indexes, annotates, and rates selected children's pages on the Web. Featured topics include: activity centers, pages by kids for kids, family and kids' home pages, games and toys, world travel, and more.

Canadian Kids Home Page

http://www.onramp.ca/~lowens/107kids.htm

The Canadian Kids page is a Web "starting place for both the young and the young at heart." Pointers are provided to "great Canadian pages" ranging from Theodore Tugboat and SchoolNet to Street Cents Online and Women in Canadian History.

CyberKids Home

http://www.cyberkids.com/

Mountain Lake Software's CyberKids Web site features a free online magazine and games galore as part of its effort to help kids learn about the Internet while having fun. Users can enter a writing contest or explore the world through the CyberLaunchpad.

Cyber-Seuss

http://www.afn.org/~afn15301/drseuss.html

The Cyber-Seuss page features biographical info about Dr. Seuss (Theodor Geisel) plus links to Dr. Seuss images and stories—and everything you ever wanted to know about the Grinch.

Edge
http://www.jayi.com/jayi/Fishnet/Edge/

Edge is the bimonthly cyberzine for high-performance students. It's filled with provocative, cutting-edge stories, reviews, and insights for teens who want to go the extra mile.

FishNet
http://www.jayi.com/jayi/Open.html

FishNet is a Web space for academically talented teens. It features a college guide, a conversation forum, and a huge database of articles and information on educational opportunities.

Fox Kids Network
http://www.foxkids.com/Kids/index.html

Fox Kids, a service of the Fox Broadcasting Company, offers a variety of entertainment, news, and resources for children. Visitors will also find contests, games, and Fox television program listings.

Headbone Interactive
http://headbone.com/

Headbone Interactive is the electronic home of the Headbone multimedia projects, from "The Gigglebone Gang" to "What the Heck Will Elroy Do Next?" Visitors will also find demos, product information and links to hot Web sites.

Hyperman
http://www.hyperman.com/

Fans of TV's Hyperman won't want to miss this chance to go on a mission with him. Along the way, they can check out Emma's cool links, or take the agent test at mission control with the Comptroller.

Interesting Places for Kids
http://www.crc.ricoh.com/people/steve/kids.html

Compiled by the parent of a 10-year-old daughter, this page points to a wide variety of sites of potential interest to children. Indexed by topic, categories include art and literature, music, museums and other exhibits, science and math, toys and games, arts and crafts, and more.

Kids on the Web
http://www.zen.org/~brendan/kids.html

Kids on the Web contains an extensive listing of children's resources. Visitors will find fun stuff, educational sites, children's books, and information for parents.

KidSource
http://www.kidsource.com/

KidSource is an online source for kid-related education, healthcare, and product information. Whether it's for newborns or teens, visitors will find books, articles, organizations, software, and forums to assist in making the best choices for their families.

Kids' Space

http://plaza.interport.net/
kids_space/

Kids' Space is a showcase for children's art, stories, music, and letters. Kids can communicate with one another via e-mail and bulletin boards, and the site includes a page of links to other kid-friendly sites on the Web.

Kids' Window

http://jw.stanford.edu/KIDS/
kids_home.html

Kids' Window is a service of Japan Window, a U.S.-Japan collaboration for Internet-based Japan information. It provides many resources for education about Japanese culture such as a picture dictionary.

North Pole Web

http://north.pole.org/santa/

It's Christmas all year 'round at the North Pole Web site. Visitors can talk to Santa, Rudolph, and the elves, decorate a digital tree, or listen to Handel's "Messiah."

Nye Labs Online

http://nyelabs.kcts.org/

Fans of PBS's Bill Nye, "the Science Guy," can enter his online laboratory and explore the world of science. Be sure to check out the Demo of the Day and the Nyestore's home videos.

Pocahontas

http://www.disney.com/
DisneyPictures/Pocahontas/
?GL=H&referer=^DisneyPicture

This Web site features images and clips from Disney's *Pocahontas*. Visitors are also treated to a behind-the-scenes look at the making of the movie.

Questacon

http://sunsite.anu.edu.au/
Questacon/

Take a virtual tour of Questacon, Australia's national science and technology center. The Questacon home page also features a "KidSpace" full of exhibits, games, and activities.

School House Rock Page

http://hera.life.uiuc.edu/rock.html

This site helps revive the educational "Schoolhouse Rock" TV spots from the '70s. Visitors will find lyrics and audio files for musical lessons in grammar, history, science, and math.

Science Hobbyist

http://www.eskimo.com/~billb/

Amateur scientists will find this Web site a hot temptation. It's chock-full of demos and exhibits, "weird science" experiments, and contains loads of links to science-related resources all over the Web.

Splash Kids Online

http://www.splash.com/

Splash Kids Online magazine features news, art, chat, and games. Ask Dr. Beta your technical computer questions, or find out what holidays are being celebrated around the world today.

The Yuckiest Site on the Internet

http://www.nj.com/yucky/index.html

The Yuckiest Site on the Internet teaches kids everything there is to know about cockroaches, all by way of fun exhibits and activities. It's an offering of New Jersey Online and the Liberty Science Center.

Uncle Bob's Kids' Page

http://gagme.wwa.com/~boba/
kidslinks.html

Uncle Bob's Kids' Page contains links to educational, entertainment, and informational sites of interest to children.

You Can't Do That on Television!

http://www.PERnet.net/~rbarrow1/
ycdtotv.htm

The home page for "You Can't Do That On Television!" features all the outrageous gags from Nickelodeon's popular TV show.

NEWS & INFORMATION

American Society of Home Inspectors

http://www1.mhv.net/~dfriedman/
ashihome.htm

This unofficial guide to the American Society of Home Inspectors, certifying inspectors in the United States and Canada, is maintained by a local Internet service provider. Visitors will find an extensive index of trade resources, including online technical libraries, industry publications, and home buyer services.

China News Digest

http://www.cnd.org/CND-Global/CND-
Global.new.html

The China News Digest-Global, a service run by volunteers, contains summaries of Chinese news. This global news report in English is provided every other day. Back issues are available.

Consumer Mortgage Information Network

http://www.human.com/proactive/
index.html

The Consumer Mortgage Information Network helps home buyers connect with favorable residential financing plans by arming them with information about the process. This consumer-oriented site provides pointers to software, articles, and reference materials related to home finance.

Detroit Journal

http://www.rust.net/~workers/
strike.html

This online version of *The Detroit Free Press*, produced by striking workers, offers standard newspaper fare—daily, business and sports news, columns, editorials, and letters—without the newsprint. Visitors also can access union news.

Edupage

`http://educom.edu/edupage.new`

Edupage, a summary of news items on information technology and the Internet, is updated three times each week as a service of Educom, a Washington, D.C.-based consortium of colleges and institutions. Visit this site for late-breaking and ongoing news stories from the cyber front.

Federal Rules of Evidence

`http://www.law.cornell.edu/rules/fre/overview.html`

The Legal Information Institute presents a complete hypertext version of the U.S. Federal Rules of Evidence. The document includes a full-text search capability.

iGuide

`http://www.iguide.com/`

Surf over to "iGuide" for the latest in the world of politics, entertainment, sports, science, and more. Visitors will also find special sections for kids, bulletin boards, and chat.

Internet Marketing Digest

`http://www.informatiebank.nl/digest/`

Internet Marketing Digest is an online magazine, published biweekly, which contains marketing and communication applications news about the Internet. Visitors can check out the current issue,

search through back issues, or subscribe to have it e-mailed to them. Information in English and Dutch.

KGTV Home Page

`http://www.kgtv.com/`

KGTV, San Diego's ABC affiliate station, posts its programming schedule and editorial policies at this site. Find children's resources, news, and technological information at the television station's home page.

MacUser Web

`http://www.zdnet.com/macuser/`

MacUser Web is the online version of *MacUser*, the magazine of hands-on Macintosh and Apple computing. Visitors here can download software, read product reviews, and browse through back issues of the magazine.

Media.Net

`http://www.synergy.net/`

Media.Net is an online information provider focusing on business, entertainment, government and education news, and resources. Produced by Synergy Communications, Inc.

National Press Photographers Association

`http://sunsite.unc.edu/nppa/`

The National Press Photographers Association, Inc. maintains this site to provide general information. Visit here to learn about its programs, conferences, and other resources. Also, find a digital gallery and short course.

National Weather Service

http://www.nws.noaa.gov/

An agency of the National Oceanic and Atmospheric Administration, the National Weather Service offers visitors to its page an operations overview, answers to Frequently Asked Questions (FAQ), and links to weather data, including forecasts and warnings, charts, and climate information.

NJOnline Weather

http://www.nj.com/weather/index.html

Find a five-day forecast and current weather conditions for the Newark, N.J., region and other U.S. cities at this interactive site. Also find the day's page from *The Old Farmer's Almanac*.

Northeast Regional Climate Center

http://met-www.cit.cornell.edu/

From the Northeast Regional Climate Center page, find a database collected by Cornell University containing useful information for climatologists who need up-to-date weather info and climate conditions.

Pulitzer Prizes

http://www.pulitzer.org/

The Pulitzer Prizes are among the highest awards bestowed upon newspaper reporters, authors, playwrights, and composers in America. Features here include a current list of winners, audio excerpts, full texts of selected news articles, and synopses of honored books.

Special Internet Connections

http://www.w3.org/hypertext/DataSources/Yanoff.html

Special Internet Connections, a personal collection of online resources, provides links to information on a variety of topics. Visit here to browse its extensive index of subjects, from business and biology to space and sports.

The Canadian Press

http://www.xe.com/canpress/

At the Canadian Press site, find today's top stories, award-winning photos, stylebooks, and information on press, broadcast, and photo services in Canada. Some information is in French, most in English.

The Daily Beacon on the World Wide Web

http://beacon-www.asa.utk.edu/

The Daily Beacon is an independent student newspaper at the University of Tennessee, Knoxville. This site features the contents of the current and previous issues, and links to campus information, as well as other student papers on the Internet.

The Internet and the Writer

http://sunsite.unc.edu/shannon/ckind/Baker.html

Wired scribes will get an overview of sources available on the Internet from this broad ranging essay. The document discusses mailing lists, bulletin boards and newsgroups, and contains tips on electronic queries and submissions.

The PIXPage

http://www.kpix.com/

The home page for San Francisco's television station, KPIX, lets visitors peek through the KPIX camera stationed at the top of San Francisco's Nob Hill, read the KPIX Radio and Channel station pages, or link to San Francisco Bay Area Weather.

The Swiss Telecom PTT Phone Book

http://etb.eunet.ch/cgi-bin/etvq

Swiss Telecom provides this online version of Switzerland's telephone directory. Visitors can use various methods to search for individual and business phone numbers.

Weather Conditions

http://www.mit.edu:8001/weather?bos

Browsers can retrieve weather forecasts here, or telnet to the University of Michigan's forecast site.

Women's Health Hot Line Home Page

http://www.soft-design.com/softinfo/womens-health.html

Current and past issues of the Women's Health Hot Line are contained here. The newsletter is designed to provide the media with information on women's health.

SCIENCE & TECHNOLOGY

A Paleolithic Cave

http://www.culture.fr/culture/gvpda-en.htm

Discovery of a Paleolithic Painted Cave documents a recent find of a network of caves in southern France containing 20,000-year-old paintings. Link to additional archaeological sites from this page. Available in French and English.

Australian Mathematics Society

http://solution.maths.unsw.edu.au/htdocs.ams/amswelcome.html

This home page for the Australian Mathematics Society provides general information about the society, its publications, and conferences. Visitors will also find items of interest to mathematicians around the world.

Evolutionary Relationships of Archosaurs

http://ucmp1.berkeley.edu/exhibittext/cladecham.html

The Hall of Dinosaurs features "a series of long hallways where you can see various amazing skeletons." It makes use of a clickable "cladogram" (or map), just like real-live paleontologists use.

Federation of American Societies for Experimental Biology Information Services

http://www.faseb.org/

The Federation of American Societies for Experimental Biology is the largest coalition of life science societies in the United States. Visitors here will find an overview of the federation along with information on careers in experimental biology, the latest news from the field, and a list of members

Forecast Systems Laboratory

http://www.fsl.noaa.gov/

A National Oceanic and Atmospheric Administration facility located in Colorado, the Forecast Systems Laboratory's main mission is "to transfer technological developments to the nation's operational atmospheric and oceanic services." Find an operations overview, meteorology publications, research data, and forecasts on the lab's home page.

Galaxy: Mathematics—Science

http://galaxy.einet.net/galaxy/
Science/Mathematics.html

This page from the Galaxy collection contains an index of links to mathematics sites, articles, guides, software, periodicals, and much more. A search engine is also available here.

Harnad E-Print Archive and Psycoloquy and BBS Journal Archives

http://cogsci.ecs.soton.ac.uk/
~harnad/

The University of Southampton, England, maintains this site for program information. Visit here to learn about its cognitive sciences or behavioral and

brain science programs or link to the psycoloquy journal archive.

Indiana University Visual Inference Laboratory

http://www-vil.cs.indiana.edu/

The Visual Inference Laboratory (VIL) at Indiana University is devoted to the study of the visual aspects of reasoning and the development of computer technology to support this type of reasoning. The VIL page provides details on current research, publications, software, and its members.

Institute for Computational Earth System Science

http://skua.crseo.ucsb.edu/

The Institute for Computational Earth System Science at the University of California, Santa Barbara, couples earth and computer sciences. It details its research here, including a look at its long-term ecological research in the Antarctic and a bio-optics project in Bermuda.

Lockheed Martin Energy Systems

http://www.ornl.gov/mmes.html

Lockheed Martin Energy Systems manages energy-related facilities for the U.S. Department of Energy. Visitors can browse through general company-related information, as well as information on specific technologies, products, and facilities.

The Complete Idiot's Guide to the Internet, Third Edition

Munich Universities Agricultural Departments

http://www.edv.agrar.tu-muenchen.de/hello.html

Links on this central server lead to the Munich University of Technology's Department of Agriculture and Horticulture and its Department of Brewing, Food Technology, and Dairy Science. Also, find the Faculty of Forest Science at Ludwig Maximilians University and the Bavarian State Institute of Forestry. Information in German and English.

National Taiwan University Department of Agricultural Engineering

http://flood.hy.ntu.edu.tw/ntuae/home.html

The Department of Agricultural Engineering at the National Taiwan University provides information on its people and programs. Includes links to faculty profiles, student services, and related resources.

New York University Psychiatry Department

http://www.med.nyu.edu/Psych/NYUPsych.Homepage.html

New York University's Psychiatry Department page contains general information about the department and its academic and residency programs. Includes links to a reference desk, textbooks, interactive testing, and the Bellevue Hospital Psychiatry Department.

Purdue University: Agricultural Communication Service

http://hermes.ecn.purdue.edu:8001//

Purdue University combines information from all its agricultural programs at the Agricultural Communication page. Categories include academics, libraries, and student and community information.

Society for Mathematical Biology Gopher Menu

gopher://gopher.nih.gov:70/11/res/SMBdigest

The Society for Mathematical Biology provides a searchable archive of its "SMB Digest" at this gopher site. Also, find information about the society and a membership application.

The Mercury Project at USC

http://www.usc.edu/dept/raiders/story/mercury-story.html

The mystery of several apparently non-natural formations in the Nevada Test Site nuclear testing grounds is posted here for research, informed speculation, and consideration of paleontologists. Some of the information of the original investigation is classified, but the government agreed to let this portion be published on the Web.

The WWW Virtual Library: Biology Societies and Organizations

http://golgi.harvard.edu/afagen/depts/orgs.html

This page, from the much larger World Wide Web Virtual Library collection, features a list of Biology Societies and Organizations with Web pages. Search by country and alphabetically, or link to other databases and search tools.

University of Washington School of Oceanography

http://www.ocean.washington.edu/

The University of Washington School of Oceanography provides information on its programs of study, course offerings, and faculty here. Site features include a look at the school's research vessels, ongoing research projects, and publications.

U.S. Department of Energy's Energy Efficiency and Renewable Energy Network

http://www.eren.doe.gov/

The goal of the Department of Energy's Office of Energy Efficiency and Renewable Energy is to develop efficient technologies that are affordable. The office gives a detailed look at its various projects and partnerships and provides extensive information about energy efficient and renewable technologies.

Why Are There So Few Female Computer Scientists?

http://www.ai.mit.edu/people/ellens/Gender/pap/pap.html

Read this report to find out. The page contains an abstract and index to the 1991 Massachusetts Institute of Technology technical report, "Why are There so Few Female Computer Scientists," by Ellen Spertus. Societal, environmental, and language factors are explored in the report.

Women and Computer Science

http://www.ai.mit.edu/people/ellens/gender.html

Visitors to this site will find an abundance of writings—from the Webmaster and others—on the topic of women and computer science. Other topical resources and info-sites are linked as well.

Women and Computing

http://www.cpsr.org/dox/program/gender/gender.html.

Is the Internet a "guy" thing? Find out with a little help from the Women and Computing site. Links to several essays on computers and gender are provided here, as well as women's resources.

Working Group for the History of Astronomy

http://aibn55.astro.uni-bonn.de:8000/~pbrosche/aa/aa.html

The Astronomische Gesellschaft (AG) hosts this site about its work group devoted to the history of astronomy. Visitors can check out the aims of the group, electronic newsletters, and member information. In English and German.

World Power Technologies

http://www.webpage.com/wpt/

World Power Technologies is a manufacturer of wind-powered generators.

Includes product descriptions, technical specifications, and instructions on planning individual electrical systems.

World Wide Web Virtual Library: Clearinghouse for Social Sciences Subject-Oriented Bibliographies

http://coombs.anu.edu.au/CoombswebPages/BiblioClear.html

Social scientists will find a bibliography of titles in the social sciences, humanities, and Asian-Pacific studies. This page of the Virtual Library provides links to an extensive collection of digital indices and archives.

SHOPPING THE NET

Absolutely Fresh Flowers

http://www.cts.com/~flowers/

At the Absolutely Fresh Flowers site consumers can have flower arrangements shipped via Federal Express from the southern California flower grower to any location within the U.S. The site accepts electronic orders.

Allegro Information Services

http://catalog.com/allegro/

Allegro Information Services is a distributor of special interest and instructional videotapes. Site features include an online catalog, ordering information, and links to selected Web pages.

Amtrak

http://www.amtrak.com/

Amtrak's official site details info on its routes, vacation packages, and promotions. Viewers can also make reservations and browse travel tips.

Auto-By-Tel

http://www.autobytel.com/

Web surfers who'd rather be driving can buy or lease a new car or truck online from Auto-By-Tel. The company claims to offer the lowest prices for the purchaser's area.

Carpeteria Store Listing

http://carpeteria.com/

Ventura, California's "Carpeteria" maintains this promotional page advertising its products and services. Southern Californians will find an online shop-at-home service, as well as links to industry manufacturers such as DuPont and Monsanto.

Concertina: Books on the Internet

http://www.iatech.com/books/intro.htm

Concertina is a Canadian children's print and online book publisher that emphasizes Jewish and Biblical themes. Visitors will find book and ordering information at this promotional site.

Diving Masks

http://www.seavisionusa.com/

SeaVision USA, Inc. specializes in producing underwater viewing devices such as gauge readers and masks. This site offers product and ordering information. Visitors will also find links to related scuba and optical Web sites.

Enter FAO Schwarz
http://faoschwarz.com/

FAO Schwarz guides the young (and the young at heart) through an online store full of fantasy, playthings, and specialty toys. Find offline FAO Schwarz stores through a directory of locations.

Equinet(tm)
http://horses.product.com/

Equestrians will find a stable of information on horse products and services here. The site contains listings of horses for sale, horse equipment for sale, and job openings. It offers information on riding getaways, too.

Faucet Outlet Online Home Page
http://www.faucet.com/faucet/

This is the online pipeline to kitchen and bathroom faucets. Faucet Outlet makes its catalog of faucets and other plumbing accessories, complete with prices, available at this site. A toll-free number is provided for ordering. Also available here is information on plumbing basics and tips on choosing a faucet.

Florida Internet Real Estate Guide
http://www.lynqs.com/floridaguide/

This real estate information service provides a variety of resources for those looking for a home in Florida. Visit here to link with home-finding services, government and business information, and more. Includes a clickable map for honing the home search.

For Sale by Owner Connection
http://www.crocker.com/byowner/

An online resource for people wanting to buy or sell houses; this site allows visitors to view pages describing available properties. Links to "for sale by owner" offices accompany a glossary of terms and real estate-related articles.

Khazana-India Arts Online
http://www.winternet.com/~khazana/index.html

Khazana, a Minneapolis, Minnesota-based retailer of collectibles from India and Nepal, maintains this site for general information. Visit here to view its wide range of handmade ornaments, statues, and more.

Maui Net
http://maui.net/

Maui Net, offering Internet connectivity to the Hawaiian island community, maintains this site for local tourism information, product catalogs, and service descriptions. Visitors will also find publications, real estate listings, online discussion groups, and more.

Moe's Bookstore
http://sunsite.unc.edu/ibic/Moeshome.html

Moe's Bookstore in Berkeley, California offers this Web site with information about its many books and reference materials. Browse catalogs for dozens of different book categories and link to ordering instructions.

Namark Cap & Emblem

http://www.accessnv.com/namark/

Namark Cap & Emblem custom prints t-shirts, mugs, and caps. Shoppers can fax or e-mail designs and place orders online.

Once Upon a Breeze

http://www.webcom.com/~mrkites/

The Oregon Coast kite shop Once Upon a Breeze highlights its online kite catalog and ordering information on its home page. The company also includes pointers to other kite resources on the Internet.

Publisher's Toolbox

http://www.pubtool.com/pubtool/

Designers and artists will find an online catalog of hardware and software designing tools. The page also posts links to publishing sites on the Web.

SpeedWay MotorBooks

http://www.primenet.com/~komet/speed/speedway.html

Arizona's SpeedWay MotorBooks sells collectible books, programs, magazines, and videos about cars and racing. Racing cards, models, and slot cars are also available.

The Chocolate Lovers' Page

http://bc.emanon.net/chocolate/

The Chocolate Lovers' Page presents a comprehensive list of shops and companies that sell chocolate on the Internet, as well as links to recipes and other chocolate goodies.

The Outdoor Network

http://www.outdoornet.com/

The Outdoor Network is a commercial site that intends to be an interactive center for team, extreme, and action sports, as well as travel and adventure. Retailers and wholesalers of travel services, gear, and sports equipment are prominently featured.

Welcome to Fido the Shopping Doggie!

http://www.continuumsi.com/cgi-bin/Fido/Welcome

Continuum Software, Inc. offers a search engine here dubbed Fido the Shoppin' Doggie to help online shoppers find products. Visitors can enter a brief product description and Fido will fetch some options. The site also contains featured vendors.

Wines on the Internet

http://www.wines.com/

Lovers of the grape will find a "cyberspace guide to wine and wineries" at Wines on the Internet. Explore "virtual wine country" or check out the "tasting room." Those seeking "unique or exceptional values" can even order selections online.

Wings America Home Page

http://www.carmelnet.com/Wings/

Products with an aviation theme are available at Wings America. Find models, clothing, books, watches, and more. Aviation links and jokes are also featured.

Wordnet

http://www.ultranet.com/~wordnet/

Wordnet is a group of language experts who translate foreign languages for companies' brochures, catalogs, presentations, and legal agreements. Languages covered are: Spanish, French, German, Japanese, and Chinese.

SOCIAL & COMMUNITY AFFAIRS

Administration for Children and Families

http://www.acf.dhhs.gov/

The U.S. Department of Health and Human Services Administration for Children and Families promotes the economic and social safety of families, children, individuals, and communities. Visitors to this site can explore the structure, programs, and services of the ACF.

AdoptioNetwork Home Page

http://www.adoption.org/adopt/

"A volunteer-operated information resource," the AdoptioNetwork offers a multitude of links to serve as a starting point in exploring the issues and procedures of adoption. Topics covered include agencies, birthparents, adoptees, adoptive parents, international resources, and more.

American Red Cross Home Page

http://www.crossnet.org/

Visitors to the home page of the American Red Cross will find an overview of the relief organization, including a list of its offices and facilities. Information on how volunteers can become involved is also provided.

Child Relief and You

http://www.wnx.com/~cry/

Child Relief and You (CRY), a children's rights and relief organization based in Bombay, India, maintains this site to describe its activities. Visit here to find educational literature, view press clippings, or donate to the cause.

Children Now

http://www.dnai.com/~children/

Children Now speaks for children in the halls of Congress, on the editorial pages of newspapers, and in local communities. It gives an overview of its work here and posts current news and action alerts. Visitors can learn how to get involved.

CMU Women's Center

http://english-www.hss.cmu.edu/womenscenter/

The Women's Center at Carnegie Mellon University provides general information about its library and weekly discussion—coffee talk. The site includes an online catalog of the center's books.

Elderhostel

http://www.elderhostel.org/

The Elderhostel home page describes its innovative, varied educational study programs for older adults. Educational institutions around the world offer courses in everything from Cicero to computers.

Feminist Activist Resources on the Net

http://www.igc.apc.org/women/feminist.html

Feminist Activist Resources on the Net provides a comprehensive index of resources, including links to indexes concerning reproductive rights, domestic violence, economic issues, and women's organizations.

Healing in the Heartland

http://benefit.ionet.net/

Healing in the Heartland offers audio and stills from a July, 1995, benefit concert in Oklahoma for victims of the Oklahoma City bombing. Links to information on the bombing and to Internet software are available here.

Lesbian and Gay New York Home Page

http://gravity.fly.net/~lgny/

The Lesbian and Gay New York (LGNY) home page features current and past issues of the publication as well as a calendar of upcoming events. Includes listings of Big Apple media and establishments catering to the gay lifestyle.

MELANET: Your Commerce & Information Center

http://www.melanet.com/melanet/

MELANET, a service for African American business people, provides an index of online goods and services. Visit here to search for companies, browse informational links, and download graphics and quick time movies.

Mount Diablo Silverado Council

http://www.emf.net/~troop24/council/mdsc.html

A profile of the Mount Diablo Silverado Council #23 of the Boy Scouts of America. Visitors can read a memo from the Chief Scout Executive, find out about the troop, or obtain division contact information.

Queer Resource Center

http://www.actwin.com/queerindex.html

The Queer Resource Center lists regional gay, lesbian, and bisexual resources across the U.S. with additional listings from around the world. Includes links to the AIDS virtual library page, Stonewall historical sites, Digital Queers, and more.

Saludos Web

http://www.hooked.net/saludos/

Saludos Web promotes Hispanic careers and education with links to job listings, internships, and scholarships. Includes articles from *Saludos Hispanos* magazine, résumé postings, and a variety of Hispanic-related Web links.

Seniors-Site

http://seniors-site.com/

Seniors-Site is geared toward people over age 50, as well as their families and caregivers. It's filled with resources for senior citizens, from government resources to volunteering opportunities to "older jokes for older folks."

Sexual Assault Information Page

http://www.cs.utk.edu/~bartley/saInfoPage.html

This site presents a wealth of information about sexual assault. Broad categories covered include statistics, counseling directories, domestic violence, child abuse, legal issues, and prevention.

Social Security Online

http://www.ssa.gov/SSA_Home.html

Social Security Online is a service of the Social Security Administration. As such, it is the most authoritative Web source for all kinds of info on Social Security benefits, forms, and resources.

The Ada Project

http://www.cs.yale.edu/HTML/YALE/CS/HyPlans/tap/tap.html

Connecting conferences, projects, and discussion groups, The Ada Project creates an electronic networking space for women involved in computing. A clearinghouse of information by, for, and about computing, this service offers women their own gateway for learning from and about the Internet.

The Aging Research Center (ARC)

http://www.hookup.net/mall/aging/agesit59.html

The Aging Research Center page provides information for researchers in the field.

Visitors will find archives of scientific papers, aging theory documentation, and links to scheduled seminars, workshops, and conferences.

The Alliance for Fire and Emergency Management

http://internet.roadrunner.com/afem/

The Alliance for Fire and Emergency Management is a network of eight professional associations whose members serve the needs of the fire, life safety, and emergency management community. Visitors will find access to a resource center, training calendar, and the associations' publications.

The Contact Center Network Home Page

http://www.contact.org/

The Contact Center Network facilitates interaction and networking for individuals and organizations who work for a better world. This page includes information about the group, its services, and how others can participate. This page also links to nonprofit-oriented sites on the Internet.

The Millennium Report to the Rockefeller Foundation

http://www.cdinet.com/Millennium/

This 1994 report, commissioned by the Rockefeller Foundation, is a key component of the foundation's initiative, The Common Enterprise, which focuses on community revitalization.

The National Organization for Women

http://now.org/now/home.html

Find general information, an organizational history, and current issues concerning the National Organization for Women. Site features also include a newsletter and listings of Internet feminist resources.

UNICEF Gopher Service Menu

gopher://hqfaus01.unicef.org/

The United Nations Children's Fund gopher offers access to a wide variety of UNICEF publications. Visitors can download reports, press releases, and advocacy information here.

Vietnam Veterans Home Page

http://grunt.space.swri.edu/

The Vietnam Veterans Home Page honors "...Vietnam Vets, living and dead, who served their country on either side of the conflict." Toward that end, the site includes information about upcoming events, support groups, and organizations of interest to veterans.

SPORTS

Amateur Athletic Foundation

http://www.pac-10.org/

The Amateur Athletic Foundation is a nonprofit institution that supports youth sports in Southern California and manages the largest sports research library in North America. This site provides a newsletter, research reports, and information on the sports library, among other resources.

Anything Goes Darts

http://www.darts.com/anything_goes_darts/

Anything Goes Darts, a North American dart equipment retailer, maintains this promotional site for product information and sporting resources. Visit here to link with dart enthusiast Web sites and virtual pubs from England, Ireland, and the United States.

Aero.com

http://www.aero.com/

Aero.com aims high with this site that strives to be the most complete online resource for aviation information on the Web. The home page features news, shopping, and the Aviation Yellow Pages.

Cambuslang Harriers Page

http://www.chem.gla.ac.uk/~david/harriers.html

The Cambuslang Harriers is a Scottish cross-country racing team. Visitors to its home page will find profiles of team members, race schedules, results, photos, and descriptions of training programs.

Coghead Corner

http://www.teleport.com/~bazzle/coghead.shtml

Coghead Corner is devoted to mountain biking in Portland, Oregon, and the surrounding area. Visitors will find information on biking trails and conditions, along with links and a trail of the month.

CricInfo

http://www.cricket.org:8001/

CricInfo provides up-to-date information on the sport of cricket. Visitors will find news, scores, statistics, player profiles, and league standings for English and international cricket.

Directory of Hang Gliding and Paragliding Home Pages

http://www.mainelink.net/
SKYADVENTURES/myhom13.html

The hang gliding and paragliding resources here feature home pages from around the world and an index of image galleries. An extensive listing of classified ads is included.

ESPNET SportsZone: Men's College Basketball

http://espnet.sportszone.com/ncb/

College basketball news and scores come to the Web through this page from the popular ESPNET SportsZone. Visitors will find regularly updated scores and standings, as well as features about the top men's basketball teams in the U.S.

Figure Skating Page

http://www.cs.yale.edu/homes/sjl/
skate.html

At the Figure Skating Page, maintained by an enthusiast at Yale University,

darlings of the sport get praised, ribbed, and profiled. Visitors can find links to skating news, humor archives, and fan-produced pages devoted to favorite athletes.

GolfWeb—Everything Golf on the World Wide Web!

http://www.golfweb.com/

GolfWeb boasts an extensive golf information service encompassing all aspects of the game—from rule books to tournament coverage to an online pro shop. Naturally, visitors will also find links to golf course descriptions and resort information.

Guide to Internet Firearms Information Resources

http://www.portal.com/~chan/
firearms.faq.html

This document provides a comprehensive listing of Internet firearms resources. Includes information on the right to keep and bear arms, pro-firearms activist groups and links to a firearms archive.

Gymn Forum

http://rainbow.rmii.com/~rachele/
gymnhome.html

Flip through a wealth of gymnastics information here, including magazine articles and reports on international competitions. The page also presents videos for sale and posts links to dozens of gymnastics sites.

Harvard Fencing

http://hcs.harvard.edu/~fencing/

Visit this site for details of Harvard University's fencing program: the people, schedules, and results. A history of the sport, answers to Frequently Asked Questions (FAQ), and links to topic-related Web sites are also featured.

Horse Country

http:// www.pathology.washington.edu/Horse/ index.html

The Horse Country site offers resources and information about horses, riding, and equestrian events. Visitors will find a riders' library, sounds, images, and links to information about horse care, breeds, and riding equipment. There are also special links for younger and beginning riders.

Hyperion's Thoroughbred Horse Racing & Breeding Page

http://www.swcp.com/~hyperion/ horse.html

Hyperion's Thoroughbred Horse Racing & Breeding site is filled with information about the sport, including links to journals, news sources, databases, and other resources.

International Rugby League Home Page

http://www.brad.ac.uk/~cgrussel/

Rugby League Football is the sport, and this site contains general information, rules, and links to related information.

Included are pages on teams and leagues around the world.

NHL Pages

http://www.wpi.edu/~defronzo/

From standings, statistics, and schedules to injuries, rosters, and rules, this unofficial National Hockey League site has it all. Included here is a listing of team pages, unofficial and official, for every NHL franchise.

Planet Reebok

http://planetreebok.com/

At Planet Reebok, the shoe manufacturer provides much more than promotional propaganda. Its smorgasbord of resources includes live chat, bulletin boards, training tips, and pages for the Women's Sports Foundation and National Standards for Athletic Coaches.

Professional Bowlers Association

http://www.pba.org/

Bowlers and bowling fans will find information from and about the PBA Tour here, including tournament results and schedules. The site also offers message boards and online chats with bowling pros.

RaceZine

http://www.primenet.com/~bobwest/ index.html

RaceZine shifts into high gear by offering visitors images, trivia, soundbites, and news about auto racing. Includes links to Sandman's MotorSports page and other online racing resources.

RSSI FAQ

http://www.skatefaq.com

The UseNet newsgroup rec.sport.skating.inline has posted its Frequently Asked Questions file here. Find answers to questions about technique, consumer information, and organizations, as well as a geographical index of places to skate.

Speedway Home Page

http://amed01.amg.gda.pl/speedway/speedway.html

Speedway motorcycle racers are not afraid to get dirty. Learn all about speedway racing worldwide on this page, which offers events listings and news. Includes answers to Frequently Asked Questions (FAQ), a photo gallery, and information on ice, and long track and grass track racing.

Stanford Cardinal Women's Basketball

http://www-leland.stanford.edu/group/wbball/

The women's basketball team at Stanford University offers information here on its upcoming games, results, and players. Browsers also can link to other athletic department pages at the school.

"The Boys" Unofficial Dallas Cowboys Fan Site

http://theboys.com/

Fans of the Dallas Cowboys will flock to this site for news, commentaries, statistics, and player information. During the National Football League season, previews and results of games are available.

UCMAP—Martial Arts Program

http://server.berkeley.edu/ucmap/

The University of California at Berkeley's Martial Arts Program is the topic of this server featuring an introduction to and overview of the program, club schedules, and related biodynamics course listings. Information on upcoming demonstrations and self-defense classes, and links to related sites are also featured.

Ultimate Frisbee Sites

http://www.contrib.andrew.cmu.edu/usr/mj1g/all-frisbee.html

Athletes who delight in the organized chase of the flying plastic disk can find pointers to Internet resources relating to their sport at the Ultimate Frisbee Sites page. Find links to team, league, and instructional sites.

World Squash Federation's Home Page

http://www.ncl.ac.uk/~npb/

The World Squash Federation provides information on its activities, tournaments, coaching, and 2000 Olympics. Includes links to player profiles, publications, and online mail order.

Yesterday's Games

http://www.instantsports.com/
baseball/YesterdayGames.html

Instant Sports, Inc., an Austin, Texas-based online sports news service, maintains this site for results of the previous day's Major League Baseball games. Visit here for linescores and links to recaps and box scores.

THE ROAD LESS TRAVELED

50 Greatest Conspiracies of All Time

http://www.webcom.com/~conspire/

The 50 Greatest Conspiracies of All Time home page delivers exactly what it promises: theories on aliens and UFOs, JFK's assassination, AIDS as a U.S. biological warfare operation—if you suspect it, it's here. Includes a tool allowing visitors to search the site by keyword.

Abuses of the Bureau of Alcohol, Tobacco, and Firearms

http://www.access.digex.net/
~croaker/batfabus.html

This page provides an "unofficial collection" of anecdotes relating to alleged abuses of power by the U.S. Bureau of Alcohol, Tobacco, and Firearms. Includes article reprints and a section entitled "Strange Things BATF Agents Do."

Area 51/Groom Lake

http://www.ufomind.com/area51

Individuals who think we're not alone will find scientific fuel for the fire at this site, maintained by the Area 51 Research Center. Visitors can look up current news stories and testimonials concerning UFOs allegedly housed at the U.S. military's mysterious installation.

Collected Writings of Ivan K. Goldberg

http://avocado.pc.helsinki.fi/
~janne/ikg/

Search the articles written by "maybe the most active psychopharmacologist on the Internet" by keyword (a list of suggested keywords is provided) or link to the Mood Disorders Page, and read Depression Frequently Asked Questions (FAQ) and access support mailing lists and newsgroups.

Hypnosis.com

http://www.hypnosis.com/

Sort of a hypnosis mall, this site links visitors to book and tape vendors selling hypnosis-related materials. Includes information on related educational resources and a Frequently Asked Questions (FAQ) file.

Hypnotica

http://www.servtech.com/public/
hypnotica/

This page offers a primer on the art of self-hypnosis, offering advice on using the process to lose weight, give up smoking, improve concentration, and gain confidence. The site includes offline references.

Interlude

`http://www.teleport.com/~interlud/`

Interlude, an "Internet retreat" maintained by the Cybermonks, offers poems, prayers, and weekly meditation suggestions. Visit here for "a few moments of peace, composure, and mental expansion." Includes an extensive bibliography of related texts.

Mysticism in the World's Religions

`http://www.realtime.net/~rlp/dwp/mystic/`

Elements of mysticism in the world's major religions are explored at this Web site. Includes examinations of different aspects of mysticism as they relate to Christians, Jews, Muslims, Buddhists, Taoists, and Hindus.

Penny's Skulls of Fate

`http://www.dtd.com/skulls/`

Visitors to this page are invited to ask a question that can be answered with a yes or no reply. Penny's Skulls of Fate will then divine the answer.

Real Stories for Real People

`http://www.io.com/~mjg/visionary/`

The Visionary Publishing site contains games, fiction, and a journal designed to showcase new talent and to focus on the interaction of myth, legend, role-playing, and storytelling. Includes information on conferences, contacts, and links to related e-mail sites, newsgroups, and writers' home pages.

Rutgers UFO Site

`http://ftp.rutgers.edu/ufo.html`

Maintained at Rutgers University, this site is devoted to Unidentified Flying Objects and features a UFO bibliography. A UFO guide and links to UFO groups' home pages also are provided.

Search for Extra-Terrestrial Intelligence Institute

`http://www.metrolink.com/seti/homepage.html`

Scientists engaged in the Search for Extra-Terrestrial Intelligence project publish their research strategies, goals, and findings here on the SETI Institute's home page. Visitors can link to researchers, investigators, and summaries of current projects from this site.

Search for Extra-Terrestrial Intelligence League Inc.

`http://seti1.setileague.org/homepg.html`

This group, dedicated to the electromagnetic Search for Extra-Terrestrial Intelligence, offers up general information about itself. Linked pages offer related articles, membership information, press releases, and meeting schedules.

Shamanistic Healing-Energies on the Internet

`http://www.prgone.com/bus/dpedro/`

A shaman instructs visitors how to absorb healing energy from this page. The process involves watching an image on the computer screen for 10 minutes

377

at specific times. The page includes testimonials from the energized and information on the shaman himself, Don Pedro.

Survival Bible 2001

http://www.io.org/~richard/

Whether you fear revolutions or earthquakes, you'll find handy advice for filling your basement with provisions from the Survival Bible. With research drawing on events from "2001 BC to 2001 AD," you'll find one-stop information shopping for surviving in all climates and conditions.

Terence McKenna Land

http://www.intac.com/~dimitri/dh/mckenna.html

Visitors can get a dose of druggie/philosopher Terence McKenna's consciousness-altering studies of ethnopharmacology and shamanism. Includes an indexed quote collection, interviews, book reviews, and McKenna's travel schedule, along with information on hallucinogenic drugs and flying saucer theories.

The Contact Project

http://sunsite.unc.edu/lunar/alien.html

This page, maintained by the fanciful Lunar Institute of Technology, presents a puzzle: Visitors are invited to try their hands at decoding a fictional message from an alien intelligence. Explorers who find this site are provided with a history of the project and links to sites of interest to science fiction fans.

The Internet Science Education Project

http://www.hia.com/hia/pcr/

Those who wander into this mind-bending site will encounter fiction, scholarly essays, and "a Web forum for critical and poetical inquiry into controversial ideas in the post-modern physics of time travel and consciousness research."

The Kooks Museum

http://www.teleport.com/~dkossy/

The Kooks Museum keeps kookdom under one roof, taking a lighthearted look at the unconventional disciplines of crackpotology, kookology, and psychoosmology. Check out off-the-wall gifts, useless research, and politically incorrect ideas here.

The Original Tarot Web Page

http://www.facade.com/Occult/tarot/

At this interactive site, visitors can have a look into the future via a Tarot card reading. Easy to follow instructions and card interpretations are featured.

The Secret History of the United States, 1962-1995

http://ucunix.san.uc.edu/~taylorrm/Welcome.html

Robert Taylor doesn't buy the state-sanctioned official version of U.S. history, and instead publishes this online work. He weaves together the darker side of the country's history, quoting from Noam Chomsky, Philip Agee, and others. Leaning heavily on conspiracy theory, he delves into nuclear testing, drugs, and UFOs.

Unarius Academy of Science
http://www.serve.com/unarius/

The Universal Articulate Inter-dimensional Understanding of Science Academy of Science is a nonprofit, educational foundation that publishes books and video programs on the "new science of the mind and the universe." This site provides information on the institution's library, seminars, and workshops.

Will of Nature
http://erg.ucd.ie/won.html

Para-natural organization Will of Nature publishes its eponymously titled magazine here. Visitors will find articles exploring virtual reality, "magick," body art, and drugs, plus music samples and pictures, presented by a neopagan group that aims to "fight the techno/Christian materialism."

Your Personal Horoscope
http://www.realitycom.com/webstars/order/personal.html

True believers can buy a personal horoscope reading here that contains aspect, element, and quality charts. The British-based site takes orders over the Net or via fax.

THE WORLD

A Guide to the Great Sioux Nation
http://www.state.sd.us/state/executive/tourism/sioux/sioux.htm

This South Dakota online guide to the Great Sioux Nation provides information about landmarks and legends, artifacts, art, and powwows. An index of links to an overview of each tribe is also featured, along with photos and maps.

Australian National University Faculty of Asian Studies
http://online.anu.edu.au/asianstudies/

The Faculty of Asian Studies at Australian National University provides information on its programs, courses, activities, services, and publications. It has centers on Japan, Asian history, Southeast Asia, and more. Includes several links to other resources for Asian studies.

Country Studies/Area Handbook Program
http://lcweb.loc.gov/homepage/country.html

The Country Studies/Area Handbook Program is a project of the Federal Research Division of the Library of Congress, sponsored by the U.S. Army. Visitors to this page can find books and supporting documentation about the world's many countries.

Date and Time Gateway

http://www.bsdi.com/date

This index provides the time and date for cities around the world in Greenwich Mean Time. City listings are arranged alphabetically within continental categories.

Friends and Partners Home Page

http://solar.rtd.utk.edu/friends/
home.htmlopt-tables-pc-english-

Friends and Partners is a joint project between Russian and American citizens to create a meeting place for people of these two countries to learn about each other. This site includes links to a wide range of sites about art, health care, education, news, travel, and much more. An electronic mailing list and an interactive coffee house are also provided.

Hispanic Heritage

http://www.clark.net/pub/jgbustam/
heritage/heritage.html

Visitors to the Hispanic Pages in the USA site will find links to all Hispanic countries, Hispanic cybernauts on the Web and the Spanish language magazine, *Coloquio, Revista Cultural Hispana.* Site features also include a review of famous Hispanics in the world and history.

Houston Information (RiceInfo)

http://riceinfo.rice.edu/RiceInfo/
Houston.html

This page from the Rice University home page features a categorized list of links to resources in Houston, Texas. Among

other categories, visitors will find arts and entertainment, consumer information, government, and media.

Map Maker

http://www.pcug.co.uk/~MapMaker/

The freeware Map Maker is designed for people in developing countries who need to create and manipulate maps on basic personal computers. This page allows browsers to download the software, a simple Geographical Information System.

Massachusetts Map of WWW Resources

http://donald.phast.umass.edu/misc/
mass.html

This clickable map from the University of Massachusetts escorts browsers on a virtual tour of the New England state. Visit corporate, educational, and cultural organizations from Boston to Great Barrington, and link to home pages where provided.

National Flags

http://155.187.10.12/flags/nation-
flags.html

Dozens of links are provided to images of national flags, from Argentina to Yemen.

On-Line Visual Literacy Project

http://www.pomona.claremont.edu/
visual-lit/intro/intro.html

From Pomona College in Claremont, California, the On-Line Visual Literacy

Project presents audio, animation, and text to explain the rudiments of visual communication. Among the basic visual elements explored are dots, lines, shape, hue, motion, value, and direction.

Rasta/Patois to English Dictionary
```
http://www.willamette.edu/~tjones/
languages/rasta-lang.html
```

This Web site offers an extensive text version of a Rasta/Patois to English dictionary. The dictionary was originally posted on rec.music.reggae.

Saskatchewan, Canada
```
http://duke.usask.ca/~lowey/
Saskatchewan/index.html
```

This information page for travelers and residents of Saskatchewan, Canada, features information about its government, towns and cities, recreation, and businesses.

soc.culture.thai Frequently Asked Questions (FAQ) Archive
```
ftp://ftp.nectec.or.th/
soc.culture.thai/
```

This FTP site contains the Frequently Asked Questions (FAQ) files for the USENET newsgroup soc.culture.thai. Visitors can read FAQs covering Thailand's culture, language, and travel opportunities.

The Computational and Language E-Print Archive
```
http://xxx.lanl.gov/cmp-lg/
```

This site serves as an archive and distribution center for papers on computational linguistics, natural language processing, speech processing, and related fields. Includes search instructions, additional information, and online proceedings.

UNESCO World Heritage List
```
http://www.cco.caltech.edu/~salmon/
world.heritage.html
```

The 469 World Heritage Sites, as designated by the United Nations, range from the ancient city of Butrinti in Albania to the sacred city of Kandy in Sri Lanka. Many of these sites are hyperlinked, so visitors can learn more about them.

VICTORIA
```
http://www.csu.edu.au/australia/
vic/vic.html
```

If you're headed Down Under to southern Australia, and Victoria in particular, prep for your trip with a visit to this page, where you can examine maps, climate data and the weather forecast, air and rail timetables, holidays, and fact sheets on the government.

Welcome to the Organization of American States
```
http://www.oas.org/
```

The Web page for the Organization of American States Web aims to further the mission of the group through strengthening the peace and security of the Western hemisphere. The organization includes the U.S. and the 35 sovereign states of Latin America. The site features history and news.

World Flags: An Incomplete Collection

http://www.adfa.oz.au/CS/flg/index.html

This site provides an admittedly less-than-comprehensive collection of flags for a world where boundaries change like the weather. Visitors can browse the archive, read about the patriotic customs of various nations, or link to information about flag-waving associations around the globe.

World Wide Web Servers in Hong Kong

http://www.cuhk.hk/hkwww.html

The Chinese University of Hong Kong maintains this index to sites based in Hong Kong. It is organized by subject and includes links to government organizations, music and entertainment sites, commercial and academic sites, and news outlets.

WWW Servers in Japan

http://www.ntt.jp/SQUARE/www-in-JP.html

This site, provided by Nippon Telephone and Telegraph, offers an index of Japanese World Wide Web servers arranged by geographical region. Visit here for links to government, commercial, and educational resources in Japanese and English.

WWW Servers in Korea

http://flower.comeng.chungnam.ac.kr/sharon/www-server-in-korea.html

Korean Internet resources are highlighted here with links to government, network management, academic, organizational and research institute domains, as well as personal home pages.

Xerox PARC Map Viewer

http://pubweb.parc.xerox.com/map/features=alltypes/ht=1.41/lat=44.99/lon=-0.57/tahiti=1/wd=2.81?244,121

This world map viewer, sponsored and developed by Xerox Corporation, offers users control of map detailing, display options, and zoom in/out.

Yamada Language Center Font Archive

http://babel.uoregon.edu/Yamada/fonts.html

This typeface archive, maintained by the Yamada Language Center at the University of Oregon, provides non-Latin character fonts. Download the fonts for creating documents using Czech, Hebrew, American Sign Language, and other languages. A guide to built-in Macintosh capabilities is also included.

Index

Licensing Agreement

By opening this package, you are agreeing to be bound by the following:

The software contained on this CD is, in many cases, copyrighted, and all rights are reserved by the individual software developer and/or publisher. You are bound by the individual licensing agreements associated with each piece of software contained on the CD. THIS SOFTWARE IS PROVIDED FREE OF CHARGE, AS IS, AND WITHOUT WARRANTY OF ANY KIND, EITHER EXPRESSED OR IMPLIED, INCLUDING BUT NOT LIMITED TO THE IMPLIED WARRANTIES OF MERCHANTABILITY AND FITNESS FOR A PARTICULAR PURPOSE. Neither the book publisher nor its dealers and distributors assumes any liability for any alleged or actual damages arising from the use of this software. (Some states do not allow exclusion of implied warranties, so the exclusion may not apply to you.)